THE LIVING LIGHT DIALOGUE

Volume 7

THE LIVING LIGHT DIALOGUE

Volume 7

Through the mediumship of
Richard P. Goodwin

Living Light Books

The Living Light Dialogue Volume 7
Copyright © 2015 Serenity Association

Through the mediumship of Richard P. Goodwin.

All rights reserved. Printed in the United States of America. No portion of this book may be reproduced—electronically, mechanically, or via internet transmission—without advance, express written permission of the publisher except in the case of brief quotations embodied in critical articles and reviews. No derivative work—games supplemental material, video—may be created without advance, express written permission of the publisher. For information address Living Light Books, P.O. Box 4187, San Rafael, CA 94913-4187.

Cover design copyright © 2014 by Serenity Association

Cover photograph by Serenity Association, 2014; copyright © 2014 by Serenity Association.

www.livinglight.org

Library of Congress Control Number 2007929762

FIRST EDITION

This volume of teachings is dedicated to the spirit friends who brought to Earth the Living Light philosophy. With eternal gratitude, we pray that we may demonstrate these principles and continue to bring to publication these teachings.

CONTENTS

Acknowledgement ix
Preface xi
Introduction xv
Consciousness Class 187 3
Consciousness Class 188 14
Consciousness Class 189 23
Consciousness Class 190 33
Consciousness Class 191 49
Consciousness Class 192 57
Consciousness Class 193 67
Consciousness Class 194 74
Consciousness Class 195 89
Consciousness Class 196 97
Consciousness Class 197 106
Consciousness Class 198 122
Consciousness Class 199 134
Consciousness Class 200 154
Consciousness Class 201 167
Consciousness Class 202 177
Consciousness Class 203 195
Consciousness Class 204 208
Consciousness Class 205 232
Consciousness Class 206 247
Consciousness Class 207 264
Consciousness Class 208 280
Consciousness Class 209 293
Consciousness Class 210 301
Consciousness Class 211 327
Consciousness Class 212 338

Consciousness Class 213 350
Consciousness Class 214 361
Consciousness Class 215 371
Consciousness Class 216 384
Consciousness Class 217 403
Consciousness Class 218 417
Appendix. 439

ACKNOWLEDGMENT

Grateful acknowledgement is made to the many friends and associates for invaluable aid in compiling this book, for their helpful suggestions, for their loyal interest and encouragement.

Special acknowledgement is due to those who painstakingly and selflessly transcribed and proofread the text.

PREFACE

It was through the mediumship of the Serenity Association founder, Mr. Richard P. Goodwin, that a philosophy known as the Living Light was given in more than 700 classes over a twenty-five-year period.

To be specific, the philosophy was imparted through Mr. Goodwin by a magistrate who had lived on Earth some 8,000 years ago. The former magistrate is known to Living Light students as "the Wise One," and he narrated the journey of his soul on the other side of life, the experiences—especially the difficulties—he encountered in having to face himself, as well as the teachings he earned to help himself through the realms in which he traveled. It was his decision to share the teachings with souls on both sides of "the curtain."

Prior to the advent of the Wise One, Mr. Goodwin had prayed for a teacher from the realms of light. Mr. Goodwin, since age fourteen, had been the instrument through which spirit was able to communicate with those seeking help. But he saw that his mediumship brought only temporary solace, because the people he was trying to help soon became fascinated with the phenomena and ignored the help that spirit was imparting. He prayed for someone who would bring forth teachings that would benefit any soul seeking a path to a greater awareness of himself and of God.

His prayers were answered in 1964 when the Wise One came through for the first time. Mr. Goodwin, at first apprehensive about what this new teacher would impart, was taken into deep trance and not able to control what was being revealed through him. Upon hearing the recorded classes afterward, however, he became convinced of the goodness of the teacher and of the value of the simple, beautiful teachings he had to impart. This, then, was the beginning of the Living Light philosophy given to Earth through the mediumship of Richard P. Goodwin.

In carrying out the request of the Wise One and Mr. Goodwin, students of the Serenity Association transcribed from audiotape the classes that had been brought through. Because most are in the form of teacher-student interaction, the classes became known as *The Living Light Dialogue*; and the students were instructed to publish the classes as a multi-volume set of the Living Light philosophy. *Volume 1* was published in the autumn of 2007.

The present book, *Volume 7* continues with three semesters of spiritual awareness classes, from CC (Consciousness Class) 187 through CC 218, covering the time period of September 7, 1978, through July 10, 1980.

These particular classes were given to a relatively large group of students who were organized into small circles and sat facing one another. Classes began with one student reading a discourse from *The Living Light*, the first book of teachings published by Mr. Goodwin and Serenity in 1972 and often referred to as "the textbook." After the reading, the class spoke in unison the "Total Consideration" affirmation (located in the appendix), which was followed by a short meditation period on peace. Then the class began.

The foundation of the classes—the foundation of the Living Light philosophy itself—is the Law of Personal Responsibility which states, in part, that we are responsible for all our experiences, and that our experiences are the return of the laws that we have established with our thoughts, acts, and deeds. Through greater awareness of our thoughts and by exercising our divine right of choice, we may choose to establish laws of greater harmony and goodness.

The Living Light Dialogue teaches that we have come to Earth to learn the lessons that are necessary to free us from the dictates and limits of our own thoughts and judgments, which are the mental patterns that we follow through our own lack of awareness and are so very potent, forceful, and limiting. This book guides us in making the necessary changes in our thinking in order to free ourselves from those patterns and to express our soul consciousness.

The choice of guiding the direction of our life, as stated by the Wise One when he speaks of being with a person, place, or thing, is, in essence, of being in this world and not a part of this world. He further explains that no matter what experiences we encounter, no matter what we do or do not do, we—our spirit—may view the experience in objectivity from a soul level of consciousness where peace reigns supreme.

The teachings of this volume help us to restore harmony or balance in our life by flooding the consciousness with spiritual affirmations and prayers, a few of which can be found in the appendix. When reason is restored, by balancing our sense functions with our soul faculties, we will consciously experience peace. Without annihilating our ego or our sense functions, we will find a pathway of expression for our soul. Where there was once disturbance, now there is acceptance. Where there was disease, now there is poise. And where there was hopelessness and despair, now there is reason, divine neutrality; and peace shows the way.

If you make the effort to apply these laws, such as, "If man is a law unto himself, what are you doing with the law that you are?", and demonstrate the wisdom of patience, the truth of this philosophy will be your living demonstration.

As the Teacher states in CC 130, "My journey of many centuries and much experience has brought me here to Earth to share with you these simple teachings that have come as the effect of a long, long, long journey. Let not *your* journey be so long in the realms of illusion. For it is not necessary for you. For in your evolution, you have earned an awakening. But it is up to you to do something that is constructive and worthwhile."

INTRODUCTION

[This introduction was written by Mr. Goodwin and originally appeared in *The Living Light*, which were the first teachings of the Living Light Philosophy published in book form. The entire text of *The Living Light* was republished in *The Living Light Dialogue*, Volume 1.]

> "Think, children. Think more often
> and think more deeply."

The teachings in this book were given as a progressive series of lessons to a group of four students who were sitting for spiritual unfoldment with me beginning in January of 1964. The communications were regular until October of that year, when nearly a seven-year silence ensued, and resumed in 1971 to the present. They were received in three ways by me as a channel. The main text was taped from a direct control of my voice in deep trance at special sittings of our group, during which I had no experience of the voice or what was being transmitted. A few scattered verses were given independently when I was privileged to see and hear our teacher clairvoyantly. I have also been a channel for this communicant when speaking from the podium at church and in answering difficult questions at our public seminars.

Nearly all we know about our teacher is contained in the lectures. He reports that he had tried for sixteen years to break through an interference barrier that the channel had to deep trance. When our conditions were in resonance with his patient wisdom, he came through ready to teach his understanding. I have seen him as an old man dressed in white with long flowing white hair. He has blue eyes, slightly smiling and deeply compassionate. I have always called him the Old Man. The students liked to call him the Wise One. He is surely one of those often called a Teacher of Light. I do not know his country, although he indicated at one time that he was from 6000 B.C., and a form of a judge in his time.

The text is often difficult, but it is complete, having been transcribed word for word from the original tapes recording the trance voice. It is presented with a minimum of punctuation to be freer for the individual interpretation of each reader. The lessons given before the long silence are phrased with many allegories often paradoxical. There are repetitions and renewals of theme, but it is explained that if an understanding is not perceived, compassion dictates that it be said again. Some of the topics have but a simple mention with little development but all are revealed, we are told, according to merit.

The Old Man is a fine teacher. He has in a hundred ways intertwined his allegory, progressive explanations, unfolding exercises, and timely references to reach a multitude of levels of individual understanding. A notable change is his more direct style of presentation beginning in 1971.

There is an endearing intimacy of person that can be felt through his lectures, a meaningful and loving encounter with a wise friend. Like an old man, he makes a mistake and conscientiously corrects himself a few paragraphs later. He listens often and carefully to our earnest discussions of his words. He consults with a group of experts on evolution and cites their learning in his lesson. His use of the direct address "children" or "my children" is not patronizing but infinitely loving and supportive.

A word must be said about the teachings. The Old Man makes clear that his lessons are not dogma, a creed or a narrow way, but simply his own understanding offered to us as a form of instruction to aid us in our own individual progression. When he speaks of Laws, he does not refer to man-made rules or moral traditions but to the cosmic and atomic way-things-are, the natural world of what-is, the universal laws of life, part of the original creative design and through which creation is fulfilled. These laws are beyond the possibility of being changed, suspended, transcended, or destroyed but they are ever a tool of mankind, not his master. First, through our awareness of the universal laws and then slowly through our developed understanding, the powers of creation are accessible to us. Not power over men's minds or circumstances, but power over whatever is selfish and imperfect in ourselves is the way up the eternal ladder of progression. When the Old Man cautions us concerning the Law of Responsibility or gives us a thinking exercise to explore the Law of Identity in a dynamic manner, he prepares us to take another step. And all move in accordance with the Law of What Can Be Borne.

Our teacher shows us how the two worlds are drawn together. In his realm, he describes, there is a great diversity of thought, many schools of understanding; but the Light is always known by the Light. Because of the interdependence of the two realms, listening to our discussions helped to clarify his teaching to others on his side of the curtain. His love and gratitude he humbly equates with ours.

The lessons to be perceived are not new, they are very old, but they are new to certain levels of our being. I would personally advise the reader, after reading this volume of discourses in full, to make a daily habit (or when there is a feeling or need) to sit quietly with the book. Open it at random and be guided to the Light by the passage that is there for the day. This technique is still used by the original students who were given the lessons and by many students after them who have studied in unfolding classes with me through these teachings.

Go beyond the words into feeling, into the immediate meanings for you. Touch into the inspiration that flows into the form of this book. It is from the Divine.

RICHARD P. GOODWIN
San Geronimo, California
June, 1972

CONSCIOUSNESS CLASSES

CONSCIOUSNESS CLASS 187

Students, I know it's a few minutes before 8:00, but I wanted to take these few minutes to welcome the new students into our classes and to also tell you about some of our procedures during class. Now, we begin our classes in this philosophy with our Healing Affirmation, which, I'm sure, you are all familiar with, which is followed by a few moments of concentration upon peace and meditation. We, after that, we have a reading from—*first*, we have a reading from our book [*The Living Light*] of one of the discourses by one of the students, then we will follow with our Healing Prayer and our concentration and meditation.

Now, there are over a hundred and some, almost 200 classes that have already been given. And so to those of you who do not have, as yet, a foundation in the philosophy, it would behoove you to make yourselves available to some of the classes that have already been given. For this philosophy is an expanding teaching. It is not something that you can come to a semester and grasp it in its entirety because it is in a constant process of expansion, as we, as humans, as all form, in truth, is in a constant process of expansion.

Now, the philosophy will give back to you, of course, whatever you give to it, through the Law of Application. The truth is given in many ways because we understand that there are eighty-one levels of consciousness and, hopefully, by giving the truth in so many different ways, one of those levels of consciousness that you may be on at the time, you will be receptive to it.

As new students to the philosophy, you must remember that all of life is an effect. It's an effect of our attitude. It's an effect of our thought. And so when we begin our study along the spiritual path, if we will first accept the living demonstration that we, and we alone, are responsible for all experience in our life, that qualifies us in that moment to make whatever changes are necessary in order that we may grow and expand in this universal consciousness.

If we refuse to accept that demonstrable truth—that life is reacting to our own thought patterns—then we are stunted in our growth, but remember, my friends, not forever. Because evolution is inevitable. And evolution is only made possible through the Law of Change. So we understand that through repetition, the Law of Change is made possible. And therefore, do not be discouraged if the lessons that you are given are repeated in your lives over and over and over again, because that is what is necessary for you in order to grow and, in time, be free. Remember, no one and no thing outside can give you freedom. You cannot be given what you already have. No one and no thing can give you truth, for you cannot be given what you already have. You already have freedom. You already have truth. It is simply a matter of, once again, finding it inside of yourself, because that's the only place that it exists.

As we go through our daily experiences in life, we are frequently tempted to put the blame of the experience, the credit, upon another's shoulders. But in so doing, we must ever be aware that by doing that we are giving our freedom and our truth into the control of another human being. Whenever we blame outside, we establish the very law that puts us into bondage and we are controlled by that level of consciousness. That, I personally believe, is man's greatest struggle: giving away his eternal freedom, giving away his eternal truth by placing responsibility for his life outside of his own universe. We are so frequently tempted to do that because it seems that, to our mind, it's easier to do that than to face those patterns of our mind that must be changed, that will, in time, be changed.

[*At this point, Mr. Goodwin goes into a trance.*]

Greetings, students, and welcome to our class.

We shall begin these classes with a discussion on the Law of Life. As the formless, free Spirit is the essence of the Law of

Life, and the Law of Form, known as the Law of Creation, runs parallel to this Law of Life, man becomes, through the Law of Identity, form in a mental and physical world. And so it is man, through that Law of Identity, stands between creation and the formless, free Essence which he is in truth.

As we continue on in our journey through life, we create many forms, for we identify with many, many things. And so it is for man to experience what he truly is—the free essence of life itself—he must, slowly but surely, gain, once again, control of the Law of Identity. For the Law of Identity is a mental law and, therefore, is in the power and control of each and everyone.

From this great Essence a spark, known to you as soul, was created by identity. And as time marches in your world, seemingly ever onward, never forget you are, have been, will always be this Essence that is life itself.

Throughout your journeys, you often will become the victim by over-identification, which is contrary to the natural laws of balance. You become the victim of these created forms. Remember, my friends, it is the very purpose of your being to experience through identity, but it is not the divine design plan to become the victim of the identity.

In my years of experience, in your earth world and in this world, I lived with the multitudes of forms of my own creation, but I did know that they were my creation.

Whatever you have and whatever you have not is always, and shall be forever, in keeping with the law you establish. To encourage oneself is to open up the soul faculty and to open the doors of eternity, called hope. Without hope, life diminishes. The purpose of its being diminishes. And so man must ever have before him what is known as hope, but with hope, the faculty of patience and the faculty of wisdom must ever rule.

The balance between the soul faculties and the sense functions is the balance between the Law of Life and the Law of Form or creation. Whenever we direct the infinite, intelligent energy in an overbalance to the left or to the right, we become controlled by those laws.

And so it is, my students, as we view the universal whole, we once again awaken within our consciousness that universal wholeness that is within us. The need that we experience in our daily life is an awakening to us that we are rejecting that which, in truth, we already have, for each rejection, as we know, a denial is a destiny.

If it is difficult for you to give forth to the universe that which disturbs you, it only, of course, reveals the degree of control it has upon you.

When you get closer and closer to your victories in life, you must choose: you must choose the faculties or remain with the functions. And the functions, which are the magnetic control of your universe, have a greater pull upon you. It is often said that man moves more quickly into the negative than he does the positive in life. But man would better understand if he would only realize and accept that the magnetic pull in our universe is the pull of that which is stored in our memory. It is our conscious mind, through which the faculties of our eternal soul, through which the essence of the Law of Life, flows in the light of reason. Therefore, for years we have asked you to think and think and think more deeply, that you may make the changes in a more gracious and harmonious way, that you be not disturbed with the passing panorama of forms that plague your universe.

Wherever we go in this great eternity, we shall ever take with us what we have. We shall not only take with us, of course, what we have, but we shall take with us what we have not, for we cannot escape the thoughts we have created. We can grow through them, but we cannot just leave them.

Responsibility, the ability to respond to all life, is something that is inherent within us. We had that before we came to earth. We will have that long after we leave.

We have spoken to you in classes before on the will of God, the will of the Divine, known as total acceptance. And then we must ask ourselves, "Do I have total acceptance?" And the answer must rise affirmative. We all have divine will, for without the will of the Divine we would not exist. It is the limit that we place upon the divine will. We have total acceptance in certain areas of our life and we have it not in other areas of our life.

We must ever be on the alert to understand the purpose of our evolution. We are calling forth into our universe everything, my good friends, that is necessary: each and every lesson that we must, someday, grow harmoniously through. If we become weary of our experiences today, be rest assured we are standing at the gate of victory. Do not step back before the victory. Persevere.

Be not concerned or judge the time that it will take, for that is a mental law and binds you to your dictate. Let us, in these classes, make the effort to apply that which we feel harmonious with, for that which we feel harmonious with we are then in a position to use more wisely. Do not press or force your way, for in so doing you are, in truth, stepping backwards. That does not, of course, mean to imply that effort should not be made. But let your efforts be ever under the guiding hand of reason that will grant you the beauty and the joy and the wonder of peace itself.

We have given to you many, many affirmations. We have spoken to you on the flooding of your consciousness. My good students, the consciousness is constantly being flooded with the dictates of the mental world. It is wisdom herself that dictates to choose what you wish your consciousness to be flooded with. Your feelings, your emotions, your experiences are effects revealing what is being broadcast in your mental world. Surely it takes effort. It is the frequency of effort—not the length of time each day—but the frequency that is the most valuable to you. Be on guard. Be a frequent and alert guardian of your soul.

Do not rest and hope that someone else is on duty. And then, my friends, you will move through this stream of consciousness without these great upheavals and struggles in your life.

Remember that you, your mental vehicle, serves a good purpose when it is kept in the light of reason. When you, the formless, free spirit, are able to rise in any moment, then you are free from being the victim of old creation.

Throughout the universes you have already traveled and throughout many universes yet to be shall you travel. The forms are varied, but they are an effect of your evolution. Some time ago we stated to you, you shall not find the missing link of evolution of man on Earth, for from Earth it did not come.

And so it is, your journey has indeed been long, but indeed is it far from over. Remember, this is a short stop in evolution. You will not leave your earthly vehicle and gravitate immediately to some spiritual realm of heavenly heights. That is a slow, but sure, process. You have many guides and teachers around and about you constantly making the effort to inspire and to encourage you. But you must be receptive to your encouragement in order that you may hear and be guided by theirs, for the law is ever equal.

You are doing, this moment, and each and every moment of your life, that which you have made necessary for you. It is in a process of changing. And, oh, so many changes are yet to be. The teaching to hold not to form, for form shall pass is a very clear and demonstrable teaching. Thought is form. Hold not to thought. Hold not to things of creation. Hold not to attitudes of mind, for in so doing you become their slave. It is not your purpose in life, nor is it mine, to be the slave of creation. To stand between the Law of Creation and the Law of Life, that is where we flow in the divine neutrality, that is where the light of reason ever shines upon our path. But to stand there firmly upon that principle requires frequent effort on your part. For how quickly we forget when we become over-identified with any thought in the mental world.

You will view, and can view, this moment in this great moment of eternity the realms that are around and about you. But you must still the mental world. And to still the mental world is to rise with the power of your eternal soul. To be freed from all mental dictates is to become aware of your true being. It is the very purpose of these classes to help you to help yourself to become aware of your true being. To be freed from the over-identification of who you think you are in order that you may know beyond a shadow of any doubt who you really are.

And now, I shall be happy to answer the questions you have prepared.

Thank you. Is it taught that we change through our heart, not our head? Then, why are we encouraged to think and think more deeply?

In reference to your question, without the change in the heart, which is the vehicle through which the eternal soul truly expresses, then there is not, in truth, a change at all. And so it is that you become aware that you have changed certain attitudes and you rise with the function of pride and tell the world how hard you've worked and finally made a certain change. It's like the reformer, once having reformed in a mental world, becomes the victim and the slave to reform everyone else because there is no security for there is no spiritual substance in the reformation he has made. Man is a triune being. He is the formless, free spirit and, through the Law of Identity, has a covering known as individualized soul and has a body. Therefore no change is a permanent change when it only takes place in a mental world. You are, and have been, encouraged to think and think and think more deeply. Do you not see, my good students, that there are many levels of the mental world? Then there is the Law of Identity. As you believeth, you becometh. That *is* the Law of Identity. And so when the changes come, they must come not only in your mind; they must come within your heart.

Thank you. Please explain the effect of there being no time in both your dimension and ours.

As time is, in truth, a creation of mental substance, whenever the true being frees itself from the magnetic pull of the mental world, there is no time. Man becomes aware of what he calls time-pressure when he loses control of his mind and experiences the bombardment of unfulfilled desires. And so it is that man finds time passing slowly or man finds time passing quickly. It is ever dependent upon his own mental judgments. There is no time in truth, for there are no judgments, there are no mental forms in the great eternal truth known as peace.

Thank you. There has been an explanation of the so-called Bermuda Triangle as being caused by deadly ultrasonic sound vibrations, which are caused by the friction of wind passing over water. Can we parallel this friction to the friction between man's conscious and subconscious? If so, and we accept that man's vibrations affect nature, what is the conflict or friction between man's conscious and subconscious that is creating the vibrations which affect the wind and sea and then result in ultrasonic vibrations?

Yes. In answer to your eight questions in one, we will speak first on this delusion of the so-called Bermuda Triangle. Some time ago we shared with you our understanding that there are certain magnetic pulls in various parts of your Earth planet. The so-called Bermuda Triangle is, in truth, one of those magnetic pulls.

In reference to the friction, so-called, between the conscious and the subconscious mind, let us look objectively at the constant panorama of moment-by-moment desires. How quickly our desires seem to change. Many times have we spoken to you not to suppress desire, the divine expression—to educate desire or fulfill desire. For the subconscious mind is already filled with a multitude of unfulfilled desires. They are constantly crying for their fulfillment. The conscious mind is in a constant process of creating ever more desires. The desires of the moment are rarely harmonious and in keeping with the desires of the moment before. It has become that way for man has not made the effort to control that vehicle that he is using for his little soul to ride in, in its journey through life.

How does man bring peace into a mental world of such discord and such distraction? By first becoming aware that he is not the form, but he is using the form. And by becoming aware of that simple truth, he gains control of that which he is using, control of the vehicle known as the human mind. It was not designed to take you where it decided to take you. It was designed to take you where *you* decide to go. This is something we must be consciously aware of constantly. But first we must separate truth from creation. We must stand firmly on the Law of Identity that we not become controlled by the Law of Creation. Creation is a vehicle to be used by the eternal soul that it may express through form, that it be not controlled by the forms of its creation.

Long ago we stated to you the soul can and does all things, for you, create. It creates each moment, for it is that Law of Identity. The covering of the formless, free Spirit, the very essence of the Law of Life, the covering *is* the Law of Identity. Your soul is individualized because the formless, free, intelligent energy, that spark, that essence, entered and became individualized. When you no longer are in the Law of Identity, you are no longer individualized. You are then, in that moment, the universality, the cosmic consciousness, the moment of peace and truth. There is no spiritual awakening, there is no full awakening as long as you are in and controlled by the Law of Identity. For the Law of Identity moves you into form, into duality, into discord, into all pairs of opposites, known as creation.

My good friends, I am not speaking of something for you to attain in centuries yet to be. I am not speaking of something for you to attain after you leave your physical body. I am speaking of that which is attainable for you this very moment. Practice each day. Make the effort to remove your consciousness from the Law of Identity in the things that disturb you. For that that disturbs us is that which controls us. It has been given to you, in earlier classes, as redirecting the intelligent, eternal energy. If you make the effort frequently and you do not falter by the wayside, you will, you *will* become aware of your eternal right.

When this free spirit enters this great pull of identity and moves into the Law of Creation, in the Law of Creation it judges. And it is our judgments in life that deprive us of the beauty and goodness of life.

Man on the Earth planet, the highest evolved form upon the planet at this time, has earned what is called the divine right of choice. But he has forgotten that the right is divine. He no longer uses his divinity in his choice. And because he has forgotten that the right is divine, he has sold out that right to the mental worlds of form and must pay the price that the mental world offers to him. But that price need not be paid from this moment on.

In a very simple truth: we put God in it or forget it. To put God into anything is to put the light of reason and common sense into it. To put God into it is to accept any and all possibilities, is to be free from that dual Law of Judgment, to be free, to be free. And so whatever you think and whatever you do, put God, the goodness of life, in it. Then you will not be discouraged. You will not be joyous and you will not be sad, for you have put no mental dictate into your endeavor. Therefore, there is no dual reaction. It is indeed the glorious path of divine neutrality. That does not mean you do not make the effort, but it means you are not controlled by the effect.

Let us look at our lives and ask ourselves the honest question, "O, Lord," which, by lord we mean the law, "O, Lord, am I controlled by my experiences or am I awake and conscious? Am I awakened and controlling my experiences?" It is your divine right to control that which you create. That *is* your divine right. It is when that which you create and you forget you have created, that you become controlled by them.

Each time, my good students, that we blame outside for any experience, each time we do that, we are forgetting that we are the creators of it. And so the more that we blame another for our experiences in life, the more we give to them power and control over us. Think and think more often, my good friends, what we are permitting our mind to do to us. Designed to serve your eternal soul, your soul is serving it. But each effort that you make each day, slowly but surely, rises your eternal little soul to once again take the reins that you may do what you have in life to do, for you have come to earth, for you have work on earth to do. You cannot leave earth until that work is completed.

It is true that many people think (from a lack of understanding) that some people come to earth and they only stay, perhaps, a few years and they do not get their work completed. That's only from a lack of understanding the great universal process, the many worlds that you have come from and the many worlds you've yet to go to. They did what they had to do on this earth and they have gone to another and another and another.

And so you, too, shall do and complete what you have come to earth to do. Be rest assured, my good friends, of that. You will complete in physical form what you came to complete. You may or may not hover in the magnetic pull of the earthly realm when you've left the physical body. That is ever in keeping with the laws set into motion. But be not discouraged by the Law of Destiny, for each and every moment, each and every moment you face the choice of establishing, slowly but surely, all the changes necessary for your greater good.

It is the goodness within you that is a light unto the world. Let it shine brighter each and every day, for that, in truth, is the true purpose of your being.

Good night.

SEPTEMBER 7, 1978

CONSCIOUSNESS CLASS 188

Greetings, friends. This evening we shall discuss, for our class lesson, affirmations and how they work for you.

As each experience in our life, the effect of a thought pattern, reassures our belief in the thought pattern, so man continues to experience a repetition of those patterns of mind. And so it is given to you many different affirmations to use that you may help yourself in changing these attitudes of mind that you have found so detrimental in your life.

When man, in his efforts to be free from continuing experiences, begins to make a positive affirmation, the defense of these levels of mind rise up within his consciousness. They have all of the intelligence that is within your mind, for they are created by your mind. And so it is when man uses affirmations, he must ever, having used them by the mind, use the very principles of the mind that established the thought pattern in the first place. For example, when you fill your consciousness with the firm belief that your life and your experiences are in a process of getting better, those patterns that dictate they are worse immediately rise in defense. Therefore, wisdom dictates, when you speak forth these affirmations of demonstrable truth, you must remember the mind already believes the opposite and the mind uses the principle of justification to support the opposite. Therefore, you must use that same principle in making the changes within yourself. When you declare that things are getting better for you, you must also justify to the mind how they are getting better. Therefore, my good students, remember, things are getting better because that is the Law of Evolution of which you are an inseparable part.

You are now, have been, and forever will be, in form changing, constantly changing, experiences. So whatever it is that your mind is dictating, whatever disaster you may entertain, remind yourself, this, too, is in a process of changing. The less attention you give to the seeming disaster or struggle, the more quickly it shall pass.

And so it is in using affirmations. You cannot use them now and then, for to use an affirmation now and then is to experience now and then results. Not only is it to experience now and then results, it reinforces the negative patterns, for they have been awakened within you. When you awaken these negative patterns—awaken in the sense they are brought into your conscious mind—then you must be religious with your affirmations. If it is a thousand times a thousand each and every day, then be rest assured that victory is at hand.

Whenever we wait for a result, there are many judgments that rise in our mind. But let us be awake and alert that those judgments are indeed and in truth the very voices of the patterns, the attitudes that we are trying to change.

It is interesting to note in your world the scientific, material advancement that is taking place. And I have also noted great interest with some of my students in what your world calls the test-tube babies and the cloning of the form. Broaden your horizons, my friends, and then you will graciously and harmoniously evolve. We spoke to you once before in reference to these laboratory babies. Yes, indeed and of course, they are soul. For whenever the negative and positive poles of creation come together, in that moment it is possible for the eternal soul to enter the form of your earth.

It is not important, my friends, whether or not it takes place in a laboratory or takes place within the womb of a human being. What is important is the infallible principle of life itself. Many minds have questioned if these children, given birth in laboratories, will be normal. It is of the utmost importance that these forms, these babies in laboratories, be receptive from the very moment of conception to harmonious sound, music, and the vibratory waves of the higher colors of the universe.

There are many changes already in process in your world. And in reference to this cloning, which you will see in your lifetime on earth—most of you—the soul is in the form, but is not limited by the form. As your scientific advancement creates these so-called duplicates or copies of your present form, the eternal soul within you expresses through how many forms man chooses to duplicate of himself. That does not mean that each so-called duplicate or clone has an individualized soul. It does mean that they are expressing from the soul that is already within you.

There are benefits to material, scientific advancement, for they are, in truth, instruments through which man, begrudgingly, must make drastic changes in his thinking. For life *is*. It is everywhere within and without. There is no place in all of the universes that you can go that you will not find life, for life is everywhere, for everywhere is life. The forms, they vary, ever dependent upon the elements of the planet through which the life force is expressing. But be rest assured, my good friends, that life force is an intelligent life force, regardless of the forms. For that intelligent life that is flowing through you this moment is the same in the rose or the tree, the blade of grass, the dog, or the cat, the horse or the cow. It is the same intelligent, eternal life. That is the life that we must, in bowing in humility, strengthen by the wisdom of patience, awaken our limited mind to.

All of these souls in the universes are only a thought away. Why is it that these intelligent forms and beings are only a thought away? For, my friends, it is the human mind that builds boundaries. It is the human mind that limits the goodness and the experiences of our life. When you make the effort to broaden your horizons to expand your consciousness, then you will see and you will know that you are, in truth, an inseparable part. You cannot, no matter what you do, separate your true life from the truth that you are a part of an infinite variety of forms. For as I view you, your world, by that very law, may you view me and my world. It is only the limited thoughts that rise in your mind that restrict you from the broadening beauty of life itself.

So each and every day and each and every moment you are constantly experiencing the opportunity to expand and to grow. Whatever it is that you are experiencing, remember the good that is in it, that is waiting for you to experience. No matter where you wander, God is there. When you permit your mind to accept that truth, then you will be freed from fear; you will be freed from the plague of the human mind and its pairs of opposites and you will know that you are all of the goodness that the mind is ever seeking. You already are the goodness, for you already are inseparably a part of the good whole, known as God.

Let us, as we continue on in these classes, begin the small, but sure, effort of encouraging ourselves, for not to do so is to deny goodness within and deny the abundant Source of life itself. And each denial, we know, becomes a destiny. None of us truly want the destinies of disaster and deprivation. We cannot experience abundance until we accept its possibility. We cannot accept its possibility until we accept the source from whence it comes.

My friends, each dictate of the human mind is a law established. And we follow those laws because we make those dictates. Do not dictate the limit of the goodness of life for you. Accept the possibility of your birthright. When you accept the possibility of your birthright, you will begin to experience it.

It may take a few moments; it may take a few years. That, of course, is ever dependent upon your effort and what you are willing each day to do.

It is the Law of Continuity that is the lifeline to the goodness of all experience. Whatever it is you choose to do, do it often. That is how the law becomes firmly established in your life. Don't start and overwork, because if you do in any endeavor, you establish the Law of Judgment, for the motive is not pure. It takes time in your world to sow and it takes time in your world to reap. But I assure you, you will not reap in vain if you have sowed under the light of common sense of continuity.

And remember, each time you think you failed, each time that thought arises within your mind, you may be rest assured you are standing at the very gate of victory.

You have already had many experiences in your life. And many times your minds have told you that you have failed and been a fool. But pause when you hear those thoughts within you and ask yourself from whence they come. What is it within that is the true cause and moving force of that thought? And you see so clearly it is a pattern of your mind. A pattern that is very old—old and time to pass on, for you have much to do. You all have a purpose in life. As I have a purpose, so too, have each of you a purpose. Each one knows their purpose in this life. Each one knows that purpose. And when you make the effort to be at peace, you know what it is; you need not be told.

And so as you go on with your mundane acts and activities, so goes the Light. It shines in ways your mind cannot yet imagine. Someday you will see. When you go from your present world and you cross the border into this other realm, you will see the record of your life on earth. And indeed will you be surprised at the credit points, for your mind never dreamed you would have credit for such simple thoughts and such simple, small deeds. Remember the record of life, the book of life, is an infallible recording. May it balance in your life in the debits and credits that you may go on in a brighter and lighter path and truly be the lamp of the world that you went first to the world to be.

The greatest teaching of life is known as the living demonstration. Whatever it is you tell another, be sure you have first told and accepted yourself. If you, your mind, wishes another to change, then remember, they will change in keeping with the law you have established: if you are making the effort, then like attracts like, they are making the effort. Remember, we all, in some way, are making some effort. And surely it is a credit to any soul that is trying to better their lives, to improve themselves and to once again declare and demonstrate their birthright to abundance goodness in their life.

You may ask your questions at this time.

Thank you. Are first impressions good impressions? For example, where one takes an instant like or dislike for another person and cannot explain why or how, any reasonable basis for the feeling, can these first impressions be trusted? And are they also judgments?

In reference to first impressions in anything, it is ever, of course, dependent upon the level of consciousness of the person receiving the impression. But in speaking of first impressions that are received from the inner being, from our own spirit, there is a great positive knowing that rises up within us. Our minds have no reason for the experience and the impression is always correct.

Are they judgments? My good students, we must surely understand someday that in a world of form, there is a world of duality, which is known as choice. Whenever man makes a choice, he is free from the Law of Judgment if in making the choice he accepts fully the benefit of either path—the goodness that is in either path. For God is in all and when we do not see God or Goodness in all things, then we establish the Law of Denial and follow our destiny. And that is known as judgment.

So let us see, though our minds do not agree, let us see the principle, the God or Goodness that is in all of life, that is in all of thought. Then may we choose and be free from the bondage of the human mind. For he who sees the good in all things, shall experience the good in all things.

And, my friends, in your experiences and efforts today, no matter how difficult they are and no matter how much effort you find you must make to see the good, make that effort. For there is no thought and there is no life and there is no experience that God, the Infinite Life, does not sustain. Without God or Goodness, no thought could rise. It is our minds that see the difference; it's not our soul. There is no difference to the eternal spark that is in everything. Let us awaken the flame within ourselves and let it burn brightly that we may see that spark of divinity, that eternal flame, in every thought, in every act, in every deed. And then, the truth and the freedom that you are seeking, it shall burn ever brighter within you. And then, your purpose, and mine, will truly be served.

Thank you. How does the divine Law of Acceptance heal both present and absent ones who are in need of help? [See Appendix for the complete text of the Divine Healing Prayer.]

How beautiful your question. "How does the divine Law of Acceptance heal both present and absent ones who are in need of help?" Absence is only, of course, an unawareness of presence, for when you speak forth that divine truth, "I accept," you first have accepted; the flame within you is first burning. That little flame of light is seen by many. Those who are present in your physical world and those who are absent from your physical world but present in your spiritual world, for the eternal flame is a spiritual flame and it burns bright or dim ever in keeping with your own acceptance. And so, my friends, those who have gathered amongst you ever in keeping with the Law of Attraction, though you see them not, they hear your thoughts, they see your forms. And therefore what you do and what you think has an effect not only upon you, but upon all of those who are attracted to you.

You all, I know, will agree that, dependent upon how you feel and your moods and emotions at any given time, those who are attracted to you are affected by you in keeping with the Law of Attraction.

Acceptance, the will of God. We all have acceptance. It is the limit of our acceptance. It is the limit, the effect of judgment, that truly is our problem in life. Look at the struggle and ask yourself the question, "Am I accepting the right of this expression and, in so doing, moving on to something better? Or am I denying this experience, the effect of my own thought?" You see, my friends, it all comes back to the very foundation of personal responsibility. When we accept that life is an effect and we, deep within, are the cause, when we truly accept that, then we accept all experience the right thereof. We accept its right to return unto us. And once having done so, we flood our consciousness with that which we have chosen to become.

Many ways this same truth has been given to you. Place your attention—the door through which the intelligent energy flows—place your attention on what you have chosen and desire to become; remove your attention from that you choose to overcome. When you remove your attention from the obstruction in your life, the way will appear. But first you must accept the right of that expression. And once having done so, when you truly accept something, my friends, especially when it's those chickens that have come home to roost, when you accept them, in that moment you face the personal responsibility of having created them. When you continue to deny and to refuse the return of those chickens, the ones you have created, then the battle goes on and on and on and on and on.

Accept the return that you may move on in life to gain what is yet waiting for you. But you cannot see when you permit the mind to view the door that has closed. Look for that which is in front of you. It's ever within. It's waiting patiently for your acceptance, but you cannot experience it as long as you are expressing denial. As long as you battle the return, the return will continue to control you. It is the very purpose of these classes: to show you a way, through applying the laws revealed, to be free from these experiences. But, my friends, it is taking place in many ways.

And when our hindsight becomes our foresight, we will then have insight. And it is insight—the looking within—that's where your gold mine is; that's where all things precious to you are waiting for you. Do not chase the universes looking for them. You will not find them. They're waiting within you. But you must first establish the Law of Going Within. And you cannot, nor can I, do that until we accept that's where it is. Truly, my good students, that's where it is. Many a philosopher for many and many a century has told the same truth to the world. It is within.

Accept the Law of Personal Responsibility, for that is the first door that must be opened to go within. Open the first door and the other doors will not be so difficult for you. Open it today. Open it this moment. There is nothing to fear, for faith, the very principle of the Eternal Being, will light your path through the forest and you will find that sanctuary that is yours, that you have wandered from out into these mental worlds back, back to you, the true you. All of the coverings, they're in a process of going. Walk along the path this moment. As you go deeper and deeper within, you will see that tiny spark. And then it'll get brighter and brighter. And then all of these forms, they will pass—the forms of the mind and the forms of the worlds of creation. There, you will find the warmth, the comfort, and the great peace that is truly you. Find that this moment within yourself, for that is the light, the light of your path. And it will take you to these heavenly heights, where all worry and all activity of the human mind doth pass. Above and beyond, that is your home. Though you have wandered far, you shall return. If you, in those efforts of meditation, return each day, then your flame of life will be brighter and brighter and brighter.

Remember, out of the eternal void an idea was given birth. And from an idea, a law—the law—was established. And once being established, like a great circle, it has no end. For it goes around and around and around. To some, they call that the wheel of karma. But because you are the idea and because from you, the idea, law, the circle, was given birth, you, the idea, can remove yourself from the law. It's known as becoming the observer: to watch the forms that travel upon the wheel of karma, to know that they are forms that have been created from an original idea. But never forget: you are the idea.

Good night.

SEPTEMBER 14, 1978

CONSCIOUSNESS CLASS 189

Greetings, students. This evening we shall spend our class in sharing our understanding over the questions you have prepared.

Thank you. You have taught the meaning of various parts of the physical body and the meanings of various colors. Does size also have a meaning in relation to various parts of the total size of the body?

Because form not only involves color and substance, which is vibration, but also size, indeed it does.

Thank you. If there is an injury to the right side of the brain, which scientists say is the creative side—does this mean that the spiritual part of the person's development will be impaired?

No, it does not.

Thank you. Does the soul express in the same gender in each incarnation? Please elaborate.

No, it does not.

In reference to elaborating upon your question, one need but study that which is ever before him: the laws of nature. The infinite intelligent Energy expresses through all forms of life. Ever in keeping with the laws of evolution, the individualized soul has, finally, upon your Earth planet expressed and is expressing through what is called the human being. In order that the soul may ever continue to unfold or expand its consciousness, the multitudes of forms yet to express through are ever in keeping with this Law of Evolution and this Law of Refinement.

When man broadens his horizon by freeing himself from the limited identity in which he has placed himself, he will no longer be concerned with what forms he is yet to be in or what forms he has already been in. For it is only a vehicle through which this Intelligence is expressing. It is born and has its death, as all forms and all vehicles do.

It is one of the purposes of these classes to help you to expand your consciousness, to broaden your horizons that you will not be limited and controlled by this narrow thinking. For when man truly accepts, then he flows in the divine will and all obstructions melt in his path by the light of reason. For it is the light of reason that frees man, through his own efforts. And the light of reason is what will transfigure you into the paradise, into the heaven that waits the moment you broaden your horizons. For the broadening of the horizons is the freedom from the limits of judgment.

Thank you. Please clarify the difference between aspiration and desire.

Aspiration, a soul faculty, is the balance of the divine expression, known as desire. It is not desire that is the problem of man. It is not desire in and of itself, for that is the expression of the Divinity. It is the judgments that precede the expression of desire. And so it is when man balances desire, any desire, with the corresponding soul faculty, then he is freed from these continuing, repeating payments. Each and every time that we dictate to the Divine, we pay the price. We pay the price of the error of our own ignorance.

Thank you. Picasso once said, "Art is a lie which makes us realize the truth." Would you please discuss this in relation to the Living Light statement, Art is the essence of life?

Indeed art is the essence of life. Art, to the mind, to any mind which is controlled by judgment, becomes a lie. For it is the judgment that makes the illusion or the lie; it is not the art itself, which is, in truth, the essence of life. It is what man, in his judgment, does with it.

Thank you. What is the meaning of the terms growth, expansion, *and* evolution *as used in the Living Light philosophy?*

They are inseparable: growth, expansion, and evolution. You cannot have evolution without growth and you cannot have growth without expansion. And so the soul is in a constant process of evolving, in a constant process of a broadening of the horizons. Now, the soul in and of itself is not, in truth, where growth is taking place: it is the form through which the soul is expressing. That is where the expansion and the evolution and the growth is really taking place. You cannot expand on Infinite Intelligence, but you can expand the vehicle through which the Infinite Intelligence is expressing.

Many times we have spoken of man's problems being in keeping with his identity. You see, my good students, we identify with so many things and each thing that we identify with, we become controlled by. And these many things that we identify with are not all in harmony. Therefore, we do not experience the harmony that we know is rightfully ours by the very right of our divine birth.

Thank you. It is stated in the November 1977 Serenity Sentinel *that man merits heaven. Is there then ground for pride in heaven?* [The Serenity Sentinel was a monthly magazine that was published by the Serenity Association from February 1969 through June 1983.]

Pride is a function and does not express in heavenly realms. The functions and the faculties, spoken to you so many, many times, must be brought into balance. When the function of pride is brought into balance with its corresponding soul faculty, that *is* the heaven. For each faculty and each function, whenever they are balanced, man experiences his own heaven.

Thank you. Having studied some astrology, would you please give us your understanding of the so-called adverse aspects (squares and opposites, mainly) and how these may tie in with your—with our philosophy regarding denial?

As you know, as students, and as you know from your own personal experiences that denial, in truth, is destiny, for whatever we deny, we direct an infinite and intelligent energy to. And by so doing, we create the form in the sense of our individual relationship to it. Now, a person may say, "Well, if denial establishes our destiny, then let me begin by denying the things that I, in truth, desire." But that is the way a mind of logic would think. It would not see that a house divided cannot stand, let alone experience what it desires. No, my friends, we must consider much more deeply than the mind of logic to find the truth that lies within us.

We deny in life many things and therefore we have many experiences. We desire many things and we have also many experiences. But remember, acceptance, being the will of God, denial, therefore, must be the will of man. So we see clearly that the will of man and the will of the Divine must be brought into a harmonious relationship through the Law of Balance.

Take a good look at your functions. View them objectively and you will see: they are all limited, for they are all formed and controlled by mental substance. Take a look at the faculties of the soul. You will see that they are limitless. They are free, without boundaries.

Now, my friends, with each thought that you have, there is something that has caused the thought. And it is only in finding the cause that the cure truly lies.

We are, our vehicles, an expression of what is known as desire. It is in our own best interests that we bring a degree of balance into our desires; that we do not permit our minds to judge they are not being fulfilled.

Time and time again I have asked that you make some effort to encourage yourself, to know beyond a shadow of any doubt, beyond the illusion of the limited mind that you are on a path that is leading you to higher heights than your mind can yet imagine, a path that you alone have merited. Upon that path, of course, as in all paths, are many stepping stones. But it is when we mistake the stepping stones along the path for the plateau itself—we do not see an end, for to view an end is to view, in truth, a beginning.

Whatever thought is ending in your mind, by its process of ending, another is being born. And so it is in a world of form or creation, this constant process has always been and will always be. For the mind to be without activity is for the soul to express without obstruction. But the mind must first bow its authority and that can only take place when you find you. Not the image you have created, for they, in truth, are many. That is not you. That is only a passing and changing form.

Each day in every way remind yourself that you are the peace that passeth all understanding. For what you are doing, in truth, is telling the mind, for you, the soul, already know. It is the vehicle your soul is using that doesn't know. Therefore, it is the vehicle that needs to be reeducated, for it is filled with many, many, many judgments that are not serving you well. Learn, my good students, to speak to your mind. Learn to disassociate that which is truly you from that that you are using. You are not what you are using. And what you are using—the mind—must be reeducated in order that you may find the true purpose of being.

Thank you. Please explain the card in the Serenity Game which states, "Freedom in creation ever seeks to find the part of self that loves, the joy with which to bind."

Freedom in creation ever seeks to find the part of self that loves, the joy with which to bind. Without bondage, there is no individualization. The moment there is individualization, covering, or form, there is limit. And that substance from which the form was gathered, the form is subject to or bound by. For example, your physical earth body is composed of the elements of your physical Earth planet. Your life on Earth has revealed, and continues to reveal to you constantly, that so-called Mother Earth rises to claim that which is hers. And so your physical body that you are presently using returns to Mother Earth. She claims that which is rightfully hers. Therefore, freedom in creation, the infinite, formless free Spirit ever seeks to find the part of self that loves. Without form, there is not love expressed, for form is the effect of love. When we love all life, then we will know the Light.

We understand life to be the movement or expression of the divine, eternal Light, which man's mind calls the great void. Therefore, your physical body is reclaimed by Mother Earth who gave it, as a loan, to you. In keeping with that very principle of form, each body that you are using is reclaimed by the very realm of which it is composed. Your thought is loaned to you by a world of thought. It is substance. From the substance you gather and you shape and you use. Your spiritual body is composed of spiritual substance that you gather unto yourself in keeping with the laws that govern the realms of spiritual substance.

Therefore, there is no thing you may call your own. Some time ago we spoke to you about man, the greatest borrower known in the universes, for he borrows many things to use in keeping with the law. When man permits his mind to say that this is his and that is his, he establishes the very law that he may see clearly: he has been loaned it for a time. If he uses it wisely, then the loan may be extended indefinitely. And how does man use wisely what he has been loaned? By never forgetting who the owner truly is.

Because we forget the rightful owner, we go through much suffering in life. There are rulers of mental realms and there are rulers of spiritual realms and there are rulers of astral realms. We have borrowed from these rulers—rulers in the sense they are responsible for the wise use of the substance of the matter in their domain. To awaken to this simple truth is to benefit your life in the now. To remember that whatever you have that you use wisely, it will remain with you until the purpose of the loan is fulfilled. If you fail to use it wisely, it shall be reclaimed by the very realm that loaned it to you in the first place.

How does man know what is wise? All men know that all things must be considered, for all things exist to serve a purpose. And when their purpose is no longer served, they return to their source from whence they cometh.

Our minds have forgotten, conveniently, it seems, that we are, our forms, indebted. And being indebted, we are bound. And being bound, we are not free. When you truly are ready to give up all form, you will know your freedom. But remember, my students, a thought is form, a feeling is form. And if you feel you are not yet ready, then you are not yet ready. When you are ready, you will be in the world and not a part of it. When you are ready, you will be with a thing and never a part of the thing.

Through your efforts in practicing the exercise of disassociation that has been given to you, you can, slowly but surely, wrench yourself free from the bondage of form. That does not mean that you will not continue to express through form, but it does mean you can be free from its control.

In speaking to you before on freedom, the effect of self-control—because self is form and there is no control of the form by you, the light of reason, then you're bound by whatever it does and wherever it takes you.

Many have asked, in reference to these astral and spiritual realms—many books have been written upon the untold number of souls who continue to serve in those astral realms. You see, my friends, when they were on earth, in an error of their mind, they tried to get something for nothing. There is no something in life for nothing. It's only an illusion that you may be in for a time. But your payment—everyone's payment—comes due. It will always come due as long as you permit the vehicles that you are using to forget that you, in truth, have created them from the substance of which they are composed, that you alone have formed them, that you alone have given them birth, that you alone are responsible to what you have given birth to, that you alone can educate them.

Many times students become discouraged in their efforts. They forget their starting points along the spiritual path and they become discouraged. And the discouragement—a devise of the patterns of yesteryear to once again rise up in their authority to control you. Sometimes they take the soul from the Light, once again, for a time, but never forever. And so the faculty of encouragement, the handmaiden of the faculty of reason, must be used wisely, must be used frequently to flood the consciousness that you may see more clearly. For everyone, their forms, in truth, are changing. But you, you will always be the principle of life, for that is what you are in truth. It is when these forms that we use become temporarily greater than their creator—yourself—that we experience these seeming disasters in our life.

And so along the path we sometimes, in the early days upon it, feel that it's impossible for us to make a change in our thinking. And as the years pass on, we find it even more impossible, because we're closer to the victory. But this thought of the impossibility of our changing our attitudes in life is supported by the many forms of the attitudes of yesteryear. They don't want to go to sleep, those forms. They enjoy this upliftment of energy that you give them by your attention directed to them.

The joy in life is when these many forms, under the light of reason, begin to work harmoniously and united as servants of your eternal being. They have forgotten that you gave them birth that they may serve you well. They have forgotten that because you have forgotten that.

And so you find often that you are no longer directing your own evolution. The forms of your mental substance have gained control. But do not be discouraged, for in so being, they will gain even more control. Pause. Pause more often. Do not give forth the power of the spoken word until you are united with the light of reason. And remember, there's no escape from personal responsibility. They are your children. Many have grown very strong, but they're never greater than their creator.

Throughout your history on earth the philosophies have taught a God of creation. But that is not the God that we understand. Oh, yes, there are many gods and goddesses of creation and they create many things, but there is one neutral, intelligent, infinite, divine God that sustains everything. We shall evolve through the mental realms of created gods and in so doing, we shall learn the great blessing of self-control. For each moment that you express control of self, you are gaining control over the many forms you have created. When you lose control of self, you are serving the forms of your creation. Forms that you originally designed to serve you, you are now serving them. No one, no one wants to be a slave, let alone a victim. When you feel these thoughts rising in your consciousness, grab ahold of them. For if you don't, they are destined to grab ahold of you.

Along the path many things will distract us. But let us never forget they are all things that we alone are responsible for. Let us make greater effort to stop blaming outside. For with each thought of blame that we direct away from ourselves, we give greater strength to those forms who have enslaved us. As we begin to accept the responsibility, as we begin to accept that each and every moment of our life is dependent upon what we are thinking, as we do that, my good friends, we begin to gain control.

Let us become more aware of the frequency in which we are blaming outside for what, in truth, is going on inside. That is where our growth truly lies. When we say to our mind, "Peace, O, mind, for I have created you out of the substance of the universe to serve me wisely. Peace. I order you to peace, that you may be truly a servant to fulfill a good purpose in life. For only through my direction do you exist." Remember, when you speak to these things, that you alone have the power. Having brought them into form, you alone have the power to send them back to the formless. Remember, my friends, that is the power that you, in your evolution, have earned. It's when you forget, then things no longer are harmonious. Disaster rises up its ugly head again and again and again, showing you clearly that you have forgotten. You have forgotten for a time.

To take hold of the reigns is to direct your own evolution. You see, each thought you permit your mind to experience, each thought, *each thought* is a form. When you harbor a thought, you are feeding a form. You are directing neutral, intelligent energy. You are causing it to move, to act, and to be. Each and every thought, it goes out into the universe; it gathers up like kind. If it is a pleasing form, a good form, a constructive form, it goes out into the world and all of the forms that are like it are attracted to it. Let your forms be angelic that your life may be the peace that is your true home.

Good night.

SEPTEMBER 21, 1978

CONSCIOUSNESS CLASS 190

Good evening, class. You'll kindly turn your books [*The Living Light*] to Discourse 36.

We have a little change of our regular format. For a number of years now, you have been privileged to ask questions concerning this philosophy and spiritual matters. And so this evening you will be called upon to answer questions that we have for you. Without participation, of course, in anything that we are interested in, there is no growth. And our purpose for being here is to grow in the most harmonious and peaceful ways that we can find.

Now, rather than call upon you individually, I shall ask the questions concerning the philosophy that you have already studied and you may volunteer the answer by raising your hand, please. And so we'll begin with one of the very basic teachings of this philosophy and that is, What is the difference between the faculties and the functions and what purpose do they serve? So if you'll kindly raise your hands—those of you who are interested in answering. [*After a slight pause, the Teacher continues.*] Of course, we're in hopes to conclude this class within an hour, but if it's going to take this long for the first question, then it looks like it'll be longer than what we anticipated. Yes, please.

My understanding is the functions are expressed through the brain and the faculties, through the soul. And the purpose is to have them balanced so that we have balance in our expression.

Thank you very much. Yes.

My understanding is that the faculties are used to develop the soul and that the functions are, kind of, of the physical body and the mind—and then to balance them, but put more emphasis on the faculties.

Thank you.

The purpose is to bring balance. The soul expresses the faculties; the senses express the functions. And they're both necessary, but we, in this creation, express the senses to such a degree that that's the reason the emphasis is on the faculties, when we're starting, because we express the functions anyway all the time.

Thank you.

Well, it is our understanding that the basic purpose of expression and balance of the soul faculties and the sense functions—as the infinite, intelligent, neutral Energy flows through the vehicles of creation, as this Energy is directed in the mental realms of consciousness, it creates its forms of like kind. Also, in keeping with that inevitable law, as this energy flowing through us is directed to the soul faculties, it creates the form in the spiritual realms.

Now, you have, here, in your study book [*The Living Light* or *The Living Light Dialogue*, Volume 1], where it clearly states that the functions form and deform the astral body. Whenever we express what is called the functions, which are in the mental realms, we, unless balance is kept through expressing equal energy through the faculties, we become, as has been stated many times, we become the victims of our own created forms. Long ago we spoke to you about the war within. Now, this war within is the battle that goes on. All philosophies teach this battle of the forces of darkness and the powers of light. It is only an imbalance between the corresponding soul faculties and the sense functions.

I was in hopes, however, that more students would be willing to participate with these questions, but we will go on, however, with our class.

Why is the Law of Personal Responsibility the only path to freedom of the eternal soul? Yes.

Personal responsibility is that you accept whatever happens to you is caused by you. You can't blame the outside for what is happening to you. You have to take full responsibility for each act and activity. And when you realize that—I think that it will be easier for all of us if we accept that. Thank you.

Thank you. Yes.

Well, it seems as though we go into—or we're born into this world of creation with certain lessons to learn. And that seems as though man just suffers and puts the blame outside, not willing to really face it—the responsibilities. But when an awareness does come or something important does come to his life, that through the expression and re-expression of those particular laws that he has set into motion, of the Law of Repetition, that he is finally able to at least get some awareness and view his patterns and view and express to himself, "Well, I've been doing this for some total of my years here on this world of creation. And I can change this because this is all inside." So we really have to really look at ourselves and view the Law of Personal Responsibility as something that is caused by us. It's not caused by anything outside. But if we make the changes inside, we will then make the changes outside.

Thank you very much. Yes.

It seems that when we give energy to the way things are that—when they don't satisfy us the way it is and we blame it on outside circumstances, then we are, in truth, giving our freedom away. Because we gave energy to the circumstances that are outside of us, instead of seeing that it's not anything outside of us that got us to that position but ourselves—and the freedom that we have in choosing to be there, instead of taking ahold of that and giving that to the divine will and trying to move in harmony with, with the changes that result. If we are attached to how we want it to work out and we give that energy to the way things didn't work out, we attach ourselves. We give the key of freedom away and give power to the thing that we want to stay away from. That resistance brings it closer to us.

Thank you very much. Anyone else? [*After a slight pause, the Teacher continues.*] Why do we find in life attachment to be our greatest struggle? Yes.

Because, without seemingly knowing it, we make a judgment that that which is close to us or that which we derive satisfaction from is that which we possess. And when the time comes for that object or experience to leave us, the very nature of the possession creates the struggle because we have not granted God his right to express through that experience or through that object.

Thank you very much. Yes.

When we're attached, we're over-identified with self and we are not realizing our fullness of being part of the Allness. And therefore, we cannot be free as long as we're identified with self.

Thank you. Yes.

As all is a manifestation of the one great Energy, by attachment, we cling to the manifestations and not to the essence, which is making it. It is the source.

Thank you very much. Yes.

I believe it's also a lack of faith that anything we value will come to us again and we attach to the things that we do value, not realizing other good things are on their way as well.

Thank you. What is the primary difference between the duality of creation and the trinity of truth? I'll ask the question once again. What is the primary or principal difference between the duality of creation and the trinity of truth? Yes.

Truth never changes. Truth is individually perceived, but truth simply is. In creation, the mind will say something is black one moment and the next moment it is white. And it is constantly fluttering between its desires. There is no truth in the duality of creation. It isn't stable. It's just a fluctuating kind of view of the mind. Truth is on a soul or spiritual level. And truth simply is, although it may be individually perceived in different ways by the mind.

Thank you. Yes.

Truth is eternal and the duality of creation has a beginning and has an end.

Thank you. We're discussing the basic principle and primary difference between the duality of creation and the trinity of truth. What is it that brings stability or balance to the Law of Duality? Now, we all know that through the trinity of truth we experience what is called manifestation. We all know that without the duality, there is no form or creation. So what is it that brings about this balance in creation? Yes.

The light of reason.

The light of reason. Thank you. Yes.

I would think divine, neutral energy. Reason.

Thank you. Has anyone ever had experience without faith? Now, we see very clearly that without faith, there is no experience, for without faith, there is no manifestation. Without faith, there is no form, there is no creation. So all that we experience in all of our lives is in keeping with the very principle of the trinity of truth, which brings balance to creation through the principle of faith. Whatever we have faith in, we have identified and directed energy to. Now, we may have faith in experiences that we decide and we judge are not beneficial in our life. But it is the same faith. Faith itself does not change. Truth does not change. Faith does not change. You may have faith in whatever you choose to have faith in, but ever in keeping with the expression of your faith and the continuity thereof will your experiences be.

The changes that man is seeking are changes we all know that must take place within ourselves. And if we have spent our time, of course, in a life that is imbalanced between the soul faculties and the sense functions, then we must experience this war within and all that it has to offer. But we can direct the faith that we already have into something that is more harmonious and beneficial in our life. We all have the potential of equal faith. No one has more faith than another. In that respect we all have and are receptive to a great abundance of this wonderful principle called faith. We direct the faith where we choose to direct it. That's entirely up to us.

When we are discouraged and we feel discouraged and we experience what our mind says is even more discouraging experiences—that is all made possible by our own faith. That's where we are—have chosen, through errors of ignorance, to direct our faith. So if we continue to tell ourselves how bad everything is and how many bummer experiences that we are encountering each day and then we wake up in the morning we say, "Oh, no, here I go again," then we are directing this great power to the continuity of those experiences. Now, the power itself is intelligent. It does whatever you direct it to do and it does it very intelligently. So if you choose to direct this great intelligent power, through this wonderful faculty known as faith, to limitations and discouragements, you will see how great your faith is.

The word *faith* does not apply exclusively to religion. It is a principle. You use faith all the time. It's only a matter of seeing how well it works for you and making a change to redirect it. You know when you are feeling badly, how badly you really feel. It is your faith that is sustaining the thought that you have chosen, first consciously, to experience.

Now, we, I am sure, can easily relate with these bummer experiences. It's interesting to note about the human mind: it well remembers the struggles and the tough times it has had in life and usually quickly forgets the times when things were going rather well. Yet, it is the same faith that brought about both experiences. We chose to do that.

Now, we are here in these classes to become aware that each experience in life is an effect of our choice that we may ponder and think and think deeply, beyond the surface, that we may see that each thought is more than just a seed: it's a guaranteed growth taking place in consciousness.

Now, all of these forms and things and all that this planet has to offer and, yea, even the planets we are yet to experience on, they all come and they all go. There is no experience in eternity that is so disastrous that we can escape from it. Each one, each experience that we have—we alone have chosen the experience. We have first consciously chosen it and then it is sifted into the very depths of our so-called subconscious mind, where the great magnet of the universe truly exists, and just pulled it right to us. But we can choose more intelligently this moment, today, if we want to make the effort to pause to think.

Our use of the great power of faith has put us where we are today. And our intelligent use of that great power called faith will move us to where we want to go if we make the choice now.

What is the purpose of our being on the Earth planet at this time? Yes.

Well, it's the fifth planet and it's to demonstrate our faith. And to have faith in everything around us.

Thank you. Yes.

We're instruments of the Divine. So that the Divine can work through us.

Thank you.

To help humanity.

Yes.

The way we would help humanity is to grow in consciousness so that we can train and teach the forms that have controlled us to be controlled again, once again, by us because we created them in the first place. And to redirect the energy to create angelic forms, which go out into the universe, bring back its like kind and, in so doing, spread harmony . . . back for us, too.

Thank you. Yes.

To love all of life and know the Light.

Thank you. Why is the function known as money the first and most predominant of all of the functions? Also, what is its corresponding faculty? Yes.

It's faith, is the corresponding faculty. And the function of money deals with security and when you're concerned about security, there's a lack of faith on that level.

Yes. Thank you. Yes.

We have made money our false god because money many, many times is much more important than faith. And it controls us to the point, sometimes, that it's uncontrollable. And in truth, it's only paper. And money is only as important as we make it, because, in truth, it burns up. It has no value. But faith never disappears.

Thank you. Yes.

I noticed on the dollar bill a long time ago and I couldn't understand why it said, "In God We Trust." And I think people have gotten so they trust money as god, instead of who God really is and who the source of our true supply is. And it isn't dependent on a piece of paper or coins.

Thank you. Yes.

I feel that money is a way of depending on oneself for survival, while faith is depending on something greater than self for survival.

Thank you. Yes.

Money can be used to represent support. We support ourselves with it and we support the things that we're interested in with it. We work to earn it and so we've created an attachment to it, just in the earning of it. And we're born into a world where it's already being used. Naturally, our mind wants the most energy that we can give it. So when we find ourselves supporting other interests with money, the mind sometimes wants to hang on to it more and more and give itself the most of any group. And then we find ourselves very attached to it.

Thank you. Yes.

Well, one thing about money—a person never really has enough. The more he makes or the more that—the amount of money—the more that he has, it's usually never enough to the mind. It usually wants more. It doesn't make any difference if it's a dollar or if it's a million dollars. I mean, it's still never enough.

It's a very good point. Why is it that we believe there's never enough of the function of money? Do we all believe that? Why do you think we believe that? Yes.

I think because we want an optimal security. But we like to derive it in terms of the world, and not from God.

Thank you. Yes.

It's lack faith on certain levels of consciousness.

Thank you. Yes.

I think it's just a matter of reeducating the mind, because we've all grown from small children knowing how dependent everyone seems to be upon money, because of the programming you get through your education. And I think it's just reeducating the mind and realizing who the true source is. And, as you said, that money needs us. We don't need—or money needs us. We don't need money.

Thank you.

Now, we're bringing up this primary function because it's in keeping with our discussion of this faculty of faith. But I'm sure that we all agree, there never seems to be enough. No matter how much we have, no matter how much we have not, there never seems to be enough. If we have those fleeting moments that there is enough, they're only moments. I'm sure we will all agree. And then our mind rises up to tell us that, once again, we are short. And so we seem to ride the crest of the waves of creation on the highs and on the lows, ever dependent, of course, in keeping with what we believe: that we have enough and we don't have enough. So therefore, we do find, as we look at it objectively, that money is not bringing us the security that we think that it is. For if it was bringing us the security, we wouldn't be constantly riding the crest of the waves that we have enough and we don't have enough.

You see, our desires are constantly bombarding us. And as the desires bombard our consciousness, our mind has made the judgment that to fulfill these multitude of desires that are bombarding us, it takes money. Because we have made the judgment—that judgment—then, of course, we must pay the price, that price.

But it does—money, that function, our use of it, our abuse of it—certainly does rob us from the feeling of security and from the feeling of well-being. I well recall some years ago the very discussion of the function of money caused a phenomenal trauma, emotionally, in the group of students at the time. There has been some changes. There certainly has been some growth with the various attitudes expressed at that time concerning that particular function.

When we experience a so-called shortage of that function, if we would just, in consciousness, step aside and look at what our emotions are doing, we would not only receive a great education, but we certainly would be able to view what the very thought of that function is doing to us.

Now, we have taught in these classes, and continue to teach, that money, like anything in all of life, is an effect and it never is, nor will it ever be, a cause. It is an effect of directed energy. Whereas everything in life is an effect of directed energy, it is within our power to redirect the energy. Therefore, there is no reason for us to be discouraged. There is no reason for us to gripe and complain, because we have, within our hands, the power to bring about whatever it is that we choose in life. What we choose in life, if we keep ourselves free from the delusion that it is dependent upon someone else to come to us, then we will have. But if we insist upon holding onto this delusion that our desires will be fulfilled depending upon if and but such and such happens outside, then we continue, don't you see, to be the victim of the very law that we alone have set into motion.

Some time ago, to one of my students, it was stated that man is a law unto himself. And if man is a law unto himself, then what is man doing with the law that he is? Now, this is the question that we must ask. If the answer to that question is discouraging to us, then we can change that discouragement by redirecting the intelligent Energy, called God, that is sustaining the thought of discouragement to the thought of encouragement.

Whereas we are, in these mental forms, truly robots of patterns of mind that have been programmed into us—of course, in keeping with our own evolution, there's nothing outside to blame. It's called the robotical consciousness. Now, as we look at our lives and we see our various patterns, if we are happy with them, then we can continue on with them until they have served their purpose in keeping with our own evolution. But if we look at these patterns and we are not happy with them and we are not happy with the effects of them, then we certainly know beyond a shadow of any doubt that we can change them. And we can change them, of course, at any time that we choose, but we alone must make that choice. And once having made that choice, then it's up to us to stick with the choice that we have made.

I'm sure that we will all agree, even though we know the Law of Personal Responsibility, and even though we know that nothing happens to us that is not directly caused by us, we still seem to slip into the patterns of old: "If only so and so hadn't done such and such, then I would be happy today." This is the greatest delusion of all delusions. Nothing robs us of our peace and abundant good more quickly than the thought that the cause is outside of our control. Nothing takes away our peace of mind, nothing takes away the abundant goodness—those are the robbers of robbers. They come in the night, in the darkness, when you are not making the effort to be on guard—that the guardian who is supposed to be standing eternally vigilant at the portals of the mind, that guardian has gone to sleep. Whenever you go to sleep—and by that I mean when you are not thinking—then the robbers come and rob you of all the goodness that you have stored up.

And so what does it reveal? What does life show to us? We must be on guard constantly. Not in fear, for to be on guard is a spiritual duty. The goodness of life is a spiritual substance. If you permit fear to rise, then it is your mind that is trying to be on guard. It is not your mind that needs to be on guard. It's doing enough as it is. It's your spirit, your eternal being, that needs to be on guard constantly. It's your eternal being that knows the law and it knows it beyond a shadow of any doubt. It sees the robbers before they arrive. So keep your spirit alert. Keep your spirit on guard and on duty.

How does man keep his spirit, that light within, on constant guard duty? By educating his desires through a simple process of the faculty of reason. Not annihilating his desires; not pushing them down, for they'll only rise again, but by educating each and every desire that is bombarding the human consciousness twenty-four hours a day, day and night.

Many people, over the years, have been interested in seeing into these other dimensions or listening and hearing these other dimensions. We have never put that as a primary interest in these classes, because for man to try to force those doors to open, before he has gained some degree of control of his own desires, is absolutely disastrous and certainly not beneficial to anyone. It is one thing to experience an unfulfilled desire, day and night, year after year after year after year; it is something else to see the form of the desire, to listen to it. So be grateful if you see not yet, for that means, simply, that a little more effort is to be made on the control or education of the desires in the human consciousness.

The education of desire by the faculty of reason is a very simple process. We have said, a moment before, not to try to annihilate or to suppress it, but to educate it. Well, how do you really educate a desire? We've discussed this before. If you tell a desire, your desires, "Now, you will be fulfilled. You will be fulfilled under the guiding light of patience. It shall come to pass," then you are introducing into the form of the desire a spiritual substance, known to this world as plain old common sense.

That's one thing we do need is common sense—just plain common sense. When you speak to your desires that plague and bombard you, be reasonable with your desires. They are your own creations. Use some degree of intelligence. If your desire is not contaminated with the dictates that say it is dependent upon what someone else does or does not, then it is an uncontaminated desire; it is yours. The birth, then, is a clean birth. It's not filled with judgments. It's not filled with dependence on others for its growth. Now, that's putting light and reason over desires.

Then you will move on through evolution and you will see, "Ah, yes, that came to pass. And that came to pass. And that desire was so long ago I even forgot I had it, but, look, here it is. It has come to pass." I tell you in all honesty and truth that whatever you are seeking in life is also seeking you. And like the hands of the clock, they are destined to meet. Now, what day they will meet is dependent upon the many variables of the human mind and the individualized evolution of the eternal soul. But they will come to pass. All of your desires that you feed energy to, they shall come to pass. You cannot dictate the day, nor the hour, but they shall come to pass.

If it is your desire to be a millionaire, then a millionaire you will be. You cannot tell the Divine how it will come about, but I can assure you that it will come about, for the law of the Infinite is indeed infallible.

But remember, with all of these many desires, there's always a payment for attainment. It's when the payments come due—and the payments come due before the desires get fulfilled—it's when those payments come due that we start to go down into these forces of pity and discouragement and resentment.

You know, I said to some of my students the other day: You can always tell how attached a person is to anything: just cast the light of reason, through exposure, upon it. Now, if they rise emotionally, that reveals their attachment. It's just like these classes, my friends: there's a little change now and then. All you have to do is to remember how you felt when it was announced we'd have a change of class tonight. Now, if you felt a little bit of emotion, a little bit of anger, a little bit of resentment or any of those things that the functions have to offer, that reveals how much attachment your functions had to the pattern of things being the way they were.

Everything in creation is in change, is constantly changing. We all are changing. The part of us that has attached doesn't like that. We attach because of our need to control. We have a great need to control—and if some of my students don't control their sleeping, then classes will get much, much shorter.

Why do you think there's a need to sleep in class, please? You may rise.

I think it's—it's my understanding that we're in creation. I mean, right at this moment the light of reason is being shed upon all these tapes that we've created. And being in form, we identify with the tapes and we think those tapes are ourselves. And in this process we're attached to, well, because of the identification, we're attached to the tapes. When the light of reason is shed on this, it's like separating ourselves from the creation. So that's separating truth from creation. And the mind does everything it can, I feel, to not let us become fully aware. So it's, it's, I feel it's a mental defense against the truth. And I don't know what else to say. Thank you.

Thank you very much. Yes. Yes.

Well, I was about to say what the other student said. I think that the teaching, the subject of teaching goes above the level of the mind. And the mind cannot grasp it. And by not being able to grasp it, he just quits. And he also sends messages to the body of, "Well, you can't participate in that anymore." It's not used to it. But I think by doing this again and again that your mind—it's like gymnastics—it gets smooth and elastic to it and it's able to have this on a level for it to intuit. And you won't fall asleep anymore.

Thank you very much. Because it has been most interesting to note it is only at certain times—and those are always in keeping with discussions concerning the way the human mind truly works, and the spirit and the soul—that some of the students fall asleep. Now, what the mind cannot cope with, it will work very diligently to blot out. But the mind is an instrument for gathering and garnering, but gathering only in keeping with that which is in harmony or rapport with what it already has.

Now, why does the human mind work so diligently to accept only what is in harmony or compatible with what it already has? Someone care to answer that question? Yes.

I think the only reason that it's not compatible is because it just has no prior reference or experience and therefore it has no acceptance for that particular, for that new experience or discussion or whatever is being discussed at that particular time.

Thank you. Yes.

I think that the mind was originally a helper to secure life, to secure physical and mental creation, as you call it. And, oh, yes, it can only grow, well, it starts from . . . so what is already there. So that's why it allows only what has reference for that part. So it's going from the root to the tree.

Thank you very much. Now, we all know that the human mind ever seeks to control. It is, and has been, designed to serve the eternal being. It is a temporary vehicle and it is designed beautifully to serve the purpose of being the servant of the soul. But the human intelligent mind learned very quickly in evolution a very basic principle: that it could only control what it knew. And it could not control what it did not know. Therefore, the human mind resents and rejects anything that it judges it does not know, for it must control whatever it has. It must control whatever it is exposed to. And it can only control it by knowing it. Now, this is why we teach that knowledge knows much but reason knows better.

Reason is a soul faculty.

So if we reject what we do not, in our judgment, fully know, then we can keep control of whatever it is that we have judged that we already have, for what we have, we know. This is why participation is so important in these class studies, because our minds know many things. And many of my students know very well this philosophy. But that's the problem. We know it and are in waiting to fully apply it. Knowing a philosophy does not bring about the transformation and the changes. That's only the first step. Application is when the soul gets into it. And we know that the voice of the soul is the heart, the human heart. The changes in our life cannot come about until we apply what we are learning.

I have heard many of my students speak to others and beautifully speak the truth of this demonstrable philosophy. But in speaking we have left out an integral part, known as demonstration. For the law is very demonstrable: what one can or does accomplish is within the realm of possibility for all to accomplish. The philosophy goes to the world through demonstration. If we apply on a continuing basis only a microscopic fraction of the philosophy that we are learning, we will rejoice in the changes for the better that take place in our lives. But we cannot learn a philosophy that teaches the abundant divine flow of goodness in our life and then demonstrate the opposite, for a house divided cannot stand.

We all know the way, but only we can apply the way that we know. Now, if you teach another about a God that is infinite and abundant, that is the true and only source of supply in your life, then the effort to demonstrate that truth must be made or it shall fall, that great truth, on deaf ears.

I've always said it's never the amount; it is the principle that is involved. When we give, it is ever dependent from what level has motivated us to give, that is the law that will dictate our receiving. And many people, many minds, relate the Law of Giving only to the primary function of money. They don't seem to relate to the giving of a good word, a good thought, a good act, or a good deed. It's good thoughts, good acts, and good deeds that we're crying for in our life. But we must first make the effort to give the good thoughts, the good acts, and the good deeds in order to have them return.

Of what value is the function of money, if the goodness of life is not there? Then it surely—if we are robbed of our health, if we are robbed of our peace and our happiness, of what benefit is the function? It is of no good and no benefit at all.

Remember, my friends, there are no special incarnations that I am aware of on this planet or any other. So whatever one has, the God that granted it to them grants the same to you when you become receptive to it.

Thank you very much. Thank you.

SEPTEMBER 28, 1978

CONSCIOUSNESS CLASS 191

Good evening, students.

In our journey through the mental realms of consciousness known as time and space, we encounter many forms—the effect, of course, of our thoughts. However, beyond those mental realms are the dimensions of pure spirit. There, as we evolve further into the Light, we speak our word and the manifestation is instantaneous.

And so it is these realms of pure spirit are not something that you must wait centuries to attain, for there are fleeting moments in your lives on earth when you become aware of this spontaneity and, in so doing, in that awareness, have the sense of responsibility of your life and your path.

With all of the words that are spoken, there is but one eternal Spirit. There is but one you, inseparable from that Infinite Intelligence. It is when we pause in our thinking, it is when the faculty of reason rises supreme in our consciousness that we truly become aware of this unity of all, of this inseparableness of the Infinite Intelligence which, in truth, we are.

As we have already noted in our lives that we are moving through many levels of the mind and that each level, though offering experiences both pleasant and opposite, are only forms created by mind stuff. That which is temporary is certainly not reliable. And so it is that in our efforts to find this great peace, this abundant good, there is a giving of what we think we have that we may gain what we think we need.

We have spoken before on the greatest gift that you can give to the Divinity: the gift of what is known as self. For it is the illusion known as self that is the only obstruction between your true being and the reuniting in consciousness that you may experience the abundant good, the heaven that waits for you to make the effort.

But what is, in truth, the struggle and the difficulty in giving up the illusion known as self? It is the mind that forgets. It forgets the things that it judges it cannot hold. For it forgets whatever it judges it can no longer possess. And so it is in this great evolutionary process that this light of reason within you, slowly but surely, is refining the many forms that are created by your thought.

Those who have made, and are making, the effort to control their minds, their thoughts are surely well aware of the struggle and the difficulty in so doing. But it is only a temporary struggle. It is only a temporary difficulty. And it is a difficulty and a struggle because it is a new effort to your conscious mind. It is a new effort, for the effort has not been made since your first arrival upon your planet. The effort has not consciously been made.

We all know that we are the effect of our thought in a thought world. As long as we identify with illusion, we are controlled by illusion. And, as I stated earlier, the greatest illusion of all is the illusion of self. It is the thought of I—and not the I—that is the illusion that stands before you. For the I is the I of eternity. That is what you truly are. The thought of I is a mental, created image that you have placed before you, ever chasing the image and never really becoming the image. For the image, being an illusion, has no real substance. Therefore it is not a reality and can never be.

Look at the many forms you call experiences in your earthly life. Are there any that you would care to have for a constant, eternal companion? I am sure you will all agree there is no form, the effect of your thought, there is no experience, the effect of the form, that you would care to have as your eternal, constant companion. For to do so is to place your eternal being in the limitation of a world of form.

It is our view of form that is the problem we create. For we view it as a substance, we view it as something necessary, we view it as something to strive for, to work for, to suffer for. As form is garnered up from the substance of the realm in which you experience it, so does it disintegrate and return to the elements in the realm of which you experience it.

Is there any thought that you have held for eternity? There is no thought that has eternal endurance. Thought, which is form, must be constantly fed infinite, eternal energy in order to survive, in order to exist. And so it is the forms, when you are aware of the mental world, it is the forms that place their demands upon you. We are never left without the divine eternal grace called birthright. The birthright of choice: to choose wisely in our daily activities which form, which thought will we continue to feed. When these thoughts come demanding the energy from your eternal being, that is when you stand firm on the rock of principle and make your choice, ever guided by the faculty of reason.

We have stated to you some time ago that wisdom lives in the faculty of patience. But how does the human mind view the word *patience?* Because the mind does not see a definite end, because it does not see a definite beginning, it is confused with the word *patience.* And when our minds view that soul faculty, in which wisdom truly lives, the mind rises up with many dictates and judgments. And those dictates and judgments become the law that we alone establish.

We all know that like attracts like and becomes the Law of Attachment. We all know that we are known by the company that we keep. We are known by the thoughts that we form. And the thoughts that we form are the experiences that we encounter.

When we truly accept the responsibility for our thoughts, for our feelings, for our experiences, when we truly accept the responsibility for them, we will be freed from them. It is our refusal to accept our own experiences in life, it is our refusal and our denial that we were the cause of the experience that causes the experiences to continue to repeat themselves in our lives.

This is why we have stated to you that our denials in life are, in truth, our destiny. But they are ours; they are not someone else's. So our destiny is ever at our command. We alone are choosing them and we alone can change them. For man, the human mind of man, to accept the very basic truth of this philosophy, the demonstrable Law of Personal Responsibility—when man, his mind, thinks about accepting that, he goes into a trauma for he must give up the judgments of yesterday. No one, no one left to place the blame upon. When man stops blaming outside, man starts growing inside. But first he must stop the blaming—the blaming of others for his own experiences.

Think, my friends, what takes place in your universe, in your life, each time you blame another because you don't feel good. Each time you do that, you feed a form of judgment that keeps you the victim and the slave of its whims. Think before you blame another and then that light of reason will rise within your consciousness. It will light your path to heavenly heights in the here and the now. Each time we permit the human mind to think of the illusion, the image known as self, which is, in truth, in a constant process of changing, each time we permit our mind to think of that illusion, judgment rises supreme within us. And for each judgment that rises comes the feeling of rejection. For without judgment, there can be no rejection. And without rejection, there can be no judgment.

No one truly wants to suffer, the feelings, the hurt of rejection. That can change for you if you are willing to give up the self. Because when you give up self, that illusion, you give up the throne of judgment, you give up the hurt, the illusion in life itself. What you are giving up is nothing compared to what you are gaining. But when you permit your mind to say, "This illusion and image of self that I have is all that I know. And I cannot give up what I know for that which I am not sure of getting"—My friends, it takes faith to hold to the illusion of self. It is the faith that you are directing to the illusion of self that is to be used to give up the self. Your faith is the greatest power in the universe, for it holds all things that you direct it to: it holds it in your sphere of action. Think of the power of the faith that you are using. The experiences that you wish to overcome are kept in your life by your own faith. There is nothing outside of you that's keeping it in your life. *You* are keeping it there. Use the power that you are already using to keep the experiences that you don't want in your life, use that power in what you do want in your life.

Because, my friends, life moves ever onward. There are many things your mind will yet create until the day comes when you know beyond a shadow of any doubt that, yes, you are indeed the creator. You are the beginning and the end, the alpha and the omega. You are all those things. You are those things when you permit the illusion of self to control your being. To be with the things of creation and not be a part of the things of creation is to give up the illusion of self. Then, you can use the forms of your mental creation wisely: to serve you well, to be instruments through which you may experience the goodness of life. That is what you have before you to gain.

Why does man have the illusion of self, when to give up that illusion he gains the paradise of heaven? Because man, in his evolution, has earned the right of choice, that he may have the experiences of limitation as well as the experiences of limitlessness. A great responsibility have humans merited in eternity: the responsibility to be the instrument to illumine and to refine the forms of identity that are limited by the law of their own creation.

Wherever you go—and many places do you go in the course of a single day—wherever you go, you have the golden opportunity to serve the Light. The Light is not limited—only by your judgment. For each and everything you do, the Light is there if you, in your thought, pause and recognize its presence. Then, its presence will bring about the necessary balance for you to experience the goodness wherever you go. For the Light is the divine Neutrality. It is the great healing balm. And it is ever with you, for you are, in truth, an inseparable part of it.

But remember, when you do not use it, you are abusing it, for it is the power designed to be used, to bring about the great healing in your life and everything within the sound of your voice, within your touch, within your thought.

My friends, to recognize is to accept. It is the first step. But we must recognize that something greater is ever present in our life. It is wherever you are. You have that opportunity. It is up to you to use it. No one can free you from this image of limitation called self. No one, no one can do that for you. You can do it anytime you choose. Certainly, it takes a little effort. It takes effort in any change in life. It took effort for you to be where you are today. It's going to take effort to put you where you want to be tomorrow. But it is there. It is always there for you.

When we look for the good in a experience, we are recognizing the possibility that God is there. That God, that Light, if we hold on to it in consciousness, will see us through any and everything.

It is said ofttimes no is God's direction. But we never know when the no will become a yes. That is dependent on how strong we are in our judgment. When we experience a no to that which we desire, we are receiving, in that moment, the opportunity to give up the illusion of self. When we give up the illusion, the divine, neutral Intelligence that knows how to work—for that is its purpose—goes to work. No longer limited and controlled by mental substance.

So think, my friends, what you have earned in life. And think a bit more deeply what you are doing with what you have earned. You are capable of anything that your mind can imagine. And your mind can imagine many, many things. You are capable of accomplishing each and every one. You are not capable of dictating the moment, the hour, and the day that you shall experience them. For to be capable of that, you must rise beyond the mental realms known as effect and view the cause and the law that governs the effect. Do not seek the effects of life, but seek the causes of the effects. For he who has the light of reason knows the cause of anything and, therefore, is in a position and qualified to control it. Control your life, for that is your right. Don't permit the temporary forms that you have created yesterday to dictate what you're going to do today.

Many a wise man has stated wherever there's a will, there is a way. There is a way. The way appears when the judgments bow. For the obstructions are only the judgments. They are nothing more and they are nothing less. There is within you that power. No matter what the judgment, no matter what the obstruction, it is within your power to rise in consciousness to the true cause and, therefore, experience the transformation.

We have stated to you many, many times: Keep faith, my friend, with reason; she will transfigure thee. So ask yourself the question, "O Lord, to what am I directing my faith?" And if your mind says it does not know, all you need to view is the experiences of the moment. For your experiences are sustained for you by the faith, the power that you direct to them.

We stated in one of our earlier classes to redirect the intelligent energy, for that is the great power that you are using. You are using this power every moment. There is never a moment when you sleep or when you wake that you are not using the infinite, intelligent power. You are using it through the vehicle known as faith. But remember, that faculty is inseparable from poise and humility. Do you think it is not an experience of humility to bow your judgments in life? It certainly is not an experience of pride. Therefore, use the philosophy that you are studying. For it is brought to you to be used. Use it wisely and reap the harvest that is your just and rightful share.

We all know that it's up to us. Now, my good students, let us grow to that state of consciousness and apply what we have received, what we have merited, what we have earned. Become the living demonstration through the Law of Application. You can do it. No one else can do it for you. But you can do it through the faculty of faith, poise, and humility. Humility is a beautiful faculty, for it is a faculty that views through the Law of Total

Acceptance. It is the love of all the universes. And he who awakens his faculty of humility stands in the universe poised before the God of gods.

OCTOBER 5, 1978

CONSCIOUSNESS CLASS 192

Good evening, class.

You may turn your chairs, if you wish. I wish to speak to everyone for a few moments before we get into our regular class this evening.

There is a saying in this philosophy—I'm sure you are all familiar with—given some time ago that states, If the Light is too bright, 'tis best they see it not now. And I'm sure that some of you, at least, are aware that as these classes proceed, as more and more light and truth is revealed, there is the reaction from the recipients, namely the students. And so, like the plague, it spreads.

Now, all of you, I know, are aware that we have certain rules and regulations which govern the organization in order that it may survive and prosper. It is those simple, considerate rules and regulations that are being repeatedly transgressed, such as the rule and regulation of being prompt, on time, to fulfill a commitment that you, as individuals, have voluntarily made. These transgressions, as they continue to increase, which has been happening over these past few weeks, is not only detrimental to the transgressor, it is detrimental to the others who are a part of the student body and in these classes. And in this sense, it simply means that the Spirit that gives the classes will not give as much of the truth. The truth will still be given, but not the higher truths. Because the organization, if it does not survive and prosper, then there is no organization in which the classes can be given and, of course, they will not be given.

So we face the very foundation of this philosophy: that foundation being the Law of Personal Responsibility. That's what is meant when it is stated if the Light is too bright, 'tis best they see it not now.

Each time there are more and more higher teachings given, in creation, of course, the price must be paid. That price being those who are not making the daily effort, rising up to retaliate, to buck the system, and then there is discord. There is no longer peace. There is no longer harmony. There cannot be a continuity of the classes that are given. That is the choice that we have to make midway of this semester. We can have review upon review and, as long as that is not a threat to the levels of consciousness that we, as individuals, are addicted and attached to, then you can continue on with the philosophy.

If you wonder why the philosophies that are in your world are not evolutionary philosophies, why they are philosophies that have been given—and many of them very beautiful. But they do not present, if they are popular, a threat to the levels of consciousness that you find yourself addicted to. This philosophy is a working philosophy. Because it is a working philosophy, it presents a threat to certain levels of consciousness. As you experience those threats to your levels of mind, pause for moment, for that level that you feel is threatened is, in truth, your created obstruction to your heart's desire.

Many, many, many students have been attracted to Serenity and the Living Light philosophy. A few are still here. Their numbers are very, very small. This philosophy is not a popular philosophy in application. It never will be a popular philosophy in application as long as man insists upon his authority of his mind over his eternal soul.

We all have to face these choices. These choices are not something that we face in life and then it is over, because that is not how our minds created these obstructions. Our obstructions in our life were not created all of a sudden. They were, slowly but surely, fed the necessary energy to become as great as they are. If we do not make the daily effort to take control of our thought, then we have to experience the victimization of those errors of ignorance. Because we all know, deep inside of us, we all know the truth. And because we have spent so much of our lives denying it, we are destined by our own denial to find it.

Now, we chase over the universes and we run on vacations and we run here and we run there looking for the something that we know is inside and we absolutely refuse to make that effort. We know it is inside. We know it's not in China. We know it's not in Europe. We know it's wherever we are.

So if you, as students, truly desire the continuity of higher teachings—your classes will continue, but whether or not you'll receive higher teachings—more of them—is entirely dependent upon you, as a student body, and how much effort you are making to take control of the levels that are having a detrimental effect upon the organization as a whole.

If each member and student of Serenity was allowed to justify, "Well, I'm late because I'm in self," if each of us was allowed to do that, you would not long have the Serenity organization. If each of us was allowed to express, in reference to the rules and regulations that are considerate of the whole, if each of us was allowed to transgress them, then the organization, as an organization, cannot long endure.

I have always been one who was not particularly fond of rules and regulations. But each and every rule and regulation that the Serenity Association enforces within its organization has come about, has been given birth by a student and a member's transgression. So if you wonder, at anytime, why there are so many rules and so many regulations within the organization, then take a look, for each was given birth by someone's transgression.

Now, I know that you have paid good money to come to these classes. They will continue through this semester. Whether or not there will be another semester is entirely dependent upon a minimum of 51 percent of the student body. If there is 51 percent that are truly making the daily effort, then the classes will continue. If there are not 51 percent of the student body making the effort, then this will be the final semester in this organization.

Thank you.

[*At this point, Mr. Goodwin goes into a trance.*]

Greetings, friends.

This evening I should like to speak to you on the second soul faculty of humility, poise, and faith. As we have often stated, peace is the intelligent power of the universe, available to all life form. And so it is that man becomes fully receptive to this intelligent power, known as peace, when he opens this soul faculty of humility, of poise, and faith. Learn the true meaning of the word *humility* that you may, through its demonstration, bring poise or perfect balance into your life. And then direct consciously this intelligent power through the door of the faculty of encouragement; this great power called faith will move any obstruction you may have created.

Remember, my good students, that your present experiences are sustained by this great power. You, at any moment, through your own efforts and through that soul faculty, may redirect this intelligent energy and bring into your lives what you are truly seeking. Each and every time that we permit our mind to dictate the struggle and how great the effort is, we, by this great power, cause a greater struggle. We cause a greater obstruction. In many ways the same truth and the same light is spoken forth. Some of your levels of consciousness have already recorded the way for you. And so it is you find yourself against a stone wall, so to speak, or you find yourself on smooth, serene waters of time. Do you not yet see that only through your constant effort is peace and harmony and goodness the experience of your life?

You indeed are living in the door of opportunity. Each time your mind, each time it thinks, you have an awareness of knowing where it is taking you. It is the pause that is the lion's strength, the pause for but a moment. You are aware of your thought. The next step is the awareness of where it is taking you. For each thought takes you in consciousness somewhere and in time the experience enters your physical mundane world. Garner up these thoughts within your consciousness, that you may intelligently use the vehicle for the true purpose for which it was designed.

When you think the going, for you, is getting rough, remember, it is what you have chosen. Nothing outside has chosen it for you to be that way. But because you have chosen it, you can change it. Change your thoughts, my friends, and change your life, change your experiences, and truly enjoy each moment of your conscious awareness.

There is good in all things, for it is God that sustains all things. So no matter how distasteful you have permitted your mind to make the experience that you are encountering, remember, for you, God is in it if you will put God there in your thought. It is this God or goodness in your consciousness that will bring the Light of the world into your universe.

Is it worth it? So many times I've heard untold thousands of students ask that question. Thousands upon thousands in the astral and mental realms cry out as they travel along the path, "Is it worth it?" Well, I can say to you what I have often said to them, "It is inevitable." And does inevitability have any worth? We all know that that that is inevitable, of course, is worthy. It would have to be or it would not be inevitable. And so, my good students, no matter what your minds may think or think not, it is worthy and it is worth the effort. Because you have the opportunity now upon your earthly realm, you have earned the opportunity to awaken your minds to the truth that frees you. There are millions upon millions who do not awaken until the centuries pass in other dimensions and if you think the struggle is great while you are still clad in earthly flesh, you will see the day when the earthly flesh returns to its source and you will know what struggles are truly like.

Let us not be so discouraged with these passing experiences that come and go. Let us use these faculties wisely to bring about the balance that will bring the success that we are after: the success of good living. Good living, my friends—to accept that it's all where you are. No matter what you think, no matter where you go, happiness and joy and laughter, they're all with you wherever you are. You don't need to do anything outside to experience the goodness and abundance and joy which is inside. Try to accept that simple truth. There's nothing outside you need to concern yourself with. It's all inside.

And if you will place your attention upon the inward journey of life and remove your attention, your energy, from all these outward experiences, from all of this deception that ever directs your attention outward to find what you think you need—pull it all back. And when you do that, you will free yourself from those deceiving forms created from mental thought stuff. And you will find that heaven within and all that you desire. It's all inside. But as long as those thought forms that you have created in days of ignorance can direct this intelligent energy outside of you, to chase after what you think you need, then they will ever remain in control of you.

When you speak to yourself in your daily activities, when you say, "It's inside of me. It's not out there. It's inside of me," that is an exercise that will bring about the greatest goodness that you will ever experience in all eternity. For each time your soul rises and states that truth, "It's inside of me, this experience. This fulfillment, this desire is within my consciousness," each time you rise and declare that truth, you begin to gain control of your life. You begin to stand upon the rock of principle of truth and no longer worry and fret and chase the world over for something that's waiting for your recognition within.

I strongly encourage all of you, each and every day, to make the constant effort in every experience during your days and nights to rise up within you and declare that eternal truth. Whether it is what you judge to be a good experience or the opposite, rise up and declare that truth: "It's in my own universe. I will no longer be deluded that it is in someone else's universe. I will no longer be deluded that it is outside of me." If you practice that religiously each and every time you have a thought or an experience, if you rise up and declare that truth, "It is within me," you will live on earth, having filled your soul with gratitude that you have awakened, you have grown and accepted the Law of Personal Responsibility and, in so doing, are once again the captains of your ship and once again the masters of your destiny. I do sincerely pray that those within the sound of my voice will make that exercise religious to their very life each and every day.

You, if you are religious with your effort, you will very soon experience the change and the transformation that starts to take place within your sphere of action. You will start to take command of your destiny in life. You will no longer worry nor concern yourself with how experiences are going to come about, for you will have declared the truth: it's within your own consciousness and, being within your own consciousness, you can accept it in any way that is beneficial to your life, your peace, and your happiness.

Of all the teachings that been brought to your world, the greatest of all is to declare the truth that *you* can, once again, take command when you remind your mind that it's inside of you. I assure you, my friends, to those who are ready, willing, and able, the transformation will be a living demonstration of your divine birthright to the goodness, the abundance, and the greatness of life itself.

You are not upon earth to suffer. That is an error within your thought. But because it is within your thought, you can always change it. There is more than enough for all God's children. And when you declare the truth that it is within your realm of thought—and you create the thought, you can change the thought—and it is no longer (your goodness of life) dependent upon anything or anyone outside, then you will know the paradise that has been waiting for you for so very, very long.

You may ask your questions at this time.

Thank you. What exercise are you referring to in order to learn disassociation?

My good students, there have been many exercises that have been given to you, stated in your study book [*The Living Light*], to disassociate yourself from that that troubles you.

We have just spoken to you on declaring the truth, though it may take you a thousand times or more a day, to free yourself from these delusions that keep you the victim of suffering.

To disassociate oneself from that which troubles them is to free oneself from the control of it. One does that by accepting that there is only one place in which the experience is taking place and that one place is within your own mind.

Thank you. Please further explain the meaning of the parable in Discourse 6, "As the bird flew / And the snake crawled, / The lion said, / 'Of what good are those?' / And now my children: / The mouse doth chase the cat."

That has already been given to you in one of these classes and I refer you to that class.

Thank you. Please tell us, are the soul faculties of peace, joy, and harmony triune or is unity a part of that triangle?

That particular faculty has not yet been given in its entirety, but shall be as the students progress.

Thank you. What is the spiritual significance of the third eye or pineal gland?

The only significance to what you call the third eye or the pineal gland is through the faculty of reason.

I have stated to you many times, to keep faith with reason; she will transfigure thee. Now, reason is the light that is brought to the world through a perfect balance of the faculties and the functions. It is the light that shows us the way, the way that we all are going. So, my friends, when we are out of balance, when a thought takes control of our mind, our body reacts. There is no balance. The balance is: when the thought, created by the function, is brought into an equal balance with the corresponding soul faculty, that we are lighted on our path and peace reigns supreme.

Thank you. Could you further clarify two cards in the Serenity game which reads, "The essence of dreaming is the law of life, and the law of life is Divine will or God's expression"?

The essence of life, the dreaming of life. Try to ponder for a moment what your mind calls void. When you ponder the word *void*, do you experience void? We know that we cannot experience that which is void. Therefore, our minds create and fabricate what is satisfactory to the mind as void. And so it is that man experiences only through the creation of form, which takes place in mental substance.

The difference between mental substance and spiritual sustenance is in refinement and evolution. The darkness is but the lesser light. And so what we call the light is more refined or the brighter light. And so it is with spiritual sustenance and mental substance. Mental substance is the lesser light and spiritual sustenance, the brighter light.

This is why we teach to keep faith—faith being a soul faculty—to keep faith with reason, for she will transfigure thee. It is our faith that sustains for us the experiences within our consciousness. Without faith, there is no experience. Now when faith enters the mental realms of your universe, it is known as belief. And so we have given to you some time ago: awareness, belief, become.

Through the door of encouragement, the great power of the universe, called peace, moves along the vehicle of faith. And in the mental realms, you believe. And in the spiritual realms, you understand. And so, my friends, as you, in your journey inward and upward—for man moves onward and upward as an effect—not a cause, but an effect—of first moving inward. As you make that effort to move inward, you, slowly but surely, begin to educate your desires.

There has been much confusion in reference to what some understand as the educating of desire. To educate desire, man uses the soul faculty of reason. He casts the light upon his multitude of desires and he places them into a priority. He organizes them before they organize him. Now, most people upon the earthly realm at this time of evolution are organized by their desire forms. Their desire forms are not yet organized by them.

As we make the daily effort upon this inward journey, we begin to educate our desires. We begin to organize them. And so they rise up, for, not being organized before, being unruly, in total license and doing what they want to do when they want to do it, they cry out. But because they're yours, they must, in the final analysis, they must respond to your light of reason. As you continue to use that light of reason, you begin to gain control. You don't worry about your yesterdays. You don't worry about your tomorrows. You don't worry about your money and you don't worry about your health. The reason that you don't worry is because you know what's going to be, for you have taken the inward journey and you have begun to take control of creation: your creations. And having taken control, you are now, once again, restored to the captainship of your own destiny and you direct that ship intelligently with the light of reason.

And when you know, you know that you know. You will no longer have to wonder about what's going to be. You will no longer have to live in discouragement, for your path will be lighted from your own daily effort.

Thank you. Are children born to couples in the spirit world?

Well, if you mean by that question, Is there sexual intercourse in the realms of spirit? In that sense, there is not. The soul enters form upon your earthly planet and it enters at the moment of conception. Now, if the soul leaves the earthly form after it has entered—be it a day, an hour, a month, or six—it continues to grow. And in that sense, those couples who have merited the experience of caring for children receive those little forms as they are developing and in that sense they have children.

Thank you. Good night.

OCTOBER 12, 1978

CONSCIOUSNESS CLASS 193

Greetings, friends.

As we continue on with our studies and efforts along the inward journey, we soon realize that our experiences are but the embodiment of a thought that we have entertained within the realms of consciousness. And so it is through this daily effort, we open the door of truth and view the many varied creations in these mental realms.

It has often been said by many that things get always worse before they get better. What does that statement truly mean? When things seemingly get worse, it simply reveals to us that there is, indeed, a change in consciousness that is taking place within us. Because we have yet to make the great moment-by-moment effort—through acceptance of all life experiences are caused within our own sphere of action—we are often deluded that these struggles and these difficulties are the conditions of circumstances beyond our control.

However, that veil that stands between us and the light of reason disappears before our view and we begin to see clearly that each and every experience in life, be it one fulfilling our own desires or be it one obstructing the fulfillment of our desires, is directly related to a level of consciousness. For that that we experience as denial is only the outward manifestation of a denial within our own thought realm. For he who controls the thoughts that he entertains soon finds the path of freedom, abundance, and success in his life.

There is no way that I have ever found outside. No matter what we do and no matter what we think, we must ever go on the inward journey. And no matter how long we entertain our minds with the distractions of creation, sooner or later we shall take that inward journey. We shall take that journey consciously and we shall choose our moments consciously and not have them chosen for us by the patterns of old—patterns born in own errors of ignorance of the times.

Whether or not you choose to fulfill your life in your present earth form or you make that choice of fulfillment in another realm, another planet, and another time, the principle of the Law of Personal Responsibility will not change. The moment that we accept that demonstrable principle, in that moment we stand at the very head of our ship. Each moment that you declare that truth, each moment that you fully accept that truth, you are freed from the control of the forms that have already been created in your mental universe.

Think, my good students, of that principle. Whatever your experiences of the moment, when you declare that truth, "I accept the responsibility within my own realm of consciousness. I and I alone have created and I and I alone can change," when that is truly faced, in that moment—and each and every moment that you face that light of truth—you are in control. To remain in control of your life takes that moment-by-moment choice. It is worth the effort. It is the inevitable journey. It is in your own best interest to declare that truth each moment of your conscious awareness. Remember that acceptance of that truth puts you in control of your destiny.

That that has passed has passed and exists only through the power of recall. It has an effect upon you only because you do have that power of recall. You, however, have the eternal moment where you can change all that faces you. You can do that. No one can do it for you. It is time to do that which you know will free you. It is time to do it, my good students. Tomorrow may never come. It may never come in the realm in which you are presently conscious. So whatever it is to do, this is indeed the time to do it.

As I spoke to you some time ago in reference to the many forms and the experiences that I had encountered long ago in these other realms, it did indeed take me a long time to finally bow that which was to be bowed, to finally accept. But in that acceptance, my freedom came. That has a greater value to me than all the many tempting forms of creation. For he who makes that choice is above and beyond those limited forms that rise and fall. Is it not better to sail upon the eternal sea of peace than to be pulled from shore to shore by the ever-changing tides of creation? To rise above those realms of duality is where your true home and your real soul truly lives. Those moments that fleet into your consciousness are moments that you have the power to consciously choose whenever you so desire.

In all of these many, many, many classes that have been given to you, it is the repetition that, slowly but surely, is bringing about the changes to help you, step by step, come to make the conscious moment-by-moment effort to stand in command of your destiny. Think, my good friends, what a great and valuable tool that you have at your command. The light of reason to make that simple effort and to make that effort frequently is to transform your entire life.

When you find the struggles, you are only reacting to the changes in consciousness that you have set into motion. But which you is doing the reacting? Is it the you that is eternal and has had an untold number of experiences in untold eons of time? Or is it that part of creation, mental forms that you have created, that have blinded you to such a degree that you believe that those forms are you and you experience the reacting? I assure you that they are not you. But because they have received so much energy by a direction of your thought, you are blinded to believe that they are you. We gave to you an exercise so valuable so long ago: an exercise of disassociation, of consciously choosing the direction that you will permit this intelligent energy to flow through your life.

We have many likes and dislikes. They are ever, of course, in keeping with experiences we have set into motion and judged the effects thereof. We are not the experience. We are not, in truth, the cause thereof. We are, through directing of intelligent energy, in that sense, creators of the forms. We are not the cause. We are only the instruments that are directing intelligent energy. Therefore, it is our responsibility unto ourselves, to direct the intelligent energy to that which is beneficial, which is good not only for our true being, but for all who come in contact with those forms of creation.

As the changes become more evident within your life and within the student body, we shall move on, above and beyond these mental forms of creation. As, through your efforts, you gain, slowly but surely, control, you begin to choose more wisely how you will permit this energy to express through you.

Throughout the universes there is one common cry: all forms cry to be free from the limit, which is known as their prison.

They all cry the same cry: "Free me from this house of clay." Why do all forms cry the same cry for freedom? For they all know they have wandered from the true source of freedom—that the walls in which they find themselves imprisoned are walls that are created from realms of judgment, from realms of dictate. It is the error in our thinking that we often view as experience in our life.

It is one of the basic purposes of these classes: to help you awaken your minds to the simple truth that you have the right, have always had the right, and will always have the right, to choose intelligently how you wish your lives to be. When we permit our minds to dictate that because of yesterday we cannot enjoy today, that is not the truth that is speaking through us, but that is the patterns that are not about to change.

Think, my good friends, stop and think. You can be in command of your life and your destiny if you will only accept that you alone are responsible. When you accept that great, but simple, humble truth, all the forms in your universe bow in respect. For in that moment, they know that you know you are the master. That is the most valuable teaching that you will ever receive in all eternity, for that places you home, in the birthright and the declaration of your true divinity. Practice every day, every day. Every moment that you can pause for just a moment to think. When you declare that, every form you ever created bows its head in respect of the very power that sustains them. But remember, they rise quickly when you forget to declare that truth. The more that you declare that truth, the sooner will your lives change and bring about, to you, that which is rightly and justly yours. To some of you, you may find a bit of a struggle, for those forms do not want to bow. But as you repeat the truth, the truth will rise supreme.

You may feel free to ask your questions at this time.

Thank you. Are awareness and acceptance and forgiveness triune soul faculties?

No, they are not.

Thank you. It is our understanding that a clone has the same soul as the original. When the original dies, does the soul return to spirit or remain in the clone?

In reference to your question concerning duplicating or cloning, you must realize, my friends, that you are speaking of forms created from your Earth planet. This soul enters according to laws established, regardless how the positive and negative poles are brought together. The duplicating or cloning process, as you will learn in time from your earthly science, is a bringing together of the positive and negative poles through what is called a cloning process. Whereas the original form is already imbued with an eternal soul, the soul is not limited in its expression in the sense that it cannot expand itself by an expansion of the original form. Therefore, when the original form is expanded through the duplicating or cloning process, there are the negative and positive poles of creation brought together and what you have is what is known as self-reproduction. Thank you.

Thank you. Can a clone be cloned? If so, is it then possible to keep the soul in form indefinitely?

In reference to the question as to whether a clone can be cloned, you will find in your earthly science in time that the clone is an exact duplicate of the original, that the eternal soul is expressing through the clone. And in that sense, a clone can be cloned. And in reference to the soul's incarnation being kept into form indefinitely, in that respect you are not dealing, my good students, with a science that is new, but one that is eons old.

Thank you. Was psychokinesis the method used to build the pyramids? If so, please explain.

It was one of the many methods used. Your science of laser beams of light energy was the very basic principle upon which they were built.

Thank you. Where is the Earth in relationship to the spheres?
To which spheres are you referring, please?
I'm sorry. the question does not expand on that. [After a short pause, the next question is read.] *Next question. What is the breathing exercise you referred to in order to reach peace?*
There are many breathing exercises. Each one, properly used in a consistent way, will bring you to a state of consciousness known as peace. Those exercises have already been given.
Thank you. In playing the Serenity Game, how can the themes be best determined?
Well, that is entirely dependent upon the motive of the player.
Thank you. We have been taught that hidden in failure is the secret ingredient for success. Could you please explain what the secret ingredient is?
Yes, I will share with you my understanding. Anyone who has experienced failure knows within their own conscience what they have or have not done in order to bring about the experience known as failure. Therefore, because they know what they have or have not done to bring about what is known as failure, then they know beyond a shadow of any doubt what to do and not to do to bring about success.
Because what we call failure is a demonstrable effect of directed energy, success is nothing more nor less than a demonstrable effect of directed energy. We all know how to direct our energy to bring forth into our lives the negative experiences that we say we do not enjoy. He who knows how to bring into his life the negative, by that very knowledge, knows how to bring about the opposite, called the positive. So failure, in truth, is the doorknob on the door of success.
We quit at the level of consciousness known as failure. But if we stood firm, we would soon find that we can turn that doorknob of failure and open up the door of success. So often we quit

upon walking the stepping stones because we have yet to fully open the faculties of our eternal soul, especially the one through which wisdom flows unobstructed: the faculty of patience.

We can stop at any moment in any area of our life and we can say to ourselves, "I have not really been successful in this particular area of my life. Therefore, I shall spend no more time or energy or effort and I shall turn my back and say that I am a failure." That, of course, is ever our divine right of choice. I assure you, anyone who experiences success has touched the doorknob of failure, often many times. But, you see, my friends, failures in life become successes in life when we awaken the faculty of patience.

Thank you. Good night.

OCTOBER 19, 1978

CONSCIOUSNESS CLASS 194

Now, this evening I would like to share with you my understanding of this philosophy and how it works for me.

You will find, as you study this philosophy, that without the effort to demonstrate the basic principle, which is known as total acceptance, that the philosophy itself, without that acceptance, cannot and does not work. Total acceptance, which was explained to you long ago, is known as divine will or the will of God.

Now, when we consider total acceptance as the will of God, our minds immediately begin to question: a God that chooses or a God that judges. But if we will think for a few moments on those words *total acceptance* and we will study all life's forms, we will see that there is—or has to be—an intelligent energy that is sustaining all of the forms of life. In our activities and in our experiences, if we view each and every one of those experiences in a total acceptance of the right of the expression of the experience, what takes place in our consciousness is a freedom in that moment from the bondage of judgment.

Now, each time we permit our mind to make any judgment, we establish what is known as the Law of Destiny. In other words, we place ourselves in a position where we will experience everything necessary in our destiny that we may reeducate our senses and grant the right of the Divine, which is known as total acceptance.

Beginning our efforts in this philosophy on that basic principle of divine will or total acceptance, it necessarily follows the Law of Personal Responsibility. When we begin to realize, in the fullness, that every experience that we are having within our own consciousness is in keeping with laws that only we are setting into motion, then we can start upon the path of making the necessary changes in our thought patterns, the necessary changes in our own attitudes.

As we take stock of our daily experiences, we cannot help but soon become aware of how negative our thinking really is. For example, we have varying desires. And with each and every desire, we have a judgment. And with each judgment is the denial that is in the judgment, for there is no judgment possible without denial. So we find ourselves constantly, moment by moment establishing the laws of destiny through judgments and through denials.

When this philosophy teaches that our denials are our destinies, we cannot accept that as a beautiful, spiritual truth and not work with it. If we truly accept the philosophy, then we know from our own experiences that those experiences that we are encountering are effects—never causes—effects of our denials, which are effects of our judgments.

Each moment our mind is sending messages into the atmosphere, into the universe. Over 90 percent of those impulses and messages leaving our consciousness, over 90 percent are negative. You have learned in this philosophy that fear is nothing more nor less than negative faith. That fear is the mind's control over the eternal being called the soul. Each time that you have an experience—and experience is taking place at all times within the mental realms of consciousness—there is a negative projection going out in the universe. It just doesn't go out and disappear, of course. It goes out and it gathers like kind. So one negative thought multiplies by the hundreds, the hundreds of thousands.

This philosophy teaches that God, the Infinite Intelligence, is the true and only source of our supply. To demonstrate the opposite, by permitting the mind to rise with its fear and its dictates and judgments, is to be hypocritical in one's own efforts of study. For not to apply that which one believes is definitely a level of hypocrisy.

Now, in order to help us to gain, perhaps, more incentive and hopefully a little inspiration to apply in our daily activities what we are studying, I think it's only necessary to consider how hypocritical we are when we study anything and do not apply. To declare that we believe that God is the source of our supply and to demonstrate the opposite is certainly a house divided against itself. To permit the human mind to dictate that, "Well, I'm short today, but I may have something tomorrow," is to be the victim, the victim of the errors and the ignorance of our own mental experiences.

When we say those things, we establish laws. You see, when the human ego speaks, it speaks and goes to work to prove unto itself that it is right, no matter what experiences it will take us through. It is like a self-prophecy. If we say that next year is a difficult year, then we set laws into motion that will create for us a difficult year in order for us to prove to ourselves that we were right all along. The human ego, until it is educated, has a great deal of need. And because it has much need, it is very insecure. For that that has need, that that has want is never secure. It never can be secure.

The benefit of this philosophy, the true and only benefit of it, is in the application of it.

Each of us, on the path to free ourselves from all of these dualities of experiences, each of us have before us the obstructions created by our mind that we must face. We can leave one place and go to another and we can travel the universes over, but the obstructions in our path are ever waiting for us. For they have been, of course, created by us. What keeps us from facing these self-created obstructions is the level of consciousness that refuses to accept personal responsibility and places the blame outside of one's own control. The longer that level of consciousness is allowed to control our thinking, the greater the obstructions become that someday we will have to face.

There are many things in life that we say we like and there are equally many things in life that we say we don't like. But when we say that we like or we don't like, what do we really mean? We find ourselves one day saying we don't like something or someone, only in the next day to say that we do like someone or something. Of course, it is dependent upon whether or not they are acting harmoniously with our own levels that have judged and dictated to us how things should be.

Many times I have mentioned to many students the benefit of flooding their consciousness with the simple truth. For each thought that rises—and, as I say, over 90 percent of our thinking is negative—for each thought that rises, to immediately, *immediately* declare the truth of the positive. Most people think the only time to use the affirmation that God is the true and only source of their supply is when their minds have dictated that they've got money problems. No, my friends, God is the true and only source of our supply when we find difficulty staying awake and God is the true and only source of our supply, when, by our own transgressions, we feel that we are no longer in the health that we have a right to be in. God is the true and only source of our supply is not limited to green paper. It is not limited to this old material world. It is all encompassing.

When you find yourself, from the transgressions and the errors of ignorance of your own mind [not experiencing harmony], then you need God as the true and only source of your supply for peace and happiness, for harmony and for joy. Because it is obvious that your mind is not offering it to you, because if your mind was not offering it—if your mind *was* offering it to you, then you would have the peace and the harmony and the abundant good that you are truly seeking.

So let us consider here in this class—and I'm happy I get to speak this evening because I can see very clearly who's having difficulty still, after all of these many classes in staying awake. Because, as you will recall, those of you who were in our other semesters, that this one was shortened by one week. And we were promised—and I'm always grateful to the Friends when they make a promise, because I know it's absolutely guaranteed to happen—we were promised that if the students insisted upon sleeping during the classes, we would shorten it again. And then, perhaps someday it would be so short there would be no more.

Now, we must ask ourselves, why make the effort to go to any class—philosophy or mathematical is immaterial—to make the effort to go to any class and not make the effort to apply it.

The way to build anything is not to try to build it overnight, but to build from within each day in every way. Whatever it is that you seek in life, it must have enough value to you that you are willing to make the effort seven days a week—no matter how you feel or don't feel—to have the wisdom of patience to go through whatever years are necessary until you have accomplished some of your goal.

Don't ever permit your mind to judge that you have accomplished the fullness of your goal, for if you do, you will have nothing left but the fear of keeping the position that you think you have attained. You see, goal is our lifeline as long as it's never totally completed. Because the moment that we permit the mind to think that we have finished, that we have grown through this level or that level, or we have attained what we set out to attain, we have nothing left, nothing left, you see. This is why this philosophy does not teach retirement. It believes that the workers win; that there is a purpose for being on earth; that there is a purpose for being in the world; that when we no longer serve the purpose for which we came to this earth to serve, then we should not hover in these physical bodies of clay, but that we should move on.

Some time ago the teacher of this philosophy brought through the understanding that we and we alone establish the day when we're to leave this earth realm. Now, wouldn't it be nice if we would make some effort to grow inside, to awaken inside, so that we can know not only what we're doing in this moment, but what we're going to be doing in the next moment.

But we must be willing to face ourselves. Now, we're not as bad a people as sometimes we like to think we are. We have created these many different images, these different faces. And depending upon the circumstances and conditions that we alone, of course, have created, we present a different face to different people. And we spend so many years presenting these different faces to these different people that the day finally arrives, we've presented so many different images, we no longer know who we are. We no longer know because we've created so many different forms, so many different images.

Now, how do we go back home to find out who we are? Well, it's very simple really: we start taking some time each day to be honest with ourselves. How does one become honest with himself? By starting to consider what level of consciousness they are in—number one. For unless we awaken and become aware of what level we're in, we're never really sure who we really are. Because one moment, we're one way and the next moment, we're some other way.

My personal experiences in working with people over this number of years—and one thing that helped me more than anything in my efforts to work on the faculty of duty, gratitude, and tolerance was to remind myself, in working with people, "That's not the person. That is a level of their mind. That is a level of consciousness. In a few moments, a few days, a few weeks, or perhaps a few months or years, they will express entirely differently. Right at this moment, they have trapped themselves as a victim in that level of consciousness." Now, if you will remember that and if you will always remember that you have the same level yourself, then the first soul faculty of duty, gratitude, and tolerance, slowly but surely, will begin to open.

Because without duty and gratitude and without tolerance, that triune faculty, there is no real success in life. There cannot be. So when we make the effort to realize that these levels that we view in others, number one, exist within ourselves and we start to make some effort to face the level within ourselves—for the one we cannot tolerate in another is waiting to be educated, to be recognized within ourselves.

So when you work with people and, being in this church, working with people, there is no other way, because it takes people for the whole thing to work. So we have to, some of us, adjust our priorities. Now, many of us, I am aware, have spent a good part of our life, when we wanted something done, we did it ourselves. But when you're in a church or an organization, you can't do everything yourself. It is humanly impossible. Therefore, that means that changes have to be made within our own mind. Each one, I know, is making some effort, because it took some effort to get to class. So that's some effort. So we must not, you know, play our self-pity, discouragement tapes. It does take some effort to get in a car and drive to class, sit here for an hour or so. Let us just, perhaps, expand this little bit of effort that we are making—not expand it all of a sudden, for, remember, a fast growth is not a healthy growth. It is the slow growth over a period of time that has proven, in every area of life, to be the stable and the secure growth.

Everything, we know, is vibration. And vibration is created by our own attitude of mind. It is, in truth, much easier, once the effort is made, to be positive than it is to be negative. Once in awhile, as some of you are aware, I will play some negative tapes and you, as students, get terribly upset, not once considering that I hear your negative tapes all the time. I find it most interesting. Perhaps I should play some of my negative tapes more often. So that you would stop forgetting that I am a human being. But then, I don't think I would be too good an example to try to help show you that the positive vibration is the better way; that if you make some effort to keep a cheery attitude of mind, that you spend some time declaring the truth of God is the source of all your goodness and that when you're not experiencing that goodness, then you're simply out of God—that your mind, like a black veil, has dropped between you and your true source of goodness.

Now, I do try to make the effort every day to flood my consciousness. Because, you see, in this type of work—I live in a material world, like everyone else lives in a material world. And I have a mind, like everyone else has a mind. And I have all the beautiful levels that you have. And so I have chosen, and I continue to choose, which is my divine right—not to judge, but to choose, for I have seen, year after year after year through a little effort made constantly to flood the consciousness, that the experiences in my life are more harmonious; that the mind, which has nothing to offer but its fear, it bows.

We must consider that everything we encounter, whether we like it or not, is an effect, an effect with a potential cause. For cause and effect are eternally married; they are inseparable. Each time you experience an effect, in the experiencing of the effect, you become the instrument for establishing the cause of the next experience yet to come.

Now, this philosophy teaches that only through the Law of Repetition is change made possible. So now you see how that really works. Each time the experience is repeated, slowly but surely, your attitude begins to change and your attitude is the very ingredient that sets the Law of Cause into motion. So every time you have an experience, which is the effect of the cause you set into motion before, remember, in that experience you are setting the next cause or the next experience into motion. Now, this goes on all the time day and night when you sleep and when you wake.

How many students have truly listened and applied when it was given in one of these classes, to flood your consciousness as you go to sleep at night and to flood your consciousness upon awakening in the morning and to flood your consciousness during the entire course of your day? You see, there's no spirit that I've ever found that waves a magic wand that keeps me positive. No, no, that's never been my experience. I have to make the effort all the time. But when you truly become aware that in all of your experiences you are setting new laws into motion, new causes are you setting into motion, then you will pause to think, because you know that you alone will be experiencing those effects.

When you go into any endeavor or any project—it does not matter what it is—it is your attitude that establishes the vibration and the law under which you have bound yourself. And you are bound to that self-created law until it is fulfilled. Now, if you think that there is any escape from these things, then it is only, I can assure you, a temporary, temporary illusion. It will not last. We escape nothing. And it isn't a matter of waiting until we leave a physical body that we pay our dues. We're paying our dues here and now as we go along the path.

So why shouldn't we, when it's such a simple thing to do, why shouldn't we change our attitude and change our life?

You know, when we get our feelings hurt and when we find it difficult to tolerate some people, let us think of the golden opportunity that we have merited. To become aware, not that our feelings are hurt, but to become aware of the cause within ourselves. To make the effort not just to say, "Now, that person has hurt my feelings." *We* hurt our feelings in our attitude towards that person. When *we* make the judgment that it is difficult or nearly impossible to tolerate some people, well, we're the one that is suffering. We are the one that chooses that negative path.

Why do we want to beat ourselves and suffer when it's not necessary? Why do we insist upon doing that to ourselves? We cannot, if we are applying this philosophy. Because if we are applying this philosophy, then we have, number one: total acceptance, granting the divine right of expression of all things and people. And we have—most important of all—the Law of Personal Responsibility that only *we*—not someone out there—only *we* are responsible.

It has been interesting to me, in these many years in counseling and in this work, that whenever a married couple has come to the Spirit for counseling, it has been most interesting that the person who complains about the partner's difficulties is the one who gets all the counseling. I have always found that most interesting, because the one that is having the difficulty, because the other one is not making the changes, is the one that truly needs the help.

How do we bring about changes within another? We must ask ourselves that question. We become instruments to bring about changes within another by bringing about the changes within ourselves and no other way! Truth is individually perceived. And the demonstration is the revelation. We can talk until hell freezes over, but it is the demonstration that is the light. It's not the talk.

So when we truly want to help another, we begin by helping ourselves. Because by helping ourselves, God begins to help us. And that's where you hear that statement that God helps those who help themselves. Because I never ever found a God that helped anyone that didn't make the effort to help themselves. We must first make the effort to help ourselves.

Let us not misunderstand what that truly means. I know that there are some levels of consciousness who understand the words *to help oneself,* means to go around the universe and helping yourself to whatever you want to take. That's not what I'm talking about. To help oneself is to make some effort to bring about whatever changes in consciousness are necessary to enjoy life to its fullest.

See, everything that we need is right where we are. Everything we need is right where we are. And we can be any place in the universe and all that we need is right there. For everything is within us. Now, a person says, "Well, now, that's ridiculous. I need a car. That's not within me." The car is an effect, like a house is an effect. A coat is an effect. It's not a cause. But within the effect is the potential of the birth of the cause. Until we accept within our own consciousness that we have what our mind in its error says we don't have, then it cannot be. So it's inside our own head.

Now, for example, if we are having difficulty with a person because we have decided, for example, that they don't communicate, we have, therefore, created within our consciousness a communication problem. Now, think about this: What we see in another that we find difficulty in tolerating, we have yet to educate within ourselves. Now, if we find in another a problem, for example, in their lack of communicating, we can be rest assured that the problem of the lack of communicating has recognized the problem outside in another and is waiting to recognize itself within.

Now, think about this in all areas of your life. Now, a person says, "Well, I do everything I can to communicate with that person. They just don't communicate." But we believe we communicate. Now, with this particular person we may have made some effort to communicate, but let's look at all those people over there that we make no effort to communicate with at all. Because we don't want to be bothered, we say.

Why do we say we don't want to be bothered? What we really mean is we do not want to face experiences of the past, we don't want to be honest with ourselves, go in consciousness through the memory par excellence and take a look at early experiences in our life that brought to us what we judge was painful or suffering, and so we blotted it out. And rather than tell a person, "I don't want to take a look at those past experiences. I don't want to face that," of course, we usually say we don't want to be bothered.

I assure you that we all have fluctuating priorities. And I know that you will all agree. It really does take some effort every day to keep some priorities where they should be: on the highest of our list. For all of this in this world that you see has come into our consciousness and will go from it. But that something that brought you here to Earth in the first place and that something that's taking you on any minute—you know not the hour unless you know yourself very well—that something is the real you that you have been living with for untold centuries and you will continue to live with for centuries yet to be.

This philosophy has shown, repeatedly, ways of broadening one's horizon, of expanding their consciousness and not being limited by the Law of Identity. Now, I know we'll all agree: that that troubles us, controls us. So when we find something that is disturbing to our mind, if we over-identify with it, we very soon find that we are controlled by it.

Now, no one, no ego, including my own, likes to entertain the thought that we are controlled. But we are. You see, we think, we think we have free will, but that's only 10 percent. The other 90 percent, we're chasing around, waiting on those levels that we have created that control us. It's nice to have a 10 percent breather. Why not make the effort and enjoy that 10 percent each day?

To become aware of the thoughts of our own mind—that's very important.

You see, as we make the effort and as we start to grow, as we get closer to the gates of victory, what happens to us? It's very simple: we always get worse before we get better—don't ever kid yourself—in anything. For we, in our minds, set those laws into motion. Just before the victory—and I can assure you—and it's a spiritual victory—the price is ever in keeping with the victory that is yet to be. But this is where most of us, we stumble and we fall, only to rise up again, again and again and again and again and again.

I assure you, it takes a mighty, potent, strong ego to make it on the path of Light. It is not that we should ever try to annihilate the human ego, for it is the very instrument, once it is educated with the light of reason, that brings us to the eternal Light. Because it takes the determination and the tenacity of the human ego to get us through the jungle of creation. Now, that's exactly what it takes. And this philosophy in no way ever teaches to annihilate the human ego. It can and it does serve an excellent purpose once it is educated. But remember, education of the human ego includes all the soul faculties, beginning, of course, with total consideration.

Now, in this philosophy you've heard much discussion about self-will. I think even a more proper wording would be "limited will"—limited to a level of consciousness that has total consideration for the level, the one level out of eighty-one. Because that's where the problems are. That's where the discord, the disunity, and the disturbance in our life is: that we limit this will of ours to blind desire. There is nothing wrong with desire if you put a light of reason over it.

But remember that each of us in the universes is a part of a whole. We're not some unique, special entity that bears no responsibility to all the rest of creation. No, everything we think, everything we do, all of our feelings register into a universe that has an effect upon the whole. My goodness sakes alive, the American Indians knew that for untold centuries—and many races before them. Each of our thoughts and our attitudes, our acts and our deeds is having a beneficial or detrimental effect upon the whole. Now, let us start considering our responsibilities in life. We just cannot run rampant in the universe, because there are other creatures in the universe that that level is having an effect upon. If our thoughts are discordant, negative, and disturbing, the weather—the elemental spirits get upset and the weather conditions become discordant and unpredictable. Because that is the level of consciousness that we have poured into the universe. If your health begins to break down, take a look inside. And get rid of those discordant thoughts.

When we free ourselves from the thoughts of self, we find the paradise called heaven. Now that, surely, is a very simple truth that every great philosopher has taught in this universe and all universes. But before you can give up self, the thought of self, you see, you've got to find something that has a higher priority. And that's what this philosophy is trying to show you. That something is all the universes. That, certainly, to any mind, is a higher priority than the limited, little delusion called self. Because this little delusion we call self, it just keeps on changing. It's not the self it was twenty years ago and it won't be the same self twenty years from now. So why feed so much energy to something that is constantly changing, that certainly is not reliable. That's not a very practical thing to do.

Well, everything works in Serenity. It always has and it always will. Because when you make the effort to accept something greater than the duality of the human minds and the errors of the so-called self-will, and you remind yourself constantly who, in truth, is at the helm—each time you remind yourself, you establish that law. And if enough people in Serenity remind themselves who they're truly working for and what they're really working for and if they will keep that in their consciousness—the true source of their supply—they won't have to be concerned about what day that the church will be built, for one day it will appear. You won't have to be concerned about how soon *The Living Light* (book) will be printed—because we're almost sold out of this one—because one day it will appear. So, you see, my friends, it's dependent upon your own acceptance.

If you will bow the dictates of the mind that's filled with so much error and is so limited and you will just accept, then it will be. Because the law is very impartial and whatever you want is dependent upon you. But never forget, it's within your power to attain it and that anything standing in the way is just a little kink in your consciousness that you straighten out with the light of reason.

It's interesting when students come to Serenity. It's most interesting when they begin to experience the simple, but considerate, discipline that it has to offer. For without discipline, there's no spiritual light. If there was spiritual light without discipline, then we'd all have the spiritual light and none of us would be making the effort to even be here.

Discipline. But how we react to simple and considerate discipline. When we do something, do we stop and think, how is this going to affect the whole? My friends, how can we consider our responsibilities to the universal whole, including the dogs and the cats and the squirrels and the birds and the fish in the brooks and all those other universes, how can we possibly grow to consider that greatness if we cannot consider just a small little group called Serenity Church? If we cannot consider the people within it, how can we possibly expect to grow out of the personality of self and consider the principle of the whole? We have to start with the crumb. Because if we don't start with the crumb, we'll choke on the loaf. So let's start with the crumb. You have to begin someplace. Your feet have wended their way here. This is the place that you have found to start.

Now, perhaps you'll make it all the way in this particular little school, and perhaps not. That depends on how strong and how determined you are and whether or not you educate your ego and use it for the greater good which is justly and rightfully yours. That depends entirely upon you. Here, you have the opportunity to grow through personality, to place principle, the good of the whole, of which you are an inseparable unit, above and beyond all judgments and feelings of your mind. You will begin somewhere. You have earned the opportunity to begin right here.

Thank you.

OCTOBER 26, 1978

CONSCIOUSNESS CLASS 195

Greetings, friends.

Some years ago we spoke to you on the power of imaging and to image constructively. And so at this time we wish to expand on the understanding of constructive imagery.

As most of you, I am sure, are aware that all experience that comes into your life comes in keeping with the natural laws and that these laws are ever under your control, under the faculty of reason and the light of wisdom, if you choose them to be. For example, all of the experiences that you have with people, places, and things and the material world with which you all are so familiar, is ever in keeping with the image that you are entertaining in your mind.

And so it is that these schools of positive thinking that have been with you for some time, they work only when your feelings are united with your thoughts. For each image that your mind creates is created through this thought process and through the feelings of your senses. For example, it takes the effort of the forty senses; it takes the force of directed thought to create and to sustain a mental image. When we say to change your attitude, we are saying to you that your experiences, with which you are not pleased, which you find not beneficial to your life, are only the effects of these images that are created by your thoughts and feelings.

Whatever endeavor it is that you have in your life that you are thinking about going into, remember that it is within your power to create a constructive and beneficial image which will bring you the experience that you are seeking. Whenever we permit our mind to dictate to us that the cause of anything that we experience is beyond our control, then what we, in truth, are doing—we are creating an image in our mental universe that becomes a servant of the thoughts and the feelings and directions of another individual.

In our relationships with people, the first thing that we think about is how they are affecting us. Seldom, if ever, do we consider that what they do, or do not do, is an image in our own mental sphere of action; that this image that we, and we alone, create is what brings forth into our experience that which we call good or bad. We can and we are, slowly but surely, changing ourselves. We can never change another, for that is contrary to natural law. But by changing the images that we have created in our mental worlds, we do, in that respect, have an effect upon those around and about us.

When we see something in another that we find distasteful and displeasing, we must not forget that it is an image that we created. The image we can change. By changing the image, the experience that must fit into the image goes through a process of transformation. If you have an image of abundant good in your life, if you make the effort to support and to sustain and maintain that image in consciousness, by the very Law of Creation, you can only experience abundant good in your life.

Whatever it is that you have to do, it is the first step of creating image that establishes the law for you. We stated to you some time ago that man is a law unto himself, that man and man alone must ask the question, "If I am a law unto myself, then what am I doing with the law that I am?"

Personal responsibility does not seem to be something that the mind readily and willingly accepts. And yet without the acceptance of personal responsibility, man does not start on the path of reason, for he is still the servant of old creation. Creation, like a tool, was designed to be used. It was never designed to be the master of your life. When we use that that was designed to be used, we begin to flow in the realms of peace and the realms of harmony.

When we put a stop—when we make that effort to stop the constant and continuous broadcasting of our mental realms, that is the first step on gaining control of our own life, of our own destiny.

How often, in the course of a day, are we practicing the demonstrable truth that "I am what I am because I am who I am"? But who are we? If we do not pause to think, how can we know? For one moment we think we're one; another moment, we think another. That, my friends, is creation. That is not who we are. That is what we are using. Think about the many thoughts that your mind entertains. Those thoughts are not you; they are tools. Sometimes they are well organized and when they are well organized, they begin to serve the purpose for which you have created them.

It is the natural design of living to be free. To be free is not to do what you want to do when you want to do it, because the true you is not a wanting you. The true you is not a you of need. The true you is not a need of desire. The true you is not a need or lack or limit. The true you is an intelligence that is ever expressing itself. That intelligence, we call God.

It is the forms created by the mind that are discordant, distracting, and not united, because they are yet to be organized and brought under control to serve the purpose for which they were designed. Look at your life today and ask yourself the question, "All that I have created, is it serving me well or am I serving it?" It is an easy thing to see, when we pause to think, if your creations in life are serving you or if your creations in life, you are serving them. If they are serving you, then there's a peace and a harmony within you that is expressing itself. If you are serving them, old created forms, then you are racing and running, never fulfilled, ever in want, need, and desire. For those tools that you created have taken control over their creator.

Whatever it is you think you have in the world of creation, pause for a moment and see how you feel if you accept their passing. If you have any emotion, then you are attached. If you are attached, you are bound. If you are bound, you are not free.

Creation comes and creation goes. Creation is not good, for creation is not bad. It's good and bad only in your thinking. It's good and bad according to your use or abuse.

Much time in this philosophy is spent upon the mind and mental realms. Because it takes much effort, not only to understand this mental world in which the soul is moving, but it takes much continuous effort to bring it into an organized light of reason that it may serve its true purpose and design.

We know that the lack of use is abuse and we know that overuse is abuse. But how does man know balance? It is within the forty soul faculties that the light of reason transfigures the form of creation and brings about what is known as balance.

Have you not noticed before in your own life, or in the lives of others, whenever you are given choice, there is difficulty within your mind? And yet, if you were deprived of choice, there would be terror. We believe that we consciously choose and yet only 10 percent is within our power to do so at any moment. Why is it we have such difficulty in facing variety in anything? Why is it we have such difficulty in making a choice?

If we are given the opportunity to arrive at some appointed place between the hours of 7:00 a.m. and 10:00 p.m., many, many different things will take place in our mind, upon first being given that opportunity. We may choose to be there at noon. But no longer have we made that choice, then something else rises in our mind and we decide to go at two o'clock. And as we near the hour of two o'clock, something else speaks up and we postpone it 'til four. And as the hour of four arrives, we may show up at four-thirty or five. Can we honestly call that an organized mind under the guidance and control of reason or common sense? No, my friends.

One of the greatest difficulties on the evolutionary spiritual path of progression is the difficulty that we make in commitments. Why is it difficult for us to commit ourselves to anything? The degree of difficulty in that respect is ever equal to the disorganized mind that is controlling our life, that is tossing us from shore to shore. And yet, we think we are making an intelligent choice. I assure you, my good students, whatever you choose in life, demonstrate the courage of your conviction. Do not quit before the gates of victory, for in so doing, you weaken your character and your courage is left waning.

The days, the months, the years, and the centuries, they pass. You have everything that you could possibly desire. If you think you have not, then you have yet to find it within you, for that's the only place it will ever be. It is the illusion created from the errors of ignorance of the human mind that keep you searching and seeking outside of your own realm of responsibility. It is an error in thought, I assure you. For you may travel the universes over—I know, for centuries I searched—you will never find it outside of your realm of responsibility, for outside of your realm of responsibility it does not exist. It is a reflection in a clear lake. That's all that it is. And when you finally arrive at that lake, you will know, for it will disappear. If it is not within you, it is nowhere. Any other thought is an illusion, a very thin illusion that the light of reason and common sense can easily pierce.

When you enter the great void, you will know: it's what you have within. That's what you are. That's what you'll find. We all enter the void. It is not dependent upon coming to the realms of spirit in the sense of losing your physical, earthly bodies. Some of you have had moments of experience with the void and your minds do not like it. Remember, the mind does not like anything that it cannot control. And how can the mind control the great void? The mind needs form, for the mind *is* form. And the mind can only control that which is composed of its own substance and under the guiding laws of its own principles. And so to still the mind is difficult and the mind says, "Impossible." But a thought begins and therefore it ends in time.

Whenever you say that life is a struggle, you support and create that form that told you it was a struggle. You see, my friends, when the forms are created, when you image, you establish the law. And so if you image a struggle, the form of struggle is created. And in time, it becomes strong because you direct, through attention, life-giving energy to it. And the day comes, it tells you, when you say that life is beautiful, you call forth the form of your own creation, your own image, to tell you it's not. And so we call that the duality of creation.

This philosophy continues to teach the benefit of daily affirmation. Considering the affirmations of negativity that are already flooding the consciousness, one can easily and quickly see the benefit of the positive. For each negative thought, we must make the effort for positive, in order to bring about the balance that we may rise above the realms that are not serving us in the way they were truly designed to do. As we get closer to these gates of victory, as we view the realms of success in our endeavors, be rest assured, the armies of pity, the armies of negativity, the armies of discord and disaster rise up.

You can always know when you're moving forward, for all the negative thoughts you ever created will rise up. They will do everything within their force to hold you back. It may seem selfish of them, but they were created from selfishness, and therefore, of course, they are selfish. For those images of yours—of all of us—they want to survive. They cannot survive if you leave them behind. They have the intelligence of your mind, for they were created by your mind. Therefore, they know what's going to happen to them if you move forward. They know they've got to go. And as you move ever onward on this path, you will hear their whispers and their shouts. You'll hear them say, "I've got to go!" And unless you are awakened within, you will think that's your thought. It's an echo: it's known as an echo of the uneducated ego. For that's when those images were formed—when the ego was yet wanting to be educated.

The battles in creation are won and lost. But the battle within is eternal in form. If you permit your mind to say you're weary, then remember, you're being pulled back by those forms of creation. Each time you're pulled back, your step forward takes more effort. Many, many are called to the Light. Few remain with it. Our minds, they come and go until we rise in full control. And as that light dawns in your consciousness, be rest assured, the activity of your mind will increase. But we all must face it someday. And we all shall.

You have come this far. You have tried many times before. You have fallen back to rise again. And each time you fall back, you work harder to move ahead. There's no need to fall back anymore. You know the way. You know how the mind works. You know the laws of creation. For whatever it is you fall back to, it's always the same. It is no better or worse. It is within your hands and your power.

You have made, in many respects, you have made much effort. Now is not the time to stop. As you experience the torment of your own mind, remember, it is passing. Remember that you are, in this moment, the strongest you will ever be. For this is the moment that you test yourself. You have the strength, you have the common sense to stand firm and pass any test that that realm of creation puts you through, because you, and you alone, you, my friends, you are the creators. God didn't put the pebbles in your path. God doesn't take them away. God sustains your choice to get them out of the way. That's the God of truth. You choose, and God gives you all the support that you alone permit yourself to be receptive to.

You have heard much discussion on the divine will of total acceptance. And think: we have such total acceptance in certain areas of our life. When things are bad, we totally accept that they are bad. When we are struggling, we totally accept that we are struggling. When we are short, we totally accept that we are short. All we need to do with this total acceptance, this great will of God, is to choose common sense.

We are all well qualified with what a powerful force a negative thought is, for we have all experienced the effects of negative thoughts. And at times some of us have experienced the wonderful, great power of a positive thought.

As we come to the conclusion of this semester, in the few weeks ahead, let us make a choice. Let us choose the greatness and the goodness of life. Let us not choose it once, for once is not enough. For we have chosen the opposite so many times. Let us choose the greatness and goodness and the fullness of life. Let us choose it each and every moment again and again and again and again, that we may live in a world and experience the demonstrable truth of the very philosophy that we study. For that, my friends, is the application thereof.

No greater service can you do to yourself, to this philosophy, to truth, and to the world in which you live and the worlds of which you are yet to be consciously aware, no greater good can you do than apply the philosophy that you are studying, that works beyond a shadow of any doubt the moment you choose it to work. It teaches the freedom from want, need, and desire. It teaches the abundant goodness of life. Do yourself, my students, that service. That is your birthright. That *is* your birthright.

The thoughts that dictate the opposite are not what this philosophy is all about.

Demonstrate what you study. Demonstrate it every moment of your life. Declare your right to the fulfillment of your own being that you may go forth in the world the living demonstration of truth, that in the midst of the Philistines you declare the truth, "I accept the personal responsibility of my thought. I accept the personal responsibility of my experience. For it is my experience. The cause is not another. The cause is not the world, for I am the world. I and I alone am the cause and the cure." Accept that truth, in that moment, ye shall be transformed. And to remain transformed into the fullness of life, repeat the truth until no other thought floods your consciousness and you will be the living demonstration of an abundant goodness, known as God.

Good night.

NOVEMBER 2, 1978

CONSCIOUSNESS CLASS 196

Greetings, students.

This evening we are discussing beyond the human mind of creation. Much time and effort has been spent in sharing with you our understanding of these mental realms of consciousness. And some time ago we gave to you that great, demonstrable truth that peace is the power of the universe. And so it is, each time you think the word *peace*, you direct intelligent energy to the support of that divine principle which, in truth, you are, that principle known as peace.

In your times of need, in your times of struggle, if you will use that principle by flooding your consciousness with that great power, the power of peace, you have within your hands all that is necessary to help you rise to higher realms of consciousness. But that can only happen for you as you make the daily effort to direct this energy that you may use this great power, which you are, to constructive good, to the fulfillment of the very purpose of life.

Above and beyond these mental forms, there are the realms of harmony, the realms of abundant good and fulfillment. They're here this moment in the now of your consciousness. Do not look to the future for the fulfillment of your life. Look to the eternity which you are. This eternity is the moment of your awareness. Only in that moment of your awareness, only in that demonstrable truth of eternity can you use this great power that you may have all that is right for you.

And what is right for man? That that man makes right is what is right. For all of life is only an effect. In going within to that silent sanatorium—that *is* our home. That is the moment that you choose. You will soon discover in your efforts to maintain this great principle of peace within you, you will soon discover the struggle that the mind has to offer. For as you, in your efforts, rise above and beyond these mental forms of creation, you must remember, being your children, they cry loudly for their sustenance.

But it is not man's purpose to live forever and ever in these mental realms of form. It is man's purpose to evolve. And what is evolution, but the very principle of change. And what is change?

That which is form. We cannot change the formless, for there is no form to change. We only change the forms. We change our thoughts. We change our experiences. And all substance of the mental and physical world is subject to the evolutionary process called change. But we do not change that which we truly are. For we are the formless, free Spirit and, therefore, are not subject, our true being, to the evolutionary process called change.

The unfoldment of the soul—and remember, the soul, being individualized, is subject to the laws of change and evolution. It is the spark of Divinity that is the true being that is formless and free. Each thought that we entertain in our mind is governed by the very Law of Identity. And so it is that it is the divine energy, the divine principle, directed through this Law of Identity, that brings about the evolutionary process.

But remember, my friends, in all of your choosing, in all of your identification, there are times in form for beginnings and there are times in form for endings. Thoughts that have served their purpose must be released from the realms of consciousness. For if they are not, then we become their slaves. The worker begins to serve the tool, for the tool no longer serves the worker.

Above and beyond all that earth and the astral and mental realms have to offer is the beauty and the harmony, the peace and the joy, the goodness of life itself. Each moment, each moment thoughts arise within your mind. Are they serving you? Or are you serving them? It is soon that we will see, when we pause and reflect, when we look in that great body of water and we see the reflection, the illusion of mental substance.

As we rise beyond those mental forms, we begin to see the unity, the wholeness and the oneness which we are. We must become united within our own house in order that we may be a part of the unity of the One. Let us no longer seek without for that that is knocking at our door within. Practice each day that wonderful principle: it is within. Remember, each time you declare the truth, "It is within," you rise supreme. You rise each time you accept responsibility for all your thoughts and activities. Each time you accept that great truth, you once again begin to steer your ship of destiny. You chart your course through eternity. You chart it intelligently with your eyes wide-open. You will see clearly.

Practice frequently during your days. Practice, "I accept. All of this that I think, all of this that I feel, all that I see, all that I hear, all that I sense is within my realms of consciousness. And because it is within my universe, I am the master of my universe. I and I alone can change it." So whatever you see and hear and sense and feel and experience in your life, when you speak that truth, the light of reason floods over your consciousness and you become transfigured in that moment. I cannot overemphasize to you, as students, the great value, the eternal value of declaring that truth: "It's within. I am the master of that which is within. And because all things that I experience are within, I am the master and can change those things."

It seems, of course, at first a difficult path to go within. There are many obstructions that have been created in our errors of ignorance of the past. But the value to you, the great transformation that is possible for you, it isn't something that's a long way off. Each time you stand firm and declare that truth, in that moment and in that time does this transformation take place.

When you are angry, when you are discouraged, when the struggle is the greatest, pause and accept the truth. You will find the freedom. You will not have to search for weeks and months and years. No, you will find it in the moment that you speak it. I assure you, in my untold centuries of experience, it took me a long time to learn that wonderful, simple truth. But I am so grateful to my guardian angel who guided and directed me over and over and over again. I learned about the law—that change is possible through the Law of Repetition. I learned that from experience. And from experiences untold I learned the freedom from all creation is the acceptance of responsibility for it.

When you want to be free from a thought and feeling that insists upon plaguing you, accept it. Accept the adversity as you accept the attachment and then you can do with it as you choose. But you cannot change that that you have not first accepted, because that is contrary to the natural law of things.

In all of the classes that have been given and in those yet to be someday, you will find they have, slowly but surely, been guiding you ever inward on the journey to what you call heaven, to the home of peace and happiness. When you make this effort each day, many times a day—a good student, dedicated to the principle of truth, will make the effort at least a hundred times a day. And even [with] that are we short of the mark. For the mind rises in its falsity. It rises up to ever place outward what is going on inward. So you see how many times it takes to declare the truth. Inward, ever inward, your paradise is waiting for you.

The journey in the wilderness—surely, the centuries have passed. It's time. Indeed, it's time to go home. To go home where it really is. For you have traveled far. You have seen and experienced many things and you have found all of them, in the final analysis, all of them outside are empty. They'll always be empty. It is only a glitter. It has no substance, for it has no principle. And that without principle is temporal and passing.

All of form is passing. Your form, that which you are identified with this moment, is in a constant process of change and passing. Each thought you entertain is changing and passing. There is no security in creation. It was never designed as a security. For it's not your home. You are using creation. It is there for you to use in your awareness of the realms of creation. But only for you to use, never to own nor possess. And he, through error, who believes that he owns or possesses, establishes firmly the law in consciousness that he may learn the greatest lesson of all. All of this, the Divine has placed for man, the eternal being, to use and not abuse.

When you find yourself in want, when you find yourself in need, you may be rest assured you have not used wisely that which was designed to be used wisely. And because you have not used it wisely, you must learn the lesson of your error. But that, too, is passing. All is passing, my good students. All that you think and all that you think you have and all that you think you have not is in a process of passing. Let us move, on our little ship of destiny, let us move serenely on the sea of time for, in so doing, are we fulfilled; in so doing, do we experience the joy of living.

Reflect in peace that you may experience the greatness of life. The greatness of life is not only around and about you. It is the reflection of your vibration. Everything, *everything* is vibration. And it's all dependent upon you. This may be the greatest day you will ever experience if you permit it to be so. Think. Think about life. Think how it has been for you. And then think, you made it that way. You make it the way you choose to make it. Why not choose the way of peace? Why not choose the way of fulfillment? It's your choice. The power is in your hands.

No matter where you run, no matter where you go, you will know it's your choice. It is ever your choice, my friends. No matter what your mind thinks, no matter what it does, everything, *everything* is dependent upon you. Your God, your greatness is ever your choice. For your God cannot be greater than what you permit your God to be for you. Your truth is your truth, for that's the way truth is: individually perceived. But whatever you have found your truth to be, remember, if it is secure in you, you won't need to depend on someone else to support it. For it's yours and you know deep within you, for that light has awakened in your consciousness.

Though many have come and many have gone, many more are yet to come. And so the world goes on and on and on. You look and see the multitudes of disturbances in your world of creation, only from a lack of understanding the very purpose of life itself.

You may ask your questions at this time.

Thank you. What should we image when speaking forth the word success *in order to have that word do what we have sent it forth to do?*

When you speak forth the word *success,* all you need to do is to remain in the vibratory wave of peace, for peace is the power and success an effect thereof.

Whatever it is (your endeavor), do not forget the principle of continuity. Your life and experience this moment is an effect of much energy directed in a certain way. So your efforts to change must carry that very principle of continuity. The principle of continuity is not something you have to learn. You have demonstrated fully the principle of continuity. Your experiences and the repetitions thereof are a beautiful demonstration of the principle of continuity. If you have experienced failure, then you are familiar with the principle of continuity. And everyone, in some way, has experienced failure. It has simply been the continuity of directing energy through a certain thought vehicle. You wish to make the change? Then demonstrate the same continuity to the great power of peace, to the image of abundant good, for abundant good is indeed the effect of the power of peace.

Thank you. If the principle of expansion and contraction is universal and universally applied, does it follow that this principle is also applied to the Allsoul and its never-ending absorption and shooting-off of souls on their evolutionary journeys through the ethereal?

Indeed, indeed it does. When the soul, through the expansion and contraction principle, individualizes, it takes a form in keeping with the process of identity. That which expands—and the individualized soul is in a constant process of expansion—also contracts. For expansion and contraction, that principle, applies to form. Therefore, the soul, being individualized, is form. The effect of the individualized soul are the vehicles that you are presently aware of: the physical form, for example. Now, the strengths and weaknesses of the ever-expanding individualized soul is revealed in the bodies that cover it. And so it is your house of clay has all that is necessary for your soul's expansion and final contraction. Each and every part of your little house reveals the strengths of your soul faculties or the strengths of your sense functions.

Therefore, in this great journey through so-called time and space, your little house is in a process, constantly, of change and refinement. We change our identities. Some of us are conscious of that process—most of us are not. But regardless of our awareness of that principle, we are still changing identity. The hairs on your head—it is known by all religions—are numbered. The color of your eyes is ever in keeping with the laws established by you in this eternal evolutionary process of form. Your height, your weight, and everything about your house of clay is revealing to you the varying changes that are taking place in your own evolution. These houses are revealing the effects.

But when you accept responsibility of everything that's going on within your house, you will start on the inward journey and find the cause of all of these things. As we come ever closer within to the light that transfigures us, we must pass through the very depths of self. We must pass through the depths of loneliness before we can enter the great void. Many have sensed and viewed the void and fear has risen and they have retreated from it. But as we retreat from the void, the inevitable, we find an ever-deepening feeling of loneliness. For we know if we go forth with the soul faculty known as courage that the light of faith will see us through this great void, because we cannot return home until we pass through the void.

Many philosophies and religions have taught you that all that you have, give away. They have taught you that that you may be free in your mental realms from the distracting forms that stand between you and the great void. But I say unto you, you can give all that you have and still not enter the void because you have yet to give the greatest gift. To give all that you think you have is to give nothing in truth. It is the very thing that thinks that it has, that must be given. It is the thought of I. All that you have gathered is not the gift. The gift to give is the thought of I. It is the thought of I that separates you from the universal principle of truth itself. The thought of I, the very principle of separatism, stands between you and that which is justly, divinely, and rightfully yours.

When you give the greatest gift of all, known as the gift of self, the thought of I, then you will enter the void. Courage will move you strong and firm. Character will rise supreme and faith will guide you on. Reason will light your path and love will be your constant companion. As you pass through the great void, then you will enter home and beyond all doubt the Light will shine. There will be no shadows. There'll be no doubts. There'll be no fears. There'll be no sorrow, for there'll be no self. But you will be you, you, the universal whole. Home. That's what home is. Everything, everywhere, the absence of want, the absence of need, but not the absence of desire. But not the desire of the human mind. Desire, the principle called divine expression.

This is what these classes are designed to do: slowly but surely, through the very Law of Change, called repetition, to take you on the inward journey, to pass through all the obstructions you have created in errors in the centuries past, that you may enter the great void and go home. And once you go home, it doesn't mean you're going to lose your physical body. It doesn't mean you're going to lose your mental body. It doesn't mean that you are forever going to lose the thought of I. But it means when you return, you will know that the thought of I is a tool to be used in a world of creation, but it is not you. It never was you. It never can be you.

Good night.

NOVEMBER 9, 1978

CONSCIOUSNESS CLASS 197

Good evening, students.

Over these years and these many classes that have been given to you, I'm sure that you're aware that a few have stayed and many have gone on their way. Sometimes, of course, we do not see clearly our own evolution and the changes that are taking place in our lives because we are blinded by the attention to the many things that are in our lives. And therefore, in this philosophy is a teaching: When our hindsight becomes our foresight, we will gain insight. And so it is in the study and the application of this philosophy.

It seems that we are quickly aware, most of us, when we are discussing spiritual matters with others in other spiritual endeavors; we are able to see the many differences. And then, for fleeting moments, we gain some awareness of our own evolution. No one becomes transformed overnight. It sometimes seems in our life, as we go on, that we do make a great change. But that great change is the effect of many years of effort. We are often blinded by the stumbling along the path of evolution and in that blindness we become discouraged.

Many years and many, many words have been spent by the founder of this philosophy on the human mind and how it works. There is a part of us in our mind that has an insatiable need—an insatiable need to be right, an insatiable need to be wanted. And so we do many, many things in our lives to fulfill those insatiable needs.

The human mind is like a bottomless pit: you can never fill it. You can try to fill it, but you will never succeed. There's no bottom to that pit. The mind is an instrument that has this great need to gather and to garner, a great need to ever search. Some of us perhaps believe that it is our soul that is searching. I can assure you it's not our soul that's doing the searching. It is our mind. Our soul knows where its home is. It is our mind that is in the constant process of seeking, of gathering, of garnering.

When we speak of the great word, called *peace*, the great power—though we do not seem to use it frequently, it is recorded in our memory par excellence. And there are moments, there are moments when we do use it. And in those moments and the moments that follow, we become aware. We become aware that it does work. That indeed it does work. But because we have not yet established a firm pattern in our minds to use that power wisely, we slip back to the old patterns that we're trying to change. To permit ourselves to feel discouraged or despondent is simply to support the levels of consciousness, the patterns of mind, the vibrations that have already gained control.

It's been said by many that before things get better, they're destined to get worse. Of course, that's ever in keeping with the Law of Creation. It is ever in keeping with what the human mind has to offer. So when we are experiencing what we judge is getting worse, we can be rest assured, if we will only take a moment and accept the demonstrable truth, that things are getting better. For as one thing gets worse, something else gets better. That's just the way that it is in creation. You cannot have a day without a night, and you cannot have a yes without a no. Now if you'll accept that that is the very principle of creation or form—and by that acceptance, when you face these so-called struggles and difficulties in your life, you will then place yourself in a position, in an attitude of mind of accepting that something better, in truth, is happening.

As all of life, as we all know, is only an effect—and we all know that it takes a great deal of control of the human mind in order that we can move through these multitudes of forms that are all around and about us; that we can more frequently, more often experience the happiness and the health and the wealth that is our birthright. For of what benefit can it be to speak of health, wealth, and happiness, to speak of abundant good, to speak of the peace and joy of living, if we are not experiencing the effect thereof? Time and again this philosophy has taught, and continues to teach, that everything that we experience is vibration. It's always dependent upon our attitude. It is never dependent upon someone else's attitude.

It seems that one of the things that plague us in this material world the most—and it seems to plague us almost daily—is our attitude towards what we call money. All you have to do is mention the word and become aware of what your mind is doing the moment the word is mentioned to you. If you experience emotion whenever that word enters your mind, whenever it rises up from the depths within—because, you see, my friends, there is one thing about words: when someone speaks a word to you, it is *your* word in *your* consciousness that causes you whatever feelings you have. It is not the word that is being spoken to you. It is your relationship; it is your vibration that rises from within your universe.

Now, time and again a person says, "If so and so had spoken to me a little differently, if they had spoken to me in different words, I would not have had this effect or this experience."

It is your own relationship to the word that is recorded within your mind that causes your experience. So if someone speaks a word to you and you become emotional, you become upset, pause for a moment that you may go within your own consciousness and you will find all the experiences related to that word in your head. And then you will understand why you're upset, why you're sad, why you're discouraged, or why you're happy.

You cannot teach one thing and manifest the opposite and experience success. You cannot teach to another until you have taught yourself. To attempt to do so is not only a waste of time and a waste of energy, but it is feeding the realms of illusion and delusion and we just sink that much deeper. So whatever it is that you want another to do or not to do, first be sure that you are doing or not doing it unto yourself.

We've spoken many times on the joy of living, known as the Law of Giving. But giving seems to be such a misunderstood word. When we think of giving, we think of things external that we have accumulated or in the process of accumulating. It is very rare that we ever think of things internal in reference to the Law of Giving.

To become aware of what is standing between you and all that your mind says you are seeking ofttimes creates a great deal of emotional trauma. It creates trauma because, like the onion, we must peel away layer after layer after layer of experiences that we have had in our life. Now, when these layers begin to peel away—and they peel away, of course, in keeping with our own efforts—the mind comes up with a multitude of justifications why we shouldn't make that effort.

We can always know when we're getting close to victory in any area that we have chosen, for all of the defenses in our mind rise up to keep us, the true us, from going home in consciousness. For example, if we are working with someone and we are getting close to the cause of the problem, the mind will rise up with its justifications. It might even say, "Well, there's such a thing as over analyzing oneself." That very statement is a revelation that we are close to the cause. We are now working with the defenses of the human uneducated ego. That's not the time to quit. That is not the time to quit.

Now, I'm just as human as everyone else. And I have thought—my mind—many times, for several years, that really, enough classes have been given. I mean, after all, surely the untold hundreds of thousands of words that have been spoken in these classes, surely is sufficient for anyone to find some degree of peace and prosperity in their life. But that doesn't seem to be the way that it's working out. For the classes are continuing. When I was informed this morning that these philosophy classes will continue, I wasn't informed that they will continue for only one more semester or five semesters. I was just informed that they will continue.

Now, it takes some degree of acceptance for any of us to be told something and, after being told, not to be satisfied with the answer, taking a look, and the mind judges very quickly of the possibility they [*the classes*] may continue on the rest of my earth life didn't seem particularly pleasing to that level of my mind. But, you see, if you learn to accept whether you like it or not, in time, you will have all the fullness of life that you could possibly desire.

But you can't rest upon the stepping-stones on the path. You may pause for a few moments now and then, but this resting and this retiring is a slow process of digging one's own grave. As long as the mind is kept active and under some degree of control, as long as there is interest in life itself, then life has a meaning. It's only when we become grounded, when the thoughts of self bombard us, revealing to us that more effort is needed to control our own mind—that's when we become despondent.

I firmly believe—and make some effort, I hope, to demonstrate—that to the Infinite Divine Intelligence all things are possible. When you have these different judgments rise up in your mind, when you begin to fear and when you begin to worry, look at it for the golden opportunity that it truly is. For it is in those moments, when your mind is in full control and you are experiencing all of the fear that it has to offer, knowing that it is the mind's way of controlling your life, in that moment is your golden opportunity. In that moment, you have the divine right to choose.

You know what the mind offers you. You know, here in these classes, we come hopefully to listen and not to sleep. Those are the moments. Those are your opportunities. I hope that it may be in my divine merit system—for we all have a divine merit system—that I can be left consciously awake so I can see which of my students the classes have any meaning to. For that that has meaning to us, we are awake and alert.

Now, this new system of a nine-day limit to registration is a good sign to me. These classes are becoming more evolved and more selective. They were never designed to raise funds for the Serenity Church Association. That is not their function. Therefore, because they were not designed for material purposes exclusively, that wonderful freedom of choice of quality—not quantity—can be maintained and sustained. If they were designed to be a fund raiser for the Serenity Association, then they would not be the classes that you are receiving. We have bake sales and brunches. We have a ladies' guild, a men's club. We have bazaars. We have a multitude of ways of raising funds. We've never been short on ways of raising money in this church. And spiritual truth is not to be contaminated with raising funds.

We live in a material world and so it is through using the vehicle and the tools of the material world that we gather up material substance that the organization, the ship, may continue to sail on smooth waters. It is very important to all of us to remember and never forget: to try to sell spiritual truth is not spiritual truth at all. For it is ever subject to the fluctuating desires of the human mind. And spiritual principles do not fluctuate. They are the same today, yesterday, and tomorrow. For they are unchanging. They are not of the human—they are not of mental creation. I do hope in this the last class of this semester that that is clear to everyone. I have seen many organizations and I have said time and time again when the gold of the earth enters the temples of the spirit, the temple is no longer of spiritual substance. So let us separate in consciousness our physical, material efforts and let's keep separate that which is of the spirit from that which is of the mind.

Now, in reference to your coming semester, I am indeed pleased that a nine-day limit has been placed on the opportunity of registration. It is in our own best interest, for if we cannot make a decision, in reference to whether or not we choose to continue on in a spiritual class, in nine days, then what guarantees we're going to make it in nine weeks or months? When you have something to do and you have weighed it out for seventy-two hours, that gives you the opportunity to know beyond a shadow of any doubt what it is you want to do.

The more time you take in making your decisions, the more difficulties you guarantee for yourself. For example, with eighty-one levels of consciousness, in a seventy-two-hour period of earth time, you are able to go through each of those levels of consciousness. And so finally, it's either yes or it's no. But if you take more time than that to make your decisions, you introduce—for example, say that you have fifty levels that say yes and thirty-one levels that say no and you're not satisfied with the way you feel. You establish a law for you. It's known as self-prophecy. You establish a law to introduce experiences into your consciousness in order that you can make a decision. My friends, you are then the victim of circumstances. That's what happens when you wait and you think and you think and you think: you open up all these doors and then so-called circumstances make your decision for you. Think about that, for that applies to everything. It applies to everything. It applies to going on a trip or not going on a trip.

And so this evening—we still have time—I want to speak to you about when you seek spiritual counseling and assistance, because it seems that some of my students still do not understand or not aware what really takes place. You know, religions in our world that are extremely popular are religions that have a little genie in a bottle that fulfills all your desires and does just what you want it to do when you want it to do it. Now, someone once said that religion is the opiate of the masses. Depends upon the kind of religion you've got. If you've got the kind of religion that some little genie in a bottle out there is going to come and just take care of all of your desires, while you continue to demonstrate the direct opposite of their fulfillment, that's the genie in the bottle religion.

Now, when we come to Serenity, one of the first things we hear is about the Law of Personal Responsibility. Now if you accept the Law of Personal Responsibility, you can't have that and the genie in the bottle religion, too. Because they just don't mix. They're like oil and water.

When you come into Spiritualism, it isn't the spirits that are going to do this or that for you. No spirits that I ever met ever guaranteed anything like that for me. In fact, they never even implied that they would do such a thing. And whenever I've asked for help in a situation, the standard slogan that I seem to get is, "Well, just go to work and work it out." They do offer some alternatives: there's this path, there's that path, and there's that path.

Now, some time ago, I learned from bitter experience that when they made a recommendation and I didn't agree particularly—I couldn't see the wisdom of it—well, they'd make a second one. And if I didn't really like that, why, they'd even make a third one. And if I still wasn't satisfied, they'd make a forth one. And finally they would come to something that I could agree with. And what a price I had to pay.

When you ask for help, I hope you have a little bit more common sense than I did at that time. I admit that was several years ago. But I hope you have a little more common sense. And you really weigh out what they first said. Because they'll give you all the alternatives that your little mind needs, that you may have all of the experiences necessary for your own growth.

You see, my friends, the spirits, friends in the other world of Serenity are not, they are not, I assure you, genies in a bottle. They do not balance the budget of Serenity. They do not come down and pay the bills. They do not come down and raise the money. If you asked them for help, they're very practical. They're very practical. Now, were they all business people on earth? Of course, they were not all business people on earth. They're from many different jobs and professions. But they do counsel when you have questions. They do look at the laws that you alone have set into motion. They do make great effort to encourage people. Because encouragement is a very positive vibration and all experience is an effect of vibration.

Why not be positive for a change? We've certainly spent enough time being negative. Why do we let our minds say, "This is all I got"? Why don't we help our minds to say, "There's the whole universe and I'm a part of that. And because I am a part of the whole universe, there is no limit." How can there be limit to that which even our physical eyes look out and cannot see the beginning nor the ending of? We cannot see the ending of the universe. We cannot see the beginning of the universe.

Let us think more deeply when we rise up from fear, from fear. None of us are starving. None of us are without a little roof over our head. What is there so valuable about fear? Fear keeps us where we are. Faith puts us where we want to be. Now, it's really that simple. Stop and think how simple. What a simple truth. Fear keeps us where we are and faith puts us where we want to be. So, of course, when we take a look at our life and say, "Well, I'm used to what I've got. I don't like it. I'd like to have a lot more, but I'm used to what I've got. I don't want to give up what I've got to gain something I'm not sure of." Now that's where faith must rise in consciousness. It is the negative faith or fear that keeps us where we are.

The world is filled with all kinds of so-called financial problems. You will face more of it in the five years [*at Serenity*] than you've probably faced in your entire earth time. For the universe is filled, in this earth realm, it is filled with the fear. It is polluted with fear. But I can assure you, a great change is coming. A great change is coming. For out of that mud of fear will bloom the lotus of heaven. And that will take place for not only you who are here, but for the whole world.

Of course, like watching an accident on a freeway, it excites the senses. As terrible as it sounds, it excites the senses. When we hear about a fire, that's the topic of discussion. Whatever the disaster may be, it really excites the senses until, through our own effort, we evolve slowly, but surely, into other types of thinking and other vibrations.

Now, two days away—that's Saturday—we have our regular annual bazaar in this church. The bazaar, like any endeavor, is not dependent upon the weather. Therefore, I don't want to hear any of my students say because of the weather it's this or that, for it is not dependent upon the weather. I used to be in a church where, when the attendance was light, it was because of the weather. Or when this or that wasn't going the way that some were used to, it was dependent upon the weather. The success of the Serenity Bazaar is not dependent upon the weather. It is not dependent upon anything but vibration and spiritual motive. If our motive is right, we can be rest assured, then all will be well.

But how do we know if our motive is right? Well, you know how you feel. And you know you feel the way you feel because you think the way you think. So if you feel right, then your vibration is right. If your vibration is right, then no one can make it wrong. So if you feel good, don't let me hear you say that you felt good when you came in and you feel, now, lousy that you've been here a while. Because you're the one that makes you feel well and you're the one that makes you feel—yourself—bad. No one else does it.

I am pleased to see, after these years, that there are some students, in spite of themselves, who've stuck it out. I am well aware that it hasn't been easy. For their egos are no stronger, no weaker than mine. And it hasn't been particularly easy for me. After all, I have to sit here—it's my merit system—and do the work I have to do. And it's like the vice-president said the other week, "Well, you know, the students can kind of sit and rest, but you have to stay alert and work."

What is so valuable about sleep? I'd like someone to really explain that to me. What is so valuable about a lapse of consciousness? What is so valuable about it? I mean, my friends, you know, you can believe that when you're dead, you're dead. So then it's going to be very valuable for you. Why not die this minute? Then if you want to believe that way, just sleep on and on and on and on and on. What is so valuable about a lapse of consciousness that most of us are spending one-third—minimum—of our life doing? Amazing. Just amazing. It's because of a judgment that we made. I can assure you, as man evolves here on this planet, he will sleep less and less and less.

Your body is not rejuvenated during sleep unless, somehow, during that sleep, you become totally relaxed—that there's no more mental activity. It takes nine minutes to rejuvenate yourself—totally rejuvenate yourself. If you could only see how hard you're working during that lapse of consciousness, you wouldn't believe it. You would not believe how hard you work while your conscious mind is unconscious. That's why you wake up tired. That's why you wake up irritable. That's why you wake up with the blahs. Because you worked so hard with all those other bodies—just worked your tail right off. And what were you doing working so hard? Well, if you want to find out, just take a little stock of your thoughts during the day. All those unfulfilled desires, you know, that rise up and bang at your head—you were fulfilling them while you were unconscious the night before. That's what's really going on. I wish you could see what really takes place while you lay down on your couches or your chairs and *zzz* [*The Teacher makes a snoring sound, as though he had fallen asleep.*]—excuse me—snooze. Then all of the beauty and the goodness of life, you're lucky if you can experience a tenth of it because of what you're doing with the sleeping.

Now, you've all been given, and have been informed how very important it is—what kind of thoughts you have as you're losing conscious awareness. Because this is how you guide and gain control of these other bodies that are out there doing their thing, you see. That's how you gain control of them, as you lose the conscious awareness, as you're drifting off to what you call sleep. Then, not only is it critically important to do it at that time, but it is just as important to do it as you are waking up.

Now, why is it as important to do it while you are waking up? Because, you see, while you were sleeping, these different bodies were out doing their thing. And when you wake up, those bodies are still active and they are *still* doing their thing. So if you want to gain control of them, then you must make the effort when you're going off to sleep and you must make the effort when you're waking up from sleep.

Now, if the mind says, "Well, I'm not so sure even if those bodies exist. After all, I can't see them." But you sure can feel them. Those are the things that put you in what they call these strange, foul moods. Now, no one likes to be around a person who's in a foul mood—no one. I've never met a person who liked to be around anyone who was in a foul mood. You know why no one wants to be around a person who's in a foul mood? It's very simple: the person that's in the foul mood doesn't want to be there either! But they just haven't made the effort to get out. So if they don't want to be there, how can they expect anyone that they're around to want to be around? Because they don't want be around, you see.

No one really wants to be miserable, not really. I've never met a person that really wanted to be miserable. And surely nobody wants to be around a person that is miserable. So it's a place that none of us want to be. If it is true—and it is demonstrable—that being miserable is a place that none of us want to be, then how come some of us go there? Now that's a very good question. How come some of us go to a place of misery when we don't want to go there? Does that reveal—going to a place we don't want to go—does that reveal any degree of control?

So when we find ourselves in the realms of misery, a place where we don't want to be, we don't need to concern ourselves about the misery that we're in. All we need to do is to concern ourselves about the way of getting out. And that's called self-control: to gain some degree of control of our mind.

Well, I will say one thing for the students of this class and the students of Serenity: they have demonstrated, beyond a shadow of any doubt, a great degree of tenacity. Tenacity serves a good purpose if it's directed in a positive way. I don't think anyone can say that my students are weaklings. No, they are very strong. And when they direct that great strength, that they're demonstrating all the time, to what they choose for good for their lives, then they will experience all of that.

You see, I know how strong they are because I know what it takes to help them change their patterns. But just think, when they choose some patterns that are going to be positive and beneficial in their life! You see, that same tenacity that is now holding them to these patterns that are detrimental to them, that very same tenacity is going to hold them to these patterns that are being introduced into their consciousness. That someday, by the very laws of repetition, they'll make a sigh of relief and crawl out of. But it takes not only effort, it takes some time.

So we have made some changes. But just because we've made some changes, that doesn't mean in any sense of the word that no more are necessary. Why, we need the continuity just to hold on to the thin thread of change that we've already made, you see. It's very, very important—very important.

And I suppose, the Friends are very well aware of the necessity for repetition, which is the law through which change is made possible, that I couldn't get a vacation at the first of the year. I've been looking forward to a vacation for some time. Now, I don't want you to feel bad and to think because of your tenacity of holding on to those detrimental patterns that you're depriving me of a vacation, even though that seems to be evident. But I don't want you to feel bad about it. Because I want you to be encouraged. Because if you're discouraged, then those patterns are going to take that much longer [to change]. And I was kind of in hopes not to be totally white-haired by the time I did get a vacation.

So let us be a little more cheery about life itself. Because if we're not cheery about it, it sure isn't going to be cheery to us.

Now, we all know the way. There's no question about that at all. But the only time they did have a break in our semesters was when they [the Friends] were building the house. And I guess that was out of necessity and my vacation is not considered a necessity. However, I don't feel bad about it because I would rather see one student going along the path, even though they're terribly bullheaded, at least they're still on the path. And that's more than many who have come through these doors.

And after all, this little church has long been known as the court of last resort. When we've tried everything else, we found our way here. So there's a chance: when you've reached the last, well, there's nothing else. So there is a chance.

But I would rather have it be a court of last resort than have it be a smorgasbord of the masses running in and tasting a little and running out some place else to this and that and that and that. Because the day always comes that we have to get off the merry-go-round and stick to one thing, at least long enough for us to see if it's working for us or if it isn't working for us. But we do have to give it a chance.

Now, I don't think that there are any students present that haven't applied something that's in this book [*The Living Light*] or this class at some time. In fact, I know everybody's applied a little of it. And I also know that when they do apply a little of it, something works. Now, what does this say right here?

Do you want me to read it?

Yes.

"What is the motive of one desiring to be a Master? On the strength of the soul we aspire; and in humility we lose desire. Then in truth shall we become Master." [One of the Sayings in The Living Light and in The Living Light Dialogue, Volume 1.]

Now, think about that little, simple truth. Just think about that. It's when we give up everything that we gain the whole. So we're all in this process of giving up everything. Yes, indeed we're all in that process. But I assure you, when it's all given up—everything—when everything is gone, that that returns is multiplied infinitely and you're no longer in bondage to it. You use it; you don't abuse it. And you're freed from its control. But first you must follow the path and give up everything.

Now, by giving up everything, we're not discussing that you must give up all your physical, material supply. No, you must give up your attachment to it. Now, if you can give up your attachment to these things of creation without them physically leaving your universe, then they don't need to physically leave your universe. But you'll tell, on your path—it's different for each one—whether or not they must physically leave your physical world. You don't consciously say, "Well, now, I'm going to give up all this and be free," because that just is not how it works. And if you think it's easy to just say, "Well, I'm just going to give up all that," just ask—or have someone ask you for a donation and you haven't judged that you want to do so, and you'll see how easy it is to give up.

It's the giving up of the thought of I, which possesses and builds the barrier between you and the infinite abundant supply that is everywhere around and about you. That's what we give up to have the whole, the abundant flow of life.

Ofttimes, you will see that, by seeming so-called circumstances, it's being taken from you. But remember, you're the one that created the circumstance. You're the one that created the attachment. It's your child. It's growing up and it's going out into the universe. Let it go joyously and then when yours, that is yours, comes, it will come joyously. And it will be free and you will be free. No longer to fear and to live in those kind of feelings, for everything, *everything* is everywhere. You are moving in consciousness through it. It's all around and about you. Each time you say, "I have not," you move deeper and deeper in the darkness, into the illusion, where, for you, it cannot exist.

This philosophy teaches the abundant good, the prosperity of life itself. We bear a great responsibility, knowing that that is demonstrably true, we bear a great responsibility to demonstrate it by our thoughts, our acts, and our deeds! We cannot afford the luxury of the illusion of lack, of the delusion of denial, and then preach to others the Living Light philosophy. For then, we become an instrument of the darkness, instead of an instrument of Light. We cannot say that God is the true and only source of our supply and then demonstrate the direct opposite. That is the worst form of hypocrisy! That is not what this philosophy is all about.

The abundant good of life is ever dependent upon your vibration. It is dependent upon you. Give up this fear. Demonstrate your faith. And flow with the endless, the ceaseless, abundant good of life itself.

Thank you.

NOVEMBER 16, 1978

CONSCIOUSNESS CLASS 198

Good evening, students.

Before beginning our classes this evening and in keeping with our philosophy—that change is indispensable with the Law of Evolution—we'll have a slight change in our format in this new semester.

Now, this evening begins our 198th public class—and by the way, you may all turn your chairs, if you wish, those who care to do so. Like any class on any subject, man will only benefit from it, what he puts into it through his attention and through his own efforts. Now, on the spiritual paths in our lives, in order to experience anything that we have not yet experienced to our conscious recall, it is necessary to make certain changes within our own mind.

Now, students come to these classes with, of course, varying motives. But each of us will receive: whatever we put into anything is what, of course, we get back from anything.

In walking along what is known as the spiritual path, we face within our own consciousness many distractions and many obstructions. The patterns of mind, the various attitudes, and the thought patterns that we have—they were not born and did not grow in a short period of time. If they are very strong and tenacious attitudes, it simply reveals they have been given much energy by much repetition of our attention.

We all seek to be free from the things that disturb us in life. We know, in this understanding, that the things that disturb us are, in truth, the things that control us. So it is that we seek to be free from being controlled.

We all are aware, within ourselves, that we are controlled by different things. It is a matter of bringing an awareness to the conscious mind of those different things that we are controlled by. When we make the conscious effort to bring about these changes, those patterns, which are forms that we have created by our thoughts and our feelings, they rise up to defend themselves.

We all interact emotionally with the world that we experience and the world that we experience is very personal to us. It is governed, that world, by the various acceptances and denials of our early childhood. Whenever we permit our minds to think of self, we open the door to these patterns that are very old and very strong.

So if we want to make changes in our lives—and it is evident by our very presence that there is something that we are seeking—then the first step is to make the effort not to think of self. Because, as I said a moment ago, thinking of self opens the door for all of these attitudes and judgments to rise up in defense. In these many years of teaching, I have seen many, many come and many go. There are a few who still are making the effort.

We all are going to face these obstructions. And we all will have to make constant decisions whether or not we will quit before the victories in life that we are seeking and return to the patterns of yesteryear, which, if they were so beneficial, we would not have made the effort to leave in the first place. Or, by directing our thought to something greater than the limited self, we will continue on the path of evolution in a harmonious and peaceful way.

No matter how much we study and learn in life, there is no automatic cure for the control of our mind. There is no particular affirmation that will wave a magic wand in our universe and free us from our own self-created obstructions.

Now, the Old Man said some time ago that selfless service is the only path to spiritual illumination. We first must make some effort to understand exactly what we mean by "self." The moment that we identify with any particular thought, self is born. It is the process of identifying that limits our consciousness and shrinks our world into a very limited, struggling, and suffering experience.

Now, we all have been born with the divine right of choice. We can consciously choose the thoughts that we wish to entertain. But many of us have lost that ability. But that which we have once had, we can always have again. For hope is not only a soul faculty, it springs eternal in the universe—our universe.

The reason that we are not more often on guard of our thoughts is because it has not yet, in our lives, become a daily pattern. Someone speaks to us and a certain feeling rises within us and, of course, with that feeling comes the judgment. For the feeling is the child of a judgment that we have made at some time in our life.

This philosophy teaches the law, the first Law of Personal Responsibility. And so whenever we permit our mind to think that someone or anything outside of our own universe is the cause of our feelings, is the cause of our unhappiness, is the cause of any obstruction that is in our path, we have, in that very moment, given power to things beyond our control. And in so doing, in that moment we become the victim—our own victim. We don't have to live that way. But to live a better way requires a conscious effort on our part to be aware of ourselves. To be aware, first, for without being aware, we cannot make intelligent effort to control our thought; we cannot make intelligent effort to control our feelings.

Whenever we permit our mind to entertain thoughts of fear, then we are controlled by that fear that we are thinking about. We are controlled by the things that we permit our mind to think and to feel. Therefore, it behooves us, when we awaken in the morning, when we go to sleep at night, it behooves us to think more often of what we're doing to ourselves. Remember, we, and we alone, are doing—whatever experience we have—we are doing it to ourselves. This is the very first step: the acceptance that our life is the direct effect of what we are letting our mind think about.

Now, for many years, the teacher of this philosophy has emphasized that your mind, which is the vehicle of your eternal soul, must be harnessed by the harness of reason. For it is only with the soul faculty of reason that the transformation of our lives is possible.

When we take those moments in the course of a day and when we pause to think, when we consciously choose—consciously—what it is that we desire to experience, when we weigh that out in our mind and we know that to God, the Infinite Intelligence, all things are possible to he who has the wisdom of patience—this seems to be where we falter. We falter with the wisdom of patience. Why is it that man is so impatient? Well, it's very clearly demonstrated: he who has little or no control of his desires is a very impatient person.

So therefore, we know, we know from our own personal demonstration—for the demonstration in life is the revelation—we know how much control, at any moment, that we have over our own desires. For the degree of control is revealed in the wisdom of patience. If we are a very patient person, that is the revelation of what we are doing to control our own desires.

You have heard many times in these classes that desire, the divine expression, is not something to annihilate; it is something to educate. The education of the desire is the controlling of the desire. It is not good or bad to have desire. That is simply an expression of the Divinity. It is when it is educated, when it comes under the control of the faculty of reason, and the wisdom of patience lights the way, that we move harmoniously onward on this evolutionary path of life.

We all know, I am sure, that we did not begin here on earth. And because we didn't begin here, we will not end here. That that came from the earth returns to the earth: and that's our physical substance. But that that motivates this physical body of ours has long endured, for it is without a beginning and, therefore, without an ending. It moves through a multitude of experiences and different vehicles. This is not, this moment, the same as a moment before. There is this constant process of change that is taking place in all our lives, in all the universes. Therefore, a wise man does not attach to that which is destined to change.

You see, my friends, to be free, we must first accept, we must be ready, willing, and able to accept a constant process of change—the stream of life. For that is what we are doing: we are constantly moving. It is when we try to hold to things—we try to hold to form. We try to hold to thoughts. We try to hold to feelings. Those are the chains that bind us. That's where our real suffering begins. You cannot hold to that which is beyond being held.

Life is a constant movement. Your consciousness is a constant process of movement. So when you look at things that are in a process of change and you permit yourselves to be emotionally disturbed, you are only working against yourself. You then become a house divided.

If you let go of that which is in a process of going from you, if you let it go freely, if you let it go with feelings of joy and gratitude, the new experience, which is being born from the one that is leaving you—from the very essence of that that is leaving you—the birth of that which is coming, that you see not yet, is therefore formed or deformed by your feelings, by your attitude, and by your thoughts. So when something is in a process of leaving, be joyous and be of good cheer, for that energy from that soul level of consciousness is what is going to control the new experience in your life.

Now, this is taking place each and every moment. This is not something that happens now and then. You have children. They're born, they grow, they change, and they leave. You have friends. They come and they go. You have husbands and wives and brothers and sisters, relatives and acquaintances. They all come and they all go. So is it not in one's own best interest to accept the going as joyously as the coming?

As you, in this semester, study and apply what has already been given, what is yet to be given, you will find yourself slowly, gradually going through a process of change. The change was taking place anyway, but you become aware of the change. You see, all of us are changing, but few of us are aware of the process.

We seek pleasure and deny pain. But if we are going to permit ourselves to think of self, then we must accept pain as readily and as joyously as we accept pleasure. For to seek one thing at the denial of another is to guarantee that which we do not desire to experience. For example, in the teaching that our destinies are born from our denials, we direct energy, intelligent energy, to whatever we deny. And anything that we direct energy to, through the vehicle of thought, we give birth to: we assist it in its growth.

Many people, many students have experiences and they wonder why. What did they do to attract that experience in their life? And sometimes they are very persistent in wanting to know exactly what they did. The most interesting thing is, they already know what they did, for we all know the cause of all the effects in our life. We do know. It is the levels of consciousness that are striving to defend themselves, to continue to be in control of us that speak out and say they don't know. Now, think about that for a moment. When we are truly honest with ourselves, we know beyond a shadow of any doubt not only what we have done, but what we are doing. We know better than anyone else. We really do know.

So let us begin this semester with an acceptance of the truth that already lies within us. We know where we are. We know what we're doing. We know where we're going. But the question must be asked of ourselves, Are we willing to make the changes that we know, we alone know, we must make to bring about the experiences that we desire in life?

With all of the teachings available in this world to you—and some of you have studied many of them—what works for you is whatever you work for. Each one works for themselves in a variety of different ways. But it is a conscious awareness that is the true light of our path: to become truly consciously aware, that we don't continue to react to other people's feelings, to react to other people's thoughts. To be in a constant battle within ourselves because we are frustrated in our efforts to try to get someone else to do what we desire them to do.

What is it within us that causes this frustration, when we get emotionally upset because we tell someone to do something and they don't do it or they do it their way, which is not our way? So let's take that experience, that many people are going through daily, let's take that experience and accept the Law of Personal Responsibility. And let's see what we're doing inside ourselves.

The law clearly states, like attracts like and becomes the Law of Attachment. Well, how beautifully, demonstrably true. So we ask someone to do something and they don't do it. And if we think of asking them the second time, we usually get upset inside. And we ask them perhaps the second time and they still don't do it. Do we ask them the third, the fourth, the fiftieth, the hundredth, the thousandth, or the ten-thousandth time to do it? I don't think many of us make that much effort. But what we're truly missing is, we are not making that much effort inside of ourselves. Because in keeping with that law that like attracts like, we are attracting into our universe, into our life that experience.

We can change the experience by changing our level of consciousness, by changing our thought and our feeling. You cannot change someone else. It is a great waste of energy. It is a great waste of life. When you are willing to give up the delusion that you can change anyone else—if you are willing to give up that great delusion—then you will begin to see the light of reason. You cannot change anyone else. You can change yourself. And when you change yourself, that that is in your universe will change with you or it will leave you.

Now, this is the most important thing in facing personal responsibility: If you don't like the things that the people who are in your personal life are doing, change your thought, change your attitude. And they will grow or they will go. If you are willing to accept whichever path they choose—the going or the growing, with you or without you—then you will be freed from their control over you.

The first thing in this type of teaching and philosophy that the mind rises up to say, "Well, am I to allow my wife or my husband total license that I am to do everything for them?" But take a look at that type of thinking. Who are you thinking about? Well, it's very evident, of course, in that type of thinking, we're thinking about ourselves. Self-preservation rises up to preserve our judgments, to preserve our thinking, to preserve the status quo. So that type of thinking has to go. And when that goes, some other thinking will rise up and possibly entertain that maybe, just maybe, if you are real strong inside, if you really gain control of your emotions, and if you stand firm on the rock of principle within your own thinking, then everything around you will react accordingly.

You see, it has been said by many a wise man that life is but a stage, and we are actors on it. Now, they didn't say that we are reactors on it. It said that we are actors on it. So we have a choice, constantly, of either acting or reacting. Now, each time that we react, we are controlled; each time that we act, we are free. We make the conscious choice to either act or just to react. So in your daily lives and experiences and activities, think. Begin to think. Are you going to act? Or are you going to react? Now, who, who would consciously choose to be the victim of the whims and fluctuating thoughts of another human being? Now, we don't consciously want to be that type of a victim. And we cannot be, unless we are first the victim of the fluctuating thoughts and feelings of our own mind. People who permit themselves to be controlled by another human mind are first controlled by their own.

Now, these classes are designed to show you a way—for there are many—to free yourself from that type of slavery and from that type of bondage. But we must first consider, if we are bound and controlled by the emotions of another individual, we have first bound and controlled ourselves by our own emotions, by our own thoughts, and by our own feelings. How many of us awaken in the morning and make the conscious choice, the conscious choice to say, "This is a beautiful day"? How many of us, having made that conscious choice, are able to sustain that thought and feeling throughout the course of one entire day?

We must first begin with our emotions. For it is our emotions that are depriving us from the true inner awareness of our own divinity, of our own eternal spirit.

This philosophy teaches an Infinite Intelligence, called God, of divine neutrality. Not good, not bad, not black, not white—a divine neutrality. So do not seek pleasure unless you enjoy pain. Do not seek all these things of earth unless you enjoy being deprived of them. For whatever you seek in creation, you are receptive and responsive to the Law of Duality: the highs and the lows. He who puts his security in a dual law is destined to the trials and tribulations of what the dual law has to offer.

Does that mean that we should not be joyous or enjoy the abundance of life? No, it does not mean that. It means simply our perspective. To some, they see, in pain, the pleasure. To others, they see, in pleasure, the pain. How many times people in the midst of pleasure think, "Oh, what's it like when it's over?"

And so here is the constant cycle. Here is this great treadmill, this karma of creation. That, we shall, in time, evolve through and see the peace and the beauty which is the life of this eternal moment.

When you have these experiences, you must remember they guarantee the continuity in keeping with how much attention you give to them. If you are feeling bad and you direct intelligent energy to that thought, you are guaranteeing to feel worse. If you are feeling what you call good and you direct intelligent energy to that, then you will feel, yea, even better. But remember, whenever you think of self, you are controlled by the dual law of life, you're controlled by those pairs of opposites.

And so if you will kindly turn, now, in your study books [*The Living Light*] to Discourse 46, we'll begin our class.

[*At this point, Mr. Goodwin goes into a trance.*]

Greeting, friends, and welcome to this class.

In coming forth to speak with you in this semester, let us consider the divine will, the Law of Acceptance, and accept the possibility, always, of something greater. For in accepting the possibility of anything, we establish the law which is necessary for it to enter into our universe.

I note that you have prepared many questions. And for the remainder of our class this evening, I shall attempt to share with you my understanding.

Thank you. What is the eighty-first level of consciousness?

The eighty-first level of consciousness is the Essence, the Principle, the Divine, or God.

Thank you. Is it possible to create an allegory [allergy] within your body through a judgment that you may—that you will never be allergic to anything?

By making the statement that you will never be allergic to anything, you have already accepted the condition and, in so doing, must make great effort to battle those accepted patterns of mind. To deny is to destine oneself to the experience. Therefore, it is not in one's best interest to deny an allergy or to deny anything. But to accept the right of its expression and to choose oneself—to personally choose—to rise above the level through which the particular pattern or so-called allergy is expressing. For to deny its existence is in truth to help it grow.

Thank you. Can it be that the human race is an effect of cloning on another planet, sent to Earth long ago as an experiment? Please give us your understanding.

My good students, there is nothing new under the sun, the Light of eternity. And so some time ago we spoke to you about this delusion of being so unique. Where there is nothing new under the eternal Light—and, in that respect, one might consider themselves to be a so-called carbon copy. You cannot have uniqueness and unity. For that considered to be unique, therefore, must be separate, and in truth, there is no separatism. There is but one united, eternal consciousness of which we are an inseparable part.

When you understand the levels of consciousness within yourself, you will see the similarity in all people. For one may seem to be unique in their particular appearance, but they are only unique in a limited consciousness and do not see the whole. Remember, my friends, that that is, has been and shall be. And so it is that the light of reason shines brightly in the eternal moment of the now. It is the light of reason that guides your path. And remember, it shines brightest when your thought is in the eternal moment of now. And so in respect to your question on duplicates and so-called cloning, we spoke to you before that the so-called missing link of the human race will not be found upon the Earth planet because it did not originate upon the Earth planet. As all planets have been populated, so was the Earth planet populated by intelligences from other spheres.

Thank you. Was psychokinesis the method used to build the pyramids? If so, please explain.

The pyramids in your question—and I see you refer to the Egyptian ones—were brought about by a very advanced race of people, at that time, who used the power inherent in all human beings: the power of the mind. The reason that man on your Earth today uses so little of the great power within him is because he is blinded by self-thought and self-created desires. They draw a wall between his eternal soul and the divine intelligent universe of which he is an inseparable part. To speak to the mountain to move and for the mountain to move, man must *be* the mountain. And to be the mountain, he cannot be separate with the delusion of the identity of self. To build a pyramid one becomes the pyramid, for that is the power that lies within the human being. So whatever it is that you choose to do in life, become that which you choose and the experience will follow.

Thank you. Please explain the meaning of the card [from the Serenity Game], "The foot is bigger than its children of toes, therefore, understanding is greater than decision."

Because, my friends, from understanding all things are born. But, like the child that leaves his home, he soon forgets his home. He soon forgets the source from whence he came. And so it is that decision, once made, forgets understanding, that which gave it birth.

Thank you. Could you please give a precise explanation of the meaning of the word principle?

To the questioner who has judged what "precise" means, it would be more than difficult. We have discussed principle many, many times in these classes. To understand fully, one must first fully become. To understand principle, one must permit principle to rise within themselves. Because the mind of the questioner has made the judgment, the prejudgment, therefore they cannot be receptive to an answer that would not fit into the mold of the prejudice that has been made.

Thank you. Please expand upon the teaching [from the Serenity Game], "The greatest cancer of the soul is guilt. Guilt comes from rejected desire, and desire is rejected by the educated brain."

Yes, for each desire that is rejected and not educated, but rejected—a rejection is a denial. A denial is a destiny. We understand that desire, its very principle, is the divine expression. To deny that expression is to create what is known to your mind as a frustration, as a guilt. You separate yourself from the universal stream of life and, in so doing, must pay the price of that separatism. Therefore, he who educates desire holds the torch of wisdom, is guided by the lighted path of patience, knows the welcome hand of reason, and opens wide the doors of opportunity.

Good night.

JANUARY 4, 1979

CONSCIOUSNESS CLASS 199

Good evening, students.

To help us, so that we won't get into any particular ruts of any particular pattern or format with our classes, the classes in this semester will vary from time to time.

Now, as we've all come here to class this evening from our many acts and activities and all of our various unfulfilled and seemingly fulfilled desires, we will have little discussion this evening. We notice, all of us, I'm sure, that we're often, it seems, plagued with different thoughts and different emotions. And when we are having those experiences, it seems to be almost automatic that our minds find someone, something to put the blame upon. Facing personal responsibility in life, which is the very foundation of this philosophy—the ability to respond to all of the experiences in life, for they are but the effects of what we have sent out into the world.

The teaching that like attracts like and becomes the Law of Attachment is a wonderful thing to remember—most beneficial—when we are having experiences that we find distasteful to us. For when we are having those experiences—you may turn your chairs, if you wish—when we are having those experiences, those distasteful experiences, those seeming difficulties and struggles, in those moments, especially those moments, if we will say to ourselves, "Now, like attracts like and becomes the Law of Attachment. This disturbing thought and feeling in my mind, I cannot seem to get rid of. Therefore, it is evident that I am attached to it." Then we will begin, at least we have opened the door of opportunity to begin to trace that thought pattern inside of ourselves to find out what law we alone have set into motion in keeping with the Law of Personal Responsibility.

I had a discussion with one of my students the other night and they were a bit surprised because they were able to see objectively that what they were experiencing was simply what is known as greed. Now greed, our minds usually relate to money. How unfortunate. For greed is something that we experience in many ways. Many people have the greed, the need for constant attention. And it just grows and grows and grows and grows and never seems to be enough. Many people have the greed of judgment: that is, as soon as they go to work on themselves to bow one judgment in their minds, twenty thousand other little judgments rise up to get bigger.

So what is the application of this, the Living Light philosophy? Well, I think we will all agree that it's quite simple: the application of this philosophy is to make the constant effort to control our own mind. Now, why do we say the constant effort? That seems like a great deal of effort—the constant effort. That means every minute, every moment.

When we understand that our mind—the average mind is never still; it is constantly broadcasting a judgment out into the world. Now, they go out into the world and, of course, in keeping with the law and the demonstrable truth that like attracts like and becomes the Law of Attachment, they return to us someday. And they've attracted their kind out in the universe and that's referred to, in this philosophy, as when the chickens come home to roost. Now, the chickens don't come home to roost all at once, you see, because we did not send them out all at once. So all those eggs don't get hatched at once. And so we find a constant stream of chickens returning to roost. I mean, after all, everything in the universe is sustained by an Infinite Intelligence, even the chicken. And it knows its home. It knows where it was born. So every thought and every judgment that we give birth to, it knows where home is. And as I said, it goes out and it always comes back.

Well, we're all, of course, seeking something better. And we all want something better than what we already say that we have. So our mind that constantly is working, creating all these forms—we'd like to have them be angelic forms, something beautiful, something that will bring some good into our life.

The seeming most difficult thing in any philosophy in any religion is for those who claim to believe in it to accept that it's all inside. We cannot step on the path of reason until we make the first step: that it *is* inside. This is why so much time and effort and energy is spent in this church to get people to accept that truth. The moment that you accept, that you truly accept that it is inside, that it really is inside, that it's your thought and it is your feeling, that you alone have caused it—if you go out into the world—and in your study book, you'll find what is listed here as auric pollution. Well, you made the choice to expose yourself to it. Therefore, you still have the responsibility for it. There is no God that I have ever found that dictated you must go here and there, that you must expose yourself to levels of consciousness that you choose not to.

Now, some students will say, "Well, this particular job that I have, well, those people and that job are very negative. And I have to work for a living because I have to eat and I have these different needs." But you made the choice to find that particular job. No one else made that choice for you, you see. You set all the laws into motion necessary to have that particular job. You can set new laws into motion and you can get a new kind of job. It's quite possible, if you have not learned and opened up your faculty of tolerance, a soul faculty, that you'll probably merit a job even more negative until you begin to open up those soul faculties.

Now, the soul faculties and the sense functions, as we have discussed before, once brought into balance—that means equal energy expressed through the corresponding function and faculty—bring about a harmony, a rhythm that brings to us the peace and the joy and the happiness which is, in truth, our birthright.

Now, many of those faculties and functions have already been given. The various levels of consciousness correspond to the forty functions and the forty soul faculties. To list all of those functions and faculties for you in a definite, concise way deprives you of the opportunity of learning them for yourself through your own experiences. If a person, trapped, for example, in the function of greed, makes the effort to free themselves from it, by that very effort they will learn for themselves, within themselves, the corresponding soul faculty to that function.

Now, this philosophy teaches that truth is individually perceived. The purpose of the philosophy is simply to share with you a way that has proven, through many centuries, to be successful and beneficial to those who are willing to apply it.

Many times there's been questions on principle. We've discussed principle many times and we will discuss it again. Whenever a person is truly expressing principle, there is total consideration. But what we seem to misunderstand, in reference to that word and its meaning—principle—is that we say, "Now this is principle. Therefore, it applies to everyone." It applies in keeping with the law for which the principle is established. Now, you cannot take twenty people at any given time and say that they're all in the same level of consciousness, because I don't think you're going to find that in any group.

The difference between principle and rule is very simple. Principle has total consideration of all the various levels of consciousness. A rule or a regulation is an effort to bring about harmony in anything through an authoritative action. There is a vast, vast difference. Every rule and regulation that this organization has given birth to is the direct effect of transgressions. Now, for example, whenever a person is in total consideration of self, they are controlled by what self has to offer. Being controlled by what self has to offer, there is not consideration for others. If an individual consistently remains in that level of consciousness, it creates problems for those around and about them. That is when these transgressions give birth to rules and regulations.

We must, at some time in the course of our daily activities, ask ourselves honestly, What are we doing to ourselves? We must ask ourselves that. Don't ask what you're doing to someone else until you know what you're doing to yourself. You see, once you know what you're doing to yourself, you won't have to worry about what you're doing to someone else because you'll already know. Because you'll know yourself. So let us make the effort to become aware of what we're doing to ourselves in order that we may know ourselves. We cannot know ourselves unless we know what we are doing.

When we wake up in the morning, what is the first thought we have? How many students present can honestly tell themselves, and then me and the rest of the group, what was their first thought upon conscious awakening this morning, just this morning—not last week, not last year, not even last month, not even yesterday, but just this morning? If we truly and honestly know what our first thought was upon awakening this morning, then there is obviously some effort being made by the student to become aware of themselves by knowing what they're doing to themselves. But if you are not aware of the first thought—your first thought this morning on awakening—then you do not know what you are doing to yourself, for you are not truly considering yourself. You are only considering desires that rise up in your mind. And you trace those little desires blindly from one to another and another.

Now, will any student present who is honestly aware of their first thought this morning kindly raise their hand? Yes. All right. I'll come to you. But this lady here, first. Would you rise, please? What was your first thought this morning? Yes.

It was that I had to get up immediately in order to make an appointment.

That was your first thought—all right. Thank you very much. Do you know why that was your first thought?

I've been giving a lot of attention to not being late—trying to prevent being late.

Would you say the thought that you had just this morning, would you say that that was a conscious awareness of God in your life? Or was it a limited level of consciousness that expressed?

Probably limited.

The thought did not consider your health, your wealth, and your happiness, did it? [*After a short pause, the Teacher continues.*] Pardon?

No.

Did it consider the animals of our kingdom here on earth or anyone else? I'm only trying to help you to see how you set your day and your law into motion. For the level of consciousness that you awaken to when you awaken, unless nipped in the bud, if it is not one that you consciously choose, is the level predominant to control you for that day. Therefore, does it not behoove us to understand a bit more about the so-called computer known as the human mind?

Now, why did the student—and does the student know, truly know, why *that* was the thought and not some other? [*After a short pause, the Teacher continues.*] Pardon.

No.

All right. What it reveals is that that level of consciousness, that particular level was the strongest broadcasting level when you went to sleep and lost conscious awareness. That's what it reveals. Now, when you know, when you make that effort—and this particular exercise, if you wish to call it such, was given some time ago to the students here in class. You were shown very clearly how, by programming your mind as you're losing conscious awareness, you establish the law for your tomorrows. Whatever level of mind that you are in when you lose conscious awareness goes to work during the time that you are sleeping. Everything of like kind is working within your mind. And [then] you awaken in the morning and that's the first thought.

So if you become aware of your first thought, you will know what you are doing. You will know what you are doing to yourself. Now, that really doesn't take much effort: to be aware of your thought when you go to sleep and to be aware of your thought when you first awaken. Then you start to find out what's going on. You'll be very surprised. And soon you will no longer be surprised about your experiences in life. You won't have to worry, you see, about being a Dr. Jekyll and a Mr. Hyde. You won't have to be concerned about some level just seemingly spontaneously rising up and controlling you. You won't have to live any longer being deceived by the subtle workings of the vehicle known as the human mind. You won't have to be sad and angry and not know the reason why. So often we get angry and our little deceiving mind says it's because our wives or our husbands didn't do what we desired when we desired it to be done. But that's such a sad deceiving of our own mind. You see, that's just—the little door was opened that we can have the experience. But we and we alone created everything that's behind that door.

Now, isn't it certainly more practical, isn't it certainly worthwhile to become aware of the vehicle you're using? Do you realize, my good students, that we are much more aware of our physical body than we are our mental body? We have spent more time and more energy on our physical bodies—how they look and shine and how we comb our hair and how we keep it in such a way and how we buff our nails. We are much more aware of our physical bodies. We are little children just crawling to become aware of the body that moves the physical body, of the body that brings all of these experiences into our life.

Some time ago we discussed the principle of honesty—honesty, which is a soul faculty. There are many soul faculties. There's duty, gratitude, and tolerance. There's faith, poise, and humility. There's patience. There's understanding. There's harmony. There's faith. There are 40 triune soul faculties (or 120) and there are equal corresponding triune sense functions.

Now, the only obstruction between our soul, our true being, and the awareness and experience of the universal Whole or Infinite Intelligence known as God, the only obstruction is the blindness that is created by an imbalance between our soul faculties and our sense functions. And if you will make this effort of becoming aware of your thought, at least in the evening and in the morning, at least that much—that's so little to do for our own good, so very little—then you will become objective to the many desires that are taking place within you. You will be able, then, to view them.

You see, desire, that divine principle of expression, if it is not balanced, instead of being a vehicle through which God, the Divinity, expresses, we become the victim of creation of the form of our desire. You see, when the tools no longer serve the worker, the worker begins to serve the tools. Now, the mind, the body, the form, it's a tool designed for us to use. Now, we can very quickly tell whether or not we are using the tool or the tool is using us. I mean, it's a very simple thing to become aware of that this very minute. We either are serving the tool—we are either using the tool and it is serving us or we are the servant of the tool.

Now, if you have a thought in your mind at any time that you cannot control—in other words, it keeps repeating itself in your mind—or a feeling that you know that it is not beneficial for you and you do not want to experience it anymore, if you cannot say to the thought or to the feeling, "Thought, I no longer choose to experience you. Feeling, I no longer choose to have that feeling," and if, when you say that to yourself, the thought does not return to its source, the feeling does not disappear from your awareness, then that is a revelation, you see. It is a demonstration. And the demonstration *is* the revelation that you, that tool, thought, and feeling, which is a tool, it is not serving you anymore. No, because if it were serving you and you told the thought to go and you told the feeling to go, then it would go. So, you see, that tool is not serving you anymore. You are serving it.

Now that is something—my friends, it certainly is time—that we really begin to consider. When we cannot change our thought in the moment of our choice, when we cannot change our feeling in the moment of our choice, *we* are the victims of it. Indeed we are the victims. Now, we don't need to be the victims. There's no law of the universe that says we have to be. We can, once again, declare our divine right for the tool to serve us and to serve us well. But we cannot do that without the awakening and the expression of the soul faculties.

Become aware, when you find that you are serving the tool, when you find that you cannot control the thought and the feeling, become aware and direct your attention, your energy to the soul faculties and you will very quickly see which ones are not in balance with your functions. You will see very quickly.

So often in life we sell out. We sell out and do things in our life that we know are not right. We know in our heart, deep within ourselves what's right and what's wrong, for we all have a conscience, a spiritual sensibility with a dual capacity that knows right from wrong. We don't sell out because of our faith in God. We sell out because of our fears in life. I can assure you that whoever sells out is controlled by the fear of the human mind. But if you will stand firm and free yourself from fear, if you will, in those moments, demonstrate your unshakeable faith in God, you won't have to sell out. You won't have to do things that you know are not right for you and your eternal soul. You won't have to do that. My good students, there is not enough gold in all the universes to sell out for. For you'll always come out on the short end of the so-called stick. If you will stand firm, you will not be hungry; you will not be cold. You will have your health, your wealth, and your happiness if you will stand firm inside of yourself on the rock of honesty within your own being.

You see, we do take it with us. We take all our thoughts, all our fears, and all our feelings. I wish that all my students could see the forms that the mind creates from fear. For there is no horror that you have yet in your life experienced on earth that can possibly compare with the forms that are created by fear. They are directly contrary to the beautiful principle of harmony. Therefore, they are distorted and discordant. In the midst of the great fear, that's where you'll find your God, if you don't sell out. If you sell out, you'll not find your God, not then. No. You will find what the Bible speaks of as the false gods of creation.

But they all have clay feet and the moment that you have found them—it lasts but a moment—you stand still and be patient and you will see how quickly their feet crumble—the feet, the symbol of understanding.

And so when we sell out, we see that we are yet far from finding that great God, that beautiful principle known as Life itself. For whatever we fear is that which we are serving. So become aware of what you fear and then you will know who your master is. And you will find and you will see how many masters have been created.

Now, long ago in ancient religions there were many gods. And in some civilizations today, there are still many gods. There is the god of rain. There's the sun god, the god of the wind, and all these different gods. They all have form because all created gods have form. Only the true God is formless and therefore free. For whatever has form, has limit. And whatever has limit, is not whole, is not universal. And so we see in ancient religions many, many, many gods. Each one born from fear. We understand in this philosophy that fear is the mind's control over the eternal soul. And so we see that creation (the mind) gave birth to these gods of form. As long as we believe in them, we are controlled by them. We know that from our daily experience. We are controlled by the things we believe as long as we permit our minds to be in control.

Speaking so much in this philosophy on the mind, I don't want my students to entertain the thought that the mind is not a beautiful instrument that was designed to serve a beautiful purpose. It is not the design of the mind that should our interests be directed to. It is what we are doing with it. If an automobile takes you where you want to go, there is no need to be concerned with what design it is—if it takes you safely where you want to go. And so it is with the human mind. It is designed for you to express through on this planet and in other dimensions. It's what you choose to do with it.

But we don't even know what we're choosing to do with it unless we are aware, by making some effort to [become conscious of] what it's doing. And if we don't know every morning, upon awakening, and every evening, upon going to sleep, what thought is there, then how do we know where it's driving us? Because, don't you see, my friends, it is driving us into many, many different experiences and places in our life.

And so it is that before we open our eyes to other dimensions, let us become fully aware of the one that we're already in most of the time. By becoming aware, truly aware of the one that we are spending most of our time in, then we can consciously choose our direction. We don't need to live with these false gods that have been created by fear. We no longer have a need to serve them. But to make that change, we will have to become aware of our own thoughts. Surely, when we pause to think, surely, we cannot help but be surprised how little effort has been made by ourselves to become aware of our own thoughts, how little effort when it is so very important.

Every philosophy in the world has taught the same principle: O man, know thy self and ye shall know the truth. And the truth shall set you free. Now, that's the only way we're going to be free. And if we're not willing to make that effort to know ourselves, then it is just a waste of time and energy, for we can't be free if we won't make that effort.

Does anyone present have any thoughts on why we do not make greater effort to know ourselves? I mean, we spend so much time in self. Does it not seem logical? Does it not seem practical that we would make some effort to know this little house in which we reside? Most of us know our cars and our clothes and our homes much better, much, much better than we know the thoughts of our mind. Surely, we know these propelling desires. We certainly know the things we can't tolerate. We certainly know the things that we insatiably desire. You see, we're spending so much of our energy and so much of our time on the physical forms of creation that we can no longer see the cause of it. We've lost sight of the cause and, therefore, lost the cure.

Now, let us encourage ourselves. Let us truly awaken and place that thought of knowing thyself higher on our priorities. How many people spend their days in discussion—five or ten minutes—with anyone in an effort to know why we feel the way we do? How much honest, *honest* communication is there? How much honest communication do we find in our life? My friends, honesty is the only thing that's going to lead us through this jungle of creation. Why do we have difficulty in being honest with ourselves? What is it that we fear that honesty may reveal?

I've never been known as one who is lost for something to say. I'm a firm believer that God gave me a mouth to use and a mind to direct it and hopefully a soul to shed some light of reason upon it. How many of us honestly, truly are communicating with ourselves? We know right and wrong. No one has to tell us right or wrong. We surely know that. What is it that we fear that we must be dishonest with ourselves and, therefore, can only, of course, grant that dishonesty to those with whom we come in contact?

I would rather lose all of the so-called wealth of this world of creation and have my honesty, for my honesty will go with me throughout eternity. That, surely, to any mind, is certainly more valuable to anything that this physical Earth has to offer. Why—and I truly emphasize—why won't we be honest to ourselves? What is such a great force that we are so fearful that we must sacrifice the principle of honesty?

You see, when you speak of honesty, most minds think, "Well, I'm an honest person. I don't cheat anyone. I don't try to deceive anyone. I don't try to get something for nothing." But is that where honesty begins and ends? What about the honesty of how we really feel? What about the truth that frees us?

You can't tell me this can be truth when there's no honesty. That's impossible! That's contrary. What keeps us from being honest with ourselves? We judge if we speak honestly, we judge; we judge and we fear. We fear the experiences for we presume what they will be.

This philosophy has tried to show you a way to be free from fear. For with fear, you cannot have a full and good life. If there is something you don't like, why don't you be honest with yourselves and speak it out? You see, it is better to speak it forth in a kind way and work with it so that you may begin to understand yourself and, in so doing, be honest with yourself.

The cause of all divorces and separations in our world is very simple. Two people live together, not being honest with themselves, then they cannot be honest with each other. If they won't admit to themselves how they really feel, how can you expect them to possibly admit to anyone else how they feel? But why won't they admit to themselves how they feel? What is it that they fear?

When we've lost sight of God, we experience fear. When we experience fear, the functions take over and we live an imbalanced life. Then our little minds work very hard to try to fulfill the multitudes of desires that it has and we do all kinds of things, all kind of games. And someday, we become the victim of the games that we play, when we don't need to live that way.

When this beautiful, simple truth shows you a way that you can stand up and declare the truth to yourself: that you have a right to your life; that you don't have to deceive and be dishonest; that God, if you truly believe God, if you truly, truly in your hearts have accepted God, then you cannot have any fear. And if you remove fear, you remove dishonesty, you remove deception, you remove all of those games from your life. And then you can breathe and you can be free. I assure you, you will not lose. I assure you, you can only gain. You can only gain a greater life than you have already experienced.

I am not telling you that you are dishonest, for we all know where we are, you see. No one needs to tell us. We all know. We all know. We all know what we fear. And we all know, because we fear it, we do these shady things, so-called. We know. Oh, yes, we know. Our little conscience, it whispers within us and it says, "You know. You know that's not right." Oh, it knows very, very well. It knows so well.

Now, do we really understand why we are not aware of our thought as we go to sleep and we are rarely, if ever, aware of our thought when we awaken? Because our little minds have worked so hard to blot it out, you see. Because it doesn't want our little soul to see. But the eye of eternity never sleeps. Our soul is ever present, ever urging us onward to accept responsibility for our life.

To commune with God, we must first commune with the vehicles through which the God within is expressing. And so one of man's major problems is his lack of communication. We are our own best friend and we are our own worst enemy. Now, when we are our own best friend, well, everything's beautiful; everything's just great. But then, when the chickens come home to roost, revealing to us that we have been our own worst enemy, those are not happy moments. And we immediately blame outside for all those little shenanigans that we've been doing inside.

That's one thing about this little church: it's a little church and for that I am very grateful. Because with so much to be done—you know, I like to stay afloat and if it was too big of a church, it's going to take a lot more people to work on a lot of other people to keep it on the rock of principle for which it was founded. I have always believed that truth really frees our soul. I have always believed, therefore, that it is better to speak forth the truth as you know it than to hide behind the cloak of fear. For the day comes in eternity that you not only begin to wonder who you are, you even begin to wonder what you are. In fact, we had a whole class on the hindsight years of the forties—that's the age of forty. It was a few years ago. Because it's usually when man reaches his forties that he starts to look back and say, "Well, how come I didn't do this or that?" Well, if we had grown to that point, of course, we would have done that, absolutely.

To ask ourselves each day what it really is we want is to set a law into motion to find out who we really are. We chase so many things and they never last. The only thing that's going to last is that which is the truth. We blink our eyes and we see it. And we close our eyes that we may go back to sleep in the slumbers of satisfaction. How long does anyone stay satisfied with anything? If you go to a church and you only go to a church and you get into a religion and you only get into the religion because it satisfies you, open your eyes: it won't satisfy you forever. For satisfaction is a slumber and when you wake up, you won't be happy. For the motive, you see, is limited to a level of the mind.

If a marriage is based upon the principle of satisfaction, it does not endure. For there is no woman or man that can satisfy any other woman or man forever. So it has to be something greater than the slumber of satisfaction. I mean, everyone, of course, can be fascinated and hypnotized for a time, but by the very laws of evolution, they wake up someday. So there has to be more than that, you see. It has to be a lot more that.

That—about temptation—the one thing good about it, the one, real, beautiful thing is that it doesn't endure, you see. We can be tempted to something for only so long a time and then it dies. Now, we can be tempted to something else and then it too dies. For whatever is born, dies. So, you see, even the Lord's Prayer clearly states, "O Lord," meaning, to us, the law, "lead us not into temptation but deliver us from evil for thy name's sake." So the Lord, being the law of our universe—what is that? It's our mind. Our mind makes life a law unto ourselves.

Now, I know that, to some, it certainly would be more pleasing if the Light, perhaps, at times wasn't so bright. But I am sure it's in keeping with what we're able to bear. Because, if it wasn't, we wouldn't even be here, of course, this evening.

Some of my students are wondering why our spirit teacher hasn't come in each time. Well, he'll come when he comes because, you see, I don't—I'm not familiar with any kind of spirits that I can tell when to come and go. Now, I am aware that some people have those kinds of spirits or at least they tell me they have those kinds of spirits. But I never found any spirits like that. Years ago, I used to think there was something wrong with me, because I heard so many people—mediums—tell me that their spirits did this and their spirits did that. I haven't been able to find any of those kind of spirits. And I wonder, perhaps, if it's because I never believed in having slaves or servants. You see, that thought has passed through my mind many times. Like attracts like and becomes the Law of Attachment. And perhaps because I never believed in slavery and in having servants around the house that I just, of course, cannot attract those kind of spirits that do everything for me.

My friends, so many people get, in conception, that to get into Spiritualism, there are some spirits that are going to do everything. Well, if that was the case, after thirty-nine years—going on my thirty-ninth year in this work—then how come I haven't been able to get any spirits to fulfill my desires? I can assure you I haven't found one spirit, including my own mother, to fulfill *my* desires. Whenever my mind thinks I have a need, she tells me the same old story. And I say old story—"Just go to work"—because that is a standard answer for any problem that I think—that is, my mind thinks—that I might have.

Now, so considering I've spent so much time of my life working with them, it's difficult for me to understand any student, *any* student of mine that has any spirits doing all these things for them. Because it just doesn't seem fair to me! It just doesn't seem fair. [*Many students laugh.*] When I have to raise money to pay the bills, no spirit comes in and says, "Don't worry, Richard.

Here, that's all done." No, I have to work through the emotionalism of my own students, which, of course, I merit.

I am so grateful that things are getting better. And, as I've said to my students many times, a part of my little brain many times says, "Well, if we only had compulsory tithing, then I wouldn't have to go through all of this." But then, of course, I know better. How do you grow if you don't face your own levels? How are any of us going to grow? You know, we don't grow sitting on the mountaintop basking in the sun like a toad, you know. We've evolved beyond the toad stage. We grow climbing up the mountain, you see.

So don't get tired—God forbid—that reveals a grounded vibration into self, you see. You know where I first got that? I'll never forget. Years ago I said, "O God, I'm so tired." And my mother said, "Tired? Oh, Richard, you're grounded in self. Just get out of self." And it made me so mad. [*Many students laugh.*] Then, all of a sudden, in just a matter of minutes, I thought, "Well, how'd I get all this energy? I just feel great. I'm not tired at all." Because the spirit was right, you see.

When we start thinking of self, then we get all that negativity and how exhausted we are, because—don't you see?—we stand in our own light. When we get into this lack and limitation and we get into all of these different things, we're not in God. We're totally locked into the limitation of what our mind has to offer. Of what good is a philosophy if it teaches the health, wealth, and happiness that is available to all God's children if those who are preaching and teaching it and those who are trying to learn it are not demonstrating it?

I tell you it is only an error in our thought that keeps us from the goodness of life. It's an error in our thinking that keeps us in lack and limitation. It's an error in our thinking that keeps us from having all of the goodness that our heart desires. You see, it is our mind that judges and depends upon what the limited experience in our computer has to offer. And as long as we depend on those limited experiences, we cannot open up the door to higher levels of consciousness where things flow harmoniously and we don't have to spend so much of our time and energy in constant self-concern whether we're going to make $20 or $5 or $50,000. What difference does it make? It makes no difference if we will only accept that God is the only source of good; that God, to us, does mean good. And when we are in that goodness, there is no concern over all these other things.

You see, it is our thought that's doing it to us. If we'll only let go of that thought, then we won't have to worry so much, you see. Because we're literally killing ourselves off, literally, moment by moment. You don't have to worry about what you eat. You don't have to worry about your smoking or your drinking and all these other things. That's not where it is. It's our thoughts that poison our body. It's our judgments that break down our health, which is the effect of harmony, you see. You see, if our thoughts were in the harmonious flow, then we don't have to be concerned about, you know, what we're eating or what we're drinking. We don't need to be concerned about that. It's our thoughts that poison our body or permit us to be in the health that is our birthright.

Now, we can say the Healing Prayer, but if we do not accept the first two words of it, then let us forget saying it. Because the first two words very clearly say, "I accept." [*Please see the appendix for the entirety of the Healing Prayer.*] Now, think of that. In one of our classes, our teacher clearly stated that the obstruction to this great goodness is the thought of I. Now, let us relate that to this Healing Prayer that we have. It doesn't say, "You accept." It doesn't say, "We accept." It doesn't say, "Accept." It says, "I accept." Because the moment that the thought of I, that which you have identified with as you, the moment that it accepts, truly accepts, it moves in the will of God. For acceptance is the divine will. Therefore, if you want to continue to establish these negative mental laws, then continue to direct your attention and your energy to denial. Now, think about that. Denial—denials become our destiny in life. The law is so clear.

Is a man who entertains fear in acceptance or denial? When you have fear, are you accepting or denying? Would anyone care to raise their hand? Yes. Would you stand, please?

Denying.

Denying. You see, if we fear—most of us fear what is the three major functions: *m-e-s*—money, ego, and sex. We fear that we may not have enough money to fulfill our desires because we are denying that we have. And because we are denying that we have, we establish our own destiny and have less. And so the wonderful prophets of the Holy Bible said clearly, "To those who have, yea, even more shall I add. But to those who have not, even that shall I take away." Now, I think that that truth is very clearly stated. To those who have—they could not have if they had not accepted. They have accepted. And because they have accepted, yea, even more shall be added. To those who have not, who have denied the source, yea, even that shall be taken away.

And so in this philosophy is the simple teaching, speaking of God, "He who loves himself more than he loves me shall lose himself to find me. But he who loves me more than he loves himself has found the truth, eternity." So our choice is very simple: we all love, but do we love ourselves so much, do we love ourselves so much that there is no room for the goodness of life, that there is no room for God to get in? We all have a great abundance of love. Where is it directed?

Now, if we don't know whether or not, yet, that we love ourselves more than we love God, all we have to do is to make a little effort to become aware of our thought and feelings, to communicate within ourselves and we will very quickly see who we love the most—that which is the true and only source of our being or the little being that by the laws of evolution is in a constant process of change and decay.

Thank you very much.

JANUARY 11, 1979

CONSCIOUSNESS CLASS 200

Good evening, class.

Now, in this semester we've had a few informal discussions here on the philosophy. We, surely, are all well aware of the importance of thought and the importance of our attitude of mind, of our various patterns, and the things that we are working to grow through.

Now, it was stated that it would behoove us, as students, to become aware of our thought, to become aware of the first thought we have upon arising in the morning and the last thought we have upon retiring in the evening. Now, how many people have made that effort this past week? If so, please raise your hands. Well, I am sure, to those who have made that effort, they've had, perhaps, a few disappointments, some surprises, because we alone put our house in order. What goes on in our house—this house, this mental body, this physical body and these other dimensions, that some of us are aware of and many of us are not yet—is dependent upon us.

Personal responsibility is something that has been taught in this church for many years. It's the very foundation upon which the philosophy is based. And when we make the effort to become more aware, when we find ourselves blaming outside for what's going on inside, then we can take control and we can move onward in what we choose to move onward with. We very soon find that we do not have as much control over our mind and our emotions as we thought we had. We find ourselves, in the course of a day, blaming someone else for how we feel, for the circumstances and the experiences that we are having. And this blaming outside, from years of usage, has almost become a habitual pattern.

Whenever the Law of Personal Responsibility and the thoughts of our mind are discussed, some of us become very nervous inside. We find our minds being distracted with things other than the discussion. We should, at those times, ask ourselves the question, "What is it inside of me that doesn't want to hear about the Law of Personal Responsibility? Why do I want to shy away from it, when only by accepting it can I truly fulfill the purpose of my life, become the captain of my ship and the master of my destiny?"

Whenever we find time, it is very rare that we sit quietly and start on an inward journey to see what's going on inside of ourselves. We either have a radio playing to keep us constantly distracted or we have a television on or we're doing something else to entertain the mind. It seems that we're not very good company with ourselves. And so we must ask ourselves that question: Why aren't we good company with ourselves? What is it that we don't want to see? Have we spent so much time in our life creating an image of the way we would like to be, but are not yet willing to make the effort to really become that way?

Now, our philosophies in this world teach us that a house divided cannot stand. And so it is that in making these little efforts each day, we slowly, but surely, begin to communicate with our whole being—not just those parts of our being that have created an image for others to view and for others to hear. Sooner or later, we will become aware of who we are. Because we're spending our days in being one thing to one person and something else to someone else. And so there are many things that we, seemingly, are trying to be. But we never can really be all those different things because we will, in time, be honest with ourselves, the way that we feel, why we feel the way we feel, why we think the way we think. Become aware of all these fears that we have. Become aware of all these needs and the causes of them. Because only through that awareness can we know ourselves.

And here we are, in these classes, to know ourselves, for we are seeking to be free. To seek to be free, of course, reveals to us that we are bound by something. We cannot be—desire to be free when we are experiencing the fullness of freedom. We can only desire to be free when we have some awareness of being bound. And so we are all aware, to some degree, that we are bound by something. But first we must make the effort to find out what it is we are bound by.

We look over the world and we meet many people. And we carry on many conversations. And we have a multitude of experiences. And we continue on with experience after experience. When we know what it is we really want, what we *really* want, then we will know who we really are.

We all are seeking to find the purpose of life. Many times in our lives we have thought what that purpose is. And we have chased that thought to find that is not our purpose. We come to the earth realm with many lessons to be learned. How do we merit the lessons of life?

As we evolve, we stumble along the path. Each stumbling, through an error in our thought, transgression of the natural Law of Harmony, sets into motion experiences or lessons to be learned. And so each of us has come here to earth to learn these lessons. You don't need someone to tell you what those lessons are. For we all know what it is—what attitudes, what habits, what patterns are detrimental to us. And being detrimental, they are our greatest lessons. We will all be freed from them in time, for we are, in our ways, making some effort. And the crumbs in life, they guarantee the loaves.

So often we have desires to do different things. And we entertain those desires. And when we're about to fulfill those desires, because we do not yet have control of these levels of consciousness, we move to another level and we have a different priority. And the desire we had on one level of consciousness meets what we call an obstruction: it meets a desire with a greater priority. This, in time, causes us frustration. Obstruction after obstruction. From the frying pan into the fire and back to the frying pan again. And so it is we seem to go so often.

When we go to choose anything, first it behooves us to make the effort to face the various levels of consciousness which we, at varying times, are expressing through. Having once done that, when we make our choice, our decision, we follow that decision to its completion. If we do not do that, we find ourselves in life starting many times, but getting nowhere. We do not reach our goal. And the reason we do not reach our goal is because when we go to set the law into motion to travel along that path to its completion, we move into one of the eighty-one levels of consciousness that has another priority. Now this takes place every day. This is one of the major causes of people being tardy or late for their own commitments. They have good intentions, good intentions, but no control. And this is why this philosophy teaches that hell is paved with good intentions and broken promises.

When the word spoken by man becomes his bond, his character is sterling and all may view it. And it reflects a soul that will not sell out for any desire once it has committed itself to what it has to do. It takes that sterling character, it takes that type of commitment for any soul to reach its own home and the fullness and the purpose of its life. When you are ready to make that commitment to your eternal life, you will call forth from the world of creation a multitude of distractions. But in time—and when you look at those distractions and the causes of them—they serve to strengthen you on what you have to do in life.

Much of our time and energy in the course of our day goes to a multitude of distractions. This philosophy teaches to put

God in it—whatever it is you choose—or to forget it. If you find difficulty in fulfilling the commitments that you alone have made in your lives, if you find difficulty in being prompt for your commitments, if you find difficulty in completing what you have started, whatever the project may be, then you can be rest assured there is, within, great need to take charge and to take control of the vehicle of the soul, known as the human mind.

And so let us pause for a moment and let us ask ourselves where we are headed. Where are we really going? Do not think you're standing still, for everyone everywhere is going somewhere. We are, this minute, this moment, we are traveling in consciousness. Depending upon you, each individual, how you react within to the words you hear shows you where you are traveling.

The awakening process comes at the expense of the thought of I. When the thought of I bows to something greater, then there is an open receptivity to experience something that is greater.

Throughout all of eternity we are gathering and we are garnering, for that is the Law of Creation and our eternal, formless spirit is moving this world of creation. We all understand, I am sure, that we are this formless, free Spirit, this pure Energy, which is the motivating power of all forms everywhere. When we believe we are a thought and not the cause of the thought, then we are limited by the thought.

Our purpose here is to help you, by thinking and thinking more deeply, to grow and go beyond the limit of the thought. We can easily tell how much we believe we are the thought we think when we view how much emotion we experience when anything runs counter to it. Depending on your reaction reveals how much you believe you are that thought. It is not easy for some to separate their being, their free spirit, from the thoughts that are running through their mental vehicle. We are attached to creation by the principle of our belief. And so it is a matter of expanding our consciousness, broadening our scope in order to truly find that we are the universal whole, that our lack of experiencing that universal wholeness is by our own belief that we are these thoughts that pass through our mind.

We know that we are the creators of them in the sense that we have personally identified with them. There is only the principle of mental substance. Man's identification with that principle, sustained by his personal belief, and in that sense only is he the creator of it.

Inventions and various things that come to our Earth planet come to this planet like a ladder of progression. They do not originate here. But they originate here to those who believe, who have identified with them. We are the receiving sets and transmitters to this, the earth realm and to the dimensions that surround this earth realm. Our responsibility to life is not limited to the vehicle through which we are expressing because we are an inseparable part of the whole. And being inseparable from the whole, have the potential of the full experience of the whole, our responsibility is limitless.

So many times, especially in the nature of this religion of Spiritualism, we seek and are attracted to it to communicate with other dimensions. Hopefully, many people think, to make our paths a little bit easier, a bit more harmonious. And when these angels who surround us, inspire us and show us the way, so often it is not in keeping with the thought that we have chosen as the way. It is the very nature of the human mind to question. But we must also be aware that when we question, we have first questioned ourselves before we ever question another. And so we present ourselves to the spirit—in the flesh or out of the flesh—we present ourselves with our questions. How rarely are we aware that we have already given ourselves the answer. And if the answer we receive from another is in keeping with the answer that we have already given ourselves, then for a time we're pleased; we are satisfied. But it doesn't work that way all the time.

Sometimes a person will say, "I am undecided." What does that really mean? When we think we are undecided about anything, do we mean that we are neutral and totally receptive to guidance from any other source? How wonderful if that were true. But that's not how we go to God or to anyone. We are undecided because we have two conflicting answers that have come up within our own universe. And because they are contrary and conflicting, we say, why, we're undecided; we are not sure; we don't know just what to do. But that is not true. From one level of consciousness we have decided that that is the right thing to do, only to face, in a moment, another level of consciousness that dictates that's absolutely the wrong thing to do. And so we go with our questions with decisions that have already been made. And therefore, in a sense, we indeed fulfill our self-prophecies.

This is not something unique to the religion of Spiritualism. It is something that is very common in our world today. What does it reveal to us? And how can we benefit from the awareness of it? It reveals to us, clearly, that we are moving through realms of prejudice. That we have, before we have the physical experience, we have already prejudged it. We don't want to do that, because that's not a reasonable way to look at life. But that's what's happening. We want and have desires and we judge whether or not it's going to be possible. Depending upon how attached we are to those judgments dictates the Law of Struggle and Difficulty in our life. Say that we want to go into a new profession or a new business. When we have the desire, we also have the judgment. Now it's very subtle, but it's taking place all the time.

We go to make a purchase at a store. Before we ever get to the store we establish all of the laws in keeping with our judgments that took place at the moment we made the decision to go to the store. Now, we get to the store and we have some very difficult experiences. But if we will trace our thought and our feeling back to the moment of decision, we will see the laws that we set into motion.

In our work we ofttimes are enthused in the beginning and then we begin to experience all types of difficulties and struggles. And our mind says, "Well, that one is not doing right. And that one over there isn't doing right. And this didn't go right. And there's a shortage of supplies." And all of these different things happen. That's fine. That's all the effects and they're very clear. And they show us very clearly how we started the endeavor in the first place. How we really started it. And as these things mount up, as we're getting, hopefully, closer to the completion of any of endeavor—any of our endeavors, we turn our back. We don't want to face all of that. Because, you see, we really know what we did and we don't want to have to face it. It's called growing up.

Now, we'll all grow up. We're in the process. But, my friends, if this philosophy, which clearly shows the demonstrable truth of how to be free, which clearly shows you how to be captain of your ship and the master of your destiny—by simply, truly seeing that you and you alone are the law that's working in your life.

We go to God in prayer. And we go with hope, with expectation, and we guarantee disappointment. Because, you see, the word *expectation* means to expect. Be fine if it stopped right there: to expect whatever the Divine has to offer. But that's not where the expectation stops. Oh, it doesn't stop there at all. We go with the hope, which is eternal. We go with the expectation, which is the covering of all of the judgments and dictates of what God is going to do about this mess that we got ourselves into. And then we get mad, disgusted, and turn away from what we call God because it didn't work out the way that we judge that God should have made it work out. But what we don't see is it worked out exactly the way our judgment caused it to work out, because the law is so beautiful, because it is so impartial.

Whenever the Friends say to me that it'll work out in divine order, that means to me total acceptance of however it works out. Now, when we're ready for total acceptance, which sees the good in everything—because God is the good and God sustains everything. Though our view may dictate it to be bad or something else, the good is in everything that you choose to enter if you put God in it. And when you put God in it, that means putting God inside your conscious awareness. That's why and that is how we are freed in the midst of the Philistines of creation. We are freed by where we keep our head. Remember, it's our head. And because it is ours, because it's something that we alone have earned—somebody else didn't earn your head. Only you earned it. And because only you earned it, it's yours to do with as you see fit. But isn't it fit to be good to yourself?

When we become aware of what we're really doing to ourselves, we will start being better friends with ourselves. Because if we can't be good company, there's no sense in running out all over the world trying to find good company because the good company has to be inside first.

Now, I've taken this little time to try to show you the importance of thought and of attitude and how we question and have the answer immediately in our head. And therefore, when we seek advice, when we seek guidance, let us be aware that there is a part of us that has already dictated how it will be and what it will be. And that's the part that we must first give up, even though it's very subtle. Because, you see, my friends, you cannot have a dictate in front of a request. So when you ask for something, whether you ask a person here on earth or you ask the Divine Intelligence or you ask one of the ministering angels that are around and about you, when you make that request, you must first give up your dictate; give up the judgment that is there, standing as an obstruction to your receiving what you are after in life. And if you will become aware of how that part of your mind really works, and in becoming aware, bow that, that you may receive what you seek.

For, you see, the cup runneth over for it is filled. The cup must first be emptied in order for you to receive what you are seeking to receive. When you give up what you think you have, you will make room for the better that you are looking for in life. And by giving up, it's not a matter of giving up physical, material objects. It's a giving up of the judgment that keeps those things as obstructions in your universe.

More than we use in life is not only more than we need, it is an abuse of the divine Law of Harmony. All of the things that you have in your life, if they are not being used, they are not serving. If they are not serving, they are decaying obstructions. Now that applies not only to physical things in a physical world, but it applies to these mental things that our world is so filled with these obstructions. We don't need them. Our houses are jam-filled. Let us clean them out. Clean them out that this flow of harmony and rhythm we may experience once again.

I know that many of you have prepared questions for this semester. And beginning with our next class, we will be getting to those and a little change of format.

But it's interesting, for we see, whether it is we go to a class or we go to a grocery store or whatever it is that we do, we really walk with judgment right in front of us. We have done it so long we're not really fully aware. But that will change because as we see what we're doing, as we really see what we're doing, the changes will take place greater than ever before.

Love is the very Life and it is the Light. And it is so distorted by the errors of our mind. We seek love. It is a natural thing for all souls. It's a natural thing for the animals and the birds and the human beings. And often we seek it because we feel we don't have it. And the reason we feel that way is because we are not giving it. You see, when we give love, then we experience love.

But when we bottle it up in what is known as the greatest sin to man, the love of self, that's when our problems really begin.

We have built up so many obstructions. We've worked so hard to create so many images so that people, we think, will like us. But what it is we're really seeking is the Light and the Life, which is known as Love. When we start breaking down these barriers that stand between us and all of the universe and everything that is in it, when we are no longer concerned about what someone else thinks about us, then the energy that we have been using to create so many images for so many different people, that energy, which is, in truth, pure Love—for that's what Love is, is pure energy—then it will flow through us, around and about us. And everyone that comes in contact with us will experience it. And then we won't have to worry so much about not being loved.

The mind, it dictates what being loved is. And because the mind dictates, it creates its own experience. And so it keeps seeking and never finding. And it goes on and on and on. Often we have said, "All that you could possibly desire is where you are." But do we know where we are each moment of our day? Do we know where we are this moment?

None of us enjoys being miserable. None of us enjoys being sad and all of those other levels of consciousness. And if we don't enjoy it, then we must ask ourselves why we choose to experience it? And if we say, "I am miserable. I am struggling. I am sad," and we say, "But I have not chosen to be that way," then what does that tell us? We haven't chosen to be that way. That's what we say to ourselves. But we are that way. Then it simply reveals that something inside of us is making us that way. And that something inside of us, we are not in control of. Therefore, only through self-control do we ever experience what is known as freedom. We want to be free from many things. Then we must make self-control a number one priority.

Remember, each time we blame another for our thoughts and feelings and experience, each time we do it and in the moment that we do it, we are controlled by the error of ignorance. We are the victim of that error and we alone will pay that price. Someone else doesn't pay our dues. We pay our own dues. There is no credit in the realms of spirit. It's simply a pay-as-you-go system. Credit is an illusion created by the minds of earth. It does not exist in the spiritual realms of truth.

So each step that you take—that we all take—let it be a sure step. Let us truly be aware of where we're going. We have that right to know. And within each and every one of you, there is that Infinite Intelligence that, once you bow all of these veils that stand in front of it, that you control the mind that it may be still—for when the mind is still, you see the Light of eternity. It is not something you must chase the universes for. It is something you already have, if you will make the effort to control the mind, the vehicle. For that must be still, perfectly still, for you to see and for you to hear that which is eternal, that which is your own guiding light.

When you make those efforts to be still, you know better than anyone else how much more effort is necessary. For you know when you experience the peace that passeth all understanding, you know how you got to experience that and you know the effort that it takes. But, of course, it's worth it. It's worth it to be free. All philosophies teach that it is the truth that frees us. But how does man find the truth, if he cannot still creation, the human mind. First we must still the mind.

And when our emotions are running wild, that is our greatest moment and our greatest opportunity. When you are filled with anger and you are on the verge of losing total control, that is your golden opportunity to tell your little vehicle, "Peace. You be at peace." And when you do that, if your mind reacts, and it stills itself and the waters within you are calm, then you know you have gained control. For when the test is the greatest, you have all of the power necessary to pass it.

We grow as we climb the mountains. We don't grow as we sit in the valleys. And so when your struggles seem so great, remember, that is your greatest opportunity. When everything that your mind can possibly imagine fails you, be grateful, for then you have no place left to turn but to something greater than your mind. And that's the great benefit: when everything your mind can create fails you. For truly necessity is the mother of invention. And one way or another, we are driving ourselves out of the limits of the mental bondage that we have trapped ourselves in.

I assure you, no matter how many days or years or centuries it takes, we're all heading to the Light. Because that's just the way that it is.

Now, with all of this, ask yourself, "What is my thought?" Have we been aware, here this past hour, have we really been aware of our thought? Have we been aware of our thoughts? For indeed there have been many. For I see no one before me or around me that has sustained one, singular thought through this past hour. We find our minds what we call drifting. But it's not really drifting, no. For everything is associated and related. You see, we open up the door of one thought and then comes another and another and another and another and another. And so we find ourselves traveling constantly. We're traveling in so many different areas of consciousness.

The universe is infinite. And so is the multiplication of our thought. So is the complexity of falsehood in comparison to the simplicity of truth. Have we, in this past hour, as our little ship has taken us to so many realms of differing thought, have we been the captain of that ship or has it just drifted? Without conscious choice, what realms have we spent this hour? For each of us has been spending it somewhere.

To become aware is the first step in becoming free. Because, you see, wherever that vehicle, that ship, takes your little soul, it establishes laws all along the way. And so each one has gone somewhere in just this short hour. But have they gone there by a conscious choice? No, it just happened. But how did it just happen? Well, the mind will do many things until it's brought under control.

You see, my friends, we're drifting on the old tides of creation. And we are drifting, not aware of where that vehicle has been taking us. But remember that like attracts like and becomes the Law of Attachment. So when you sit and your mind, your ship, takes you to so many places, stop in that moment and take hold! Choose where you want to go. And if you will choose where *you* want to go and you tell that ship, "I am captain and I am master. Now, we're going there because that's where I want to go!"

My friends, become aware each moment, for your ship is taking you to many places that you really, consciously, do not want to be.

Thank you.

JANUARY 18, 1979

CONSCIOUSNESS CLASS 201

Greetings, friends. This evening's class: *The Light Within, The Path of Reason.*

As man awakens his spirit within, he soon realizes that the only obstructions to the flow of reason are the limits and errors of denials created by the mind. For example, when the mind denies, it obstructs its own flow in the divine will known as acceptance. And so it is by accepting the right of expression, man becomes freed from the mental laws that dictate a limited destiny.

In the evolution of the individualized soul, there is an ever-expanding process that takes place. And so it is as we awaken within, we find an ever-increasing amount of experiences entering our consciousness. In time we reach that point in evolution when we realize that we are ever in a world of constant change, but we are the changeless, for we are, in truth, the formless.

And so it is in our efforts in our daily activities that to pause, to be at peace, is to enter the light that is within. Whenever you find a thought disturbing your harmony and your happiness, pause in the moment of the thought and enter that silent sanctorium that is your true home. For there, the light cast upon the shadows will awaken within you the soul faculty of reason. For it is reason that is the true light in our world. But let us not confuse the faculty of reason with what our mind judges to be reasonable. For that which is reason has no need of judgment or justification for it is considering all. And being under the direct guidance of total consideration, known as divine love, there is no dictate from the mind of that which is reasonable.

All of our feelings and attitudes and thoughts are direct contacts with the multitude of forms in the universe. And so it not only behooves us to guard our thoughts that we may see our path more clearly, but we must also bear in mind and in thought that divine right of choice. Granting the right of all expression is not a dictate of the mind to deny the existence of that which is. We choose each moment, but in that choosing, because the level of choice is dictated by experiences along our path, we continue to reinforce, to support, and to sustain patterns of mind that have indeed served their purpose as stepping stones on the evolutionary path.

With all of the many forms that surround you at this moment, we must ask ourselves the question, "What is it that I, an individualized soul, must bear in this the eternal moment in which my choice to go upon the path that leads me into ever-increasing and multiplication of creation or the path that is single, that is filled with the light of reason that will guide me home, direct?" For all us are serving a purpose. To be aware of that purpose is our true purpose. For we, and we alone, are establishing the laws of our tomorrow by the very thoughts and feelings, by the constant reacting, by the patterns that have already been firmly established. In all of your efforts and endeavors, remember that you and you alone stand in the Light; that you may use it or be blinded by it.

In any teaching, in any study man is ever faced with the choice to let it enter his heart and, by so doing, become transformed. And so we stand on this evolutionary path with that choice. When it enters the heart, it is freed from the control of the mind. We know from personal experience and demonstration that that which enters the heart permits the soul to speak and to guide us in our life.

It is our purpose and our destiny to evolve above and beyond these multitudes of created forms. To serve the light within *is* our true purpose, for we are the Light when the truth rises up from our soul and expresses through our heart.

Until we make that choice to still the mind, to no longer permit the mind to justify its way in life, to get it under the control of common sense and reason—this is not something that we do once a day. It is something that we do each moment. For it is each moment—it is the moment that we must consider. The moment, and moment by moment do we grow and unfold and, in so doing, awaken within.

We all face these self-created obstructions. But when we recognize their true cause and accept their right of existence, and when we exercise our right of choice, to be attached to them or be freed from them, then we can move onward with the work that we have to do.

Ofttimes in speaking with you, I have witnessed the many friends and guides and teachers that work with you to help to encourage and to inspire you. For all things to all people are possible, when the acceptance of the possibility is freed from their mind and enters the depths of their heart. We know that our soul speaks through the vehicle known as the human heart. And because we do know that truth, we therefore bear the responsibility to make, yea, even greater effort. Greater effort, that we may be the light of peace and joy, which is, in truth, our true being.

The lessons that you experience in your earthly journey, of course, are ever in keeping with what you alone have set into motion. Do not be discouraged by the lessons when you find them distasteful. Recognize that they are lessons because at a point in time in your evolution to you, to a level of your mind, they were tasteful.

And so it is that throughout all eternal life there is this constant give and take. There is this constant attachment and adversity. It is when we bring these functions of the vehicles into a balance with these faculties of the higher being, known as the soul, that we move along the neutral path. We are aware of all that is around and about us, but we are no longer controlled and, therefore, no longer disturbed by them.

To be in the world—any world—and not to be a part of the world—any world—is to be free from the vehicle that the soul, the eternal being, is expressing. To be detached from the vehicle that your soul is presently using is to be free from its limits. For all vehicles, being formed, are limited by their form. To go beyond that vehicle in which you are presently residing takes effort to bring about a balance within the vehicle. For only in bringing about a balance can you be freed from attachment and adversity. For both attachment and adversity are bonds that tie you to the vehicle in which you express. How does man bring about this perfect balance? By first recognizing and then accepting that the body and the mind through which his soul, his true being, is expressing, is a tool designed for him to use. He is not the form. We are that which causes the form to move. We are not the thought. We are that which moves the thought. We are not the mind. We are that which activates the mind.

And so it is, separating truth from creation that our freedom is truly experienced. To permit the mind to dictate what freedom is, is to limit the possibility of freedom, to limit it dependent upon your denials and judgments of the past.

It seems upon your earthly planet that the greatest difficulty and struggle is an understanding of the law that is the true cause of your material world. As long as you permit your mind to chase the effects in life, you will be bound and controlled by effects in your world.

To bring the mind under the control of the light within is something that takes place each and every moment of your life when you permit it to take place each and every moment of your life.

Your journey upon your planet is indeed a very short journey. And upon your planet you have many lessons and much to learn. For unless those lessons that you, by the laws you have established, are learned in keeping with your experiences upon your planet, when you leave your physical body you are trapped, so to speak, in what is known in our world as the magnetic belt that surrounds your earthly planet. Therefore, take control of your magnetic field, which is known to you as your own emotions, for unless you make that effort to do so while you are yet in the fleshly form, your magnetic body, your emotional body, will continue to bind you to the planet of your present existence.

When this effort is made daily, when you truly, truly desire to be freed from the things that control you, that is the first step. For to take control of a desire, emotional, magnetic body, one must use the very tools of that realm of existence. For example, one must learn to use desire to educate desire. One must use the very tool that is composed of the elements that they wish to be freed from.

To understand the things of a spiritual nature, man must use the spiritual being that is within him. To understand the simple truth, one must use the principle of simplicity that exists within him.

Therefore, my good students, all of the tools necessary to bring into your life all the goodness that waits for your recognition, you already have. You have the spirit within. You have the light within. You have the eternal soul. You have all of the bodies necessary. All of the tools are in your hands. But you cannot recognize them and, therefore, by not recognizing them, cannot choose wisely their use, until you pause and begin to think.

To still the mind and accept the truth: "Indeed, indeed within me is the fulfillment. It is within my reach for it is, in truth, in my consciousness." Think, as you go through your daily acts and activities, how many times the vehicle of your soul directs you outward to fulfill your life. Ever outward until the day in eternity finally dawns—it's not out there. It never was. When that day dawns, you will find all that you possibly could desire is where you are. And where you are can be guided and will be guided by the light of reason when you accept that simple truth.

You may ask your questions at this time.

Thank you. Are all so-called defense mechanisms employed by the mind to preserve its judgments? Would you comment, please?

All defense mechanisms—for example, the reason that truth needs no defense is because it is truth. Therefore, all defense mechanisms are created by the mind and controlled by what is known as negative faith or fear.

When you pause and enter the truth that is your eternal being, you know beyond a shadow of any doubt that whatever is form begins, serves its purpose, and returns to the source from whence it has come. Knowing that and knowing that you, the formless, free spirit, flows eternally beyond the limits of the illusions of time and space, there is nothing to defend when you are in truth. Because there is nothing to defend, for you are truth, does not in any way imply that you, in a world of form, should not stand upon what you truly believe is right for you to do. The defense, which is a mechanism designed by negative faith or fear to protect form—the form of thought, the form of belief, the form of a physical or a mental or an astral body. It is those bodies that awaken to what is known as self-preservation.

And so, my friends, when you are in that great sanctuary of peace and harmony, you stand in the midst of worlds of creation knowing that they only affect you when you are attached to them.

Thank you. Would you please give your understanding of why some children are autistic, that is, refuse to speak, and how can they be helped spiritually?

Many souls enter the earth realm and bring, of course, with them the lessons that are necessary for them to grow through. And so it is when you find a child that perhaps appears not to have the desire to speak, to communicate, it is not that they do not have the desire. The obstruction in their view, created by fear from past experiences, can be quickly overcome with love. Now love, divine love, is total consideration. And so those who love a child, if they are truly in divine love, they are in total consideration, which means they are above and beyond the limited desire for the child to do as they wish.

Thank you. Please give us your understanding of the saying, "A man without courage is bound by fear, the effect of which is fascination, guaranteeing the law of temptation and eternal bondage."

A man without courage, indeed, is one filled with fear. Fear, we understand to be negative faith or the mind's or mental vehicle's control over the eternal soul. And so it is that a mind filled with fear, lacking in the soul faculty of courage, is out of balance. The human mind, designed to be a receiver of information, if it is not brought into balance with the great peace that passeth all understanding, which is in truth the light of the soul faculties, if it is not brought into balance with that great stillness, it begins to fascinate with the many creations within its domain. Once establishing that Law of Fascination within, it becomes attached and controlled by the multitudes of form that are without. And so anyone who finds that they are filled with fear, controlled by the many fascination forms, can bring about a balance in their life by directing energy, the divine energy, that flows through them, to the soul faculty of courage.

It is interesting, I am sure, to all of you to note that whenever you begin a new endeavor in your life, enthusiasm you find to be short-lived. The mind is stimulated; the human ego, which is the crown of the mind, is stimulated by what is known as challenge. It can, and ofttimes does, serve a good purpose. It serves a most detrimental purpose when the stimulation of the human ego is misunderstood as enthusiasm. When a person is truly enthusiastic, that is an expression of the soul faculties. And the enthusiasm in any endeavor lives through the completion of its original motivation. When you have something to accomplish and you feel that you are enthusiastic about accomplishing it, the end result reveals to you whether or not you were enthused or you were stimulated by the challenge to the ego.

Success in anything is dependent upon the spiritual vibration of enthusiasm. Ofttimes a person says, "I used to be enthusiastic." Enthusiasm is not something we used to be. Enthusiasm is an expression of the soul faculties. But as time goes on and things do not go the way our mind has dictated, we say we have lost enthusiasm. I say unto you, my good friends, in that respect we never did have an expression of enthusiasm; we had simply an expression of ego stimulation, known as challenge.

Many of us have found ourselves to be great starters and very poor finishers in our efforts in life. A good starter and poor finisher reveals ego challenge stimulation. A person who starts an endeavor and, regardless of the struggle, completes the endeavor is truly guided by enthusiasm, for to be enthused is to be in God and in God is good. So that that is begun is completed and we move on and on and on.

When we find ourselves in life being so-called great beginners and poor finishers, all of these loose ends, these laws that we have established, they return unto us and build untold mountains of obstructions. And then we find ourselves in the function of discouragement and no longer desiring to make the effort to do too much. We would rather entertain ourselves with the function of self-pity, which is known as failure, for, unfortunately or fortunately, much of our energy goes into the function of discouragement. Now if we discourage ourselves enough, we can justify, to ourselves, of course, that it is reasonable for us not to make any great effort. But, you see, my friends, sooner or later our little soul rises again and again and again. For those who enjoy the function of failure guarantee by that very enjoyment to someday find it a distasteful adversity.

Whatever it is in life that you have to do, do it, complete it. For it shall haunt you throughout all eternity, for it's your child and it will come home to be fed again and again and again. And so it is whatever you choose to begin, be sure you complete. For it is all of those incomplete, loose ends that bind you to the functions of failure and discouragement.

We must consider what it is in our thinking that does not find responsibility, the ability to respond to life, what it is in our thinking that shies away from the ability to respond to the greatness, to the goodness of life itself.

Indeed, we all are growing, hopefully, up. For it is up, up in consciousness where we find our home, rising above and beyond.

For you see, my friends, a straight line, which is the path of our spirit, is, in truth, a complete circle. So it is with our direction in life. Let the path be straight and narrow that we may complete the circle for only in completing that circle do we ever experience the fullness of life. And that which we begin must, by that eternal law, have its ending or completion. The circle is not a half-circle or a quarter-circle. It returns unto itself. And so it is in your endeavors in life. You cannot leave them half done or just started, for the circle is not complete and the incompletion of it takes control of you. Though you see it not, someday you will.

When we have responsibilities—and responsibilities, the ability to respond to life, for us, ofttimes are many—complete each one. Because you cannot be free until they are completed. When you leave your physical world, those incomplete endeavors in your life bind you to the realm upon which those forms are waiting to return unto their source.

Therefore, I say to you awaken within that you may be objective and no longer attached to the physical body in which you are presently expressing. For detachment from your physical body is not an automatic process by the laws of nature. When your soul has finished the work it has to do on the Earth planet, if you are still attached emotionally and mentally to that physical form, you are held in those physical realms to view the natural, decaying process of the physical body returning to the source from which it was composed.

And so it is with your creations. The law is universally applicable as a universal law. You create the thoughts and the feelings of an endeavor in your life. You begin it. If you do not finish it, you cannot be freed from it, until it has gone through the circle to complete itself and return to the source from whence it was created and formed. Those are the things that bind us and hold us.

Remember that all things must return to their source. And when you, by not completing that which you have begun, do not stay with your efforts and you build something and do not complete it, the circle is not complete. It has not returned to the elements from whence it was composed. Those are the shadows that haunt you. Those are the obstructions that stand in your path. For life marches on. And those who remember whatever goes out, returns, are aware of the circle of life. And that awareness, of course, helps man to stand upon the rock of principle and face what is known is personal responsibility. Because life is, in truth, a circle, man's foundation is personal responsibility. Accept that simple truth that is ever with you, around you, about you. Your feelings, your thoughts, they come from within you; they return unto you.

So as you flood your consciousness with the divine right, your birthright, of harmonious, peaceful flow, you send that out into the universe. It ever returns to you, the source, for you are the creator. And that that you have created, your children, know their home. Accept your responsibility for your life that you may respond in the light of reason, that you may be the living demonstration of the goodness of life. And then your whole world will brighten and you will see and know the way. There'll be no question, for there's nothing to question when you accept responsibility for all your thoughts, acts, and activities.

From home you have wandered, and to home we all are returning. But we're doing that each moment. We become aware of doing that each moment when we truly accept responsibility for all our experiences.

Good night.

JANUARY 25, 1979

CONSCIOUSNESS CLASS 202

This evening, for our class, we'll have a discussion of what we're doing with what we have already studied and what we have already learned.

Now, we all know that repetition is the law through which change is made possible. And we find ourselves in our daily activities, ofttimes, entertaining the same levels of consciousness, the same patterns of mind that have lead us into the obstructions and difficulties in life that we're trying to be freed from.

Now, we have discussed before the importance of positive affirmations. Now, you must realize that each time you use positive affirmations, each time you think them and each time that you speak them, the defense mechanisms of the human mind, which ever strive to protect the patterns that are already registered within it, they rise up. And so we all find difficulty in flooding our consciousness with the positive, with the good, and with the beneficial.

Now, the stronger that these patterns that have had control of us for so many years, the stronger they rise up is a good sign, if you hold firm to the positive that you are striving to accomplish. No one ever said, of course, that it was easy. But we all know that it is possible, for we have already demonstrated in some parts of our life, through making some effort, that we have overcome certain patterns of mind that have proven to us not to be beneficial.

The question then arises—when we find it so difficult to make the constant daily effort, it reveals to us that these patterns, that are within our mind already, are working diligently, day and night, to express their continuity. When we awaken in the morning—and hopefully we're making the effort with that exercise to be aware of our first thought, our first feeling. And we go to sleep at night with our thought and our feeling: that vibration goes to work while we are sleeping. Now, we have become so addicted, it seems, to our way of thinking that it does seem, of course, to us it's most difficult to change. As long as we think how difficult it is, we direct this intelligent, infinite energy to making the difficulty more difficult, to making the struggle a greater struggle.

And so it is that we ourselves must become more consciously aware of what we are doing to ourselves. Especially—and it's most interesting, because it appears to be a basic vibration—the after-Christmas blues, I think, some people have called it many times. That the denial of God and his abundant good appears to be the strongest in the month of January and again in the month of April. Now, we can flow with that difficulty, with that mass thinking, or we can make the constant effort to change our own thinking. When we look outside and we feel that we're not fulfilling what we want to fulfill, we're not getting what we want to get, we direct this energy constantly to those obstructions, until we finally convince ourselves and we wholeheartedly believe that that vibration, that type of thinking, is us. You see, whatever we identify with in life, we sooner or later become. So, if we choose to identify with the way—to ever flood our consciousness with the divine truth that wherever there is a will, there is a way—then the way will appear for us.

Are we, as students, taking stock of not only the things that we are thinking, but the things that we are speaking? Now here, very recently, we had a wonderful demonstration of the infinite, divine law: What goes out from us, returns to us. And so it is whenever we find ourselves trapped in a vibration of unfulfilled, blind desire and we entertain that type of thinking, we guarantee what is known as the Law of Greed. I have yet to see it fail: whenever the mind dictates that it's short of money, that the person who entertains that type of thinking doesn't have to spend more money to prove that they are right. If you understand that very basic principle, then you can use that principle for bringing the good into your life.

We must remember that we all have a vehicle known as the human ego. It has been designed by the Divine Architect to serve a good purpose for the soul's expression. When the effort is truly made to educate it, it does serve that good purpose. If the effort is not made to educate it, then that vehicle brings to our lives a multitude of obstructions.

Whenever you say that you are short of anything, you establish the law unto yourself to prove that you are right. Now, it is a known truth that the human ego will do everything necessary to prove that it is right in any experience, in any endeavor, until it has the light of reason cast over it and it awakens and becomes educated.

So remember that when—in your study of this philosophy, the basic foundation of personal responsibility cannot be disregarded. When you say that you have an experience that you were helpless, that it just happened to you, you are denying the very foundation of the philosophy that you are studying. Nothing just happens to us. There is a law established by us that goes out into the universe and, in keeping with the law that like attracts like and becomes the Law of Attachment, it returns to us.

Now, for example, if someone comes and robs us of what we have worked to earn in life, we must ask ourselves the question, "Under what vibration is a person who robs or steals?" Are they under the vibration of reason or personal responsibility? I'm sure that we will all agree they're certainly not under the vibration of personal responsibility. They're certainly not under the vibration of consideration or regard for the law. What vibration are they under? Well, I think it is very evident: they're under the vibration of blind desire and greed, with total disregard and total lack of consideration of the laws that are very clear, granting each soul its individual right to respect itself and be responsible for itself and therefore granting that to all those with whom it comes in contact. Therefore, regardless what our experiences in life may be, we must face this bitter pill when things aren't going our way, because the law is totally impartial.

I know, from personal experiences for many years, that the human mind, the ego, until it is educated, is an absolute guaranteed self-prophet. For it will establish every law that it dictates and believes. Now, this is a demonstrable truth of how the mind works. And we should indeed be very grateful and encouraged by that demonstrable truth. Because though we may have had many negative experiences in the past, we cannot live in the past. We can only live in the moment that we can do something and that is ever the eternal moment of now. This is the moment in which we can bring about any change within our consciousness that we truly desire to bring about.

And so are we, as students, making the effort to become aware of eternity, which is the moment of now? Or are we living with yesterday's experiences and yesterday's judgments and yesterday's dictates? Because if our mind is living in those realms of consciousness, then we are controlled by those realms of consciousness, by those judgments, and those experiences of yesterday.

I am always grateful and pleased whenever I see the immutable, divine laws of nature operating. Though those laws may cause distress to the student who has placed themselves under the control of that law, there is good in everything. And there is good in seeing how infallible, how divinely just the laws of God truly are.

I vividly recall the experiences of many months ago when we, as an organization, a group of people, merited what our minds, of course, viewed as adverse publicity, as a lack of understanding the purpose and the foundation of this church. But I tried to encourage my students and also, of course, to encourage myself to face the truth. We teach a philosophy of personal responsibility. Therefore, the experience was something, vibration-wise, that, as a group of people, we and we alone had established.

If you attract into your life jealousy, envy, greed and those functions, then we must pause in that experience and we must honestly take appraisal of ourselves and we must find out what it is inside of us that is attracting these experiences to us. I know that for many it is not the easiest step to pause and to honestly ask oneself, "What have I been doing to call forth from the universe the experience that I am having?" Now, if we will truly pause and we will truly ask that question, then we can move in the eternal moment of now and we can do something about the now. We can do nothing about the yesterday. But we can do a great deal from this moment onward.

If you will honestly look at your daily lives and truly make the effort to become aware of how many times your mind blames outside for what's going on inside, that's where spiritual growth really begins. Spiritual growth does not begin in studying any philosophy or religion. It truly begins when we accept responsibility for our life. We cannot accept responsibility for the lives of others. But sooner or later, we all will accept responsibility for our life. When we do that, we begin to grow spiritually. When we truly accept that the experiences in life, our attitudes, our thoughts, and our feelings, that they're all ours; that we and we alone have created them, therefore, by accepting that truth, that we and we alone create them, we, having divine choice, we and we alone can change them.

When our minds blame outside to others, we come under others' control. Now, no one, no one, no soul that I have ever met wants to be controlled by anyone. There is an inner sensing; there is an inner freedom within our soul. We all sense that great inner freedom—and that makes great effort to keep us as free as it possibly can—but when the vehicle through which it expresses (our mind) directs the cause of any experience outside to another, we're bound by the other's vibration. And we don't really know their vibration. We don't really know how it fluctuates and changes.

This happens very frequently with married people, with people who are together. In order to be together, of course, they establish some degree of rapport. But what is the danger of rapport, but bondage. And the bondage is the blindness of desire. And so we find a husband blames his wife; a wife blames her husband. And it goes on and on and on and on. And yet, if each would stop for just a moment, they would be able to trace that thought and that feeling inside themselves: they would find out how many years ago that was given birth.

We all have desire, for it is the divine expression. But when we have desire, in the moment of desire do we accept the responsibility for its fulfillment? For to accept, in the moment of desire, responsibility, wholly and completely, for its fulfillment is to awaken the soul and to bring the light upon the desire. All desire is blind without accepting responsibility for its fulfillment. The moment you accept responsibility for the desire that you are entertaining in your mind, the moment that you do that, that is when desire becomes divine expression.

I know that many of you students who have been with us over these years in these classes, having heard so much about the blindness of desire and also having heard that desire was the divine expression, certainly must have been a little bit perplexed or confused. Yet, to this day I have never been asked the question. Now, we must ask ourselves why, in years of studying this philosophy—because, I assure you, when I first heard it on the tape in these classes, I said, "Just a minute. If desire is the divine expression, then how come desire is also blind? What kind of God or Intelligence is that?" And I was given the answer. But I would like to know why, with years of classes, with the untold hundreds and thousands of times students have heard those statements, the question never rose. And if it did rise, why was it not asked? I'm a firm believer in getting the answer to anything that my mind questions, if at all possible. And I hope that my students, all of them, will speak up and question in order that they may know themselves.

Now remember, my friends, desire becomes the divine expression the moment you accept responsibility for its fulfillment. If you have desire—and we all desire—and you do not accept personal responsibility for its fulfillment, then remember, you are blinded by the desire for you have not made it yours by accepting responsibility for it. Think about that and think about your daily activities. And if you will do that, you will see how quickly your desires come under the faculty of reason. And coming under the faculty of reason, the faculty of patience, the wisdom of the universe starts to guide your path.

I am very much aware that some people think whenever I have a desire, it is very quickly fulfilled. Well, their desire does not see clearly my life. For if it did, they would never think that way. I'm grateful for a little bit of patience. All your desires can, and will, be fulfilled, when you accept that they are truly yours—and that means responsibility for their fulfillment and not depending or relying upon anyone else to do it for you. That is truly when we start to grow.

But, you see, my friends, the little baby, it's hungry and it wants to be fed. And of course, it learns very quickly. It opens its mouth, it makes a sound, and the bottle comes. But that, for us here in this class, was a long time ago. And it doesn't work that way once you're able to move your feet and your hands and your body and go to work and do it for yourself. We are no longer little infants who can open our mouth and make a sound and someone comes running to fulfill our desire. That was a long, long time ago. Now let us think what we're doing today. Are we in principle sitting on our duff, opening our mouth, making a sound, and expecting the desire to be fulfilled? I assure you that is exactly what we are doing if we are not accepting responsibility for the fulfillment of our desire. And so we now know that we must make some effort to grow up out of the infantile level when it comes to our desires. That is our real growth.

Now I am sure that there are many people, of course, who have a wife or a husband or someone else to fulfill their desires and to wait upon them, but that doesn't, usually, last too many years. They say the honeymoon is short-lived for all married people. But it doesn't have to be short-lived, if all of us will face the truth and *wake up* and *not sleep* and start to grow.

Now, I wasn't going to discuss the sleep of satisfaction, but seeing whereas some of my students appear to have that vibratory wave coming over them, like a cloud, we'll discuss for a few moments the sleep of satisfaction.

It's most interesting to note, if we'll recall, or perhaps, if we can't recall, to study how little children often act. And it's also interesting, not only with little children, but with little dogs and certain domesticated animals: when they hear something they don't want to hear, they suddenly become very sleepy. And their little eyes, they blink and finally they close and their heads nod. Now, I assure you, this not only happens to my dog, Black Hawk, Jr.—it also happens to that little Tappet [*Tappet was the dog of a student.*]—very quickly. You just sit them in a chair and start to talk to them about something they did that wasn't right and their little eyes blink and their heads nod and they're off to the sleep of satisfaction. Now, they're little four-legged souls running around, you see. They're not supposed to be, according to the thinking of our egos, so highly evolved as we are. And yet, we find ourselves doing the same thing. In this philosophy it's known as the animal instinct within us.

Well, these classes are not designed to bring you any discouragement. On the contrary, they are designed to encourage you. But they are not designed to encourage you in the sleep of satisfaction or the license of blind desire. They are designed to help you wake up. We are well aware that irritation is what wakes the soul and satisfaction is what lets it sleep. So let us not be satisfied with filling up space in this beautiful universe. Let us not be satisfied with the status quo. Let us not be satisfied with the so-called satisfactions of yesterday, for to do so is simply to deteriorate.

We are here to fulfill the purpose of our soul's journey. And the banner in front of us all in the fulfilling of our purpose is a four-letter word called work. Now, many of us, I'm sure, think we work. And to us, I'm sure that we do. But when we find ourselves with so much energy and so much time on our hands that we become self-destructive, then it's time to add more work into our daily activities. Because we're not here on our evolutionary journey to self-destruct. That is not our purpose at all. We are here to evolve. Now, self-destruct—stop and think: How many thoughts do we have in the course of a day that are destructive? Do we have thoughts of pity? Do we have thoughts of blaming someone else for our feelings? Are those thoughts beneficial? Are they encouraging? No. They are destructive. Indeed, they are destructive.

Now, last Sunday, one of our students, knowing the rules and regulations that are established in consideration of all our people, transgressed a simple rule of the church. And they went home and they made a change in their attire. But, you see, there's a difference between doing something graciously by accepting personal responsibility for our acts and activities— there's a vast difference. Because if we do it graciously, knowing that, for a moment, we lost control and we didn't do what we knew we should be doing, then we feel good about correcting it. We feel good inside. And feeling good inside, then only the good do we experience. But if we resent and we do something under duress, we don't feel good about it at all.

Now, many, many people attend this church. Much of the public comes to visit Serenity and, yea, much more is yet to come. And we are very fortunate for we've always had very positive comments concerning our church, concerning its efforts. And the people feel very good visiting Serenity. Now, why do they feel that way? It's quite simple: it means that over 51 percent of the people involved in helping to conduct a Sunday service, they feel that way, at least during the time at the church. We're hopeful they'd feel that way all the time, because if you can feel good for two hours, you certainly can feel good for twenty.

You know, each time that we make the effort, when we hear something negative, to respond with something positive, we not only help ourselves, but we help those around and about us.

Accepting the light of truth is not a drudgery. And it shouldn't be a drudgery. It's no great struggle. And it shouldn't be a great struggle. Truth is what frees us, when we stay awake and don't sleep. But if we sit in class and sleep, then the truth we don't even hear. Now, perhaps the volume of my voice is not yet strong enough to keep my students awake. Please turn the heat off. I can assure you, if I can't keep them awake by speaking, I certainly can help keep them awake by turning the heat off. It seems there's something about heat, you know. We have a little tape in our mind—when it gets warm, we get sleepy. So from now on let us have the temperature down to 30. We'll not only save energy, but I am sure my students will stay awake.

Now, I don't sit here to give classes because I have nothing else to do. I sit here to give classes for I have a responsibility that I have accepted in life.

When you find something that works for you and the years pass by and you find that it also works sometimes for others (the times that they accept it), then you do what you can to share it with those who are seeking it. Because you know the good that you have already experienced and continue to experience from its use. And so it is with this philosophy and these classes.

Now, when we have these fears—fear of this and fear of that and fear about everything that our mind can think about—we all know that the mind is demanding that it stay in control. And so we all, I'm sure, will make greater effort to free ourselves from these fears. Why is it and what did Job mean when he said, "The thing I fear the most has befallen me?" Is that not the living demonstration that we have had in our lives so far? All you have to do is flood your mind with fear of anything and you be rest assured, it will knock at your door, because it does know who its parent really is.

And with this awareness—that everything's inside—everything. Everything we desire, that it *is* inside. When we truly accept that—just accept it in one, small area of your life. The smallest of the areas of your life. The ones that have the very least priority of value for you. Try it in something in just a small way so that you can see how beautiful it works.

I'm so happy the furnace went off, because now all my students are wide awake. You know, I've always tried to be a very practical person. I don't like to spend money for anything that I don't get my—what I feel is my money's worth: value. I certainly wouldn't spend $150 for class and sleep through it. I think what we need is a new regulation: those who stay awake in class get a cassette of the class; those who sleep in class don't get any cassette of the class. I think that's only fair. So that we may be practical in financial matters and not be in lack and limitation. Now, I think that's very, very important. Why spend money for something and then not hear it?

Now, I know that many times many people don't like what I may have to say, what the Friends have to say, but I'm also sure that we did not come to this class because we liked or particularly liked what I had to say all the time. That's not why we came here. Why, we came here, hopefully, to find a better way than what we had already found. But, you see, how can you find a better way if you're not willing to give up the way that you already had? You see, the cup runneth over and nothing more can get in. It's quite a simple thing. It's like a person—perhaps they have a desire and they want to learn to play golf. And so they go to a golf instructor. And while the instructor's trying to instruct them, they go over and take a nap because they made the judgment they already knew what the instructor was going to say in the first place. Well, why spend the money for the golf instructor? Don't you see what I mean? That's what I'm talking about.

And I'm very glad that I am consciously very aware, because I like to see which of my students think they know it all and, therefore, can sit and sleep through class. You see, we wouldn't sleep through class unless we'd already made the judgment, "Well, we know what he's going to say anyway, so, you know, I'm going to rest. I'm going to sleep for awhile." Now, that's not why we come here. And if that is why we come here, then the ones who sleep are not going to get any more cassettes. No. No.

The survival, the financial security and survival of the church is not dependent upon selling cassettes or dependent upon anything else but God. God keeps us going as long as we accept that simple truth. And I do hope that all of my students will make greater effort, greater effort to accept the divine Source of their good in their life. And if they feel they're short of the good in their life, then remember, we have built an obstruction in consciousness to that divine Light from whence all good constantly and continuously flows. Now, it flows through us when we bow our judgments and permit it to do so.

And it's interesting with that understanding, because so many people, you know, they say, "Well, I'll give that a try." And then maybe it works a few times in a little way. And then they reach that obstruction within: "In this matter, there's no other way. It's not going to work." You see, that's their own test. Their mind, their own mind tests them. If God works in a small way, then God can work in a great way. But this cannot work for us unless we work for it. I can only assure you that it works. I can only assure you from my own personal experience.

And I, also, am very well aware of how, when we find ourselves strapped and we find ourselves in these difficulties, I am very well aware, because I already had the experience many years ago. I hope it may be in divine order that I don't have to repeat it because at least now, through an understanding of this philosophy, I am very well aware that I, my mind and only my mind, created the obstruction. Not someone else's mind. Not someone else's circumstances. My mind.

So, my friends, that is the most important thing in this philosophy—is to understand the human mind. For I assure you, again and again, it is only the human mind, our mind, that is the obstruction. There is no other obstruction. It does not exist. It's our thought, our mind that is our obstruction. It does not have to be.

But, you see, when you permit yourself to experience fear in anything, the moment you permit yourself to have the experience of fear, your mind, your mind is in control. So when you don't have these experiences of fear, then your little soul is expressing itself. But we must then ask ourselves the question, "How often in my life is my little soul expressing? How often am I truly freed from fear?" Just have a desire. And make the judgment it's not going to get fulfilled when you want it fulfilled. And then tell me whether or not you experience any fear. Now, we know when we experience fear. We have a desire, for we have made a judgment. We have dictated to the Divine and we have received from our own mind a negative response, one not in keeping with the judgment we have made, and we experience what is known as fear.

We're afraid of this and we're afraid of that. Every time we turn around, we're afraid of something. But do we truly want to live so filled with fear? Do we really want to live that way?

Now, we can be freed from fear only by accepting personal responsibility. We cannot be freed from fear by not facing responsibility. We all face responsibility. The ability to respond to our own desire. Think of that. We have the desire. And because *we* have the desire, we certainly do have the ability to respond to it. That's called responsibility.

Whatever it is that you desire, it will be fulfilled if you truly accept the responsibility for it. Say that you have a desire to go on a vacation. To go away somewhere. I'm sure everyone has those desires. Now, what happens when you have the desire? What happens inside of your mind? What is the first thought that you have when you have a desire to go on a vacation? What is the very first thought that you have? Now, we understand a vacation, in the sense that we use it here, is a function of our mind. And the functions are controlled by the very simple triune function of *m-e-s* [*money ego sex*]. And so we find when the desire to go on a vacation rises up in our little mind, it comes with a banner called—What would you say? Does anyone know? What is the banner that rises first, when we have a thought? Yes.

Money.

Money! The very first thought! Is there anyone present in this classroom this evening, when having the desire for a vacation, that doesn't think of the word *money* first? Yes.

I think I feel guilt—I don't know if that's the same—when I first feel vacation.

Guilt, we understand to be rejected desire.

OK.

Do you understand in feeling guilt—

Yes.

When you have the thought, the desire for a vacation, do you understand why you experience the feeling of rejected desire?

Yes.

Then you have the answer.

Now, it's interesting to note that everyone in the classroom this evening, except one, who has the experience of feeling guilt or rejected desire—experience a rejection to the desire. You see, we cannot feel or experience a rejection to a desire unless we make the judgment and are, therefore, concerned about how other people will think—Do you understand that?—which is a denial of the Law of Personal Responsibility and puts our soul under the control of other people's thinking. Good. It's very important.

But the predominant vibration is, when we have the desire for a vacation, is money.

Does everyone here agree with me that money is not necessary for a vacation? If you agree, raise your hands. Some people do believe you don't have to have money to have a vacation. Now, I'm very happy to see that, because that's the first step in freeing ourselves from that vibratory control. You don't have to have money to have a vacation. You may have to have money if you dictate and judge what a vacation means to you. You see, there's a difference between the principle of vacation and the personal judgments and censorship of the very principle of vacation. A person can have a vacation this moment. Sitting right here this very moment. For it is within your power to travel anywhere at any time if you truly want to make the slightest effort. But if, with the word *vacation*, you have lost the principle of the meaning of that word, then in keeping with your judgments shall money control the fulfillment of your desire.

And so it is that we all have these different desires, whether they're vacations or whatever you want to call them. But we've lost the essence; we've lost the principle of the true meaning. And so we go through life and we say to ourselves, "I don't get to have a vacation. Everybody around me, all the people I work with, why they're going to Hawaii. They're going to the Caribbean. They're going to Europe. Why, they're going to China. Why, they're just traveling everywhere. And I work hard. I work just as hard as they do, but I don't get a vacation. I don't get to go anyplace." Well, we lost sight of the true meaning of vacation, you see?

And so, what it is, instead of educating that level within us, we suppress it. We not only suppress that desire, but we suppress a multitude of other desires. And then the day comes that all of this suppression finally explodes inside of us. And the disaster that goes out from us returns to us! For what? Because we did not daily work on ourselves. You see?

Faith is a great power of the divine Intelligence. It moves the mountains of physical, mental, and spiritual. It is faith that moves the mountains—the direction of faith. We have so much faith in what our mind says to us that we follow it. Just like a little slave, we follow after what our mind says. That's how great our faith is in our beliefs. This is what you're really dealing with in making a change in consciousness: redirecting your faith.

Now, I know it's been many years that you've had faith in your thoughts and what you believe is you. Many years, the faith, this great power, has been directed to the human mind. I'm here to show you what that great power called faith, that you already have plenty of, simply to show you what it can do for you by directing it to spiritual dimensions of consciousness—not something outside of you. The spiritual dimensions of consciousness that are inside of you, closer than your hands and feet. Direct your faith, that great power, the greatest power you will ever know, that you're using all the time, redirect it. Direct it into accepting a greater intelligence that knows every desire before you think it, that knows every way to fulfill it.

Now, when you will redirect this great energy, this great power called faith, to the will of what we understand to be God—and we understand that total acceptance is the will of God. Think of that. Use that daily. You want God's will in your life? God, being the will of goodness, then redirect your faith, through total acceptance, which is the will of God. For God leaves nothing out. All things are sustained by God. The ant and the angel are sustained by the same God. Think of that. And do you think that your desires, no matter what they are, are lesser in God's eyes than the ant, the insect that crawls the ground? No lesser is your desire, and no greater.

And so this great God, that sustains all of these things in all of these universes, is sustaining your desire through direction of the intelligence within you through the power of faith.

You want to go on a vacation? You dictate to God how much money it's going to cost, you dictate to God how long it's going to take you to save that money, you dictate to God what you've got to give up in order to save that, you, in that moment of thinking, are greater than God. And, therefore, man, a law unto himself, must follow the law he has established. And so you make all of these dictates and you are bound by the will of self. And the will of the Divine, which is total acceptance, you and you alone have limited to your judgment. That God is so great and so compassionate: you choose to make the judgment of how you can accomplish what you desire in life, then you and you alone in that moment, God sustains your judgments. For God sustains every thought you entertain in consciousness. And then, if that's the way you have judged your vacation will be, then that's the only way you can possibly experience it.

And in that thinking, which seems so difficult for many to accept—it's difficult because we're still bound by the experiences of yesterday. We are still bound by our faith in our thoughts and those experiences, which were nothing but the effect of those thoughts.

Now, I'm just as human as everyone else. And so I have to work on my mind, just like anyone else. I've made some effort to understand my mind. And I'm grateful I continue to make that effort, for it truly is designed to serve a good purpose. But why, we must ask ourselves, should we live in such frustration when everything, *everything* is here within us? All the fulfillment is waiting for our own acceptance. And when we take a few minutes a day, every day, and we have an awareness of all these thoughts in our mind, and we say, "God, I accept something greater. I accept," when you truly accept—when you put your faith that you're already using to support your judgment, when you redirect that power to accepting something greater and you hold onto the acceptance of something greater as tenaciously as you've already held onto the judgments, you can be rest assured, you will be transformed and transfigured into all of the goodness your heart could ever desire.

Thank you.

FEBRUARY 1, 1979

CONSCIOUSNESS CLASS 203

Good evening, class.

Now, I am sure that all of you, of course, are interested in this philosophy and religion or you wouldn't be attending these philosophy classes. It's time, I'm sure, for all of us to gain perhaps a broader perspective of what it really is that we are seeking in this particular religion. I'm sure that each of us has varied views of this religion and philosophy and that those views, they change from time to time, like all mental thoughts are destined to do.

We're all aware, of course, that we are in a constant process of change, because we are all an inseparable part of the evolution of form. Our eyes see very clearly, outside, the changing of things around and about us, but rarely do we see the growth and change that we desire for ourselves. It is at these times, when we think that we are not changing in the direction of the fulfillment of our desires—because what is truly happening is that our desires themselves are changing. And so it is that as we continue to evolve, we not only go through many experiences, which, of course, are the effects of the many judgments that we slowly, but surely, become aware of, but each of us, in our efforts, reach a certain point in consciousness at which time we have to make decisions: decisions to continue on with the efforts that we feel we have been making or to change our direction.

It is very easy to entertain the thoughts, of course, of changing our direction when the struggle seems to be the greatest. Many times you've heard in this philosophy that at the gates of victory are the hounds of hell and is the struggle the greatest. Some of you already have had those experiences and have made sufficient effort to demonstrate the Law of Continuity that you may look in hindsight at some of the growth steps that you have already made.

No one has ever said in this philosophy and this religion that it is easy, because that that is worth working for is not necessarily easy to levels that do not care to make the effort.

When we find that we have passed through a certain struggle and a certain experience, we must ever remember that that level of consciousness is not something that dies, never to rise again. It only means that we have passed through that particular lesson at that particular time; that that lesson will repeat itself if the soul faculties of the sense functions that brought the experience to us in the first place have not been brought into balance.

Some years ago, there was much talk and concern about the question of whether or not God is dead. Well, any god that can die had to be born and so that type of a mental-created god is constantly in a process of birth and death.

Spiritualism and the Serenity Association, which is a part thereof, is a very unique philosophy, science, and religion. Without the science of Spiritualism, we would not have the philosophy that we enjoy today.

One of the many levels on the spiritual path is the level in which we will find ourselves, if we have not already: the level that doubts what it cannot physically see, the level that doubts what it cannot physically hear, the level that doubts what it cannot physically sense or taste. And so it is that all of us will have to, if we have not already, face that level of consciousness. And when we are honest with ourselves, we have to say many times have we questioned the existence of God. If we think we have not questioned the existence of God, then we do not understand what we think is God. For we all know, I am sure, and believe that God is a representative principle of the goodness of life. And so all of us at some time in our life have questioned whether or not we are experiencing this goodness or this godness that, at other times, we do think we believe in.

It is when we think that we have made great effort and have not yet experienced what we judged we should experience from the effort that we have made that we begin to question the Divine Principle, the Goodness of life or God. When that happens, we make a choice. We choose to turn away from that which we thought we believed in and found out, in the time of greatest need, that we didn't really believe in at all. Because if we did really believe in this Goodness of life, this God, then we wouldn't be turning away from it.

And so it is in the very nature of Spiritualism, with a science based upon spirit communication, that we ofttimes question the existence of spirit or spirits. But in those moments we must ask ourselves, if we are questioning the existence of spirit, then we are questioning the existence of our own eternal being. Because either we are but the flesh and the form of the physical and mental realms or we are indeed an eternal being. So let us awaken, in this type of thinking, that we are questioning that inside of ourselves there is anything that will endure the decay of our physical and mental body.

Now, when we look at it from that vantage point, we all, very quickly, will begin to change our thinking about the existence or non-existence of spiritual beings. Because within all of us, far beyond the limits of our intellect, far beyond the limits of any of our thoughts, is this eternal being called spirit—far beyond within our own consciousness.

I am aware that we all have different views and understandings of spirit, of soul, and of our eternal existence.

What is it, then, that rises up within us and questions the existence of eternal life? Surely, it is not our soul or spirit that is an inseparable part of that eternal life. When our minds make the judgment that we have made the effort and have yet to receive, we begin to question the validity of our own eternal existence. It is not our soul, nor the Infinite Spirit, that questions, for it is beyond question, for it knows. And that that knows has no need to question.

Now, in some religions they call that faith: to be able to accept without the need or the justifications of the limited, human mind.

Many, many years ago I spent a number of my years in what is known to this world as physical and material seances, for I come from a family of a medium who did that all her earthly life. I made a choice, those many years ago, and, fortunately, I feel, merited refraining from that practice. For I found in my early years of growing up and attending every seance—ever since I can remember—and seeing the materializing forms of the discarnate spirits and hearing their physical voices and all of the physical phenomena that can be offered by a physical medium, that it was never enough for those who attended. That if the spirit came and materialized and only sat down for a half hour, then the minds of those in attendance demanded an hour. If they answered twenty questions, then the minds of those in attendance demanded forty. For the human mind is like a great vacuum: it is never enough.

There is no phenomena, in or out of Spiritualism, that will, in and of itself, prove beyond a shadow of any doubt life eternal. You may attend these physical phenomena and you may be shocked and surprised for a time. But it is your mind that is making the demand. It's not your soul that already knows. And it certainly is not the Divine Spirit.

The purpose of spirit communication, to my understanding, is to bring to the world the demonstrable truth that man, in the light of reason, may choose wisely the laws that he sets into motion, that in so doing he may awaken: by stilling his mind he may awaken his own soul that the truth, which is individually perceived, will light his path in eternity.

And so it is in this church that there are times, as there are here in the present, when the minds of the students and the minds of the members question and doubt. But in those experiences, which obviously are necessary for them at the time, when they, in time, pass through those levels, do they pause and look and take the good from the experience?

You see, my friends, you'll never find God outside until you make the effort to find God inside. And if you are not willing to make the effort to find God inside yourself, you will never find that Goodness, that Principle, no matter where you wander, no matter how many seances you may attend, no matter what you do or don't do, if you are not willing to make that effort to control the thoughts of your mind. For only in controlling the thoughts of your mind will this great peace, this great harmony, which is your true being, will it rise in your consciousness that you may have the personal demonstration of your own eternal life.

When that effort is made and you have that experience, you will no longer have the need of your mind to doubt and to question life eternal. For that light of your soul, that faculty of reason will so shine over your mental realm that never again will you have that discord and that need of your mind.

Faith, this great power, which we have spoken many times of, is being used by all of us at all times. We see how great that power is when we direct it to our mind: we have a greater tenacity than any animal ever on this Earth planet. Our tenacity is almost unbelievable. But it is the power of faith that is behind it. And when we want something really bad, we all know, sooner or later, we do get it.

The only sadness in directing that great power, called faith, to the human mind and its fluctuating desires, is that the desire does not have total consideration. It has a limited total consideration to the fulfillment of its particular desire. And therefore, it cannot see the price tag that comes with the fulfillment of that desire. It does not consider the payment.

To those who have been given much, much shall be demanded. Not by some individual somewhere, but by the very law, for the law is the demand. And who establishes the law? We establish those mental laws, through entertaining in thought our desires and making the judgment that we—meaning our mind—and we alone shall fulfill it. All the prices we do not see.

So when we want these things of our mind and when our mind demands that we have, to our minds' satisfaction, absolute proof, in keeping, of course, with our mental judgment, of life eternal and positive demonstration to our mental judgment of communion with that dimension, then we set every law necessary into motion to pay the price before we attain it. For in the realms of spiritual dimensions, there is no credit; there is no pay later. You pay. And you pay in advance. And you don't pay with the coins of the earthly realm. You pay by facing every mental obstruction that you have created, that has blinded you in this great evolution to see and see clearly. Before our eyes open to the greater Light, they must first see clearly the lesser light. The greater Light, to our understanding in this philosophy, is the Light of the Eternal Spirit and the lesser light, the light of the limited mental world.

So first we will awaken to the lesser light and we will pay the price of every obstruction that is in the way. The seeming sadness is that we don't know what that price will be. And so we start on the journey, we get a few steps along the path and we decide the struggle is too great; that's too much to demand of anyone. But we did not consider, when we were transgressing these natural, divine laws of harmony, we did not consider the price would be extracted from us someday.

My good friends, the very simple common sense that none of us, not even the insects that crawl the ground, get something for nothing. The air we breathe, our lungs are paying for. There is no world that I have ever seen where we get something for nothing. Each thought your mind entertains you pay for. And each thought you give to God you are free from. And so the law, totally impartial.

We all have come here to this little church with varying motives, of course, for we are all different in the sense of the thoughts that we entertain in our mind. But our motives, like everything else in life, they grow and they change. Slowly, but surely, we awaken to the price that we must pay for what we do with our lives. But when we awaken to that truth within us, we must be alert and not be discouraged, for to be discouraged is only to increase the payment that we are already paying.

And so, do we, we must ask ourselves, do we really believe in the goodness of life? Do we honestly make the effort to flood our consciousness with the goodness of life? Now, we can cry God until hell freezes over and still not experience the goodness of life. It isn't a matter of crying God. It is a matter of making the effort to set the laws of peace and harmony into motion, for the effect of those laws is the goodness or godness of life. But that choice is ours. And that choice is with us every moment of every day. We are never without that choice. We can change our attitude at any, *any* moment and we can experience God or goodness at any moment. But to do that we have to give up what is standing in our way. So when we don't feel the way we know we should feel, then we have to give up that thought in our head.

Now, many of you have had experiences every day in not feeling the goodness of life. But are you making the effort to become aware of why you're not feeling that goodness? Because, I can assure you, when you don't experience that goodness in life, you have a judgment that's holding you right by the tail. But because it's your judgment, you can let it go. Now, that's where we are in this growth in this life: to exercise the divine right of choice and experience that goodness that we're looking for.

But before we can do that, we have to demonstrate to ourselves the full acceptance of the Law of Personal Responsibility: that there is absolutely nothing outside of ourselves that is the cause of our disharmony and our discord; that it is not the responsibility of someone else to prove to us that God exists. That, my friends, is our number one responsibility. That's ours personally. That is not the responsibility of another soul. That is not the responsibility of a church or anything else. That's our personal responsibility.

And if we are yet wanting in our finding of this goodness or God in our life, then we can travel all over the world, we're not going to find God—not until we stand still long enough and accept that we and we alone will have to make the effort; that no one—a husband, a wife, a brother, a sister, a mother, a father—no one outside can give it to you. No parent can give God to their child. They can give them the goodness or the God that is within them, but it is up to the individualized, eternal soul that is in the child to be receptive or not receptive to that God or goodness that is being expressed.

You all, I know, are aware of the many people—the public that comes and goes in this church. And for many years, many years, I had entertained the thought, "How nice it would be if their motive for coming was this beautiful philosophy that I know, beyond a shadow of any doubt, works and works very well." But, then again, it is not my right to deny them the motives of their choice. And so we find many people coming to Serenity. And I'm sure that we will all agree that they receive, many times, the help that they are seeking. If they don't receive it sometimes, then that is their right to their choice to their path.

But what are we doing with the beautiful philosophy that we all have received? Are we really making the effort? Are we becoming aware when we hold tenaciously to these different judgments that we have? Are we making the effort to be aware, number one: that it is a judgment; number two: that it's our judgment; number three: that we caused it; and number four: that it is in our best interest to change it?

I have seen many, many students and many people in these thirty-nine years now. I've seen them go on the spiritual smorgasbord from one philosophy and one religion to another and another and another and another, which, of course, is their right. But because they are looking outside for what is waiting for them inside, they'll never find what they're really after until they make the change and accept the truth. They cannot get it outside.

If you get married in life and your motive is to have what you have judged is security and someone to look after you and take care of you and bring you peace and harmony and happiness and joy, don't get married. Just stay single. Because if that's your motive, you're in for nothing but a downhill path of disaster. For you have made the greatest folly the human mind can make: someone else is going to do it for you. That's where all our problems lie: someone else, you see, is going to do it for us. Someone else is going to bring us peace and harmony. Someone else is going to take care of us. Someone else is going to keep us feeling good.

Well, I see a few married people here in the class this evening. If they disagree with that statement, just kindly raise your hands. Someone else is not doing it. Now when this wonderful warm blanket of what they call the honeymoon was covering us and we were in the darkness of that desire, we perhaps entertained that type of thinking. But then we all have to wake up.

Like one of my students said the other day—that I irritated them quite frequently. And it really pleased me to hear that. Because in keeping with this beautiful philosophy that irritation wakes the soul, I was happy to see their soul awakening. You see, I never did consider my job to be that of satisfying everybody I talked to. And so, indeed, I know I irritate them. And I am grateful that to some degree they irritate me. And therefore, two souls are waking up. Now, if they survive in this church—and I can assure you there's a lot of irritation in this church, but then there's a lot of awakening going on.

And when we look back at yesterday, we can say, "Well, I don't do that as often as I used to." Some of us, you see, we've got enough tenacity that we're going to make it. It takes a mighty strong ego to stay on the spiritual path. Don't ever let anyone convince you otherwise.

You see, if you want to go away on a hilltop and not have all this disturbance around and about you—that's, of course, created by you. But if you make the judgment it's everybody else's fault, you go away in some retreat and live the rest of your life. And everything is just beautiful, unless somebody comes by. [*Many students laugh.*] You see? So we can choose to live our judgments out on the hilltop or to live our judgments out here in the jungle and in the world. Isn't it better to face these things frequently and chip away at them and get through them?

And it's so nice when we get irritated. It's really quite a beautiful experience. I know. I've been irritated many times. It's a wonderful experience. And it's wonderful to watch students when they get irritated, you know. Because by watching how they react emotionally when they're irritated, you can see; you're more objective. You're not emotionally involved yourself and therefore you can see what you're like when you're irritated.

It's really quite a childish thing to view. And if you've ever seen a little four- or five-year-old child kicking his feet and having a tantrum, jumping up and down on the floor, pulling his hair out of his head, smashing the windows or whatever thing he can find to smash, then you can understand how it is—the principle that is at work: that irritation wakes the soul. Because so much energy is released in the emotional body that it finally becomes exhausted. There's no more thought. All the thoughts are still, and, you see, the soul rises up. Now, that's how irritation wakes the soul: it exhausts the emotional body. Now, some people, when they're irritated, it takes maybe days, weeks, or months. And in this church we understand that to be the forces. But aren't they beautiful to see after they have run their little race and their little, emotional mental bodies are totally exhausted? And the light shines and there seems to be such a beautiful humbleness, for that's the faculty of the soul that you're viewing.

Now, husbands and wives frequently have that experience. Sometimes day to day. Sometimes now and then. Sometimes—but at least sometimes. And after they're through with all this emotional uproar, they're perfect, little angels. Wouldn't it be nice if they could just stay those perfect, little angels? And this is why, in this church, it is taught, daily, not only do the workers win, but to those who find themselves in these forces and this emotionalism, that the church must work much harder to give them more work to do so this energy can be released in a more constructive way.

You see, if we have time to direct this beautiful, intelligent energy into our little judgments and our emotionalism, we need more constructive work to do. Because if we direct this energy to more work, then there won't be any of that left over for all that emotionalism. So it is a standard prescription for all my students who have so much abundance of this divine energy that they're walking, emotional time bombs, that they be given more work to do, for that's where the problem is.

Now, we all know that when we're laying around our houses and sitting down, perhaps addicted to our television sets or our radios or just sitting daydreaming, that we don't feel very well. No, no, after we've spent the hour sitting, we feel pretty bad after. We always feel worse after sitting around than we did before we did sit down. It's because the energy is trapped in all these self-related thoughts.

Now, I have many, many, many different methods of helping the soul of my students to awaken. There are many methods at which a person can become irritated. And so if any of my students feel that they have not had enough irritation lately, will you kindly speak to me after the class? And I will be more than happy to accommodate you. Because that's just the way this little church is. And if we have any complaints, you just kindly let me know because for every one you have, I have ten-thousand waiting to express.

So, you see, my friends, whatever it is you want out of life—and you all know what you really want—it's there if you'll keep your eye on it and you'll really make the effort to stick with it. I know what this philosophy can do for those who use it. I also know what it will do for those who abuse it.

We must become very much aware that this philosophy works when it enters our heart. That's when we use it. That's when it serves us well. It's when we play with it with our heads that it starts to become abused. Because what our heads do, they have, our little heads, its own set judgments and desires. And so it goes to work to justify, by the philosophy, its judgments that it refuses to let go of. Now, I'm not saying the intellect doesn't have a purpose to serve. It certainly does: playing with mental thoughts. That, indeed, it serves a good purpose in that way. It's like a Ping-Pong game: it goes back and forth over the net. That's what our mind does with those things. But when it enters your heart, you will see in front of you the Light that will clear a pathway through this evolution.

And you won't have to worry about how your mind can attain spiritual awakening, because it's a total waste of your energies. It's your heart which is the vehicle through which your soul expresses itself. And when your heart is truly open, you won't have to worry about how the law works, for you will be working with the law. And you won't have to be so concerned about tomorrow and how you're going to get through tomorrow because you will be so busy and so happy with the moment of which you are aware.

Now, the mental world offers you the duality of all creation: for every gain, you have a loss. When you open your heart and rise to the spiritual realms of consciousness, you'll no longer experience that duality for you will be in the very essence of things. And you will not be at the tail end and the effect of things. There is a vast difference.

So many of us, we worry about how to pay our bills and how to face tomorrow. And each time we let our minds think that way, we do not experience the goodness of the moment in which we truly are. I do not mean to imply that we should not take some wisdom from the squirrel that puts away a few acorns. But remember, the squirrel knows how long the winter will last. Nobody has to tell him. He doesn't have to worry because, you see, the little squirrel knows. And the little squirrel puts away just enough acorns for that winter. Never too many and never too little. For the little animal knows that more than you use is not only more than you need, but it is a transgression of the soul faculty of gratitude and is an expression of the sense function of greed.

We want to learn more about the laws of God? Then let's make some effort, some effort to observe nature. To see the beautiful, but perfect, balance of the intelligence that is flowing through nature. It doesn't hoard. The animals know. It is only the animal called man that hoards. And man hoards because he makes judgments. The squirrel doesn't make judgments. He has an awareness of the length of the time of the winter and he acts accordingly. He's not fearful or concerned about ten winters from today, or five or anything else. But because the little animal is in the eternal moment, then the little animal is indeed well cared for. Now, if we will get ourselves into the moment of eternity, which is the moment of now, then we will experience how well cared for we truly are. It's when we make all these judgments about what's going to happen tomorrow—the tomorrow that we have yet to experience—that we guarantee all of these problems. By taking care of the eternal moment, we are freed from the concern of these tomorrows.

For what is man to think of that which may never be? If man is in the eternal moment, he is in eternal consciousness and is not deluded by the mental realm that offers to man past and future. Man's future is a repetition of his past because man spends so much time concerned about his tomorrows, using his past as the guiding light. That, my friends, is the repetition that grinds away within us.

So if we don't concern ourselves with what happened yesterday, we will not establish yesterday's laws for our tomorrows and we can be free today.

Thank you very much.

FEBRUARY 15, 1979

CONSCIOUSNESS CLASS 204

Good evening, class.

Before beginning the class this evening, I want to thank everyone here for their kindness for my birthday and for the varied gifts and kind thoughts. And—you may turn your chairs if you wish. Considering, I guess, because today is my birthday, I have been given permission to give the class myself. Now—not that I asked for that permission, but that request, or order, was given to me earlier today. So I will share with you some of my thoughts in reference to this day and to many days that have already past.

Sometimes I think that we have varied, of course, varied views of what it's like to, to be a medium. Ofttimes we look at something that we desire and judge we do not have to be something that is all a bed of roses. And in that respect, I suppose, that you could consider mediumship a bed of roses, but somehow you have to cultivate the thorns out of those roses because I can assure you that there are plenty of the thorns along with it. And so it is with our experiences in life.

Some people, I know—and I'm sure—think that it's nice to have someone to make all the decisions for you and to guide you and to tell you what to do. And in many respects, of course, that is very fine. Except that it doesn't always agree with your own thinking and your own desires. And so when that conflict arises within your mind, you have to, of course, face it and you have to work with it. Because in my life in these past thirty-nine years in this work of mediumship, there has been untold numbers of times when the information and guidance that I receive is certainly contrary to my own thoughts and my own judgments.

And so it is that everyone, of course, in truth is a medium. There is always that something within them that is trying to guide them. But when it runs contrary to what our mind thinks, then, of course, we experience the difficulties, because it is only natural to flow with that with which we are familiar. And, of course, we're all familiar, to a great degree, with our own thoughts and with our own desires and our own mind.

Now, my day had a most interesting start, as most of my days do. As I said earlier to one of the students, "I don't recall a day in my life that I ever experienced boredom." But I think in order to be bored, one must not have desire to get something accomplished. And somehow it seems I came to this earth with plenty desire to get something done. I like to see things moving.

And so for about the—well, since we have lived in the house there on the hill, two of our audio speakers have been going through the rumba cracking up now and then. And if you know what—if you like good music, and we have plenty of good music, you know what it's like to hear distortion periodically. And so we have fiddled with it and done everything and it's just kind of been wearing itself out.

So the Friends decided that we would replace them. And I said, "Well, that's fine. Someday we'll get that done." That was yesterday. And so today the Friends said to me, "Now, we're replacing those speakers that are worn out." And I said, "Well, if you hit them, sometimes, you know, they work fine. [*Many of the students laugh.*] I think it's just something loose inside." And she said, "No, they don't work fine at all. They're just played out." Well, they were the best speakers we could get at the time, about four years ago. And so I put on a record to show them that, you know, if you hit it just so, that it does work. So I put on a record: nothing came out of those speakers at all. Absolutely nothing. So I wiggled the wire: there was nothing. I hit the back of the speaker: there was nothing. I kicked it with my foot and there was still nothing. So I put on a different record. I thought, well, maybe, you know, the tone of the music sometimes has an effect on those speakers up there. Nothing. So I toppled it over on the floor to give it the best jolt possible, put it back up. There was still nothing.

Well, you see, my mind had made the judgment—because my mind is very capable of judgment, just like everybody else's mind; in fact, it makes many judgments and I have to work with them all the time—made the judgment that, certainly, not at this time was it in the best interest to have to replace a speaker—two speakers, in fact. But that wasn't what was to be. Needless to say, we got that taken care of.

Now, that doesn't seem like very much, really, to have to do something like that. But it was most interesting considering that my mind, number one: had made the judgment it was not going to get any speakers, especially at this time of year with everything going on and all of the expenses. But the level in which I trapped myself was very interesting on this day of my birth. For it wasn't very long after that I got a call for our attorney—from our attorney, informing me that I had to go on a deposition in reference to our going to court about our church exemption for the church property. Well, what is interesting, of course, is that number one: the first deposition I ever made in my life was months ago. I didn't appreciate it. We don't appreciate things we're not familiar with. All minds work the same way. So when I got that call, after I got through this speaker bit and they all got delivered and everything, I really found that I was quite upset. And so, I was aware, of course, of the cause. But to be aware of something and to work your way out of it is two different things. You have to make the effort.

Now, in this world, there's all these experiences going on all the time. There is no way possible that my mind can see the way of how this church keeps going financially or otherwise. Yet, it always keeps going. But it is a constant test, as we test ourselves between our mind and our eternal spirit. It is a constant test.

After that experience—and I was trying to work my way back up from the level I had put myself into, which was not very harmonious—my mother said to me, "Richard, this is a wonderful opportunity for you to demonstrate your faith in God." And so, of course, it is. It's a wonderful opportunity: when your mind takes a look and cannot possibly see a way that things are going to work out, out of necessity you have to turn to something greater. Because that's just the way that our mind works.

Now, to think that a person who is a medium and communicating with the spirit, that it's always beautiful and peaceful, that it's always a positive, progressive, and successful thing is certainly not looking at both sides of the coin. In order to sustain my faith in a higher power we call God, I have to make the daily effort, the daily effort to educate my own ego and my own mind. You see, there is no spirit—or spirits—that comes in and automatically removes from you the negative thoughts of your mind. It just doesn't work that way. For me, it doesn't work that way. Now, if it works that way for someone else, I'd like to talk to them, because I'd like to find an easier way. But it certainly does not work that way for me.

Now, I not only have to work on my own negative mind, but, you see, the experience is compounded because if I don't work on *my* negative thoughts in life—and experience—and whereas I have earned the responsibility to help others, then if I am negative or discouraged, those around and about me become the same way. Now that's what's called facing personally one's responsibilities.

We all know that God helps those who help themselves. But what most of us don't seem to understand, sometimes, is that God helps those who help themselves by helping others. You see, each time that we make the effort to help someone else, we, in truth, are helping ourselves. So if we talk to someone to try to encourage them to find a better way, that is taking place within us if we believe what we say. First, we must truly believe what we're saying. And if *we* believe what we're saying, then those who are listening, you see, if they are in rapport with us, they, too, will believe what is being said.

Now, my understanding of the work of the spirit people, when they return to earth to help us through these many paths that we have to walk through in life, they do not, for they cannot, do it for us. There is no way that I am aware of that a person, a spirit who has left earth, can do something for us. They do not do things for us. They show us a way in which *we* can do things for ourselves. Their interest is not in this physical, material, mundane world. Their interest is in awakening souls who are yet in this physical flesh, that through that process of awakening they may become a light, not only unto themselves, but to those 'round and about them.

I am very familiar with the duality of the human mind, because I'm familiar with my own mind; that's how I'm aware of it. If we want guidance, then we have to be willing to accept thoughts and ideas that are flowing from the spiritual realms that are contrary to our own desires, to our own judgments, to our own fears.

What is it that keeps us from the greater goodness in life? Well, it's very simple: it's the fear. And the fear is what blocks our path, for it is a great magnet that pulls the obstructions to us. We all know that the thing we fear befalls us. So if we become aware of our fears, then we can go to work on directing this energy to something that is beneficial and to something that will bring us the peace that we're all seeking.

Now, you see, my mind, as your mind, for all minds, in principle, are the same, when it faces a new experience, whether it's a, a speaker or making out a deposition or any new experience, everything that has already been recorded within our mind in any way related to the experience comes up to take charge of how we're going to handle the experience that we're presently having. Now, what happens is that the mind does not want to change whatever patterns it's already accepted. It is those patterns that rise up and they use what we call fear, negative faith, so that we will stay right where we are. But in spite of all of the experiences that we have had in this earth life and in spite of the patterns that we cherish so dearly in our minds, evolution does take place. For evolution is absolutely guaranteed. It's demonstrated all around and about us.

Now, sooner or later, of course—and by sooner or later I mean in your daily activities—these choices that you make, you become aware of whether they are based upon the experiences of your past or they are the guidance of the spirit within you, around you and about you.

So often in this work, students have so strongly desired to see and to hear a spirit. But there are many spirits in the atmosphere that you would not consciously choose to hear, let alone to see. For the level that desires the communication is a level of self. Now, you must consider: of what benefit, of what benefit can it be to communicate with a spirit totally locked in self when you've already had the experiences, already, that being locked in self is not only not beneficial but it's extremely detrimental? So stop and think, my good friends. Do you want to attract unto you those kinds of spirits? Can you imagine being guided by someone that's totally interested in themselves? Surely, I wouldn't want to be guided by someone like that. But if we desire—you see, it's the motive that we must consider. Now, if our motive is to try to establish laws in life that will bring us some kind of light of reason, if that is truly our motive, then, of course, like attracts like and those are the kind of spirits that are around and about us.

Because I know and in times in the past when the guidance I have received has been totally contrary to my thinking and my own desires, I have entertained the thought that they were just getting a little bit too selfish with all my work and my effort and my energies. Because that's what the mind has to offer.

Now, if we think it is such a glorious path to be in this work, then we have to consider there has never been a Sunday morning that I knew with any assurance that I could serve on the podium of this church. There is absolutely no guarantee that any message can ever be given, because it is not within the power of the mind. Now, if you find that pleasing, then you're not thinking about having to go to work on a job and not knowing whether or not in any way, shape, or form you can complete the job that you're going to work on. It's a very traumatic experience for the mind; you can be rest assured of that. Because if the mind doesn't get out of the way, then none of this work can possibly get done.

We spoke here before about our faith in God and whether or not we believe in spirit or we don't believe in spirit. And the question is a wonderful question, because first we have to believe in our own spirit before we can accept the possibility that a spirit exists outside, we first have to believe that one exists inside. And I tell you, I just have that kind of an ego that's absolutely determined—in fact, I don't believe, I know beyond a shadow of any doubt that going back into the ground is not the end of me because my ego wouldn't allow such a thing.

You see, I do believe that the ego serves a wonderful purpose. And I don't even entertain such negative thinking that, "You know, I'm going to be planted someday and who knows how soon and that's the end of me. What a waste of life." No. So first we've got to believe or, at least, accept the possibility that we are this minute spirit. And because we are spirit, those that we physically see, they too are spirit. And when they shed their physical body, considering that the spirit is not composed of that physical substance, there's no longer any question for the answer is self-evident.

Now, in these classes in this semester, surely, to me, at least, I have found them most interesting, constantly changing. But if you think that your path is a heavy one and that perhaps someone else has a lighter one, someday you will have the path that you think is lighter and see how heavy it really is. Now I hope you don't get me wrong and think I'm wallowing in self-pity because it's my birthday. I'm very pleased that I've managed to survive this long on earth, because there were many times when I didn't think that there was going to be that many years left.

But what is it we must, I think, ask ourselves: What are we doing this moment? What have we done this day? Because if we'll only stay aware of this day and not spend so much time and so much energy and so much effort being concerned about all those tomorrows, being so unhappy about all those yesterdays.

I never know from day to day whether I'm going to be here or I'm going to be there. But most of you are aware, to some extent, where you're going to be because your mind makes a judgment, you follow that judgment, and you go where your mind tells you to go. But if you're going to be a medium in this work, you see, you're going to have to sacrifice that. You'll have to go where someone else tells you to go, when *they* tell you to go, and do what *they* tell you to do, when *they* tell you to do it. Are we willing to give up that precious self-will to gain something that is far greater, far broader, and certainly more beneficial?

Well, you take a look at married people. A husband tells the wife where to go—or tries to—where to go, when to go, what to do, and how to do it. And they have problems. And then the wife tells the husband what to do, how to do it, where to go, and when to go. And *he* has problems. So if we have problems because someone else tells us what to do, how to do it, when to do it, and where to do it, then how in the name of God can we ever accept a guidance greater than what our mind is dictating? If we can't accept it from a husband or wife to whom we have—with whom we have a rapport and certainly an attachment, how can we possibly accept it from some discarnate spirit floating around in space? I think it would be most difficult. Indeed, I think it would be most difficult.

And so, what do we have to give up to gain the fulfillment of our desire, if mediumship is what we want? Well, we've got to give up the self-will. And I'm sure that everyone will agree with me that is not an easy thing to give up. Because if it was so easy to give up, more people would be doing it, wouldn't you think? No. When we have over-identified with self, then we experience a great deal of self-will. So the first step we have to make is to identify with something besides self. Something much greater. Something much broader. Because you cannot give up the self-will without identifying with something greater than the self.

So in spiritual unfoldment and in going along the path of evolution, it's a matter of making an effort on a constant, daily basis of identifying with something greater than self. And then you really test yourself, when you have a strong desire and that which you have identified with does not agree with you. And you have to accept that something greater that you have identified with and bow your self-will. That's the first step on the path of spiritual awakening—is identifying with something greater.

Now, how does one move from the over-identification with this little, small self to something greater? You just cannot jump from here way over to there. That's contrary to the process of evolution. No, no. You go step by step by step. So you begin by identifying with another person.

Marriage is a wonderful institution, for it grants to each person the opportunity to identify with another individual. Now, this very clear principle is stated here in the Living Light book [*The Living Light*]: to identify. So what happens when you make the effort to identify with your husband or wife, to try to understand why they feel the way they do, what their desires are, what their problems are? Do you have the tolerance and the compassion? If you have truly identified with another person, then you have the tolerance necessary to help them; you have the patience that's necessary to help them; you have the compassion; you have the encouragement. Because if you do not feel encouraged, how can you possibly identify with them and help to inspire and encourage them to make the changes that they know are necessary, but they're still quite weak and stumbling along the path? You see, the soul faculties have to be opened. And they get opened when you make the effort to identify with another person.

Now, if you don't have a husband or you don't have a wife, there are untold millions of people in the universe with whom you can identify. Now, if you say that this person, you just cannot stand the way they are, you cannot tolerate because they cannot see, no matter how many times you talk to them, they cannot see the way, that person will do you the most good. For they are what is necessary for you to see which of your soul faculties are closed.

Now, you know in this philosophy, there's that little saying: that that disturbs us, controls us. So when you identify with someone, if you feel disturbed in your efforts to help them, as you're helping yourself, of course—because that's what it's really all about: that's how it works—then you wake up and see how they control you. They do not control your strengths! They control your weaknesses. And when you awaken that what they are controlling in your life are your weaknesses, you start to become irritated. From disturbance to irritation. Now, you're not irritated with that person. No! You are irritated with your own weaknesses, the ones you that pushed out of sight of your conscious ego and you shoved them way down below. That's what you're irritated with. You're irritated with your own weaknesses. A weakness, for example, in having the patience, the wisdom of patience to work year after year after year with a person, to constantly repeat again and again and again and again.

But what we forget, so often, is that someone along the way worked with us. For any soul faculty that we have open, someone, somewhere at some time worked with us. Whether or not we consciously recall that is not important. And so, therefore, because someone did work with us to help us to open up some of those soul faculties, we are therefore qualified to help another. Because we can't grant to another what has not already been granted to ourselves.

Now, to strengthen our weaknesses, we must first become aware of them. We do not become aware of our weaknesses until we begin to work with another's weaknesses. That's when we get to see our own. That's when we get to see whether we are short-tempered, whether we have tolerance, whether we have patience. You see, if we have judged that we can do a job in five minutes and the same job is taking someone else fifty minutes, and we find that that disturbs us, then we must ask ourselves what our weakness is. For we are not disturbed because someone else is taking fifty minutes to do a job that we can do in five minutes. That's not the reason we're disturbed. We are disturbed at the weakness that is taking control of us at that moment. And what is the weakness? The weakness is the soul faculties: The faculty of duty, the faculty of gratitude, the faculty of tolerance, the faculty of patience, the faculty of encouragement. All of these faculties, they are weak within us for we have not directed energy to them. This is why we are disturbed. We're disturbed at ourselves and controlled by the functions which are out of balance with the corresponding faculties. That's what disturbs us. And then we become irritated and we start to wake up.

Now, if we will truly face that simple truth, when we're working with people and around people—because you can't be working around people without working *with* people. And if you don't believe me, ask some of the ladies that work in the kitchen and keep these dinners going. You can't be around someone without making the effort to work with them, because if you go amongst a group of people to do a job and you want to be an island self-sufficient unto yourself, you're going to have problems because there are people around you. And if you stand there and they're doing their thing and you're going to do yours and there is no communication taking place, you're going to find out what a difficult thing it is for you, because it's all vibration.

Just like sleeping. I notice that some of my students sleep. I'm going to ask the Friends if I can't give classes more often because at least then I have my eyes open and I can see what's going on in these classes. It's very important to my mind to see what's going on.

So we see where these struggles in our life are—all these self-created things. It certainly is indeed very, very, very interesting.

We must also ask ourselves, Why don't we want to bother? When we think we don't want to bother to help someone else or that we've made some effort and they're just not going to change—to say that a person is not going to change is to deny the demonstrable Law of Evolution. To make that judgment, you see, we've got to find out what's going on inside of us that looks out at the world and sees other people and says, "That one's not going to change." Perhaps it's only a microscopic change. And if that microscopic change we are not grateful for, that's denying the crumb that guarantees the loaf.

But we find ofttimes that we don't want to make so much effort to help another person. It's just too much effort. It just takes too much energy. Why, my mind has said that about hundreds of people. It didn't get to have its way, but it certainly has thought, many times, as some of my students present know, that have been around for a few years. But I am indeed grateful because I have lived on earth long enough to see these changes take place. Very microscopic. Surely they were so small you could hardly see them. But as you look back over the years and you consider the starting point, yes, the changes are taking place. The changes for the better.

If we want to make changes—and we all do. There are many areas of our life we certainly want changed. But, of course, we want that change to take place immediately. We don't want it to be ten years from today.

You must remember, all our minds look out to see how someone else is doing. That's just the way our minds work. And if we make the judgment, "Well, let's see, that person's doing very well. I better find out what they're doing because I want to do so well myself." Now, this is the way our little minds work as it looks around the world of creation. It takes a look, it says, "Yes, yes, I can do that. I see what they're doing. And that, yes, I can do that. Because it's worth doing that if that's how they got what they got." But what happens—we do—we look around and we say, "Yes." But we do not accept what is contrary to the patterns that keep us where we are. So what happens to us, you see, we delude ourselves. We take a look and we accept that which is in keeping with the patterns we already have.

Now, how do we overcome something like that? Well, it's quite simple. If you look at a person and that person works a certain way and declares the demonstrable truth that God and God alone is the true and only source of their supply, do we ask the person how many times a day and night they say that? Or do we automatically judge they say it, maybe, once in the morning, maybe once for lunch and once at night? We have to investigate. Not just presume that they do this and do that and do that. And therefore we try that for a while and it doesn't work and that's it! The old patterns take full charge and full control all over again.

This is why I'm sharing a little bit of how my mind works. So that you won't think that mine is so different from yours. Just the same. Identically the same in principle. Just as negative. Just as fearful. Loaded with just as many doubts. It just goes to sleep for a while when the spirit has their work to do. But because of the years, you see—you know, like water flowing through the pipe, as the years go by that which is within the water deposits on the pipe. And so it is, you know, with a medium sooner or later some of it's going to rub off. And so, some, along the years—you see, after all that time a little bit of it has rubbed off. But not enough to totally blot my own self-will out of the way. No.

So let's ask ourselves that simple question, "First, what is it that is greater than my self-will that I'm ready to identify with?" During the honeymoon phase of a marriage, you know, there seems to be no problem at all. The partners have identified with something greater than themselves and everything is just peachy and roses. But why doesn't it last? Now there are married people here in the class tonight. Why doesn't it last? We must ask ourselves that question. Why do married people, after a time, it seems, most of them, start doing their own thing? I mean, one goes off in this direction; the other goes off in this direction. It's like two strangers living under the same roof. It's really quite something to witness. Why? Why do they do such a thing?

Is it because they worked real hard to get the other one to change completely to their way of thinking and they finally woke up that like attracts like and becomes the Law of Attachment and their partner has just as much self-will as they have? So they call a truce and go off on their separate little paths, except they still live under the same roof. It's really very interesting.

It would seem, I'm sure, that two people, surely, can get more accomplished, united, than one person, if they're truly united. And it would seem to me that that's the purpose, the basic purpose: to bow the self-will, self-interest for the good of the whole—the whole being the marriage itself.

Now that's what this church is about. This church has very few people. Great effort is made, constantly, to bring about some degree of unity. But, you know, you don't have unity without discipline. And you don't have discipline without some degree of self-control. So any organization is as successful as the people within it are willing to bow their self-will and self-interest to unite for the common good. And it would seem that that's what a marriage should be all about, is to unite for the common good. And the common good doesn't necessarily have to be children. The common good is the very principle of the marriage itself. However, that's my view of marriage. That's not necessarily all of my students' view, I'm sure.

Well, does anyone have any questions? They can just raise their hand. You know, it's like at my birthday party, they—somebody—said I should have given a speech. I told them that I just was not qualified at giving speeches. A lecture, maybe. Speeches, absolutely not. No. I would never make, I am sure, a good politician because I'm just not good at giving speeches.

But I'm trying to show you that not only is there something greater than the mind and all of its games—you know, it must be very weary for the mind to be working so hard to get so many things done and to tie up all the loose ends. You see, if you can just bow that self-will, there is something greater in the atmosphere—no matter what you care to call it, it really doesn't make any difference—that will guide your path serene. There really is. And you don't have to wear yourself out and be so exhausted with all that mental activity of trying to figure out everything and how is everything going to work and, and just be totally worn out.

You see, if you'd kind of visualize, "Now let's see, whatever I think I have, if it all disappears, if it all goes away, where will I be?" Well, you'll be wherever you choose to be! That's entirely up to you. Life is filled with a constant panorama of change. It's up to each individual. But why work so hard to try to mentally figure out so many different things?

You know, we make the judgment that we have not and then we follow the judgment to support the judgment of how right we are. You know, all we've got to do—you see, we're setting all these laws into motion all the time—all we've got to do is say, "Well, I don't have this and I don't have that." And our mind, it'll go to work to prove how right we are. Our mind makes constant effort to prove how right we are all the time. Because I never met a mind yet that wants to be wrong. And so, you see, it works like a, a little trooper to prove how right we were all the time. You see?

So if we say that we're having a struggle and we keep saying that to different people, we work very hard to make sure, to prove to ourselves that we were right. So if that's the way the mind works, and I can assure you it's exactly how it works—and certainly the students have had enough experience—why not make the effort to tell yourself how great everything is? And then your little subconscious goes to work to prove how right you are. And then things get greater and things get better.

Become aware of how many times in the course of a day that you tell yourself what a heavy cross you have to bear, in a million different words. The spoken word is life-giving energy. Your spoken word gives life to the forms that work to fulfill your law, the law you have, by your own choice, established. So if you're worried about your job and you're worried about the things your mind says you don't have, all that you are doing is guaranteeing the continuity of the experience. Just like a woman—she wants to get married. If she keeps saying, "Well, I'm not married. There's no one, really, you know, around or available," and she keeps playing that tape, well, that's the experience she has. Now, see, that works in everything. That works in everything.

Surely the bookkeeper of this church is well aware of what I say whenever I look at a bill, let alone a check: that "God is the source of my supply. There's a higher power." Because I know that the spoken word creates these things. And if I don't speak forth the positive, then I cannot experience the positive. And if we keep telling ourselves how tough everything is, you see, and we insist on being prophets of doom, then that's what we're going to experience: constant doom! If we need the excitement that disaster brings to us, then you can be rest assured our little minds are going to create one disaster right after another, constantly, around and around and around, until we get so weary of that merry-go-round that we step off of it.

When we think positive, we speak positive and the positive returns to us. And I, surely, have plenty of opportunity, considering that I was in hopes, years ago, that I could be freed from the fund-raising department of this church. It kind of looks like my desire was too strong because I'm still stuck with it. And I don't want to make any more judgments. I'd rather try to stay neutral in that department—haven't had, already, enough experiences.

But it's what we're saying and it's what we're thinking that's the cause of all our experience. Now, the classes have taught that repeatedly in a million different words. It's what we're thinking. It's what we're saying. We are constantly doing these things to ourselves all the time.

So it's up to us to make some effort to bring about some degree of change that we desire. Are we really making the effort to become aware of whether or not our words are positive or negative? For when we become aware of what kind of words we're sending out into the universe, then we'll become aware and know the cause of all our experiences. It takes, I know, a constant effort of reminding the human mind that it and it alone is responsible for all experience.

Now, when I got that call today from the attorney's secretary, I had to remind myself immediately, "Richard, this is your responsibility. You set the law into motion. You merited the experience. You can either wallow in the pity because you don't like depositions or you can just move forward." You see, these things are opportunities for us to make intelligent, reasonable choices moment by moment. It's like if we have judgments in reference to the employer that we've merited in our life and we choose to bring those judgments home with us, give us indigestion, ruin our dinners, ruin our evenings and everything else—we have to make a choice. Is our employer—Do we love our employer so much that we've got to take him to dinner with us and take him to bed with us and brush our teeth with him? Because if we are thinking about our employer, that we don't like, of course, the thought is the form.

You cannot think about anything, whether it's an apple or a toothpick, that your mind, in that instant, doesn't create that form. Because the human mind is a process of imaging. It has all of these images. If you say "black" to the mind, your mind comes up with an image. Everyone's mind comes up with an image. If you say "red," it comes up with another image. If you say "white," it comes up with something else. If you say the number "5," your mind comes up with an image. Now, it's those images, you see, the effect of your thinking, that darken the path of reason. This is why this philosophy teaches control of the mind, because without control of the mind, the light does not shine clearly because all these forms are in the atmosphere around you.

So, when you think of your employer and you don't feel good, you are in that instant, number one: creating the image of your employer; number two: you have not only created the image of your employer and, if you feel badly in the thought concerning your employer, you have created the image of your employer in such a way that it is distasteful to you to the degree and extent that you feel badly. And you carry that package with you as long as you feed it energy. Now, once you have established that, you have created that form. The next time that you think of your employer, that form comes up out of your subconscious. And if you think again badly of them, they're even stronger because more energy is released by emotion than any other possible way. The more emotion you have concerning a thought, the stronger the form will be that will, in time, control you. Think about that.

So if you want to be emotional about anything, why don't you choose something that's pleasing? Don't you see? Become emotional over the sunset. Because that's a pleasing form. Or over the sunrise. These forms, they are as strong as you release energy to them. Now once—they have the intelligence of your mind, for your mind created them. Now, if you have directed a lot of energy to them, they're determined to survive. And they can only survive on energy. Then the day comes that perhaps you're sitting down having a cup of coffee and all of a sudden a thought comes into your mind and the thought is the thought of your employer that you don't like. And you wonder why you can't get that thought out of your mind. If you could only see the form that you have created that is demanding its sustenance for survival, then you would understand why it is difficult to get certain thoughts out of your mind.

So isn't it certainly common sense to give more consideration to the thoughts that you permit your mind to entertain, considering that you have not only created a form, like a little child, but you are feeding that form each time you entertain that thought? Now, is that form a form that's going to be beneficial for you or is it something that is detrimental?

Now, why do you think—yes, I'll be right with you—why do you think that in this philosophy the strongest functions are money, ego and sex. What made them the strongest functions? What made them the strongest functions? It wasn't some divine dictate. It is the minds of men. Because they think about those functions so much, they have created an entire realm. And in some of the books on Spiritualism, it is spoken about those realms. Now, that's really what it's all about.

It is the nature of our mind to create. God is the sustaining intelligence. The mind is the creator and it creates many things. But when the things that the mind creates become stronger than the creator, look at the master that we are serving. If you find a thought repeating itself in your mind and you cannot control it and it robs you of your peace, it robs you of your joy and your happiness in life, then you know beyond a shadow of any doubt the form you have created is now your master and you, their slave. You don't have to remain the slave of that created form, because you created it. Therefore, you can change it. God will not change it, for that is contrary to the very nature of God. God sustains what you choose to create. But you can create a replacement of that form that has taken control of your soul. But that takes a lot of effort because the form that has become a master has been fed a lot of energy over a lot of years.

Now, if you permit your mind to say, "Well, that's just too much effort." And you become discouraged, then the form is planting that thinking in your head in order that it may continue to be your boss.

So let's take a look at all these different things. I'm sure everyone here would agree there are certain thoughts that seem to plague us at times. But they're not somebody else's. Surely, they're our own and because they are ours, we can do a lot about it.

Yes, now the lady had a question.

Concerning imagination, I understand that if it's negative, it feeds that. But if it's a more positive form—I'm thinking more of fantasies—is this something—can it ever serve the purpose of opening us to something greater? Or is it more that we are putting power into our fantasies and not into our actual lives?

Yes. Thank you very much. Now, it is very important in understanding—there is a vast difference between what we call fantasy and imagination, imaging. When we experience what is known as fantasy, to most of us, what is really happening is a desire in our mind has taken control of us. And the process, from the control—that desire having control—is that there is a creating process of the mind based upon past experiences. Now, most people think that fantasy is not based on past experience. I assure you that fantasy, definitely and positively, is based upon past experience. Now, that is what gives it the energy, is past experience. Now our mind will create different things that were not an actual experience of the past, but the driving force *is* past experience, unfulfilled desires of the years past. And so our mind fantasizes to bring it into harmony with our present desire.

Now, we'll take that as fantasy and we'll move to imaging, imagination. Imagination is a conscious choice, a conscious choice. For example, I image a white elephant with pink, pink polka dots. I happen to like that. It looks very nice. Now, I image that. I see it in front of me. I am aware that I have created it. I have created this white elephant with pink polka dots for a specific purpose, you see.

Now, the realm of imagination is ever in front of us. To use that realm constructively, as it is a doorway—it is not the realm of spirit—but it is the doorway through which we must pass to enter the realm of spirit. You can create, by the process of imaging, anything that you choose to create. I create a beautiful bridge in front of me. And I create the trees and the mountains that are around it. And the little ship that is sailing underneath of it. You see, when you can consciously do that, and anything that you consciously choose to do it with, you have gained a degree of concentration, a degree of control of your mind.

Now, to permit the mind to fantasize in these realms of desire, controlled by past experiences, is not moving us forward into higher dimensions. For example, if you choose, in your particular field, to create a new type of dance, that is within your power to do so. You can do it in this very moment through the process of imagination, you see. Therefore, that can be, and is, as you move on through that, extremely beneficial. The inventions that are in our world come through the doorway of the realm of imagination. And that's how they get here to earth.

In the creative work—and everyone truly is creative—how many presently—raise your hands, please—will consciously choose something to create in the atmosphere and therefore see it? Yes. Now it is very important to gain that degree of concentration and control. You can use that exercise wisely, because, you see, there's a fine line between imagination (imaging) and fantasy. There is a very fine line.

Now, those who were able, a moment ago, to image what they consciously chose to image, I want them to think for a moment and become aware: Was there any past experience related to the image? If there was, then you have spontaneous fantasy rather than imagination. Imagination, you must consciously choose what it is. And instantaneously it will appear.

Now, this teaching—and we're going quite long here this evening, but anyway it is important—this teaching that states,

"I speak my word forth into the universe." All right. Now we'll stop at that point. "I speak my word forth into the universe." At that point we are at the door of imagination. "Knowing that it shall not come back to me void." We now see the very image we have created. Now I'll go through this again because it's important. "I speak my word forth into the universe"—we stand at the door of imagination—"knowing that it will not come back to me void,"—we clearly see that that we have consciously created—"but accomplish that which I send it to do." We have created the form. We know it will not return to us void for we see the fullness thereof, of the form we have created. It is animated. It is movement. "But accomplish that which we send it to do."

Now, if you want to send a message to someone, you create the messenger and you send the messenger to do what it was created for. Do you understand? Now all of our lives, from this very law, that we speak our word forth into the universe, all of this is taking place all the time. All the time. We speak the negative; the forms are created; they go and do the work that they were sent to do by our own mind; and they bring back the negative experience. It's happening all the time. Constantly, day and night. For that is the law that we alone have set into motion.

So why not set the forms that we consciously choose? Not the ones that we've been choosing by our errors of ignorance. It's like a person that has a strong desire that they're without, whatever they choose to decide they're without, of course. If they would only open the eyes and see that they have created a little messenger whose sole responsibility is to keep everything away from them, in keeping with their own spoken word, that would fulfill their desire. And so those forms go to work and keep that away so that our little king inside says, "You see, I'm right. I'm right all the time! There's nobody coming into my life. I've said that for years!" That's what we do. All the time we're doing that, for all the time we are speaking our word forth into the universe. And be rest assured, we know it's not coming back to us void because it always accomplishes exactly what we send it to do. So, you see, in that respect we always get what we really want.

So whatever experience you're having, say, "Thank you, God. How beautiful your laws are. They never fail. They're supporting all this negative garbage that I'm sending out all the time. Just take a look at my miserable life. How accurate, how absolutely positive and guaranteed your laws are. They are so infallible." Like they often say garbage in, garbage out. Now this is the thing to view objectively. How beautiful and infallible is the law. It never faileth. You wake up in the morning grumpy, you guarantee: little grumpy goes out and gets all the experiences to support your grumpiness.

Don't you understand? These workers are working all the time. If you feel rejected or lonely, God forbid, or you feel your wife's not treating you just right, well, you send out all those little forms to have all these experiences come back. On the freeway, wherever you are, it's taking place.

God has given his angels charge over us, least we dash our feet against the stones of ignorance. But that charge over us does not in any way imply depriving us our own self-will. That's ever our own choice: to accept or to reject.

Our destiny is ever in keeping with our denials. And every time we deny—and we deny by declaring we have need. You see, we cannot experience what is known as need without denial. We first must deny that we have. We must deny what we have in order to experience need. So when we deny, the Law of Destiny is established and we prove to ourselves that we have not.

So considering how beautiful that law has already worked for us in the negative, why not accept? For those little workers of acceptance are just as great of workers as the workers of denial. They work just as hard. Day and night. Right around the clock. So all you have to do is to choose whether you want the abundance of life or you want the deprivation that only you can create. So if we feel deprived, you can be rest assured, the law that is working to keep us deprived will also work to keep us fulfilled, but we will have to make a greater effort to become aware of what kind of thinking that we are entertaining.

Now, I am very grateful for the students that I have merited, somehow, in life, for they constantly remind me, though I don't think consciously, what I shouldn't be doing. And that is most helpful to me. Because, being human, I have the potential and possibility of just as much self-pity as any student I have. So when I find them in self-pity and I find them in negativity, they serve very well, because I see very clearly, "Whoops, I've got to make greater effort on myself. It's so easy to slip into that."

Thank you very, very much. Thank you.

FEBRUARY 22, 1979

CONSCIOUSNESS CLASS 205

Good evening, class.

I wanted to speak to you this evening in reference to the faculties and the functions. All of us have heard about the faculties and the functions, and we've all heard about gratitude, the Law of Supply. What it seems that we often forget is that the faculties, as well as the functions, are triune. And we're all seeking an abundant good in our life. We're all seeking harmony and peace and success and all of those things, but we cannot just concentrate our efforts on duty and forget about tolerance and gratitude or we can't concentrate our efforts exclusively on gratitude, knowing that gratitude is the law through which God's goodness flows, and forget about tolerance. Because, you see, they are triune faculties and unless all three points of that triangle are in balance, then, of course, there is no flow.

Now, we all seem to have—we think we have problems with tolerance. Now this philosophy has given to us many teachings in reference to tolerance, clearly stating the things that we cannot tolerate in another we have yet to educate within ourselves.

We want to know how to be freed from the seeming struggles and problems that beset us in our daily work and acts and activities, but wanting something and making the effort to attain it are two entirely different things. To make the effort to attain the success that we're seeking, we have to wake up from the sleep of satisfaction. Now what is, in truth, the sleep of satisfaction? It is simply the unwillingness to change. Why do we find ourselves at times, so often, really, unwilling to change? Well, our unwillingness to change our attitudes and our thoughts is dependent upon how much love of self we are in. Now, the more of the infinite, intelligent energy that is directed to the love of self, the more we sleep in the slumber of satisfaction. As we, slowly but surely, make the effort to educate our ego, which, in truth, is to awaken it from the sleep of satisfaction or the love of self, when we make that effort, we begin to become a bit irritated with ourselves.

Another teaching in this philosophy simply states that irritation wakes the soul. And, indeed, it does. We all seem to have problems with the first soul faculty and this is why the teacher of this philosophy has not expanded on the many other triune soul faculties, because it would only divert the effort of opening up the very first one. Now, it seems that the greatest difficulty with the first soul faculty is that point called tolerance. Why is it that we find it so difficult to express tolerance? We must ask ourselves the question. When we look at another and we find ourselves intolerant to the way that they do things, to the way they speak and act, what we are really viewing is that exact level of expression in ourselves. But we cannot see that we, in truth, are acting the same way because if we honestly face that within ourselves, then we would have no problems with tolerance when we viewed it in another.

So we all want to know what it is—these lessons in life—that we have to learn. Well, every time you think and you feel that you are not tolerant with someone's expression, that it is so difficult for you, the way that you have to constantly repeat the lesson to them, that they don't seem to be willing to change, stop in that moment and take a look at that level within yourself, because it is waiting for you to make the effort to educate it.

And so each experience that we have in life is a mirror and it is reflecting to us our own attitude. But when we are so filled with the love of self, then our minds, you see, have made the judgment how perfect we are. And being so perfect, being so infallible in our decisions, there's no room there left for tolerance, the first soul faculty.

We look at the people around and about us, the people that we want to do things for us—we like to think that we do everything for ourselves. But we all know that no man is an island sufficient unto himself, that he and he alone can fulfill his life's purpose. That's not the way that life is. Everything around and about us is dependent upon all the forms in our sphere and zone of action.

We all know that everything, in truth, is vibration and that we and we alone are the creators of the vibration. We have these multitudes of desires that plague us and, indeed, they plague us. They not only blind us because of our attachment to them—you see, my friends, desire, indeed, its principle is the divine expression. Desire is blinded by man's dictate, by man's judgment. You cannot—no one with any common sense and reason can accept that desire is the expression of the divinity of God and then accept that desire is blind.

We must know how desire gets blinded. And, as I said a moment ago, it is blinded by *our* dictate, by *our* judgment. We all know what it is to have a desire rise up within our consciousness.

We all know what happens to our thoughts. We all know the dictates and the judgments that are made by our own mind in reference to its fulfillment. Do we express the first soul faculty when our own mind records and registers desire? That's how desire gets blind. It's blinded because, in the moment of the experience of desire, the counterbalance soul faculty is not being expressed: the first soul faculty: duty, gratitude, and tolerance.

If you want to keep desire divine, then you will have to bring balance between the faculties and the functions when the Divinity is expressing. Now that's possible, of course, for all of us, if it means enough to make the effort.

One of the first stages or steps of unfoldment is to become aware that we need to make a change in our attitude and in our thoughts. That's the first step on the spiritual path: is the awareness and the acceptance that within us there is a need to make a change. Now that's only the first step. The second step is to make the daily effort to bring about that change.

One of the most interesting—and using that word *cop-out*—one of the most interesting cop-outs or justifications that I have found with some of my students, when they know very well what they're doing—because we always know what we're doing: we may try to justify that we were unaware. And unfortunately, that's when we use this philosophy against us. We use it against our own growth. To do something and justify your doing it when you know, for your conscience is a spiritual sensibility with a dual capacity; it knows right from wrong; it doesn't have to be told. To do something and then say you were unaware is to use this beautiful, simple truth against your eternal soul. We are always aware. We don't always want others to know that we're aware. But within us we know. We really do know what we're doing.

Ofttimes, when we do things that we know are wrong for us and those around us, we like to go into the sleep of satisfaction and simply say, "I, I was just unaware, just unaware." Now remember, friends, that's not the way to grow.

We all know, when we desire something, we're very much aware of our desire. So that great, beautiful potential of awareness is ever at our fingertips. All we have to do is make a little effort. Just a little bit of effort each and every day.

Tolerance, the key to success, seems, for many, to be their greatest struggle. But we all know if we will love ourselves a little less, we will have all the tolerance and, yea, even tolerance to spare and, therefore, assure our own spiritual, mental, and material growth. Remember that tolerance is inseparable from duty and inseparable from gratitude.

So if you feel in the very depths of your heart that you are grateful, grateful for the breath of life, grateful for whatever crumbs or loaves you think that you have, and you still are not experiencing the fullness of life, then take a look at duty and see to what are you directing that faculty. To what are you dutiful in your thoughts, your acts, and activities? And if you honestly find that you are dutiful to the principle of the faculties of the soul, then the question must rise in your consciousness, "Have I included, in my dutifulness, the faculty of tolerance?" To express the fullness of the soul faculty of tolerance, we have to give up the obstruction that stands in the way. And I assure you the obstruction that stands in the way of the soul faculty of tolerance is the function of self-love.

Love, we all know, is this great Intelligence, called God. When we restrict this Intelligence, when we limit it to the thought of I, then we must pay the price of that obstruction, for the soul faculty of consideration is limited to one simple identification. The world around and about us does not exist for us without the identification of the thought of I. That, my friends, is, in truth, a struggle for anyone that chooses to remain in that limited type of thinking. But we don't have to remain there.

When we find we're having difficulty with the faculty of tolerance, we know, if we're having difficulty, to whom or to what this difficulty is directed or blamed upon. We cannot experience intolerance unless we are totally considering the thought of I. You see, when we are filled with this self-love of this thought of I, then everything around and about us has to fit in to a limited sphere of action. If it is different than what we have accepted, out of self-preservation, which grows into the great love of self, we must annihilate it. And so we work to annihilate it by what is known as intolerance.

What we are not thinking about in those moments of intolerance, what we are not thinking about is that that level that we are viewing not only exists within ourselves, but is being expressed: the identically same level that we are intolerant to in another is expressing within us in other ways. But we see it not and, therefore, are not tolerant to it. It is self-destructive to be intolerant. It is a slow but sure suicide of the self. And how beautiful are the laws of nature. For whenever we direct the infinite, intelligent energy in any direction and create in our universe an imbalance, we pay the price of that imbalance.

We all know the function of money, ego, and sex. And if we have a problem with that function, you can be rest assured—if you have a problem with it, that you are out of balance. How does man get out of balance? Only from an error in his own thought. Not from an error in someone else's thought. No, that's not how we get out of balance. We get out of balance with the divine Law of Harmony because we are not directing the intelligent energy equally to the faculties and to the functions.

The only thing wrong with the functions is the imbalance to the corresponding soul faculty. And if you direct, in an imbalanced way, the intelligent energies to the faculties at the sacrifice of the functions, while you are yet expressing, your soul, through the functions, then you've got that problem. The effect is very simple: we find ourselves, then, controlled by certain thoughts and that robs us from the harmony and the good of life.

Are we, truly, each day, making a little more effort to awaken within? Or are we dictating to ourselves that it's such a struggle? Each time you permit your mind to dictate that it's such a struggle, you create even a greater struggle. What we are really saying to ourselves, when we tell ourselves what a struggle this life is, what we're really saying is, "I don't want to make any effort to change. I don't like the experiences I'm having in life. Those experiences I would like to change. I would like all of those experiences changed, but I love myself so much I cannot face, I cannot permit my mind to entertain the thought that *I* must make a change. Because to do so, my great love of myself proves, then, that it is fallible." And none of us, when we are filled with self-love, want to accept the possibility that we have made a mistake.

Let us think about this beautiful, divine, Intelligent Energy that sustains—and will ever sustain, as it always has sustained—any thought and any feeling that we choose to entertain in our mind.

There are so many devious ways that our mind uses to keep us where we are. But in spite of all those devious games that our little mind keeps playing, in spite of all of that, our minds are not so infallible that they can stop the demonstrable Law of Evolution. In spite of our minds, we will evolve. The purpose of making the effort to bring about some changes in our mind is so that we may evolve more harmoniously; that we will not have to fret and go through all of these cyclic ups and downs; that there *is* a better way; that we can grow joyously.

There is no sane reason why we should spend time in the pity of self. My friends, the more pity we have for ourselves only reveals how much love we have of ourselves.

Now, if you find that you have any, or all, of these seeming problems, then find something, or someone, to love besides yourself. You could love the tree. But if that's too difficult for you, I suppose you could start with another human being. But in so doing, the problems that you brought to the other human being will only bounce right back to you. So, you see, it's really, in many respects, a little bit easier to start by loving a tree or a blade of grass. And perhaps then, moving from the plant kingdom to the insect kingdom, maybe love a little ant or a beetle. And then, slowly but surely, grow with tolerance with the first soul faculty: perhaps you could move to love a little kitten or a dog. And slowly but surely, as you make the effort daily to evolve, gradually gravitate to the actual possibility of loving another human being. But, like in everything, we should start small, you see. Slow, sure steps.

So I would suggest that you start with a plant. It doesn't talk to your physical ears. Oh, it does speak, if you can get out of self long enough to hear it. It has sound. It has feelings, for it has an intelligence flowing through it. That's what causes it to move. It moves, but very slowly. Few people can look, with their physical eyes, of course, and see a plant moving. But it is moving. We call it growing. But when you have made some little effort and you're starting with a little plant, if it doesn't do what you think it should do and it doesn't grow or move the way you think it should have done, do you still love it? Do you still love the intelligence flowing through the little plant, it started to grow and flourish, now its little leaves are turning brown and it's in the process of decay? How do you feel? Do you still feel the same about the intelligence that was expressing through the plant? If you still feel the same the day that you got it and you feel the same the day that you threw it in the garbage can, then you have found divine love. Now, if you have any emotion the day you threw it in the garbage can and that is not the feeling of joy the day that you received it, if it's not the same, you haven't found, yet, divine love.

So, you see, isn't it better to start with something simple to love, to expand this divine God that's flowing through you? Because you can see very clearly. Then, if you get a little pet and you're so happy that that little pet has entered your life and it brings you so much joy and so much happiness, and the time comes for the little soul expressing through that little pet to go on to another life, another expression, how do you really feel? Because that will tell you whether or not you're ready to express any love to a human being. Because if you have any emotion when the little pet, when the time has arrived to go to the other world—where we're all going—if you have any grief or any sadness, if you have any of that, you're far from being ready to have any love directed to a human being. For it is not the love of another that you are yet ready for, for the love of self, known as possession, as control, is still, *is still* the highest priority in your mind.

Now, we don't like to think about these things—a part of us doesn't—because most all of us have, surely, a plant or a little animal or another human being or children. So we don't like to think about those things. But to be forewarned is to be forearmed, if we make the effort. When you have a plant that doesn't do what you decide it should, and when you have a little pet, a little animal, and they don't do what you decide they should and you get upset and emotional, it's not the love that you have for the pet or the plant—it's the love that you have for yourself that's upsetting you. The animal may be just as happy as can be, doing what he wants to do when he wants to do it. That doesn't mean that there shouldn't be consideration for the animal. That doesn't mean that there shouldn't be some education, because the animal has a vehicle and within the vehicle is what is known as the ego. But whose ego are we making the effort to educate? Is it the little animal's ego that we are being tolerant with? Or is it our own?

So what does it really show? It shows the problems that we have in human relations. If we have people working for us and we find we have problems, have we looked inside ourselves to see where the problem really is? If we have a cat or a dog and they're not doing what we want them to do all the time, who has the problem? I think you'll find we're the ones that have the problem. Now, this is what life is all about when we open up our eyes and see what's really going on inside ourselves.

We all know that exposure frees the soul. It frees the soul if the exposure that we experience, something is done with it inside ourselves. If we permit our mind, with its multitudes of deceptions and devices, to discourage us, then, certainly, it's not helping us.

I found it very interesting today—and I'll bring this up as a point of lesson here in this class. For months I have listened to one of my students complain about the General Electric refrigerator that is at your church home. Now, there was never anything wrong with that refrigerator, except the vibrations that kept bombarding it. And for many, many months, many months, I had spoken to the directors of your church to make the effort to stop the negative thinking and complaining that was bombarding a very fine, expensive General Electric refrigerator. Sufficient effort was not made by my own students. And now, today, they have to pay the price of a serviceman to come in and correct the problem.

I always find it sad to see people waste—waste what they work so hard for. Knowing the law and having so many experiences, so very many demonstrations and yet waste hard-earned money. But then, we must look at the other side of the coin: When it costs enough, we start to wake up. Necessity, indeed, is the mother of invention. And so if it takes $30, $50 or $100 out of my students' pockets to pay a serviceman to come in and make some little adjustment, that is nothing but an effect of negative vibrations bombarding a piece of equipment, if that's the lesson that is needed and if they truly learn the lesson, then the $100 or $30 or $50—whatever it's going to be—is worth it. But if the lesson isn't learned, such a terrible waste.

To sit here or up at the house and to teach that all of life is vibration—how many times have my students viewed, and know beyond a shadow of any doubt, that if you have a harmonious, positive, accepting vibration, then things work well. It's taken a great deal of experience for many students to accept that their attitude can have an effect upon a piece of equipment. Some of my students here present have had so many experiences, so many lessons with that, they have finally accepted that demonstrable truth. But I have yet merited students who have yet to have more experience with negative attitudes to see how they affect physical objects.

And I will explain, once again, about equipment. The human mind emits, constantly, electromagnetic energy. That energy leaves our physical body invisible to our physical eyes and physical hearing. It has an effect upon equipment that operates under an electromagnetic field, whether it is an automobile, a piece of electronic equipment, or a refrigerator. When we express negative attitudes, there is an imbalance emitted from our minds, an imbalance between the electrical and magnetic field. This leaves our aura and bombards anything that is around us. Equipment that is very finely tuned is the first that is affected. Now that applies to radios, automobiles, television sets, refrigerators, and any other kind of equipment that you can think of.

One of the most interesting things to me was, many years ago, way back in—when I was living in Mill Valley—and one of my students was a computer operator at one of the big banks in San Francisco. And there were certain days in which all of this vastness of computers, he said, went emotional. And they would have to call in the servicemen and they would spend days looking it over and there was nothing wrong with it. And then, it would start working again. And it created, for the bank, a lot of problems. But whereas he was in charge of that computer department and whereas he was really very interested not only in computer technology, but in these emanations of the human mind, he began to make some effort in reference to the attitudes of the co-workers that were allowed to work with the computer equipment. And it was approximately a year later and several changes have been made with the employees and the bank had made the effort to see that the attitudes of the workers around those computers was peaceful and harmonious; they never had any more problems with those computers.

Now, when we get upset at how costly we find things are in our world, it's time to consider how much destruction we're doing. We're not doing it, I'm sure, vindictively. We're just expressing habit patterns that we know we've got to make some effort, some effort to change.

Now, one of my students said to me the other day that they didn't realize I was so human. And I guess they said that because of one of the classes you people had here a week or two ago, whenever it was. Well, I don't think I'm acting any differently than I've always acted, although I hope there's some growth. But I never did claim not to be human, because to do so would really put me in a terrible level of frustration, knowing how human I really am.

You see, it's been interesting to me over the years—and one of my other students revealed this to me a few years ago, when I was living in Corte Madera. As long as our minds can say to ourselves, "Well, things work for him because he's different. Therefore, he's not really human. Therefore, I don't have to make so much effort because he's not really human in the first place." [*Some students laugh.*] Now, I have had other students in the same type of thinking. You see, if we find someone human and things seem to be working for them, if we accept that they are as human as we are, then that simply means that we've got to make more effort. But if we can let our minds say, "Well, now that person's not quite human," and we want to remain human, then we don't have to make any effort, you see, no real effort at all.

But I am very human. But I also know, being human, that you can control the thoughts of your mind, that you can have whatever it is that you desire to have, that it is your right, if you're willing to demonstrate the natural laws through which it may flow into your life.

If you permit your mind to tell you how difficult and how hard it was to get what you got, then you can be rest assured, it's even going to be harder and more difficult to get what you yet desire. You see, if you work on your own mind, like I've been working on my mind, considering I have to—it's my responsibility to go down to that Civic Center for a deposition on your tax exemption. Now, I don't like that. I still don't like it, being human. I didn't like it when I first heard it from the attorney, but I went to work on myself. I said to myself, "You know, this is a wonderful opportunity for me to stand up for my religion and for the right of my religion and for my church and for me." So if you look at things—you see, you can always find the positive, no matter what the disaster seems to be.

Now, I know enough about the law that if I let myself entertain too long that I'm mad because I have to do something like that, then I will create, by my own mind, everything necessary to prove to me how right I was in the first place. That's what it's like being human. But you can make a change, as I'm making an effort to change and telling myself how great it's going to be and I'm really looking forward to it. I've almost got myself convinced! [*More students laugh.*] But I have to work at it. I mean, for any of my students to look and think that I'm not human and, therefore, not being human, I don't have to make any effort, of course, only reveals that they don't have to make any effort because they don't want to be inhuman. Now think about that.

I tell you there's a better way. But you are going to have to make the priority high on your own list. The problem is not outside. The problem is not your husband, your wife. The problem is not your workers. That's not where the problem exists. If you will only accept that it isn't outside. You see, if you can't accept personal responsibility, you're in the wrong philosophy, the wrong religion. If you really are making the effort each moment to accept personal responsibility, that whatever happens to you is caused by you—It's not your wife that did it. It's not your workers that did it. It isn't somebody out there that did it. You see, our minds are so programmed of putting the blame out there, you see. That's not where—that's not where you're going to find the cure. The cure does not exist out there.

Now, if you want some changes out there, make some changes in here. Because you can talk and you can do everything you want to, the changes are not going to take place out there until the change has taken place inside. You are only wasting your time, spinning your wheels trying to change people out there. They are not going to change until you change inside, for it is your attitude that is attracting and pulling those experiences to you. It's such a waste.

You see, money—and all these things—is an effect of directed energy. If you continue to spend your energy in trying to change somebody out there and you are not making the effort to change something in here—because that's where it really is—that out there is not going to change. That out there is not going to change.

When we first moved up on that, that hill there in Santa Venetia, there was a little problem of a clutter vibration from a little house down the road there. I knew—I didn't like it. I didn't like it at all. I don't like clutter. I never did like clutter. I try to work on it inside myself. And so I went to work on *me*. On my attitude. And after working on *myself*, I started to speak a few words and work out in the world. And I have lived there long enough to see the change. But first I go to work on myself. That's the only way you're going to get changes. First we've got to go to work on ourselves.

Now, I had to ask myself, when I saw all this terrible clutter, this pig vibration, I said to myself, "Now, I have merited looking at that. And I don't like it. Now, where in my life did I express this clutter vibration? Somewhere, somehow, I must have. Because if I hadn't, then that surely would not be coming to me." And so I looked over my life and I did recall that in that little room in Corte Madera—I wouldn't have called it the very neatest. It, to me, was very cluttered. And I justified its clutter because I had everything stacked in there because the place was so small. But it could have been a little bit more neat. Then I found another experience when I was eight years old and I used to throw my socks on the floor and always got hell for doing so.

So, you see, whatever it is that's outside, be rest assured it isn't going to change until we accept that it's somewhere inside and we have yet got to face it. Whether we like it or not, we are going to have to face it.

Now, most of us think, well, we're very neat. We've always been neat. We've never had any clutter. Has our thinking always been so neat? Have we never experienced frustration, which is clutter? Have we always had harmony and unity in our attitude, in our life or have we experienced clutter? You see, clutter doesn't mean somebody throwing beer cans or pop cans all over your yard. That's only one expression of clutter. But the principle of clutter is the principle of clutter. Do we wake up each morning and every thought that's coming through our mind, is it all harmoniously united with all our other thoughts and if we hear the sound, is it like a beautiful symphony? Or is it all garbled? Well, if it's all garbled, then we are certainly expressing clutter.

You see, my friends, it's a matter of our view. When you look at something, like clutter, you don't limit the principle of clutter to physical objects that you are viewing. You've got to go inside. You can say, "Now let me see, am I organized? Am I all united in my efforts? Am I always pleasing to my wife in the morning and say good morning and, and have breakfast or whatever my routine is? And am I always smiling and happy? Or am I in the depths of self-pity and filled with the clutter and the garbage of the mental realms?"

So let us think, let us think *inside* before we act outside. Let us go inside each day, every day and see if we are cluttered or clean. It's very simple. If our experiences are cluttered, then we know very well that our thoughts and our attitudes and our feelings are cluttered. And the beauty is that if we cannot see it spiritually, we guarantee to call it forth right into this old, physical, mundane world, until we make the effort to go in and clean up our act. Because only by cleaning up our act will our world become a beautiful plane.

Thank you.

MARCH 1, 1979

CONSCIOUSNESS CLASS 206

Good evening, class.

The benefit of any study of any class in any philosophy is its application in our daily activities. And so, as you'll recall, we had discussed a problem of negative vibrations on the refrigerator at the church office. And so we had the repairman come out to see what the problem was. Well after much time was spent in invest—[*A telephone makes the beeping sound indicating that it is not on the receiver.*] Pardon?

That's the telephone.

Oh. In investigating the situation, we found that it was the timer on the clock, known as the brain of the refrigerator—it's a General Electric—that was stuck between defrost and freeze. And I found it most interesting, because the refrigerator's an automatic defrost. You never have to defrost it. And the repairman said it's the first time he'd ever experienced where this mechanism was still working, but stuck between the defrost and the freeze mode. And he says it's just a frustrated timer.

Now, the revelation, of course, is ever the demonstration. And so it is that it's repaired now and it's working fine at a cost to our students and members, of course, of the church. But this philosophy reveals that the negative laws that we set into motion and the negative experiences that we have are the direct effect of our attitude, of our thoughts, of our emotions. Now, no one can free us from these negative attitudes that we alone, of course, are choosing to experience. No one can free us from them. But we can free ourselves from those negative and frustrated emotions and feelings.

Each day we have made a number of judgments in our life of how our days and how our jobs are going to be. We make decisions and we commit ourselves to those decisions until another desire passes through our mind. If we have made no effort to control our mind, then these various thoughts and desires passing through our mind, they control us. And so we establish these various laws.

We keep chasing the rainbow of success. We keep chasing this rainbow of fulfillment and we never catch it. The only reason that we don't catch it is because we don't stick to anything long enough for it to be successful. We often get to the door of victory and then we make the judgment that it's not going to happen anyway and we go off on some other tangent. And we do this to ourselves all the time. As the years pass by, we begin to experience frustration.

Now some time ago the spirit that gives these classes—many years ago—spoke about the frustrated 40's. But I don't think we have to be 40 to be frustrated. I know many people in their 50's and they're still frustrated. And I know people in their 20's and they're frustrated. What is frustration? What is it really, but a lack of effort on our part to work and fulfill the desires that we have. We have these multitude of desires in our mind and we keep chasing what we judge is the way to get them fulfilled, but while we're chasing one desire, another desire comes up and we leave the one that we were chasing to chase this new one. And this goes on day in and day out.

The Law of Continuity is indispensable to success. But to stay with the Law of Continuity, one has to open up the soul faculties, beginning, of course, with the first soul faculty. Because when you make the effort to be successful in anything, you have to pay the price and the price is the obstructions that you alone are creating in your lives.

How many times have I witnessed people wanting many things, but they never stay long enough with one thing for any of those things to really manifest in their lives. It reveals, of course, to us that we have not truly—not yet—accepted the Law of Personal Responsibility. When we feel frustrated, someone else is to blame. Whenever we feel frustrated, something's wrong outside. It has to be a person, a place, or a thing.

Had my students truly accepted that their minds, emanating negative vibrations, cause mechanical things to break down, we wouldn't have had the refrigerator breakdown, because there would have been different emanations around the refrigerator.

When we spend our time criticizing and complaining about things outside, we are far from finding out what is going on inside. Now, as we come to the ending of this semester, let us awaken a little more inside.

When the struggle is the greatest, it is said in this philosophy that victory is at hand. But when we find the struggle the greatest, how many of us think of that demonstrable truth? We are so concerned about the struggle that we cannot see the completion of what it is we're after in life. Surely, some effort is being made. That doesn't mean, however, that it is all the effort that we need to make.

Now, at the office, we have a pantry committee. And they have a responsibility to see that the system that was brought about by the Spirit Council, to see that that system is followed. We have seven members on that committee—one of the largest committees that we have. But we've had, especially recently, nothing but problems. Some of the items are completely out of stock. But why is this so with seven students—most of them members of the church—on that committee? What does it reveal? What do these things truly reveal? It's very simple: it reveals that the priorities, in reference to their spiritual duties and responsibilities, are in dire need of some type of adjustment.

Now, I have listened to the committee in reference to the problems that they seem to have. And the usual statement is that someone is not following the system. But no one has yet told me, that is, in the physical world, who that someone is. Therefore, the responsibility, the spiritual duty to see that the system flows harmoniously, as it is designed to do so, that duty is not being fulfilled. For if there were someone not following the system, then it is the responsibility, of course, of those who have accepted that responsibility to find out who that someone—or several someones—really is. Now, the mind, if you ask them, the mind rises up and says, "Well, I'm not here all the time. How can I know?" Well, I'm not everywhere all the time either, but with some effort we can know where the breakdown in any system really is.

We have to first go to work on ourselves. What is it that we have—do we feel that we have gained from these classes? That's a question, as these classes come to their conclusion, that is a question that all of us should be asking ourselves. Have we viewed any changes for the better in our life? If we have, then we must ask ourselves, "How did this come about? Have I made any changes in my attitude? Have I made any changes in my thinking? Or am I still going through my various emotional traumas and frustrations, going through my moods or have I really made some changes? And those changes, have they really brought me something that I feel is worthwhile for me?" If your answer is affirmative, then it's very simple: we make a little more effort on encouraging those changes inside of ourselves.

How many people present can honestly say that they have been able to free themselves for twenty-four hours from these frustrations and emotional negative moods, feelings of self-pity and rejection?

And speaking of rejection, there appears to be a growing interest in that level of consciousness—consider the demonstrations that I have been privileged to view these past couple of weeks. We all know if we don't make judgments, we can't experience rejections. And so we all have the answer to that terrible feeling of self-pity, known as rejection. All we have to do is put the brakes on judgment and then we won't have to feel so bad about ourselves.

Are we making the effort each day to tell ourselves what a beautiful world it really is? Are we making the effort to tell ourselves how very fortunate we are? Because if we're making that effort, then we can be rest assured that our days are becoming more beautiful, more successful, and more beneficial for us than ever before. But if we are still spending our days complaining and griping and frustrated and concerned about our great burden in life, concerned about our great struggle, concerned where our next slice of bread is going to come from, concerned about what everyone else is doing around us—because they're not doing anything right, of course, according to our judgment. I never did meet anyone that did everything the way that my mind of judgment said that they should. Well, if we're doing that, then we certainly do have a long row to hoe in life.

But if we have made some effort to really accept that it's all inside, and because it is all inside, we are encouraged to do something about it. We're no longer a defeatist. We're no longer a crybaby. We don't have to complain about the world and about our families and our relatives and our friends and our enemies. We no longer have that need, because we know and we have truly accepted that it's not out there.

Rejection seems to be one of the heaviest crosses that man has to bear. I don't know of anyone, including the animals, that enjoys the feeling of rejection. Now, we all know that animals make judgments. Humans make judgments. Because if an animal didn't make a judgment, then they wouldn't experience rejection. And we've all seen some animals, at times, that look as though they're ready for the other side of life. They've just about given up hope. They're so totally rejected because they have so much judgment.

Some time ago one of the students and members of this church used to say quite frequently that they were having a breakthrough. And each time that they said they were having a breakthrough, they were in the depths of forces and frustrations and rejection and everything that goes with it. And it was most interesting to me that if one must have all these feelings of rejection and frustration in order to get a breakthrough, sooner or later they're going to be totally worn-out.

Are we really viewing our life in the moment of the now? Are we really making that effort? Or are we still using the justification that, "Well, my mother didn't treat me right. My father didn't treat me right. And it's true, I'm filled with rejection because of the way that I was treated." Well, the only thing that type of thinking does is to push the weight of personal responsibility on to someone else. Whether it was your mother or your father, your uncle, your grandfather, your grandmother, or your fifth cousin, it doesn't make any difference. If you let your mind entertain that type of thinking—that the reason you are a rejected soul in life is because of your upbringing, totally, totally disregarding the truth that you merited the parents you had and have, that you merited the experiences, and if you really had grown through them, you wouldn't still be controlled by them. Now, anything that we have made effort to grow through, we are no longer controlled by, if we really have made the effort.

In this philosophy many, many are called. Very few, very few will choose to remain. Why will so few choose to remain? Because something beyond the self will have to have greater meaning, a greater priority, a greater value. We all face the crossroads: the choice between the limited self and what it has to offer—which we are all familiar with what it does have to offer—and that something greater, known as God. These crossroads, we don't face just once and say, "Well, I'm certainly glad I'm through with that." Because that type of thinking just sets the next one into motion. We face them, all of us, periodically. But you can be rest assured of one thing: if you stand firm, if your faith in God is truly strong, you don't have to worry about whether or not you'll stay on the path that your own soul has chosen.

Everything necessary will come to all of us. And it will, by our own choice, it will test us. That test, of course, being ourselves. We're tested in life by our own attachment to what we call self. We believe we are a certain way. And we believe that. And as we continue to grow, we, sooner or later, begin to find out we are not the way we thought that we were. We don't have as much tolerance as we thought we had. We don't have as much dedication to what we choose in life as we thought we had. We don't have as much loyalty as we thought we had. We don't have as infallible a memory as we thought we had. We don't have as much character as we thought we had. Because if we had all that we thought we had, then we would no longer be here, for there would be nothing to grow to. We would already be these angels far off in another dimension.

So we're all growing. But what the philosophy offers to you is the demonstrable laws of life that through your effort to apply those laws, you may grow more harmoniously, that you may no longer have this need for rejection, no longer have this great need for retaliation, no longer have these feelings of revenge. Because you know that it's all inside, that it's what you're thinking that brings about the joy of life. It's your effort to discipline your own mind.

You see, our emotional body is not very old yet. We can tell that very simply when we become the victim, by our own laws, of course, of another's mind that judges we are an obstruction to their desire. Then we can view, if we remain objective, we can view very clearly the little boy or the little girl that's running around inside filled with emotion and frustration because she or he didn't get their way. Now, how many times a day do we go through our work feeling that way? How many times a day do we blame outside for what we're doing inside? Year after year after year.

We know that repetition is the law through which change is made possible. It doesn't say that repetition makes the change. It says that repetition is the law through which change is made possible.

Now, many of my students in the past have mentioned, whenever there is semester break, how happy they will be when class starts again. And each student has always said the same thing: "Well, when the people are in class, they seem to be a lot better." Now, what do they mean by that? I think, perhaps, what they mean is that because once a week they're constantly reminded of what they're doing to themselves that a little bit of effort gets made to make a few changes. Well, my friends, it certainly is past time to move into the spirit of application: to apply the multitude of beautiful truths that you have already received.

Ofttimes, you know, a student will make the judgment that, "That other student has been around long enough, they should know better." I agree that they know better. Oh yes, we all know better. I don't agree that they are always able to do better. Because the thinking is something—our thoughts are something that we really are not making sufficient effort to become aware of what they are. Now, the changes can't come for us until we truly start to become aware of what type of thoughts are passing through our mind.

Now, I've been sitting here this evening for about half an hour speaking with you and I have been watching, with increasing interest, a few of my students who are taking this discussion very personal: taking the discussion about the refrigerator very personal and about rejection very personal. And that serves a very good purpose, if, in taking this discussion personal, they don't take it in personality. Because if they do, they're destined to retaliate.

Now we—most of us—have witnessed how these retaliations work. Because, you see, whatever was done—taken in personality, guarantees, absolutely guarantees retaliation. Therefore, having those experiences, we know where to begin to free ourselves. We know that we will have to make the effort to learn the difference between personality and principle. And there is indeed a vast difference. When we find ourselves attached to our fruits of action, then we can be rest assured we are in personality. When we do what we have to do and are freed from the fear of what the results may be, then we know we're moving in the realm of principle.

We have discussed in this philosophy how often we sell out. We only sell out when we're in personality when we're controlled by the fear of our own mind. When we accept that there is a supreme, higher, greater Intelligence than our limited mind, when we truly accept that, we will never again experience selling out for anything. Because what do we have to sell out for, when the greatest thing we'll ever find we have already accepted? So there is nothing that can tempt us.

Even the Lord's Prayer clearly states, "Lord," meaning the law, "lead us not into temptation." You see, my friends, you can never sell out if you are never tempted. It's when we're tempted that we sell out principle, because each time we're tempted, we're controlled by fear. Now think about that. If you have no fear, you'll have no temptation. Now a person says, "Well, I've been tempted many times. I didn't experience fear." Because you were blinded by the temptation, which is controlled by fear. You see, you cannot be tempted when you accept God. There is nothing to tempt you, there is nothing to control you, for there is no fear. Now it's really quite simple. But if you allow yourself to be tempted that perhaps something over there is better—"Perhaps if I do this, I will get that,"—that's all temptation, my friends, dictating that by doing this, you will get that; by not doing that, you will have this. That is all temptation. That's all mental control. That's all fear.

How does man free himself from all of that? By freeing himself from attachment. Remember, before there can be attachment, there has to be temptation. You cannot be attached to anything that you have not been tempted to. Attachment is the fulfillment of temptation.

But when you accept God, you have accepted everything and, therefore, are tempted by nothing.

How do we know how much control temptation has over our mind? Well, we look at our jobs in life, we look at what we do and how we feel and we say, "Well, when I make a decision to do something, do I do it? Do I spend my life or my days in procrastination, putting things off? Do I complete the jobs that I begin? Or do I leave them all unfinished?" If you find in your life that you start many things and finish few, if any, if you find in your life that you have difficulty with the Law of Continuity, if you find in your life that you have difficulty with commitments, if you find in your life that you have many broken promises, then you can be rest assured that you are filled with temptation. If you find that you have any emotion on losing anything, then you know how much you are controlled by temptation.

And so each of us has at our disposal, at any moment that we choose, this wonderful, beautiful awareness to see where our struggles in life are, what is the cause of them, and how to cure them. There's no question about that. The question is, Do we want to cure them? Do we want to really be freed from temptation? Do we really want to be freed from attachment? Part of us says, "Well, no, what would life be if I wasn't tempted? How would I feel if I was no longer attached to anyone or anything?" The times when we want to be freed from temptation is when the payment of temptation rises up in our conscious awareness. Then we see this mountain of struggles that we're trying to get through and all of a sudden we want to be freed from the payment that we alone have set into motion.

Now it's nice to be freed from that, but how long will we stay free from that when it is temptation itself that is tempting us to be freed from it? Now think about that! Because if it was anything but temptation itself that is wanting us to be freed from it, then we would stop and say, "Just a moment. I know how I got here at this titanic struggle in front of me. I know exactly what I did." Because we all know what we do. We really do know. You see, that's one thing in Serenity, if you stick around, you can no longer use, "Well, I just didn't think about that." You thought about it very well. And if you're honest with yourself, you'll see just exactly how long you really did think about it. Sometimes all night long before you did it.

Now, let's be honest with ourselves. I remember years ago a beautiful hymn came from the spirit world, dedicated to one of my students. And I'll never forget that wonderful line that says, "Honesty, honesty will lead us through." Because that's the only thing that's going to lead us any place worthwhile. To be honest with ourselves.

Now, we know that to encourage the little effort that we're making—and to some of us, I know, it seems like a great deal of effort. And, of course, it is, considering we've gone so many years making practically none at all. So, for us, it is a great effort, because we just got started. And, like anything, if you go to learn to ski or skate or anything, in the early years there's a—takes a lot of time and energy and effort. And you're working with something that's eternal. It's not as though you're learning a new trade or something. You could mark out X number of years and then you've got it. At least that's the way the mind works. But you're working with something that's eternal: you're working with your own soul.

Ask yourself why you need to feel rejected. Ask yourself why you feel you must retaliate. Ask yourself those questions.

To some, the philosophy and the discipline in this church are too much for them to bear. And, fortunately, there are many churches where they may go. But if the discipline is not enforced within the church, then the philosophy is but hypocrisy. Because without discipline, you cannot apply the philosophy that is offered by the Serenity Church. It is not possible.

There are no shortcuts. There are no shortcuts that we have found to God and to freedom. The reason there are no shortcuts is because man's mind has created so many detours for his little soul, so many different side trips we make for ourselves. You see, it's not what we have to learn in life that's going to free us; it's what we have to unlearn in life that's going to free us. All of these judgments that we've made about what life is really about, those are the things we have to give up that we may find, in this moment of the now, the happiness and joy that life has to offer.

I always find it most encouraging when any of my students, when I say, "Well how are you today?" and they say, "Well, I'm just fine. Just beautiful." I know it doesn't happen often, but it certainly would be so beneficial. You see, I know it's more difficult to say how great life is when you're in one of your moods, but if you would make the effort to say how good life is, and make just an ounce of effort when you're in those self-pity levels of consciousness, then you'll start stepping up; you'll start climbing up out of that little dungeon down there. But you have to make that effort. Your mouth has to speak forth the words, not someone else's.

And certainly, it certainly does take a little effort when you're mad at someone outside because the way you feel inside. It takes a little bit of effort to say how great life really is. But I assure you each time you declare that truth with the spoken word you step one step up on the ladder to heavenly heights. Now stop and think about that. You not only help yourself up, you help everyone that's within the sound of your voice up. Now that's just the way that it really is. And what a little, small amount of effort, really, that it takes to say good morning and to tell someone how beautiful the world is. What a small amount of energy that takes, considering how much good is accomplished by it.

Now, I don't know—I'm very human—but my students should know: Do you find it, usually, my pattern to say what a lousy world it is and what a tough struggle I'm having? Well, I certainly want to be reminded. And I would be very grateful if anyone finds that to be a pattern of mine. I don't want it to be because I know where it leads.

Now, no matter how you think you feel, you have a responsibility and a spiritual duty, not only to yourself, but to whoever hears you, about how great this world and life really is. Let's make a concerted effort, before our final class of this semester, let's make a concerted effort in this student body to tell, first ourselves—because you cannot tell another what you are not first telling yourself—to tell first ourselves and then another how great life really is. And when you can say how great life really is after you've had a little exposure, after you've been corrected for some of your shenanigans, then you've really made a step up.

You know, it's just like with the dinners here or the brunches or anything else. If we find that we haven't followed the simple rules and regulations and we haven't made whatever it is that we have chosen to make the way that the policy has been established by our church, if we find ourselves all emotional because somebody exposed it to us and somebody corrected us, we should be grateful because to the degree of emotion that we express shows how attached we are to our fruits of action, you see. It shows us up front who we did it for. Well, did we bake the pie for, for God, for a church or did we bake it for ourselves? Now, if we baked it for ourselves and somebody corrected us and said we forgot a certain ingredient or we didn't do it the way it was supposed to be done, if we did it for ourselves, for our mind—not our soul, for our mind—then we'll be all emotional and all upset.

And it's so interesting to me, although none of my students spoke to me directly about it, but some of my students were very upset because, you see, the refrigerator went out—and we all now know the reason why it went out: the brains were stuck between freeze and defrost. That's why it went out. Of course, it took a few weeks of working on it, I'm sure, to get it done. But some of my students were upset. I had left orders that whereas the freezer had defrosted and the frozen bacon, Sizzlean, that was in there and any other meat was to be thrown in the garbage. Because any time you freeze meat and it thaws out and you re-freeze it, you're asking for a fine health problem to try to eat it. But evidently some of my students are not aware of that simple health policy. And so they were more than upset, it seems—because it didn't come to me direct—more than upset because the meat that was frozen and had defrosted and now re-frozen was thrown out.

You know, let us use a little bit of common sense. Would you rather spend $200 or more for a doctor to help straighten out your health from poisoning or save $2 worth of bacon? Now, which is the most practical? And I want all my students to think about that. I believe in being practical. And surely none of us are going to go hungry if we throw out spoiled meat.

Where the attention should have been directed is on the frustrated brains that caused the refrigerator to get a frustrated brain and not work properly in the first place. Now that's what's important. It seems that we've had quite a discussion on this refrigerator, but you have to understand how much frustration there has been from the minds of some of my students to cause it to happen in the first place.

So anyway, my friends, whatever your jobs in life are, if you're not happy with them, be rest assured you're going to stay with them a long time. Because it's your own attachment to that level inside of you that brings you the beauty and the glorious lessons that you have yet to learn.

So we can take our frustrations from one thing to another, if that's what we choose to do. But be rest assured, you cannot go away from home to get home. Whatever you have now, you know what you've got. It's all inside of you and you can change it around and you can add some new things and, hopefully, move out some of the things that are in that little house of yours. Give it a spring house cleaning and start anew. Now, you can do that if you're ready. If you're not ready, hopefully, next spring in 1980 the lessons that you have heard spoken so many times, you will choose to apply. And if not in 1980, perhaps '81 or '82 or when you reach the twenty-first century. Because there's always hope, you see. There's always hope.

Some people, you know, they've asked me over these years, well, how can I tolerate this one or that one? Well, I first have to take a look at the level that the one I'm supposed to have difficulty tolerating—I have to look at that level inside of me. That's where I start. When I see someone filled with self-pity and all of these little games of the mind and these retaliations and these rejections, I stop. And I think. Now, it's hard for me to find that level sometimes. I have to look very deep, you know. But I always find it. I can find it. And when I find it, I say, "Oh, that poor thing. Yes, I remember that." Well, we'll have to be a little more compassionate with that person. We'll have to be a little more strict with them because they're going off on another one of their bulling spells. Because that's what my mother always called those frustration moods. She always called them bulling spells.

And so the ladies of the church, they should not feel alone with those cyclic [*pronounced si-klik*] or cyclic [*pronounced sī-klik*] patterns, because the men of this church, they demonstrate it quite well. Not on a monthly basis, it seems. It seems more spasmodic. But they do seem to have those bulling spells. And, of course, we all know they're only the expression of all that frustration, all those pent up judgments and desires and all those obstructions that they're creating inside their mind.

And especially, you know, here in the springtime, these feelings of self-pity are rising because the mind likes to think, "Well, you know, if only I was retired." In fact, I know how they feel because I had the thought just yesterday, I thought, "Well . . ."—I don't get to retire very long. It never goes past a day, I can assure you of that. But I do understand what that feeling is like, you know, to kind of lay around and bask in the sun, you know. And I suppose some of my students think there I am up at that house and it's spring time and I'm probably up there laying on the deck. Well, it's very rare. And if I'm out there, I'm either editing out a movie for the students or something else, you can be rest assured of that. And if you ever try editing out the commercials out of a movie on television, you're up every five minutes. Be very sure of that. Just when you're getting comfortable, the commercial comes on and you got to run inside and edit it out.

So if the spring fever has got control of you, it will pass. It will pass. Just like when you were in your teens, you know, those levels, they come and, and they go. So don't worry about your time off and your retirements and your vacations because all of those things, they come and by the very Law of Coming, they also pass.

It's been a very fine semester. I know we have one more class. I do have the request for the students—from the students who have requested private classes. I do want all of you to know they're all being considered, the ones that have been submitted. And I'm sure you all realize and understand that in keeping with the policies of the church that those who are active within the church and members and friends of the church will all be considered. But the classes are being restricted to nine students at a time. So when you're informed when your private class is coming up and seems to be, perhaps, a year or two away, do not be discouraged. Because I can assure you that nine students in class, in private class, is a full house. Because when I have private classes, I work with those students seven days a week and that's a full house. If you don't think so, just become a little bit more aware of some of the levels that some of my students seem to be in quite frequently and then you'll understand.

When it was said, years ago, that when we harbor a thought, we are feeding a form—we must be aware that these forms, they're around and about us all the time. So like we've said many times, let's make them more angelic. I never, ever met an emotional angel. Now, if you have, please let me know what it's like, because I never met one that was emotional. I never met one that was filled with sentimental soup. And sometimes I thought perhaps, you know, their faculty of reason was rather like the north pole—a bit cool. But that's just the way that I've found it to be. It doesn't mean they don't have compassion. It does mean that they're not controlled by the fluctuating thoughts of the mind and higher than a kite one day and lower than you know what the next day. No, I never met that kind of an angel.

So remember that the spring fever, like the hay fever, it will pass. And it's only been a week of spring; so as time goes on,

I'm sure you'll all be feeling a lot better. I thank you very much. Thank you.

MARCH 8, 1979

CONSCIOUSNESS CLASS 207

Good evening, class.

Now, in keeping with the basic teachings of this philosophy of personal responsibility and especially that the demonstration in life is the revelation, we'll discuss the events of the moment.

Now, as most of you are aware, considering it's your church, whenever there is any destruction, it is always, of course, at the cost of the membership and the friends and supporters of the church. But destruction of anything, especially other people's property, is a revelation always of a retaliation. Now, we can't have retaliation unless we first have a feeling of rejection. And we can't have a feeling of rejection unless we first make a judgment. And we can't make a judgment unless we're first in what is known as self. So we find that the heaviest cross that we have to bear in life is the cross of self.

Whenever we entertain self-thoughts, self-desires, we're limited by what our computer, our mind, has already recorded in it. Therefore, we are blinded by our desires.

And so today, after spending over 1200 and some dollars for a new slipper cabinet, one of the doors was damaged by one of the members of our church. Now, I spoke to the member and asked him if they were able to trace, by their own efforts, the reason for this destruction. They have not yet been able to trace that, they tell me.

So we have to take a look at these things objectively. We all know the simple principle of personal responsibility. And unless, of course, we make the effort to accept that principle—the ability to respond to our own thoughts intelligently with the light of reason.

We find in this world, just with this small group, we find these feelings of rejection, these needs of retaliation and revenge because we find that our minds are running wild with our own judgments. What does that reveal to us? We know that we are trying, to some degree anyway, to take control of our mind, our thoughts, and our attitudes. We've been going along fairly well, considering, with this destruction vibration. It isn't a matter of a physical object being destroyed. The physical object represents the effort and the energy of the people who bought it in the first place. If we're in consideration, in the faculty of consideration, we think about these things before we retaliate.

Now, I have found in life that any of these experiences, no matter how small they seem to be, whether it's a refrigerator or it's a cabinet or it's a shovel or anything else, if you will pause, you can trace the level of consciousness that you were in at the time that you did the destruction. It is, in a way, sad to see people working so hard to get ahead in life, to try to have nice things, to enjoy this beautiful world and yet be a house divided within themselves and to be so destructive within. For this destruction without only reveals a level of consciousness that is destructive within.

You see, they say that man is known by the company that he keeps. Well, man is very well known by the care he shows of all of the things that are within his realm to care for. If we do not care inside, if we have not opened up yet the faculty of care, then we cannot care outside. We cannot care for another if we do not care for ourselves. For we cannot grant unto another what we have not first granted to ourselves.

Now, what level of consciousness is it that expresses a lack of the faculty of care? You cannot express the faculty of care unless you are expressing the faculty of consideration. Now, when our consideration is limited to the functions of our mind, then we find that there is no consideration for anything outside of our mind that we are not directing our attention to. It's really, really that simple. So we see an imbalance within the human mind: an imbalance between the functions of the mind and the faculties of our soul.

This imbalance that we are experiencing from the things we destroy from lack of consideration, from lack of care, from our judgments, our feelings of rejection and our retaliation, is not something that we have acquired in just a few, short years. A little child—the soul enters this earth realm with many lessons to go through. And its little mind registers a multitude of needs in order that it may gain the attention that it judges it should have. And so we find that people who have a pattern of destroying things from the lack of care are people who indeed are suffering within, suffering very deeply because their world is very small. And it is so small and shrinks constantly from all these judgments and all these needs that the time comes their soul cries out to be freed from the prison that they have put themselves in.

This is what we are viewing. A physical object is easily replaceable. And all physical objects, all things in the material world, they come and they go. But it's what is behind these effects: the levels of consciousness, the levels of rejection, the levels of retaliation, the need of the human ego, the phenomenal need to have to destroy, to retaliate. Until the effort is made on our own part to free ourselves from this constant, constant programming of judgment, until the effort is made daily to awaken within, we will continue on in our blind needs and blind desires.

When we speak to people, do we really have an ounce of consideration for their feelings? Or are we so grounded in self-desire that we can see nothing but the great drive to fulfill our own selfish desires? What is it within us that has no consideration for other people's feelings, for their attitudes, and for their levels of consciousness? We must look within ourselves to find that answer. For no man is an island, no matter what he may think. No one can exist in the universe without the whole. Now, when we accept that truth, when we really accept that, then we will start on the path to free ourselves from this realm of constant judgment, from this viewing the world and everything in it from a selfish vantage point.

I have always said, and I continue to say, never leave a soul worse than you have found them. If you care enough to help a soul up, then you care enough to see that they stay up, in keeping with the Law of Responsibility that you have set into motion. All of my students know that I am available to help them to help themselves as long as they choose to remain in the organization. If they choose to go, I let them go as freely as they come. But I do not spend my time and my effort with those who have out grown us, for to do so would be contrary to the responsibility that I have incurred to the members and the friends of the organization who are working to keep it afloat.

It is, however—that is, I permit it to be at times—sad to see the efforts of people be so carelessly treated. It isn't a matter of money. It is what money represents. Money is an effect of directed energy. That's all that money really is. And I am concerned and interested in the energy that is being directed and wasted. So each time something is destroyed, it isn't a matter that that costs you X number of dollars. It is a matter that the destroyer, at least at that moment, had greater value for their judgments, for their feelings of rejection, retaliation, and destruction than they had for all of the energy and effort of the students and members who work so hard to keep the ship of Serenity afloat. That is what I am interested in: the cause behind the destruction and why the student is not making more effort to consider his own coworkers. That's indeed very important to me.

Now, I am aware of the cause of today's destruction. I'm very much aware of it. I am aware of the feelings entertained, although the person, the destroyer, has not discussed it with me. I am aware of these feelings of rejection. And they can be traced to a lack of consideration on the part of another.

I'm here to reveal to you what the ego (uneducated) has to offer. For nothing goes out from our universe in life that doesn't return to us a thousand fold. And the day always comes for all of us when we wonder what's happened. Why do we struggle so much? Why do things collapse? And why does it fall through our fingers, the things we desire in life, just like the sands of time? Because we have no consideration for another. Because we are so filled with considering our limited self, we must pay the price that sooner or later we will awaken to consider a broader universe, a greater horizon than the limited, fluctuating desires of our human mind.

Without organization, without tolerance, without some degree of opening of the soul faculties, there is no success in life, there is no positive success.

I have taught for many years when you awaken in the morning to put your house in order before confusion sets in. But if we don't make that effort, then we find ourselves in a state of confusion. We have no plan. We don't know what we're going to do tomorrow, for we have no plan. We are controlled by the fluctuating desires of our own mind. Now, we can justify, well, we have no plan because everything has to wait until the last minute to see how it's all going to work out. Well, that's a wonderful justification, if we don't want to make any effort.

You see, your church has programs printed two months in advance. Now, I could use the same justification and say, "Well, I'm not so sure if that person's going to be available to work on the podium two months or two and a half months from this day." But that's not how your church operates. Your church establishes the law and makes every effort to fulfill the very law that it establishes. It does not permit itself to be the victim of the fluctuating desires of the human mind of the people who compose it.

Now, to some people new to the church, they feel that that's very strict, that the discipline is indeed strict. The discipline is as strict as we are in our license. So if we see the discipline very strict, then it's very easy to view the license that we have already spent are lives in. Without discipline, there is no control. Without control, there is no freedom. There never will be any freedom until the effort is made by all of us to control this little, wild, so-called self that has us right by the tail.

The law is very clear: if we do not consider another, we shall not be considered by another. And when our need is the greatest, and when we truly have need for consideration, we will find that none exists. For we have made no effort, no effort whatsoever, to have compassion for the feelings of rejection and the hurt feelings of other people. And be rest assured, these beautiful, infallible laws are totally impartial. Whatever goes out, it returns, until our struggle becomes so great that we really do pause to think.

And so if you find difficulty in your business, if you find that things are not harmonious, if you find that there is no unity and that others do not consider the responsibilities that you have and that the burden is all on your shoulders, you can be rest assured, that's the way you made it. No one else did it. And when your need is the greatest, because you did not consider others, you will find there will be no others to consider you. And you will stand there with all of the laws that you have set into motion, all these beautiful laws of self, they'll be there in those moments to haunt you.

Now, in concluding this wonderful semester—and it has been a good semester. I believe it has. I believe that it is. I don't know when another public semester will come about, but the requests for private classes have all been considered. And each person will be informed when their class, their private class, will come about. I believe some of my students present are not aware that one of the requirements—and it has been a requirement for many years of this church—one of the requirements for private class is that they be an active, an *active* member of the Association. The reason for this is quite simple: that if it means enough to be affiliated with, then it certainly should mean enough to have private classes when they are available. I do not know if public classes will—another semester—will be open. That is not my decision to make. But as soon as I am informed, I will certainly let those who are interested know.

Now, for those of you who are not used to exposure, this is how we grow. You can't grow through anything you can't face. It is not a matter of personality, but when a new person [is] exposed to this type of teaching and the way that it works, the first thing are feelings of, of fear. Now, we have these feelings of fear because, "If it happens to one, it just possibly may happen to me someday." And that's what we fear. We don't fear the truth in that sense. We fear what we consider is embarrassment. Totally disregarding that embarrassment is an attachment to a level of consciousness that we are unwilling, at present, to change.

In our lives, we all have different patterns. Now, this must be most interesting for anyone to experience. I myself have not had the blessing, or the curse, whichever one may view it, as getting up, preparing myself for work, and never knowing what moment or what day I will not be working. So it is a wonderful opportunity, you see, for anyone who has merited that type of experience to go to work on the wonderful Law of Change. Never knowing from day to day, never knowing when you go to bed at night whether or not you will be working in the morning, even though you have a job.

Now, I don't know how many people here—students here in this church and members—have that wonderful, golden opportunity to face that trauma every morning when they awaken and every evening when they go to bed. But I would like you to take a few moments to consider your job—the jobs that you have—and to consider what it must be like to go to bed at night and never know when you call in, in the morning, whether you will be working that day. Because I am sure, although the party in question has merited the experience, for that's the way the demonstrable law really works. But if we're going to have consideration for others, then we must take a moment to try to place ourselves in that level of consciousness that we may see what our emotions do to us with that constant fear.

Now, we may ask ourselves, "How is it a constant fear?" If you work on a job and you don't know from day to day whether you're going to work the next day and that when you check in, that's when you know—fear is the mind's control over the eternal soul. Now, what I'm trying to bring about here—a spiritual lesson. You see, you can discuss this philosophy until you know what freezes over, but if you don't apply it to what you're doing this minute, it can have absolutely no effect and no benefit to you at all. You see, I'm a firm believer in being down here to earth. Let your head be in the clouds if you want, but keep your feet on terra firma—feet representing your understanding.

So, you see, with these situations, because it is costing you, the body of the church, money, therefore it is brought up as a discussion for the revelation. Now, this is not the only thing that we have to discuss. We also had a friend of the church burn the Congoleum last week with a cigarette. And, of course, now we've not only bought seven new ash trays, but we have new regulations governing smoking. You see, it isn't a matter of just the destruction: we must find the cause behind the destruction. No matter how great the destruction is, no matter how minor the destruction is, we must find the level of consciousness that caused it in the first place. Because if we don't find the cause, we will never have a cure.

And so we are discussing destruction, the effect of retaliation; retaliation, the effect of rejection; rejection, the effect of judgment, so that we can all see what we're doing to ourselves. Now, if we don't have any experience in the present to relate this teaching to, then how are we going to make the impact upon our mind sufficient to bring about necessary changes within us?

Now, we take a look at the philosophy and the teachings and we often see, as one of my students said just the other night, they see how clearly it works—these laws—in the negative, but they would like to be encouraged to see how they work in the positive. Well, all we have to do is get positive and we'll have all the experiences that are necessary. If we can only see the laws working in the negative, it simply reveals that's our vantage point. That's the level we're looking from. We can't see the positive level until we get positive inside of ourselves.

Now, whenever there is, what we call in this philosophy, an ounce of exposure, whoever is experiencing the exposure, the degree of their emotional upset reveals the extent that they are locked in what is known as the self-computer.

In reference to the burn on the Congoleum, which, fortunately, was repaired, the person, who is not a student of this Association, but is a friend of one of our members—he comes to the house a couple of times a month—when I simply said, "Well, what happened?" he got extremely defensive, extremely emotional. We must, for our own enlightenment and our own benefit, take a look at what's behind all of these experiences and all of these effects.

The door on that beautiful slipper cabinet did not get destroyed by accident. For we know and, by accepting the Law of Personal Responsibility, that there are no accidents.

Now, isn't it interesting to see what's behind a little, dented door? And we're not finished yet! We're far from finished.

You see, why do we think, honestly, that people have problems with communication? What is it within us, we must ask ourselves, that creates this great lack of communication amongst people? I guess maybe I talk a lot, but that's one thing I have never had a problem with, is communication. I believe in speaking, in speaking forth how I feel and what I think. I do try to consider the feelings of others. Because I know to leave a soul worse than you find them is a very great payment.

Now, think, my friends. If we hadn't had a damaged door, we wouldn't have had such a beautiful class. And we're not finished yet.

I am a firm believer in that wonderful teaching that exposure frees the soul. Exposure frees the soul. In fact, you see, it is the very basis of the philosophy: to be honest with oneself and to communicate. That's the whole purpose of the organization. You see, you find people walking around like time bombs waiting to explode. They just need the right trigger to erupt like Mount Vesuvius. Because, you see, there are so many judgments, there are so many images that they are working so hard to keep up that there is not the effort made at honest communication.

I don't know of anyone, *anyone* within the sound of my voice that appreciates being informed the last minute. But if we have merited that type of an experience, we must ask ourselves the question, number one: Is this a demonstration of inconsideration? The answer, of course, must return to us, "Why, yes. That person's very inconsiderate. They are so locked in self they can't even have the courtesy or the common decency to inform me the night before, if they know." Then, we must say to ourselves, "Have I ever in my life been inconsiderate? Have I demonstrated the law and are these chickens that I have created returning to me through this particular person?" And the answer must return to us, yes! We have spent energy, directed through attention, to being inconsiderate of others.

Now, when we are inconsiderate of others, we never consider that someday, when our need is the greatest, others will be inconsiderate of us. But the law is infallible. This is the beauty of God's natural, divine laws. They are infallible. You can rely upon them. Whatever your experience, it is an effect of a law that you and you alone have set into motion. Now, you can change that law by making a little effort, just a little effort, through the Law of Continuity. You can establish new laws in your life that you don't experience inconsideration, that you become more considerate of others, that in your times of need they will be more considerate of you. For the day is guaranteed when we will find that we are in need of consideration.

You see, the law doesn't just work from one person to the other. The law may come back through someone that you never dreamed would ever be in your life. The law is totally impartial and it always returns to us, for it is the infallible laws of God. And when our need is the greatest, we will not find what we are looking for, for we did not consider others along the way.

Consideration is a soul faculty. It is inseparable from the faculty of care. And when we care enough, the change for the better is absolutely guaranteed.

How often do we think of the feelings of another? We do not think of how another feels if we are so considerate, constantly, of how we feel, for there's no room for anyone else to enter our universe. For we are so considerate of self, no one else can get in. There's certainly a better way. We all know that we are an inseparable part of the whole. Why try to be an island of glory by ourselves? It's only a false bubble that's going to burst someday. That's all that it is.

And so we see here, from this little, small experience of the day—just like the refrigerator and the brain that went into frustration. So beautiful. Now it's just working fine.

No matter what your experiences are, remember, there is good in them. For the divine Intelligent Energy, known as God, sustains all experience. So it's the good or the God in the experience we want to look for.

And from this evening's class, if it has helped but one soul to make one ounce of effort to consider something and someone beside themselves, then it has served its purpose. May it be in divine order that the faculty of consideration and the faculty of care may open even wider in our universe that we may think of someone and something besides the constant needs of the limited self.

Now, from this class, one of two things happens within the minds: either the feeling of rejection, from the exposure, causes further retaliation or they take the class and the lesson that is there and make the effort to be free from those levels of consciousness.

You see, friends, we now know the only reason we ever sell out principle. We know, all of us know principle, but we know now why we sell out. First, we make a judgment and fear rises. But first the judgment must be made! That's how we sell out principle and break the back of character. Do you understand?

You know, it's just like our experience in reference to our going to court for our tax exemption for church property. We could have allowed fear to reign supreme and not gone to all the effort—which we're still going to—and all of the costs of going to court to stand up for what we believe is right. It is not important whether or not we're granted the exemption. It is important that we stand up for our right to it. This is what we must see in life. Certainly, we would like to have our exemption, as any other church has, but what is really important is that we stand up for our right to it.

And it's so important when we know in our heart—our soul speaks through our heart—we know what's right. But if we don't stand up for what's right, the day will come when we'll be blinded by what we really know is wrong. There's always a price to pay to stand up for what is right. But if you stand up for that principle of right because it is right to do right—and many things in creation will come or go, but that principle is an eternal principle. It will be with you forever and ever and ever. Without effort to stand up for that which you know in your heart is right, the day will come that you will become aware of the bondage created by the fear of a limited mind.

So, my friends, in completing this class—and it's so beautiful. Some of my students are in various levels of consciousness in the pity and the hurt and etc. But stop and think! If you hadn't destroyed church property, you wouldn't have had this wonderful class! Your business became the church business when it affected the church. Now, I have always said that to the members and friends of the church. The church is very liberal. It's very outspoken. It's very open. Your private business is your private business until you make it public and a part of your church. Once you establish the law that has an effect detrimental upon your church, it becomes church business. Otherwise, it's your business because you keep it personal. Now, if it wasn't that way, you see, your church could not long endure.

It is only right and just that those who support the organization know what's doing—what's happening with the effort that they are making. And so you have a fine piece of church property. The work of the church is being done. You have your bake sales, your dinners, your brunches, etc., etc., etc. And you are a part of the church. It should always be your interest, always be your interest what happens to what you're working for.

I feel my responsibility very deeply. Never is a burden heavier than the love of God. But if there's a shovel missing, it's my responsibility to find out where it is, because you people paid for that shovel. And if something is destroyed, it's my responsibility to find out why it's destroyed, because you people pay to repair it. Now that, to me, is part of the responsibility of being a president and a pastor of the church. Surely, it would be much easier just to tuck it under the carpet and then someday you, as members, friends, and supporters of the church, start wondering,

"Why is this church costing us so much money? What are they doing with all that money?" I would rather show you what's happening to it right along the way. If it costs so much because somebody burns the Congoleum, well, it costs so much. You see, I believe in keeping our books right up to snuff. Every year you take a look and you see where every single penny goes.

I believe when people make an effort to purchase something in life that that effort deserves the consideration and care for what it represents. A cabinet, to me, is not just a cabinet. It is the effect of people's hard work. That they go out into this human jungle and they work and they earn money and when they spend it in this church, I want to see that it is cared for and that it is considered. And whenever there is an experience from any member or student or friend of the church where there is destruction, I take a look at all of the people who donated to get the object in the first place. And the effort has to be made to expose the level, because no one wants to spend their life working so hard and ending up with nothing.

You know, it seems to be contrary to our philosophy to say that a person can work so hard in life and end up with nothing. But it's not contrary at all. We ofttimes work very hard and we end up with nothing because we spent so much along the way. You see, we paid for all our lack of effort to communicate. We paid for all our considerations. We paid for all our lack of care. Those things, those functions they're very, very costly. Very costly.

So, in truth, we work hard and if we don't have something to show for it, then we've got to take a look at the path and see where we wasted it all.

And as long as I'm president and pastor, I will not sit by and see people working so hard to keep this beautiful church together and keep it sailing on a serene sea and let anyone, because of levels of consciousness of rejection and hurt feelings and lack of communication, let anyone be so inconsiderate of their efforts.

Whatever you people have worked to attain for your church is very well considered by the Council of your church. And whatever I see at that house or in this church, what I see is what's behind it: the people who sincerely worked on a job and donated their funds to this organization. The least we can do, as members and friends, is to care for it.

If we don't care for the things in our personal life, we're going to have to make the effort to care for the things that are in the life of our church. Because, you see, we're not the only ones that are out working to try to get ahead, to try to move our church onward.

The faculty of quality has always been a very important faculty in this church. Let us have value for that faculty of quality. Let us have more care and more consideration for the efforts of other people. Let us not just blatantly be so inconsiderate and so destructive of what other people are working so hard for.

I know what it costs to run this church. And I am very grateful that God keeps us going through the efforts of the people that are within it. If it wasn't for the donations and assistance of members and non-members, the church could not be where it is today. We've always tried to include everyone that shows any interest in the church. We have tried to keep our dues at a bare minimum of $36 a year. We have tried to have committees that ask for donations within our means that we could always afford our church. I don't know of anyone, *anyone* that cannot afford the Serenity Church. If you face a committee for a donation and you can only give 50 cents, it is better go give 50 cents graciously than to give $50 begrudgingly. This is why we have always had a voluntary system. We don't have to be concerned about money and all those material problems unless we make that a high priority in our thinking. Your church has tried to show the way for you to be free and to show where the obstructions in life are. When you're truly making the effort to flow through the faculties of the soul, through consideration for others, then all of that goodness will flow right back to you.

I'm not going to ask you for a donation to buy a new door for that cabinet, because the Friends feel that with a little more sponging of water on it, that that wood will come back out, slowly. It's going to take time. But I do sincerely pray that the two people responsible for the destruction will have received sufficient impact at this class to make some effort to communicate with each other, to be more considerate of each other, to have a little care of something or someone besides self all the time. And if that little bit of effort is made from this moment on, surely, the class is more than worth it.

I'm going to kind of miss the classes for a while. I don't know when, if ever, the public classes will be reinstated. But it's always interesting about the human mind. You see, when you have to go to class, you look forward to when there'll be no classes. And then the day comes that there's no classes, and you feel kind of sad because it's the end of that. But that's what the mind has to offer, you see.

Now, I do know—and it brings to mind a teaching that came years ago, which stated, "The bridge to understanding is the unexpected." So, you see, all these wonderful teachings, they're applicable all the time. All the time.

And I find it very interesting with my students who are standing at the bridge at the doorway to compassion and the soul faculties who back off from fear. Why do we do it to ourselves? Of course, we make a judgment. And the judgment says, "Well, I'm not going to pay that price." I'm here to show you it's worth paying the price that you be not controlled by the fluctuating desires of any mind in any universe, for there's no truth and no freedom as long as fear is in control. To be free agents of the Divine, to be afraid of no man and his forces, to be afraid of no one's emotions, to stand firm on the rock of principle because it's worth it. I admit, I have experienced a multitude of forces in the work that I'm in, but I will not sell out, for I know these forces, they come and go.

I have seen many come to this church. I have seen many leave. I have seen a few stay, because it means something to them. I assure you, if you stand firm on what you know in your heart and soul is right, you will be freed from fear, you will be freed from the control of the human mind. You must remember, friends, that you cannot be controlled by the mind of another unless you are controlled by the mind of self.

So when we face, when we rise up, and we know what's right and we know what we should do and we back off, remember, it is our mind that we are backing off from. It is not the forces of a mind out there. It's our mind that is backing us off.

[*This is the end of the recorded class.*]

MARCH 15, 1979

CONSCIOUSNESS CLASS 208

We have a few moments before eight o'clock. And some of you are attending our classes, of course, for the first time. Most of you have been with us for many years. Tonight, I believe, marks our two-hundred-and-eighth class on this philosophy.

Now, it would behoove all students to make the effort to obtain some of the classes that have already been given, because with these classes we don't start just with the very beginning of the philosophy. Now, much, of course, is contained, in a very condensed form, in this, *The Living Light* book. But over 200 classes have already been given expanding what is in *The Living Light* book.

Now, you, of course, will receive from the classes whatever you put into the classes. Now that simple principle goes for everything in life. It is a part of this philosophy and its teachings that we get out of anything in life whatever, *whatever* we put into it.

And so this evening, we will have an introductory class on the basics of the philosophy and we will continue on with our understanding of this philosophy in the coming ten weeks.

Now, our format, usually, is a reading from our book [*The Living Light*]—one of the discourses—followed by a short period of meditation. We have always taught that people who meditate without prior concentration—it is not a wise thing to do, because so often in so-called meditation one finds themselves moving into a type of self-hypnosis.

Now, we're all aware, I am sure, of the many desires that pass through our mind in the course of a day. And as life is an effect of our thought, of our own attitude, of our own acceptances and denials, so it is critically important that we make some effort each and every day to discipline the vehicle that our soul is using to express itself here on this earth plane; that vehicle, of course, being our own human mind.

During this semester, great effort will be made to help guide you beyond the limits of the human mind. We all understand that the mind serves its purpose but, being a creative substance, is subject to the Law of Creation, which we know as duality. So for every positive, there is the negative. And therefore, man continues to experience these ups and downs in his day-to-day acts and activities. To go beyond the mind is to establish within the consciousness that perfect peace and tranquility, which is the true home and the birthright of the eternal soul.

As long as we believe that it is necessary to use our mind to accomplish the good in life, then, for us, the obstruction is indeed great. The mind has been designed to serve a purpose in mental realms of consciousness. It cannot perceive. It can only conceive. Conception, controlled by those opposite poles of creation, does not grant to any of us the peace that passeth all understanding. To go beyond the mental realms of consciousness is not possible without a daily effort of self-control, self-discipline. One usually looks at the word *discipline*, especially *self-discipline*, as something that is a struggle, that is difficult, that is some type of deprivation.

For every gain in the world in anything, there is some loss. We must make room in the consciousness for the new to enter. And how that takes place is by letting the old, that has served its purpose, pass on in consciousness.

The movement to higher realms of consciousness is, of course, dependent upon your own efforts. When you look at life, as you have already experienced life, you find that there are many things that you would like to change. But when it comes to making the effort to change those patterns that are no longer beneficial, no longer useful—but they continue to control your life—then only through your efforts of discipline can these transformations take place.

As we look at all of the experiences we have already encountered, we see that they have served a purpose in bringing about a change in our mind in broadening our horizons through a greater acceptance. Man experiences what he consciously chooses to experience by the divine will known as total acceptance. Man experiences what he does not consciously choose to experience by the Law of Denial. As we deny the right of expression of any thought, of any person, of any thing, we establish for ourselves the destiny of denial. This is how our adversities become our own attachments. And so as long as man insists upon his mind being in control, man will continue to have the adversities and the attachments of life. Of course, the life that is his, or her, reality.

Whenever you permit yourself to think of the things that you want, you guarantee the obstruction to your desire. For that is what the mind is designed to do. It is designed to bring about a balance in the mental realm: for each day, there is a night; for every yes, there is a no.

The purpose of these classes and this philosophy is to help you awaken to a greater life in the here and the now. For eternity is only the moment of your conscious awareness. Eternity is the now. You can think about what is yet to be, you can think about what has already been. And in so thinking, you deprive yourself of that which is in your eternal moment.

A person thinks about a better job. A person thinks about a better place to live. A person thinks about a greater supply in their life, of greater happiness. But in that thinking, simultaneous with the desire, rises from the depths of the magnetic field of our own subconscious, is the direct opposite. Because man is expressing through eighty-one levels of consciousness—and only one of those eighty-one levels is neutral and divine. Though divinity is expressed through the other eighty, they are limited by the expression that we alone will permit.

Now, some time ago it was given to put God in whatever it is that you choose to do or to forget what you choose to do. Now, what does that statement really mean, "To put God in it or forget it"? When you put God in anything, you put the infinite, divine, eternal power of neutrality—you free yourself from the duality of the human mind; you free yourself from the want, need, and desire; and you free yourself from the obstruction of self-concern. When you put God in it, then that's exactly what happens. The Infinite Intelligence moves in that moment unobstructed. The Infinite Intelligence, known to man as God or good, that's all that can return to you. When man does what he knows is right because it's right to do right, then only the right can return unto him.

Remember, my friends, without personal responsibility, there is no spiritual awakening. And so with all of the many desires that come and go in the course of a single day, remember, you can be free if you choose to be.

When you go—for example, you have a desire and you go to make a purchase. The desire is recorded on perhaps, two, three, maybe ten levels of your consciousness, leaving the remainder of those levels of consciousness out. Now, what happens, is very simple: you have a desire to purchase something that you desire. You go to purchase it and you have many other thoughts of why you shouldn't. Well, those many other thoughts are from the different levels of consciousness that you are expressing through. And because the effort has yet to be made to control those other levels of consciousness, you experience the obstructions to your desires. It is known as a house divided.

In unity, there is power, for in unity, there is peace, and peace is the power. So if man truly seeks the goodness of life, then he must express that power that will attract it to him. But he cannot express that great power of peace until he is united in consciousness, for in unity, there is harmony, and in harmony, there is power. For in harmony, there is peace.

Now, the levels of consciousness do not need to be named. We do not need anyone to tell us those levels, for we are already so very familiar with them. I know that all of you have had the experience, during the thought of desire or the process of fulfilling it, that you've had what many people call second thought. Well, my friends, it should be called multiple thought, because there's more than two levels that are dictating to you. Does it really behoove us to be the victim and the slave of these various uneducated levels of consciousness when they were designed by the Great Architect to serve us as a tool to accomplish greater goodness in our lives?

Let us pause more often. And let us think more deeply about what we are really doing. It is not what we need to learn in life that's going to free us or bring the fullness of goodness into our life. It's what we need to unlearn that's going to open the floodgates of joy in our life. We have already filled our minds with many judgments. We've already filled our minds with many thoughts. And as experience continues to repeat itself in our life, because we have yet to learn certain lessons—there is a better way. The better way is the simple way. To forget, to forget whatever you think of doing until you've put God into it so that the goodness can return to you.

We go out—and on our jobs—and meet many people. And we discuss many things. And we permit ourselves to be constantly affected by what they say, by what they think, by what they do. They do not do it to us, of course. We only do it to ourselves. And we only do it to ourselves because of an error in our thinking. It's simply known as the error of ignorance.

But in all of these different things in our life, we can pause and we can remind ourselves that there is a great intelligence constantly working through us to express itself, that it is only limited by our mind. You see, there is nothing anywhere that limits the power of the Divine except the mental world through which it expresses. Your physical body is limited by the mental acceptances of your mental body. And the expression of your spirit and your soul is limited by the judgments of your mind.

So we all know, in truth, when we feel we are deprived, when we feel that we're short, when we feel that we're limited, that's only a thought that we, and we alone, have made a law. As the teaching is that man is a law unto himself, and, being so, what are we doing with the law that we are?

We have given away the most precious thing, the most precious thing: our divine birthright of goodness. We give it away by the judgments based upon the experiences of yesterday. Tomorrow will never be better unless this moment, we make it better. But we can make each and every moment better, if we really want to do so. We know that we always get what our mind really wants, as long as we permit our mind to be the captain of our ship and the master of our destiny.

I do not wish you to misunderstand that the mind does not serve a beautiful purpose. It serves a wonderful purpose when it is kept under the control of the light of reason, which is a faculty of our own eternal soul. When it is not kept under the control of the faculty of reason, then we experience many varied problems and obstructions in our life. It does not have to be that way. There is no law of the universe that demands that you should deprive yourself of the greatness and the wonder and the joy of life itself. But what does it take to awaken to the simple truth that life indeed is ever as we make it, that life is only as we take it? Many of us put ourselves through a great torture to learn that very simple truth.

I'm trying to share with you a way that you can free yourself from these torturous experiences of your emotions, that you may accept every moment of your life, accept a greater Intelligence, who has no desire to deprive you of what is justly yours by the birthright of your own divinity.

Each and every time you permit your mind to judge and, in that judgment, you deprive yourself or another—for remember, friends, whenever we think we are depriving another, we are only depriving ourselves. For we can never grant to another what we have not first granted unto ourselves. And so whether it's deprivation or goodness, we first are doing it to ourselves.

Stop and think. Whenever we look to others and desire what we judge is the goodness that they have, in that seeking and desire, we have denied ourselves. Now, we have spoken here in other classes on the functions of jealousy, envy, and greed. Think what they do. We are looking to a false source for what we are seeking. For we are looking at what another has and cannot see what God has brought us and in so doing, are we deprived, for we look with feelings of emotion and judgment that we have not. That is what keeps the goodness from us: we're looking to the wrong source.

The human mind is a very clever and interesting vehicle to express through. If it desires to make a change in anything in our life, whether it be a change of our residence or a change of our job, if there is not great effort at self-control, our little minds will justify and will create whatever is necessary to move us on to our desire. Until we learn to take control.

It's like a man that wants a vacation. He feels that he's worked very hard for a long time. So the desire rises up in consciousness to have a vacation. The only problem is, it comes God's way in keeping with the law that man has established and not with man's conscious thought. So man finds himself someday on vacation—a vacation he didn't desire. The job he had ended. And so the vacation goes on. The only problem is another thought rises up and it feels it's deprived; it's short of money. But it's getting what it wanted.

This is what is so important, my friends: our minds always get what they really want. But unfortunately, we have yet to recognize that what we have or have not today is exactly what we desired yesterday, but it has not come to us in the way that our conscious mind says that it should have and, therefore, does not recognize the fulfillment of yesterday's desire.

So, you see, when you desire these many things, be rest assured you will receive them in keeping with the law that you alone have established. And they come in such a way that you often do not recognize they're just exactly what you wanted before.

However, if you are grateful for each and every experience—for gratitude being the application of appreciation—you will not only broaden your horizons, you will not only expand your soul faculty of duty, gratitude, and tolerance, but you won't be on the yo-yo of creation: up one moment and down the next.

We have always taught never suppress desire. Educate or fulfill desire, for when you suppress desire, such, for example, the desire for a vacation, you push it down in the mind and you say, "Oh, well, I have forgotten that." It rises up and you lose your job and you've got a long vacation, in keeping with how much energy you have expressed to suppress it. And then you're not very happy when that happens. And you work like a dog to bring about another change.

It's like a man who has to drive a long distance to go to his job. And each time he makes the drive he gripes and complains and gripes and complains about the long distance he has to drive to get to his job. Well, when sufficient energy has been put into the suppressed desire, being, of course, the desire not to have to drive so far to work, he soon finds himself without any work at all. And so, you see, his desire did get fulfilled. Now do you understand why never, ever suppress desire? Educate your desires in life or fulfill your desires in life, or you will not be happy with your experiences of tomorrow.

You know, with these many levels of consciousness, it is really indeed a constant moment-by-moment awakening. It is truly seemingly amazing what the human mind will do and will not do to get its own way. If there is something we—one of our levels of consciousness, or several—do not want to do, it's very simple: they'll go to work and they'll send us to the hospital so we don't have to do what a couple of levels of our mind don't want to do. I ask you, is it really worth it?

You see, to God all things are possible. And to the human mind many things are possible. We always get what our minds really want. So if you want to know what's happening in your life—the reason for it—just pause for a little while and take a look, review your yesterdays, see what your desires were that you pushed into the depths of your subconscious. Remember, the conscious mind is the electrical field of your aura and the subconscious mind is the magnetic. So, you see, you have a desire in the conscious mind. You send it out into the universe. It enters into the magnetic field of your subconscious and it attracts unto you what you have desired. But it doesn't come, necessarily, the way [you wanted], but in principle, it never, ever fails to happen.

If we look at our life and we see, "Now, I'm having these experiences. I don't appreciate these experiences. But what is in this experience? What is there to help me to grow, to help me to gain greater tolerance and greater understanding, greater peace and greater harmony? Because I feel so adverse to the experience I am having, let me be on guard for my adversity is guaranteed to be my own attachment."

We can already look at the years that we have lived on earth. A few of us, perhaps, when we reach a state of peace, can see the centuries before.

But think, my good students, life is as wonderful, as great, and as beautiful as you will permit yourself to experience it by taking control of your own thoughts, by taking control of your own mind. We all know that heaven is a place in consciousness that is available to us in this moment, not tomorrow's moment. Things are not going to be better tomorrow until you make them better today. Try to remember that, my friends. There are no better tomorrows. They do not exist until your todays become better. Until this moment is a moment of greatness and goodness in your life, you cannot expect your tomorrows to be great or to be good. It is a waste of energy and indeed foolhardy.

If you have a job and you don't like your job, ask yourself why you don't like it. Would you rather be without a job? You see, gratitude is the faculty through which abundant goodness doth flow. If you spend your time unhappy with what you have, yea, even that shall you lose. But if you spend your time in the jobs and experiences that you alone have merited through your errors of ignorance, and if you spend your time in awakening your soul that the faculty of gratitude may express, when you're grateful for the crumb of life that you have, you guarantee the whole loaf. But if you're not grateful for the little crumb, that, too, shall be taken, until your mind finally learns that there's something greater.

When we hit the bottom, the law clearly demonstrates there's no place left to go but up. But some time there's a rubber bottom and it keeps on stretching down, created, of course, by our own thought.

For every moment here that you express the faculty of gratitude, your heavenly home grows. Each moment is another block, a golden brick of divine wisdom in your great eternity.

But when you complain, you deny. Think of the word *complain*. What does it mean to your mind? What is involved with complaint? Is duty, gratitude, and tolerance involved in complaint? Especially gratitude? Or is judgment involved in complaint? There's a vast difference between the word *correct* and the word *complaint*. There is a vast difference between those two words. To correct is to consider. And to complain is to deny.

The human mind cannot entertain a judgment without a denial. And every denial is a destiny that, by the Law of Denial, you become the victim of. We all know that denial does not encompass total consideration, but it is indeed limited consideration. So let us correct and not complain. Let us consider and not deny, for in so doing what we give forth is what we get. Ofttimes we're not happy with what we're getting. But we should be remembered—we should remember, "If I am not happy with what I'm getting, let me open my eyes that I may not be happy with what I am giving, for what I am getting is in keeping with what I am giving. Do I give the thoughts of kindness and joy? Do I give the thoughts of encouragement? If I do, how long have I been doing that? Has it been a year? Or has it been ten? Has it been now and then or has it been consistent?"

When we over-identify with the payment in life, we lose the joy and the pleasure of life. When we think how hard we're working to survive, we no longer enjoy living. Think, my friends. You have, by the universal Law of Evolution, entered earth in a human form. Are you not greater than the rock? And yet the rock survives. Is it all that you want to do in life is to survive?

Now we come to one of the most important things to the human mind. Why is our world so concerned with material wealth and money? Does it not represent to our mind survival? Survival of the things we desire, survival of the things we dictate that we enjoy. And yet the rock survives. It desires no money. The intelligence expressing through it—perhaps we ought to let our minds become a little like the rock and we wouldn't wear ourselves out so quickly. The rock survives, but it does not have the judgment of what it needs to survive. So when our little minds become like the rock, we'll no longer be concerned with survival, we'll no longer be plagued with the thoughts of money, we'll no longer be disturbed by all those things. It's known as the principle to ignore.

We are because we are. And that's just the way that it is. It is the nature of our mind to entertain thought, for it is the creator of thought. It will create what you dictate it to do. But if you have not and do not make the effort to take control of it, it will soon dictate to you. It will tell you when you're happy, subject to a various amount of desires that are fulfilled. And it will tell you when you're healthy and it will tell you when you're wealthy because you let it take control. Isn't it better to tell it to do what you want it to do?

Because, as we have almost forgotten our home, our spiritual home, that is within us, as we have almost forgotten its peace and serenity, because we have over-identified with the basic instinct, a basic instinct to all form—called survival. We have judged what our survival means. And because we have judged what our survival is, we're controlled by the judgments in our animal instinct of survival.

We all know where we are if we will only make the effort to become more conscious of the things we do and the things we don't do. If we can't get enough of anything, we can be rest assured we've got a long ways to go to control our mind. I've always felt that a drop, not a flood, has greater value to a thirsty man. And our minds, they're always thirsty. I've yet to find a mind that doesn't have thirst, for I have yet to find a mind that doesn't have want, need, and desire. But when we try to quench the thirst with a flood instead of a drop, it never fulfills it. We're always in need. Always.

So if you want to move on from where you are, it's a simple step. It's a real simple step. How beautiful an opportunity we have in each moment of our life. What a wonderful opportunity to see how we've grown into attachment of different things. It's so easy for us to see the attachments and adversities of others because in so doing we blind ourselves to our own. But I can talk to a hundred people and they can quickly tell me about that person's adversity and that person's attachment, but they have none of their own. Well, how could they? They're totally blind to them. And when you're blind, you're blind: you cannot see. As our minds fill up with what's wrong with everyone else, we soon begin to believe that everything with us is right. Because, you see, there's no room for honest self-awareness.

But we can take some time to see the real goodness inside if that's really what we want.

I find it very interesting, as I sit here to speak with you in this introductory class, of how our little minds wander. Perhaps because we would like something to say. If so, we should raise our hand, because I would be very happy to listen. But while I am here to serve the job I have to do in life, then your attention is demanded. Because I do not want any students who do not have enough value for what is offered to endure an hour of class once a week. I have never been interested in numbers and perhaps that's why we have such a small church. Perhaps that's why we have such small classes.

Some time ago these classes used to be a twelve-week semester. But because some of my students had difficulty in staying awake for forty-five minutes or an hour, the semester was cut down to eleven weeks. My good friends, you come here to learn of a way to free yourself from the patterns that have caused you so much disturbance in life. The number one lesson is self-discipline and personal responsibility.

You will hear in this semester many things that some of the levels of your mind do not like, but you will hear them anyway. Whatever you do with them is, of course, your personal responsibility. But you may be rest assured that they are recorded in your memory par excellence.

If this class continues to have some degree of value for what is offered, then the class will continue. But if the predominant vibration is drifting off in space, wondering when it's going to end, then I can assure you it will indeed be a very short semester.

Thank you very much. Thank you.

MAY 1, 1980

CONSCIOUSNESS CLASS 209

I know that for some people it is difficult, it seems, to stay awake during the class, but—and over the years, I have been asked by students what area in their life should they really be working on. If you will pay attention to what is being said at the time that you feel drowsy and sleepy, then you will know, during the class, what area in your life you should be working on. You see, our minds will not allow us, when we hear things that are disturbing to certain levels of our, of our consciousness, our minds will not allow us to get up and walk out. And the only escape that the level has that finds the discussion disturbing or unpleasant to it is to simply get drowsy and go off to sleep. So, you see, if you will pay attention when that feeling comes over you and you will make great effort to stay awake, then you will know what is being discussed and what area you need to work on to be free.

And so I'm sure we will all make great effort to stay awake, as much as we possibly can. And if you think that I just sit here and sleep, well, I'm having to work in my realms as well as you're having to work, of course, in yours.

So I realize that you all get the cassettes—the tapes of the class—the following Sunday, but you know there is a difference between just having the recorded tape of the class and being present in the class. If there wasn't any difference, then no one would be here this evening and we'd all just wait for Sunday morning and pick up a tape.

[*At this point, Mr. Goodwin goes into a trance.*]

Greetings, fellow students.

Once again it is indeed a joy to be with you in this way. We have been studying the need of the human mind to identify with passing events. I am sure that you all realize that time, the illusion, is only realized in keeping with your identification with passing events in your life. To move beyond the realm of time and mind, we must make the effort to be freed from identification and attachment. As we make that effort to be freed, we will find a greater fullness of life, for all that is, is in the moment of eternity. And the moment, its awareness—that moment of eternity—is only possible when you no longer identify with events. When that takes place, all that has been, all that is to be, shall be in the moment of your choice.

Each day it behooves those on the path to take a few moments to free the self from identification and attachment. As has been stated long ago, man can only be affected by that which he identifies with. To be free is to be not affected by things, by creation, by form. If you make that daily effort a few moments each day, you will soon find a greater peace, a greater joy, a greater purpose to life itself. For sooner or later, as we move through the dual laws of form, sooner or later, we will grow to that understanding and grow to that great value to be freed from these dual experiences in life.

In my many, many years here in this dimension, I have encountered the effects of thoughts I never knew I had. For all that is, has been. And all that is to be, is. We are moving through a so-called curtain of time and space that does not exist in truth. It is sustained by mental substance. And only with mental substance can, and does, it exist. When you, your free spirit and your soul, move through this curtain of mental substance, you move on into the totality and the true purpose of your very being. To remind oneself daily that you are not the form, but the power that moves the form, the benefit is very simple: you, your being, is no longer affected by the flux and flow and tides of old creation.

This planet, the fifth, the planet of faith—here you have the opportunity to learn this simple, yet great, truth. But the steps of suffering and discouragement do, in time, serve their purpose to help you to make that little bit of effort each and every day. Power lies in the Law of Continuity. It is of no lasting nor enduring benefit to make effort in anything on one day and to forget it the next day or to make effort in anything for one year only to forget it the next year. People who have problems with the Law of Continuity reveal clearly the lack of discipline and the lack of control of the mind.

When we slowly but surely, through discipline, through daily effort, no matter how few the minutes may be—whoever makes that daily effort will reap the harvest in their own tomorrows.

Be grateful for the struggle, for without it you cannot grow nor be freed from the levels of consciousness that you have over-identified with and have attached yourself to. When I entered this world that I now reside in, when I found the barren desert and was granted the wonderful opportunity of learning the value of the faculty of gratitude and moved on through a multitude of experience that I may bow this great pride of mine, that I may gain balance between the functions and the faculties of being, though it seemed at the time a great and never-ending suffering to endure, without it, I could not have gained my freedom.

That, of course, that we identify with, we, of course, then become the victim of. Surely, it is not wisdom, nor is it common sense, to identify with form which is governed by dual expression. Beyond that duality lies the divine path of neutrality. And what is neutrality, but perfect balance. And what is perfect balance, but harmony and perfect peace.

When you find a need in any area of your life, you will also find that there has been a lack of balance through directed energy. We all direct our energy in the course of a day to many things. We all desire many things. And we all feel many, many things. But we must all remind ourselves: we are not the feeling, nor the thought; we are not the act, nor the deed. We are the power that moves the thought. We are the power behind the mental substance that does the deed. That does not free us from our responsibility, which we have created by the Law of Identity.

We know that our greatest obstruction is not the eternal I; it is only the thought of I. There's a vast difference between the I and the thought of I. The thought of I is a mental identification with form, but the true I is a formless, free spirit. It is known as the I of eternity.

You see, my good friends, we all are the I of eternity. But we have forgotten our birthright. And in forgetting our birthright, we do not express the greatness and the goodness of it. How does man forget his birthright? He simply entertains in mental substance the thought of I. And the thought of I limits his expression because it is the mental thought of I that denies the inseparableness of truth. It is the thought of I that creates discord, the opposite of unity. It is the thought of I that has want and need. It is the thought of I that experiences the effect of the denial of the oneness of life itself and, in the denial, denies itself.

It is said that we grant not to another what we have not first granted unto ourselves. Without the thought of I, all is. All that possibly could be desired is, when you are freed from the thought of I. When you breathe, you do not think, "I am breathing." The thought of I is breathing. No, my friends, you are a part of the breath of life itself and, therefore, have no need to think of breathing.

Health is restored when man removes the obstruction to the soul faculty of harmony.

When all thoughts flowing in your mind enter a state of harmonious agreement in anything in your life, the true you, the I of eternity, moves unobstructed. Do not waste life in chasing for things, for the price of them is not worth the sacrifice of identity. Seek the unity of your true source and things will no longer concern you. For they will be ever present for you if you will first accept the source of which you are an inseparable part.

But discipline of the mind to free you from identification to form is the first step along the path.

My students in this dimension have always enjoyed attending this earthly class because they receive so much in their recall of their experiences so very, very long ago.

We know that all things in life—and life is everywhere. There is no planet, there is no star, there is no solar system where life does not exist. But man has judged what life is. And so man travels through so-called space and sees many things and finds not life, for he has judged life and, therefore, is limited to what life is. Wherever there is intelligent energy, there is life. Oh, the forms, they vary greatly, but life still expresses. We do not see—because of our judgments—the life in the rock or the little grain of sand. We do not see that life expressing, but it is there. And someday, as we broaden our horizons, as we expand our consciousness, our judgments will broaden and we will accept that new—for us—that new experience of the expression of life.

Your breath, like the breath of all forms, is the breath of life. And when you speak your word, the breath of life goes out into the universe. Now, form and forms are created by the breath of life. And so we speak many things, and by the breath of life, we create many things. Because we are the creator by our breath of life, we are responsible, of course, for our creations and they come home, for they know where home is. And so, my friends, may we pause to think before we give the breath of life to our thought and, in so doing, gain some degree of control of our reality, of our life expression.

Many of us, I know, are aware that the trees and the plants and the blade of grass, they have their thoughts and their feelings. They have their likes and their dislikes, for there is an Intelligence—we call it God—expressing through them. The Intelligence is no different in the frog than in the man. The vehicle through which the Intelligence is expressing is the only difference. And because the vehicle is different, our mind, through judgments, creates an obstruction. Now we all know that we can't judge anything we don't identify [with]. And so identification is inseparable, of course, to judgment.

We look at the frog and the frog does not speak our language. And so we identify with an obstruction to communication. Our identification and judgment to the frog becomes the obstruction and the barrier for us to freely communicate. We look at the plant. We see that it grows. And we see that under certain conditions it appears to grow intelligently. We talk to the plant and the plant does not speak our language. And once again, we identify with obstruction and judgment. But think, my friends, the Intelligence within the plant or the frog is the same Intelligence in you.

And if you wish to truly understand, then communicate with the language of your soul. For the language of our soul is a universal language. It has no judgments. It has no obstructions. It's known as love, true love.

If you have any thought of what love is, you no longer have love. Think of that, my friends. If you have any thought, then you have identity and you have judgment and you no longer have love. You only have need. And when the needs of your mind are fulfilled to the satisfaction of your judgments, then you call that love. That is not love. Oh, no. Love has no barriers. It has no identification. It has no judgment and it has no need. It is fulfilled within itself. And if you truly want to communicate with anything in any world at any time, then all you need to do is open your heart which permits the language of your soul to express, which is love.

You know that simple truth: Love all life and know the Light. We cannot know the Light until we do love all life, for it is only in loving all life that the Light does shine. But how often do we make the effort to love all life? To love all life does not mean that we must do what all life may dictate. That is not what we are discussing.

To love is not to fear. To love is not to want. And to love is not to need. It is to be in the eternal home of your soul. You can be there this moment. You can be there every moment. For, you see, my friends, it's ever waiting and available to you. But it's up to you to make that choice. Someday we all will make that choice. Because we wander in the universe—sometimes it seems for many centuries—but we always return home. And because true love has no need and it has no want and it has no judgment and it has no fear, it's ever at peace.

Use your mind and body for the purpose for which it has been designed. But do not forget who you really are. Remind yourself of who you really are and then you will always be who you really are.

All these things have come and, by the Law of Coming, will go. But you will go on and on and on. There is no end to that which has no beginning. Today, this moment, you identify with one thing, only tomorrow to be another. And throughout the centuries it goes on and on and on. You will have this little package that you have created here on earth, that you call self, as long as you have a need for it, no matter what dimension you pass on to. But someday, when true love rises in its fullness and expresses through your heart, you will no longer have the little package called self. Tired and worn, it will lay down to return to the elements from whence it has been created. And then you'll know you've always been. And then you'll know the error of the fear of tomorrow, the error of regret of the past. Then you'll know.

And no matter what comes or goes, you will always be at home, the castle of your soul. And look out over the many universes and see the passing panorama of the multitudes, knowing that someday they, too, will find home. There's only one home and that's where everyone, sooner or later, returns to.

We have wandered from the home of infinite, divine Love. And we are wending our way back to it. It can be now. There's no need to put it off for centuries yet to be.

Remember, whatever it is we cannot tolerate in another we are still waiting to educate in ourselves. So when tolerance becomes your cross, remember: effort every day in every way. No one wants to be in prison. Not really. We all know our home. It's only a matter of making the effort to get there.

Be not disturbed with all the fluctuating experiences of life. They're serving their purpose. Your security was never, ever possible in mental substance. Your life already has taught you that simple, yet great, truth. No one is secure in the dual vibration of opposites, which the mind, by its very nature, is. Our only security is when we free ourselves from creation and continue to be in it and not a part of it.

Just to remember we have come to earth to serve a great and good purpose. Though our minds know it not, our souls are very much aware. And that great and good purpose that we have entered the earth realm to fulfill, oh, indeed, it shall be fulfilled. But your minds shall know it not. For whatever the mind knows, the mind controls. And the spiritual purpose of your soul's journey cannot be fulfilled when your mind gains control. And so it is, God's greatest work is done in the silence of the mind.

Good day.

MAY 8, 1980

CONSCIOUSNESS CLASS 210

Now, in keeping with the basic principles of this philosophy—that change is not only inevitable, but it is indispensable to evolution—our format this evening will be a bit different.

For many, many years the Council of this church has made great effort, great effort to demonstrate one of the basic teachings of this philosophy: that teaching being exposure frees the soul. Now I do realize that to some of you who do not attend our classes up at the house, I do realize that that may be new to you. So I'll take a few moments to explain that process. First of all, our eternal being, our formless, free spirit, uses this vehicle we're presently in. We are not the form. We are not the body. We are not the mind. But we are using it, as you use a car to go where you choose to go. In order for the eternal soul to be free from the restrictions and limitations of the vehicle that it is expressing through, one must first become aware of the limitations of the vehicle they are expressing through by an awareness of certain laws that they alone have set into motion, which causes them an obstruction to their own freedom.

I am very well aware that one of the most difficult steps for anyone to make in evolution is to fully accept something beyond the control of their vehicle of mind. We all try in our ways to accept this Divine Spirit, this God, this Eternal Being, but we have great difficulty in demonstrating it in our day-to-day acts and activities.

I recall listening to one of the classes in one of our other semesters in reference to a refrigerator at the church home. It was indeed most interesting and most awakening. The refrigerator got stuck in the frost and defrost mode. It didn't know what to do. Now, for some of you, I am aware that electrical equipment or electronic equipment—it's difficult for our minds to accept that we are directly affecting equipment, whether it's an automobile, a refrigerator, or a recorder or whatever it is. We are having a direct effect upon it by the electromagnetic energy that is emanating from our being. Now, this electromagnetic energy, it responds, you see, to the thoughts that we entertain in our mind. Sometimes there is an emanation that is very harmonious, very united, very peaceful, and good experiences, of course, are the effect. But that, unfortunately, is not always the case.

And so, in keeping with our policy of exposure frees the soul, we were all blessed in the sense that many months ago one of our members worked very hard to crochet, hand crochet, tablecloths for the tables at the church home. As one of our other members is working diligently to complete the china that she is painting and will finish in the months to come. And I vividly recall when I was standing present with some of the members and the dimensions—exact—were given. And I watched with great interest, great interest, when these hand-made tablecloths were sent to a professional to be blocked.

Now, ofttimes, ofttimes the Spirit will allow certain experiences to take place in order that the students may benefit from the demonstration. Whether that demonstration be negative or positive, it is ever in keeping with what is needed for the people who are involved with the project.

And so the experience took place. The tablecloths were blocked and they're about two rows around too short. Now, how do we trace these experiences back home where they originated? What does it offer to us, these many experiences that take place every day, seven days a week, in our lives? Just—you, friends, can turn if you wish, because this is a different format this evening. You might as well relax. Whether you know it or not, you're still having class. You see, to sit here and to study and not to apply is not only a waste of time, of course, it's a waste of your energy; it's a waste of your money. And so we share with you these experiences and how you trace them back to home to what's called personal responsibility.

And so it is, the one crocheting the cloths is truly blessed, for they have the golden opportunity to choose between truth and creation, to choose between attachment to the fruits of action and freedom from them. And I am sure, after these many years, they have chosen very wisely: to be freed from the attachment to the fruits of action to a tablecloth or whatever else it may be. To see clearly the wonderful, golden opportunity, the demonstration of how difficult it is, for all people, to choose something that the mind cannot control.

No matter how hard we try and no matter how many years of effort we make, I can assure you there is one thing in eternity that no human mind will ever control. And that is the free spirit which is the true you.

On another occasion, just the other day, when several people were talking about that it was going to rain, I was out in the garden watering. One of my students said, "Well, you know, it's going to rain tomorrow." And I said, "Well, I won't hold my breath. I won't hold my breath." Because the Spirit had informed me that it would not rain.

Now, you see, I admit, it's been forty years, forty years working with the Spirit. And I do admit I've had many, many experiences. And I do consciously choose to listen to the Spirit over the human mind. And I made that choice long, long, long ago. Long ago. Because I have lived to see that the human mind, of course, has nothing to offer to anyone—to ourselves or anyone else—except the limited experiences that it's already had. If you want something new in your life, then you've got to move out of the mind. Because, you see, as long as you let your mind stay in control, the only thing you're going to experience is repetitions of the past. No matter where you go, no matter what you do, as long as your mind is in control, it can only offer you what it has. And what it has is what you have already experienced.

But sooner or later, repetition, being the law through which change is made possible, sooner or later, we all have enough repetition that we do make that step. Now, we don't make it in one day in one gigantic leap into the spiritual dimensions. You see, friends, you don't pass on and then automatically land in the spiritual dimensions. The spiritual dimensions are something you're working towards here and now. The spiritual world, you see, is right where you are. The only difference is that if your mind is active, then you cannot have the awareness of the spiritual dimensions in which you truly live. So the first thing, of course, we need to do is to gain control of this little automobile we're running around in that's just gone wild, going here and there and everywhere. Without the effort, of course, to take control of that vehicle—the mind—then, you see, we don't even get the glimpses of the spiritual dimensions, which are our true home.

Now, getting back to these tablecloths, which, like the refrigerator, are such a wonderful, wonderful opportunity for growth. You know, many of my students are aware of our principle of exposure frees the soul. I haven't found one yet that likes it while it's happening to them. But after they got through it, after it's over, they feel like they just took a nice, fresh shower. They feel so good. But never while it's happening. Oh, no. No, because, you see, our mind rises up and it reacts and it goes through all of its retaliations and rejections and everything else. To the degree of the emotion expressed during exposure, which frees our soul, reveals the control that the emotions and the mind still have over our eternal free spirit.

So if you ever want to know how you're doing with your growth, you don't have to ask anyone. You just have to set the necessary laws into motion to have someone kind and considerate enough to give you some exposure and become aware in that moment how emotional you really are. If you're not too emotional, then that reveals you're more free than you really realized you were, at least at that moment.

So we see how difficult it is for us to accept, let alone to believe, something we cannot with our physical and mental senses, we cannot touch, we cannot sense, we cannot feel, we cannot see, and we cannot hear. And isn't that beautiful? Because with all those senses we cannot touch the Spirit. Isn't it wonderful? Because we cannot control it.

And yet, if we will only make the effort to still our mind, we will be aware of our home in this moment. This is the moment in which we all have the power, not only to become aware, but to live in that heavenly home which is a state of consciousness. You may go there in any minute of your choice, but it's much easier said than done because the mind, not having made the effort to control it, rises up with its demands and its dictates to control. And when those demands and dictates rise up in your mind, then they control you and you cannot enter and cannot be aware, cannot believe and cannot accept the only thing that will ever, or has ever, brought into your life the goodness which is God.

I know that there have been—of course, you've all had experience of a fleeting moment when you've exhausted yourselves in trying to accomplish something of your desire that you've had a fleeting moment, a fleeting moment of that peace that passeth all understanding.

Also, I want to discuss with you this evening something that was brought about many years ago in this philosophy, known by the Old Man—who brought us this philosophy—as pressure points. Years ago. Shortly after that was revealed, we became aware, at least here in the state of California, of the efforts to legalize what is known as acupuncture. This philosophy clearly teaches that everything is the effect and the expression of intelligent energy, intelligent energy.

Now, last Sunday it was revealed to me by one of my students that they had received a communication in reference to their pet, their pet dog. I spoke to that individual—they spoke to me, rather—after last Sunday's church service. And it seemed that during the communication of the billets that the Spirit had recommended that this animal be taken immediately, immediately to an acupuncturist. Well, they were more than willing to do that, having been told by the best medical doctors that the animal had approximately three months left to live; that he had a very large, cancerous growth.

Well, the Spirit had recommended that the animal be taken within twenty-four hours. And so within twenty-four hours the person managed to find an acupuncturist who was willing to treat the animal. Most of them were not willing. In fact, there was only one that was willing and, of course, then that was the right one. Now, it's been Monday, Tuesday, Wednesday—the animal's taken in, in the evening. Just about this time. In fact, he's there now, being treated. After the first treatment, the animal began to make a seeming miraculous recovery. Now the animal has had three treatments. The condition is making a complete reversal.

It was interesting to me that the doctors—there are two Chinese doctors—made the statement that animals respond much, much quicker to the treatment than human beings. And it should be of great interest to all of you as students. What is it that man has that an animal doesn't have that becomes an obstruction to the infinite, divine healing power? Stop and think. What is it in our minds that tells us that we are, of course, more evolved than animals? What is it? For that one thing is the obstruction to the healing. That one thing.

Now, an animal goes to a doctor. And the animal doesn't lay there and think, "Now, let's see, I'm not so sure whether this doctor knows what he's doing. And what's he going to do to me anyway?" You see, the little animal's mind doesn't work that way. The animal's mind responds to consideration, responds to all the soul faculties, has no dictates of whether or not that this doctor knows what he's doing, doesn't need to see all his certificates, doesn't need to talk to hundreds of people that agree that this is a great doctor. The animal is not interested in that foolishness. Only man's ego, uneducated, is interested in that foolishness.

Now, all animals, like all plants, like all form, have egos. Any of you who have pets, I'm sure, are aware by now, if you really love them, of their little different idiosyncrasies, are well aware of their little egos, are well aware of their feelings of rejection and etc. But the animal does not have judgment. The only difference is judgment. That is the only obstruction to the goodness of life. That is the only obstruction to the divine healing. That is the only obstruction to the fullness and the freedom of life. One word, my friends, only one: judgment. The animal does not make judgments. Only the animal called man makes judgments. Therefore, the animal does not have this wall of obstruction between himself and the Divine.

Whenever you permit your mind to make judgments, you cut yourself off from what is known as universal consciousness. Now, universal consciousness isn't something that's out there. Universal consciousness is something that's in here. And when you're in universal consciousness, you are a part of the whole; you have an unobstructed receiving of the whole of life itself. The moment you make your judgments, you cut yourself off from the Source, the very source that is your only sustenance.

Stop and think how many times, how many times your mind tries to dictate, to connive, to figure out, to conspire, to collaborate, to do all these different devious things to fulfill what it judges is a need that it has. And what a price. What a price we have to pay.

It is understandable that our minds would have more faith in the weather forecaster on the television or the radio than in the Spirit or the spirits. It is understandable that the mind would have more faith in a professional who says how big a tablecloth must be in order to fit properly than it would in the spirits. Don't you see, my friends, it takes a lot of work to have faith in God? It isn't something that we just open our mouth and there it is. Oh, no. It takes a lot of work because it takes a lot of work to calm down our minds that are so tenacious and demand that they control everything.

I think one of the greatest blessings, if you can call it that, was in facing my adversity to open up a church that I was, perhaps, intelligent enough—or something—that I said very clearly, "Then you make all the decisions. I'll have no part of that." And the Spirit was kind enough to feel that was a just agreement. Now—of course, that's nine years ago. They still make the decisions. My job is battling with the egos so they can get it through their brain that if my ego doesn't get to make the decisions on how a class is run, how a church is run, how a bill is paid, what's purchased, what isn't purchased, if my ego—which I happen to know its size, and I'm pretty familiar with some of yours—doesn't get to make those decisions, then what kind of an ego must think that it can override mine? See, it doesn't work that way. So, you see, the ego does serve a good purpose: you get a little educated. But I've been through this many times with many people.

I know we've got a small church. About twenty-four members—about twenty, eighteen to twenty active, I guess. But we have a lot of friends. I never was great on being a card-carrier, though I do happen to carry a card, being the founder. And our doors are always open to those who are really interested, but that has never really been my thing. I have seen nine years of wonderful growth with very few people. And the right ones, they always find us. And those who feel that it's for them, they stick around. And some of them, they get to carry a card and some of them don't. But I can tell you up front I'd much rather have a worker than a card-carrier. Now, if they want to be a worker and a card-carrier, that's just fine. That means $45 more a month into the church fund. And a lot more work. But it is worth it.

Now, you see, friends, because I am somewhat aware, hopefully, of my mind, I am a bit familiar with yours. So if you want to know what's going to be in your life, just find out where your mind is now. Because wherever your mind is now, that's what your tomorrow is going to be like.

One of my students said to me once, well, they love their mind. They were going to keep their mind. And I think that's wonderful. How long you're going to keep it, that will tell you how long you're going to be in the mental realm. Because there's no guarantee, you know, if you go out of the physical body and you still love your mind and you're not going to let your mind go, well, that's a mental body and it can only express in a mental level, you know. So that's fine. I don't see anything wrong with the mind if the effort is made constantly to cast the light of common sense upon it.

Now here, just the other day—I think it's a wonderful class. I love this class, myself. Might even keep going on and on and on, because [there have been] so many wonderful experiences with the members and the friends of this little church.

Now, the other day—today's Thursday. Well, it must have been Wednesday. That was last night. The Spirit decided that we would have some new flatware, silverware for the church. The reason being very simple: they—we have a dinner coming up of about eighty or eighty-one people for our anniversary. And I had asked them to take inventory of the silverware and come to find out they've only got fifty-three forks! Well, what are they going to do? Are thirty people going to share? [*Many students laugh.*] No, it doesn't work that way. I don't want to eat off a fork and share with somebody else eating off the same fork. It's like my toothbrush. I'm not going to—I'll share many things, but not my toothbrush. All right.

So it was a very simple thing: just have a flatware committee and they each chip in a few dollars—whatever it is—and you get the flatware. Well, we had that experience. And one of my students, who was assigned to that job to purchase it, I know was not thinking when she accepted delivery two days before the church dinner. So we got that worked out. The Friends demanded it would have to be in, I think it was by the tenth. And she did have the wonderful opportunity with all those con games and lies and all that stuff with stores—It's coming from here. It's coming from there. And they don't even know where it's coming from. But, needless to say, we finally got it.

So it's such beautiful flatware that the Spirit had chosen, they decided that we would get two more sets and have them for the house. Because we had so many pieces of this and so many pieces of that. And somebody had thrown one of our tablespoons down the garbage disposal and that wasn't worth saving anymore, after the garbage disposal unit got through with it. And so it came last night time to put in all the new and take out all the old and give it away or put it in the garage sale, because that's just how your church always has operated.

You see, my friends, you never have a problem receiving if you remember whatever it is that has been on loan to you from God—because all that you have, you know, is only loaned to you. And you never know when the laws you set into motion will call it back. But whatever you think you have, which happens to be on loan to you—even your body is on loan, your mind, too. Don't forget that. Whatever you think you have that's on loan to you today, if you use it and you care for it, then you're not abusing it. Now, if it sits in your house and you look around and ten years have passed and you haven't used it, and another twenty years pass and you still haven't used it, and you get upset because you have to move it around because your house is so filled with the things you're holding on to—the garage sale is the end of the month. I want to be sure and get that in [*Many students laugh.*]—then what you are doing, you are abusing it.

You see, everything that's created has a purpose. It is designed to serve a purpose. A glass is designed to hold fluids. So you drink from it. You set it on the shelf and it sits there year after year after year, you are abusing the purpose for whence—for which it was designed. Now, it's that way about your thoughts and every part of your life. And because you are abusing that spiritual principle, you find the things you want, you can't seem to get them. No matter how hard you try, you cannot get them. Because, you see, you have abused the Law of Use. You have totally abused it. And you guarantee the day, you absolutely guarantee the day, when there's something you want really, really bad, but you cannot get it. No matter how hard you try, you cannot get it for you have transgressed the Law of Use.

Now, on the other hand, if you accept the simple truth that the Infinite Divine has on loan to you all of the things that you have, that they have come into your world to serve the purpose for which they have been designed and you look around and you see that the purpose for which the object has been designed is no longer serving its purpose, you move it on. You let it go, you see. If you let it go freely, then that that you desire will freely come to you. But if you get into this old mental world, "Let's see now, maybe this is worth about $3, maybe $5. Maybe I could even get $10 if I tried real hard," you're going to find out you're stuck with it.

Now, there's many things we want to get rid of in life. We go out in the world and we grab a hold of a cold, and we can't wait to get rid of it. We don't care who takes it; we just want to get rid of it. And we work like the dickens, but we can't get rid of it. Why can't we get rid of something we want to get rid of? Because we've held on to so many things that are not serving the purpose for which they were designed and came into our life. That's why we can't get rid of it! Because, you see, the law itself is totally impartial.

Now, man is a stream of life. And things are designed to flow through your life. And when you forget that in all this world of creation, when you forget that you are the stream of life and you forget and you block up the stream, you guarantee the day you will be flooded by it. You guarantee that day. Because there will be things that come to you that you want so dearly to get rid of and you won't be able to. They may be a physical object. They may be a thought. They may be a feeling. But they hold tightly to you. For, you see, everything, *everything*, an infinite intelligent energy is expressing through. Everything. And that energy is intelligent. It knows the ones who hold and it knows the ones who flow.

I know that you're all very familiar with thoughts and feelings that you've had to work like the dickens to get rid of. You didn't even accept that they came out of your own head. They just came into your head, because they're so terrible they couldn't possibly have come out of your own head. They had to come out of somebody else's head. And you just happened to be passing by. Well, that's not how it works.

It's just like the tablecloths, you see. My students merited going to a person that would give that dictate. Don't you understand? Now, the problem does not exist, and never existed, with the person, the professional that made the dictate. That's not where the problem is. You see, we merit all experiences in our life. The law clearly says that like attracts like and becomes the Law of Attachment. So all of our experiences are beautiful mirrors to tell us where we are at any given moment. It's right there.

Now, if we don't like the experience, all we have to do is change our attitude. And if we don't want to bother to make the effort to change our attitude, then sit back and relax because millions more of like-kind of experiences will come your way.

See, everything in the universe knows its source. Everything. A thought in your mind goes out into the universe, but it always comes back home because it knows its creator. Everything knows its source and everything returns.

We all really know where we are. There's no problem with that. You just be at peace for a few moments and you can tell very clearly.

You see, many people, they pray to God when their minds cannot work out their problems. When there is so much disaster in our lives that our minds have tried every shenanigan and every device and every trip that it can possibly dream of, in total exhaustion, we turn to the slightest possibility—and that's called God—the slightest possibility that maybe there is something, possibly—that's how our minds work—*possibly*, just possibly there is something. "I better get some minimum insurance on that possibility," you see. Many people go to church because of the possibility that death is not the end. Birth was never the beginning and so death is not going to be the end.

So we must, you know, become aware, a little more aware of, really, what our beautiful, *beautiful* minds have to offer. And make a little effort each day to be still that we may experience what our eternal being has to offer, our soul, our spirit. That's where life really is.

Now, one of my students here, the other day, came with this beautiful new hairdo. I, personally, thought it was very beautiful. I admit, I had a little education from the Spirit before I met the person, because, you see, our minds react in such strange ways. You see, our minds react that, "Now let's see, is this fitting into my square head? Oh, I haven't seen that. No, it's not fitting in. It's new. It's different. It's not fitting." So I was fortunate. I did have some help. And I personally think it's quite nice. I really do. It's different. And it is nice to see that a race of people centuries and centuries and centuries and centuries old, that their hair styles are being copied by this great civilization.

I think that's just great. Of course, I think what's even more great is their hair style came out of necessity and being, simply, practical. Their hair was so difficult to have to try to comb or fix or etc., and so they braided. And I think that's just plain great. How readily do we accept something different? I tell you it's something else to witness. It's not readily at all. Believe me. It just isn't.

And yet, when we want a job or we want this or we want that, and we do not readily—we have not demonstrated that we readily accept change, well, how do we expect it to happen just like that when that's not the way we have been? That we have to dream about something and think about it and whirl it over in our minds for maybe three or four months—the possibility, you see. And then what do we expect? That we make a change just like that? I never met a person that made a change just like that.

I am going to speak, however, for a few minutes more on the understanding of the Spirit in reference to our health. In this society today, we are obviously brainwashed to what we call medical science. Medical science has come a long ways, and it's got a long, long, *long* ways to go. I've spoken to you before about surgeries. And I have spoken, also—I've spoken on cancer. I've spoken on many different health problems. But I do hope that you all understand that there is no form, whether it's a tree or a plant or an animal or a human, that does not have negative cells, which man calls cancer. Because that's exactly what they are.

Now, this animal that has had three treatments of acupuncture—it's a very simple process, you know. You see, when the intelligent energy in the form—the human or the animal or any other form—is obstructed from its natural flow, the energy still moves. And it will become concentrated—over-concentrated in an area where it is obstructed all around. And so it concentrates all this energy flowing in. Now, this energy, intelligent energy, directed to the cells—because it's obstructed from its full flow through the body—will cause a rapid growth and an increase in that area. It's just like, you know, if you fertilize a plant and you concentrate the fertilizer on it, it really mushrooms and grows. And so it's the same way with the energy flowing through your body. If it becomes obstructed in one area, then you get a double shot in another area. And if it becomes obstructed in ten areas, you get ten extra shots in some other area. And so what happens is these negative cells then begin to mushroom and grow.

Now, surgery, they make an opening. They cut it open physically and they seal it up. They don't know and don't seem interested in anything about the ethereal body that they have pierced. And experience has shown repeatedly, repeatedly, through millions of cases that the negative cells usually vastly grow. Tremendously. In most cases. There are a few cases, however, that that doesn't happen. Now, what is it that takes place with these few cases where there isn't a mushroom or growth of these negative cells called cancer? What is it that happens? They have, deep inside, an entirely different attitude. Attitude creates a rate of vibration. But it's not just an attitude here, you see. The mind can do many things, but it's the heart that really does the job.

Now, I'm not trying to teach you that acupuncture or chiropractic care or holistic this or that is the thing for you. I'm trying to show you, before you make final decisions on surgeries, that you at least investigate reputable—and I do mean reputable—alternative measures. For nothing is as final as surgery. It's very final. It's very final. And there are so many wonderful ways of restoring healing to the human body without having it all cut up. There are so many wonderful ways. But each person should make that decision for themselves. And at least be kind enough to themselves to investigate alternative measures.

Now, if you go to a medical doctor and a surgeon and you ask him what he thinks about a chiropractor—don't waste your time. And if you go to a chiropractor and you ask him what he thinks about the surgeon—don't waste your time. Because you're just going on what's called a merry, old merry-go-round. It's a total waste, a total waste of energy.

So I think, considering all factors, that the tablecloths will be finished, that the students involved with the project have learned a wonderful lesson. I'm sure they have. If they have not, the principle of the experience will indeed be repeated. It will indeed be repeated. I know, over these many years, the Spirit has always said, "Well, we're not infallible." They've never claimed to be infallible. But I've found where the fallibility problem exists, is in those poor souls trying to get the message through the egos down here. That's where the fallibility exists, believe me. It's our mental interpretations of what they mean and what those Friends don't mean.

So if you want better health, if you want a job or you want a change or you want a new job, I know you know the way. And I know that you know the only thing that's in the way of the way that you know. I hope you understand that. If you don't, you can hear it on tape a few times.

But think of the multitudes of times that we judge by doing such and such, such and such will be the result. Just stop and think how many times a day our minds do that. "Now let's see, if I do this, then that will happen and such will happen and such will happen and such will happen." But it doesn't, you see? It doesn't work out that way. You see? Someday we're going to realize that.

Another one of my students is having a wonderful opportunity of facing attachment and freedom of attachment. It's just beautiful. I am always so happy for my students when I see them going through what their brains call disaster and struggle because I know their tenacity is unreal. I know that they not only have the tenacity, but they have the will power to ride the waves, to get through it someday. I don't know how many centuries it'll take—or days or years. But I know—but I'm always so very happy for them.

When the struggle is the greatest—and if you think I sit in a plush chair and there's no struggle, forget it—but when the struggle is the greatest, you see, victory is at hand. But it's not a victory that your ego can say how many days away it is. So if you think it's that kind of a victory, just forget it. But when the struggle is the greatest, victory is at hand. And it's a beautiful thing to watch. All of these different experiences. And it's even more beautiful when I make the effort to keep my mouth shut, because I can't always say what's always going on because if I do, I interfere. And if I interfere, I have to pay the price. And I don't want their trip. I got my own to take care of—keeps me very busy.

But anyway, think about that. When you're having a struggle with this or you're having a struggle with that, think of that opportunity, you see. Especially, especially is it the greatest when your ego didn't decide that this is what's going to be and your ego didn't consciously tell you. That's when it's the best of all. I can assure you of that. It's really fantastic. It's just wonderful! Because you get to see, you get to see how those levels inside you really are. Are they little, bitty kids, crying for mommy or daddy? Are they in rejection and self-pity because they don't get their own way, you know?

Some people, you know, they call the house and if I'm not right there, they get furious. They not only get furious, they go into total rejection, you know, like I was a doctor, a 24-hour doctor, that I've got to be right there on the telephone. It doesn't work that way at all. It doesn't work that way. I don't know anybody I can call twenty-four hours a day and night. Why, I can't even call the Spirit. I wouldn't think of doing it. Calling them around the clock just to take care of my little whims and fancies. Oh, no. No. So we, of course, must not expect that from others because, you see, none of us are willing to give it. And we cannot expect to receive what we are not willing to give. Don't you see?

Now, I've been called during the night, sure. Years ago, I was called almost around the clock and I finally said, "Something's wrong with me. There's something wrong with me. There's this damn telephone ringing all the time—every time I turn around. I'm a constant slave to this telephone. This is insanity." I, I even had to have a great, big long 25-foot cord to carry out in my yard because I couldn't even take care of my roses because the phone was going round and round and round. And I finally said to myself, "There's something wrong with you, Richard. There's something radically wrong. You're an absolute slave to this telephone. An absolute slave." Well, believe me, I got freed from it. It took me a while, but I got myself freed from it. And you have, I believe it's right here in the book [*The Living Light*] that gadget called the telephone. I paid the price before I got the teaching, though.

You see, we become slaves of many things. And because we're such a slave and so addicted, we're not even aware that we're a slave! But when you can't even have a cup of coffee without the telephone ringing and you have to race to the telephone, I don't know, there's something radically wrong. I share that with you because I paid that price. It was worth every minute, believe me. The price was so great, it was well worth it. I look back—But to try to get that message into some people's head—you know, well, they haven't answered their telephone enough times yet, to get that message through. But someday, someday it will happen. Someday.

Because, you know, there's not really much accomplished when you're in that constant call vibration on the telephone. There's not really much accomplished. No, no. I'm a firm believer, you look them right in the eye, you get a lot more accomplished. Now, of course, the telephone serves its purpose. But if you find yourself constantly on it, then you can be rest assured, you can be rest assured you are totally controlled by it and cannot see and cannot be free. No.

So, what are we going to do? It looks like by the time that one of my students re-does the tablecloths—which is such a wonderful lesson for everyone. I want you all to be real happy about that and, and make it register good, so you don't have to repeat it someplace else—and the other student gets the dishes finished, it kind of looks to me as though they'll both be arriving at the same time now. Because the one doing the hand-painted dishes, she is a little behind and, of course, I'm sure she couldn't help but feel a little bit badly—not too much—but a little bit because the tablecloths were finished. And so I'm sure she'll be much happier to know they're not finished. It's going to take a few more months. And so the dishes and the cloths will probably arrive together and won't that be nice.

Now, I know it's only what you might call material things, but look at the spiritual lessons. There are so many wonderful spiritual lessons involved. You know, I well remember the years when we had a few directors and some members that, well, they were going to make the decisions. Well, each time they had that thought, they had me to meet, because I had eighty-one people over there to meet. And I had already made my agreement before the whole thing started that they would make all these decisions. Because I had been a member of a church and knew what it was like. Now, any of you people that attend our membership meeting know that it takes about eighteen minutes. Be nice when we reduce it to nine. There's no sense in taking all day with so much work to be done.

But that's something we have to be constantly on guard for. Constantly. Stand guardian at the portal of your thought and the joy of life will ever be at hand. Now think, that's all you have to do: Stand guardian at the portal of your thought and the joy of life will ever be at hand. Now isn't that a simple thing to do, really? But if you ask a person, "What are you thinking?" they say, "Nothing." There's no mind that's not thinking something. Believe me. It really takes a lot of effort to shut it up. It really does. It really does. Now, you just try it. You just try it for a few minutes a day to shut off that mind, you'll see how tenacious your mind is, and its demands and its desires and its frustrations—you see—and its judgments that things aren't going your way.

Well, you know, if you judge today that things aren't going your way, you guarantee the law for tomorrow that they won't. So isn't it better to accept, well, things are just great? I think they're fantastic! I've told myself that for so many years I can't remember, really, when I started. And I've had a terrific amount of help, because I have had students tell me how miserable life is. And every time they say that, I say, "Oh, God, thank you. I've got to remind myself. I've got to say it more often: Life is just beautiful. It's just great for me. It's just absolutely wonderful!" So I have had a great deal of help, you know, from my students, from friends of the organization and the church telling me how miserable things are because it serves—you see, I, I choose to use that input into my consciousness as a reminder to be grateful of how good my life is. You see? And I kind of like to share that. But you have to make the effort.

So perhaps if you would expose yourself a little more to that jungle of how horrible everything is, then you could remind yourself of how grateful you are, for you have your health, you have your wealth and your happiness. And if you think you don't, then, of course, for you, you don't! You can have a million dollars in the bank, you know, but if you think you're broke, of course you're broke! Because you're thinking, you're living in the mental world, don't you see? It is really so simple. It's so simple.

I hope that all of you will grow to that understanding of how simple it is. That it really does come from God. It's loaned to you only for a time. You don't know how long or how short. And it's going to move on, so something else can move in, you see.

Now, I know that there is no mind present, no mind that doesn't want something new entering their life. If that wasn't true, there wouldn't be so many divorces and so many struggles with these marriages. They always want something new. See, the mind always wants. You know, it's its nature: to gather, to garner. It's got to have this. It's got to have that. It's got to have something else. It's constantly doing that. Constantly.

This is why your mind can never offer you happiness. There's no possible way that your mind can bring you happiness. No possible way. It certainly cannot bring you joy. Oh, no. Now, it serves its purpose, but it cannot bring you peace, it cannot bring you joy, it cannot bring you any soul faculty. There's no way possible that it can. Because its very nature is to get, get, get, get, get. And it's constantly getting something. Unfortunately, it's usually getting the stuff you don't want, you see. But the reason it's getting the stuff you don't want is because you haven't taken control of it: you let it run wild. So it has this, by its nature, this principle of getting. So it looks around and just gets everything. It doesn't discriminate, you know. It doesn't use any common sense. It's just got to get, get, get, get, get. But it can't get happiness. It can't get that for you.

And for every dollar it gets for you, it'll cost you ten. Believe me. Because, you see, the moment your mind sees one dollar coming in, it has so many desires lurking back here that it will spend ten for every one you take in. Now that's just the way the old mind works. And so it lives in a constant process of frustration because it's never getting enough. There's never, *there's never* enough for the human mind. There never will be. You cannot fill the vacuum of the human mind. There's no way possible that anyone can fill it. No way possible.

This is why it's a miracle that marriages last any time at all. I mean, you know, it's really kind of a miracle. It's just a miracle that that institution even lasts. But I think the ones that really last is that they go through so many years of fighting with their minds, that their little minds finally get exhausted and then, you see, there's peace, you see? And there's unity.

And then there's no problem. Because their minds finally just got too weary. But it doesn't last, unless you remember how it happened. It doesn't last.

Well, I do hope you have enjoyed this evening's class. Of course, there was no personal exposure. However, the ones involved, I'm sure, got the message without me having to name each one individually and specifically because we all have a conscience. It's a spiritual sensibility with a dual capacity. It knows right from wrong.

Now, we've covered a lot of subjects this evening. And I'm glad that I got to give the class, because everybody stayed awake. I don't see anybody sleeping. And isn't that great? Not even the chairman is snoozing.

Now, I know we've already gone past the hour and it's going to have to go on to a longer tape. So I'm not going to waste the tape. I have a lot to say. I don't get to give class too often. Many years ago I used to give seminars. And they lasted a few hours, yes. Yes, I always—I don't know, I've never been, really, lost for words. I always have something to say about something, whether it's the weather—don't get into politics too much. But I hope, when you do listen to this evening's class, that you will pay attention to some of it, because there is definitely something there for you. There really is.

And your life will change when you make the effort to take control of your mind. That's when your life will change. Now, it won't change and—permanently—that's it. Your mind doesn't give up like that. You've got to stay on guard. Say, "Little mind, you've ran me down the primrose path long enough. I will now tell you in what areas you are to express and in other areas, you are to keep your mouth shut and sit in the bleachers. And that is it!" But, you see, the first time you tell your little mind something like that, it's going to retaliate against you. But remember, remember, it is a vehicle designed to serve your soul. And if you never forget that, it'll never be stronger than you, you see?

It is only a tool that has been designed by the infinite Divine Architect to serve your true being.

You know, once it was given that, "When the tools no longer serve the worker, the worker begins to serve the tools." And if you let your mind—if it's in control, then you're serving the tool, for your mind is a tool designed for your use. Can you imagine, you being out in the garden, laying on the ground looking at a shovel, doing what the shovel tells you to do, when it tells you to do it? Well, don't you see, my friends, that's what you're doing when you let your mind tell you what it wants and when it wants it and how it wants it and what it wants to do. That's a tool, my friends. But it became your master because you didn't keep it under control, don't you see? Think of that. Think of laying on the ground and a shovel ordering you around, crawling around down there, what you're to do. Well, that's what your mind is doing. As beautiful as it is, when you let it take control—that's what's happened—then that's what you're doing.

Because, you see, your mind has birth and your mind has death. For that that has birth has guaranteed death. That is the law. But you, your soul, your spirit, it never was born. And therefore it can never die. There's no way it can die, because it was never born. But your mind, oh, it's dying all the time. It's already dead to many thoughts of the past. Oh, yes. And even today, we find that our minds are often dead and blind to the light of reason. I'm sure that many of you will agree, working with the different employers that you have and the different associates and etc., you say, "By God, that person's dead." Dead to common sense. Dead to communication. So your mind is already dead to many things! Some minds are even dead to understanding. Dead to tolerance. Dead to patience. Dead to wisdom. Go on down the list. And ask yourself what is your mind dead to today? Because it's dead to something.

What you are this moment—if you think you are the form and the mind, if you think you are that, then you will die. Oh, yes, indeed you will die. But you are not that and therefore you will not die. But if you are attached to your mind—think of it—if you are over-identified—now, remember that attachment is nothing more nor less than over-identification with anything. That's what attachment is, is over-identification. Now, if you are attached to your mind and to your form, then you must suffer the price: pay the price and suffer its death. Because it was born and it will die. And it isn't just like [*The Teacher snaps his fingers.*] that and it's dead. No, it's a slow process. Your mind, your body, it wasn't born [*The Teacher again snaps his fingers.*] at the snap of the finger. It's a slow process and a painful process. And your death will be accordingly, in keeping with your attachment, in keeping with your over-identification.

And so it's very simple. It indeed behooves a person to spend a few moments each day, *every day*, in taking control of the mind that you may experience that which is eternal, that which never dies, that which is never born. That's what you really are. This is where the effort—if the effort is made today, every day to tell your mind the truth: You are not that mind. It's a tool that you're using. You are not that body. It is a tool that you are using. And you remind yourself of that simple truth, then, when your time comes—your transition—you will not have to go through the suffering and the decay of the mental and physical body because you will not be so attached to it.

Now, if you think you are not attached to anything in life, invite someone in to take the things you think the most of. You'll very soon see whether you're attached or not. It's really a simple process. Just say, "Come on in. Now, this I'm very fond of. I like this more than anything in my life. You take it." And then, you see, you get to see how you feel as they're walking out the door. [*Many students laugh.*] Now, it's going to go someday. A robber may come and take it in the night. A thief in the night may take it. You don't know, you see. So we all can see, for physical objects and people, how attached we are by entertaining the thought of just giving it up, all right? But how many of us will make the effort to see how attached we are to our thoughts? How attached we are to our judgments?

Now, I have a few students that are looking for work. And I assure them that work is looking for them, but they must change their attitude or they're not going to meet it. Because the only thing that keeps the job from them is their attitude.

And I must say one thing before I finish this. This is very important. On attachment. And so one of my students said, "Well, you're not going to give these away, are you?" And I said, "Yes, if somebody wants them, let them have it. Otherwise, they go to the garage sale." They replied, "But I use this knife to peel the potatoes with!" I said, "That's not a paring knife." Now, we have several beautiful pairing knives in that kitchen. And I was delighted to see the student had merited the opportunity—the opportunity they had merited, number one: to free themselves from their attachment; and number two: to accept an authority greater than their human mind and their emotional attachment to a knife or knives. It's that simple. Isn't that beautiful?

And, you see, that's where school really is. That's where it is. Up at God's house, there on the hill, that's where all these wonderful experiences are taking place all the time right around the clock. And a few people survive. Our membership is less than twenty-four. But a few do survive. I mean, some have been around since the beginning, you know—a couple, not many, but a few. Yes. They're as tough as I am, I know. They have survived. Now, you, too, will survive if it means enough to you.

We all shudder at the thought of discipline. And yet, discipline is the very thing that's going to be an instrument in bringing us the goodness that we're seeking.

Now, I was a little bit sad to see here this evening one of my students who was late last Thursday and is not here in class this evening. But we all were informed that we lock the door at 8:00. We are always given two warnings in anything. Now, stop and think, my friends. If we permitted one student, one student to come in tardy and we did not permit all of you to come in tardy, then your little church and your school would be operating in personality: granting favors to one and not to another. But that's not how we operate. We never have. The Spirit has never operated that way. It didn't matter to the Spirit in any way, shape, or form, whether it was a relative of mine or anything else. That doesn't cut any ice. In keeping with the law demonstrated, principle is ever the same.

And speaking on that subject of principle, when our minds judge what principle is and our minds judge what principle is not, we're a far, far cry from principle. Because without total consideration, principle does not exist. And when it's limited to the human mind, then that's a very limited consideration, you see, and does not exist.

When—remember this—when we find our minds demanding, absolutely demanding that we know this and that we know that and why is this and why is that and go on down the list, you can be rest assured your little mind is just furious it can't control everything. But remember, when you experience this feeling to control everything, what it really is—and we've discussed it before—your little soul is impinging on your consciousness, "Hey, you need to control yourself. You're way out of control." Your soul is not telling you to go out there and try to control everybody else. Your little soul's trying to tell you that you're so far away from control that you've got to make some effort on your own head. But then, it rises up here and the ego gets a hold of it, the uneducated part of the ego. It says, "Control? That's it! I've got to control everything." You see? "And everything I need to control is out there. There's nothing in *me* to control. It's out there I've got to control."

Well, thank you, friends. Thank you very much.

MAY 15, 1980

CONSCIOUSNESS CLASS 211

Good evening, class.

Well, as you notice this evening, life constantly offers us the opportunity to see where our priorities are, whether it's being prompt or it is facing our responsibilities of directors of the church or anything else. And so it is that your philosophy, when it is applied each day in all of your activities, will reveal to you exactly which levels of consciousness are in control at any given moment.

I want to speak to you in reference to the application of the philosophy that we all have been studying. Each and every experience, as I said earlier, is offering to each of us a golden opportunity: number one: to see what level of consciousness is controlling our life most of the time; number two: to see the benefits or detriments of the level; and number 3: of course, to make a wise choice in order that we may experience the true beauty and the joy of life.

Now, there are two words in this philosophy that the majority of levels of our mind not only do not appreciate, but immediately kick out. Now, those two words are *responsibility* and *discipline*. Let us pause and think for a moment. What judgments we have made concerning the word *responsibility* and the word *discipline*? Obviously, it's quite negative, considering how adverse we seem to be to those two words. So I'm sure we'll all agree that they have a very special negative, restrictive, limited meaning to our minds. And yet, in the understanding and application of this philosophy, we sooner or later become aware that without responsibility, personally, without discipline, we have no freedom. We are in bondage to whatever level of consciousness, whatever thought strikes our mind at the moment. And so we find our days—most of them—filled with frustration and, of course, unfulfilled desires.

We all know that life, surely, was not designed to be filled with frustrations and with all these struggles that we put ourselves through. But it's a matter, of course, number one: of becoming aware; and number two: taking control. Taking control of one's own feelings and thoughts. Ofttimes, you know, a person will say, well, they didn't—they were not aware that they felt such and such a way. So the first step, obviously, of course, then, is awareness. We become aware of our feelings and we become aware of our thoughts.

Now, some time ago it was given in one of these classes to flood your consciousness. One of my students spoke to me the other day and asked me if that meant every moment of every day. Well, I never met a person so perfect to do it every moment of every single day. In fact, in the many years that it has been recommended to flood your consciousness with the positive and the good, it's a rare person that does it ten or twenty times a day.

Now, let us understand, of course, how our mind works so that, hopefully, we can move on to our spirit. But let's get some understanding of how our mind works. Our mind is in a constant state of broadcasting messages into the atmosphere. And when I say constant, I mean constant. There is no moment that it is not broadcasting something into the atmosphere.

Now, there are times when a person becomes aware that a particular thought keeps repeating itself in their mind. A particular thought or a particular feeling. And it's very disturbing when they become consciously aware of that happening to them. But it just seems as though the thought, negative, just insists on repeating itself constantly. Moment by moment, it just keeps bombarding the consciousness. Now, what has happened is that you have somehow opened up a door of awareness to that inner mind. That's what has happened. That process is going on constantly. Once in a while, something will bother you a great deal and a thought gets in your mind and you can't get rid of it. You can't think of anything else. That's all that you can think of and you want to get rid of it real bad and it, it keeps on bombarding your consciousness. It only means that you have become aware of that mind. That's all that it means.

That same thing is happening twenty-four hours a day right around the clock. So doesn't it behoove us, considering that the very nature of that mind is to broadcast the message, doesn't it behoove us to consciously choose the message that we want broadcast? Because whatever the message is that is being broadcast—you don't have to ask what the message is, if you're not aware. All you have to do is look at your experience. Now, your experience will reveal to you whatever message is being broadcast the loudest, the most frequent, and with the most energy. Each day your experiences will tell you what is being broadcast.

So if the experiences that you have in your daily activities are not in keeping with what you consciously would choose, then you have to make the effort to reprogram. And that takes a little bit of energy and it takes a little bit of effort.

The difficulty in flooding the consciousness to bring about new, more beneficial, more positive and productive experiences, the difficulty is that the message presently being broadcast is a very strong message and it will not allow a new message to be introduced, you see. It is in control. Whatever experiences you're having, if you want them changed, you and you alone can change them. They are not beyond your power to control because they are your experiences.

Now, here in these classes and in Serenity we offer to you a program of self-discipline, of self-control, and personal responsibility. The very things that are indispensable to bringing to you the peace, the joy, the freedom, and the abundant good that is your divine birthright. That *is* your birthright. You cannot claim your birthright as long as the error, the error of thought is in control.

You see, we're living so much of our time in a mental world, in a world of thought. We have such great difficulty in receiving the things that we desire to receive because we have such great difficulty in letting go of the things that we think that we have. Now, your receiving of what you desire is ever in keeping with your willingness to let go. So if you let go easily, then you will receive in life easily, for the law is totally impartial.

Ofttimes a person feels that they, they give very freely, very freely and they're having great struggle in receiving. But we must remember that the principle of the law is totally impartial. And it only reveals that it is not in balance—the giving and the receiving—because if it was in balance, then there would be a continuous flow. If you give spasmodically, restrictively, then you can only receive spasmodically and restrictively. And so the time you want to receive and you really want to receive, that happens to be one of those spasmodic times of your giving and, consequently, it's not there when you want it.

Now, everything that we desire sooner or later enters our universe. The problem is, it enters it when we don't want it. That's the problem. But, then again, it is in keeping with our givingness. Ofttimes there is the need of giving and that is the time when we're not in the giving vibration. And so, you see, my friends, all of life works both ways.

When you decide to enter the flow of the Divine and you decide that by accepting there is no thought or judgment that is worth holding for eternity, when you make that intelligent decision, and you let the thought come and you let the thought go, then you are constantly in a flow. And you don't have to have and experience this fluctuation, these tides of creation.

One moment you're sky high and the next moment you're at the very bottom of the barrel—and many of my students below the bottom. They somehow got down underneath of there. I know they'll come back through, but they'll have to go through the same obstruction that they went down through to get back out again. Because the law says the way in is the way out; and the way out is the way in.

Now, there are levels that are very important to recognize and everyone goes through them. And one of those many levels—most interesting to me. I see it expressing; periodically it rises up in one of the students to take control. And it always gives, of course, the same message: "Well, I always used to do fine before I learned so much about this philosophy." It's a very interesting level. I have heard it from the vice president of the church years ago. I haven't heard it for several years, though, I'm happy to say. But it rises up periodically in someone's head.

Now, what does it really say? What is that level really saying? "I was much better off before I was found out. I was blind and happy in my blindness, slumbering in my sleep of satisfaction, and now I've woken up. I've got to face personal responsibility. I've got to make some effort now for the first time, perhaps, in my life to discipline myself. I've got to grow up and accept that whatever is happening to me is caused by me." I know it's a rude awakening. And because it is such a rude awakening, it expresses in a very rude way. And it always blames outside for the problems that are going on inside. We all know that there is no problem that doesn't have within it, by its very nature, its own solution. There is no disaster that one cannot, and will not, grow through.

There's one thing, if you will remember your teachings, whatever it is that you think is your struggle today, be grateful for it, because it could always be worse tomorrow. And if you push it aside, known as procrastination, you push it aside, it only knocks at your door again and again and again. And each time it gets stronger. And each time the struggle gets greater. So whatever it is that you have today to grow through, look at it with a joyous attitude, with a feeling of a golden opportunity for the experience that you may perceive the lesson that you alone have merited and, in perceiving it, will face personal responsibility and grow through it in a very harmonious way.

Because, my friends, you'll always face your own pride. You'll always have to face your own ego. You'll have to face all of the functions. And, of course, on the bright side of life, all of the faculties.

Now, you have been given the soul faculty, the first one, of duty, gratitude, and tolerance. You have also been given the second soul faculty of faith, poise, and humility. I'm sure all of you will agree that pride is a great stumbling block on our path to peace and harmony. But what is pride, really? We all will agree, I'm sure, that it's certainly not a soul faculty. I'm sure we'll all agree that it has its limits. I'm sure we'll all agree that it is the effect of the king of judgment. And I'm sure we'll all agree that it is very limited and very restrictive. So what benefit does our mind tell us that pride has for us? Whatever we take pride in—in some talent we feel we have or we take pride in some job we think we've done or we take pride in what we think we have or we take pride in what we think we don't have—be rest assured, we establish all the laws necessary to help free us from that error, that great error of ignorance.

A person can take care of themselves without the function of pride, but they must have expressing, to some extent and degree, the faculty of humility. When we feel ourselves prideful, of course we can be rest assured that our little mind is in total control and we are guaranteeing for ourselves the freedom from that bondage. Because our adversities in life, they become our attachments. You see, it isn't pride that we need, if we need anything, but it is an expression of the divinity that is within us.

Everyone feels at some time—and some people feel more often than others—a great need for energy. And we have discussed this need for energy some time ago. When you permit your mind to entertain self-thought to such an extent that it becomes an imbalance in your universe, you ground out the electromagnetic field within you. Now, when you ground that out, there's that inner vibration known—that inner, true inner thought of self-preservation that rises up. For it knows that there is a shortage of energy flowing through your being.

Now, there's no shortage on the part of the Divinity or the Divine or God. There is a shortage created by an obstruction: the obstruction being a great deal of self-thought which brings about an imbalance and grounds out this flow of energy. It blocks it like a dam. When that happens, self-preservation rises up demanding the energy necessary for your survival. And because, at those times, you are controlled by self-thought and are short of energy because of the self-thought obstruction, you can only do what your mind offers you to do. And so it does whatever is necessary to get you attention, for it knows that energy is following attention. And it is amazing, to say the least, what the human mind can connive and conceive to gain energy. It is just amazing.

Now, we see this taking place with little children, little, bitty children. Now, no one taught them if you do this, you'll get an extra charge of energy; if you do that, you'll get an extra charge of energy. Something within them—the self-preservation knows. And so they will do whatever is necessary to bring them attention, which is energy—which energy follows, which is love. For pure love is pure energy.

Now, we've all gone, here, through this earth time for many years now. We're no longer little children that have to do all these little idiosyncrasies in order to receive this necessary energy for our survival. But we have to give up one thing: we have to give up this over abundance of self-thought. So that our health, our wealth, and our happiness can be restored to us. Now, health and wealth are inseparable. In truth, they're one and the same. They are an, an effect of an unobstructed flow of infinite, intelligent, divine energy. That's really what they are.

When you find that the struggle is great and your thought concerning it is only making it worse—because that's what created it in the first place. Nothing outside created it. No circumstance created it. No condition outside created it. Only your thought created that. And when you find the struggle the greatest and you're ready to accept the possibility of something else working through you, then you're ready to give up the need for self-thought, the error of ignorance, and declare your divinity by removing that obstruction in consciousness: the self-thought. The immediate effect is new experiences of a more positive nature begin to flow in your life.

I know that many people have said that, well, they're not about to give up their mind, considering they're not sure of what is beyond—beyond the control of their mind. Well, be rest assured, I haven't met anyone that automatically or in any way gives up their mind. The tenacity of the human mind is so great it can't be given up for more than a moment or two at a time. With that kind of tenacity, don't worry, you won't be shedding the old mental body in any century in the foreseeable future that I'm able yet to see. Now that takes a long time and a lot of change and a lot of growth.

But think how simple the philosophy is that you're here to study. Think how simple that it is. Only our minds complicate it. It's only our minds that do those things.

Remember, if we don't like where we are, we know how to leave. We leave right in here, you see. If there's some experience that you're going through that you don't appreciate and you don't want any part of it, well, you have the power to leave.

You created it and you can create something better. You see, you have that power within you.

How many people feel that they're capable of changing their thought when they choose to change it? Please raise your hand. Well, there's a few people that feel that they can change their thought when they choose to change it. Now, we should all feel that way. Because that is our birthright, you see. But it isn't the way it works, is it? Many of us have great difficulty in changing our thought—great difficulty—which reveals whatever has control of us at the moment is very powerful. But remember, it's never more powerful than you who created it in the first place.

So you can always encourage yourself. Each effort that you make to encourage yourself to tell yourself how much better things are, each time you do that, things do get better. Because, you see, the universe responds to you. You are your reality.

Now, I remember when one of my students mentioned the other day about flooding the consciousness, well, [they asked] Wasn't that a type of self-hypnosis? Well, you're already in self-hypnosis, if you want to give it a name tag. I mean, if some thought gets into your head, which happens, it takes total control of you, what do you call that? Well, they call that self-hypnosis. The thing's got a hold of you. Right by the nape of the neck.

So why do we take so long to wake up from the sleep of satisfaction? But at least we do wake up. Some of us, we go right back to sleep again. And then we wake up again for a few more minutes and we go back to sleep again. Only to wake up again and again and again and again. Experiences, oh, they repeat themselves. They come back to tell us a change is long overdue, long overdue.

Now, when your minds have tried everything—and I do mean *everything*—and they've turned over every little rock in the universe and nothing has worked, then it's time to turn to God in the court of last resort. And then you wonder, when that day comes, why you waited so long, why you almost killed yourself thousands of times trying to figure out the universe, trying to control everything you looked at and everything you touched or sensed or felt. You wonder, when you've finally reached the court of last resort, why you waited so very, very long. Now, you don't have to wait a few more centuries to get there. You can get there at any moment that you, yourself, choose. At any moment.

I know that tolerance is indispensable to success. And that tolerance, that first soul faculty, which is inseparable from duty and gratitude, has to be applied within. You see, you cannot apply tolerance without, unless you've applied it within. People who have great difficulty in tolerance with other people have almost no tolerance with themselves. And there's no success in life without that soul faculty. It is not only the first soul faculty, it surely is one of the most important. Tolerance.

But what must we give up to gain in tolerance? I can tell you, and you all know. We must give up judgment in order to open up our first soul faculty. Can you imagine living in paradise one day? The one day that you give up judgment, you'll be in paradise right here on earth. That one day that you give up that king. Think of that. Think of the experiences you can have. Why don't you try it only, say, for sixty seconds? I know for a whole day that would be a phenomenal task for most students, phenomenal task. But try it for sixty seconds. Stop and become aware of how you feel in the one minute that you really give up that king called judgment. Why, you'll really be amazed at how you feel in that one 60-second time.

Now, if you're looking for a job or you have struggle with money problems or business isn't up to what your judge in your head says it should be or on down the list, try it for sixty seconds. When you think of your business, say, "Whoops! I'm freed from judgment." And just see what takes place in your head. Now, if you can do it for sixty seconds, you can certainly, slowly but surely, do it for a day.

Now, many people think, "Well"—and they've even mentioned to me—"Well, how am I going to do this and do that, if I don't make judgments?" Well, there's a vast difference between judgments and decisions. There's all the difference in the universe between the two. A decision has total consideration for everything.

Now, I'm sure we'll all agree, concerning our experiences to date, that judgment has been a very expensive luxury that we'd like to do without for at least sixty seconds. I tell you, it's a wonderful experience to make that effort each day to be free from judgment. Because it means you get free from the control of the mental world. Totally free. And that is really and truly something.

Now, we're here a very short time on earth. We don't know how many days it's going to be—or years, for some of us. So isn't it better to really make some daily effort, some daily effort? We can hear the philosophy throughout all eternity, but, you see, it won't help us until we apply it. It's worthless without application. You can listen to 200,000 tapes of this philosophy, it'll register in your memory par excellence to be of benefit in the day that you apply any of it. That's the only time it's going to do any good. It won't do any good otherwise. None at all. It'll just be recorded in your memory par excellence waiting for someday in eternity to benefit you when you apply it.

Now, if you're ready, you'll start on that path of freedom from the bondage of judgment and creation by taking sixty seconds once a day. That certainly isn't much effort and much time. Sixty seconds. You certainly can't be concerned about self-hypnosis with a 60-second effort. Sixty seconds to consciously be aware of freedom from judgment.

Now, you'll have to work at it in those sixty seconds, because those thoughts will rise up and bombard you. And they won't be happy with the tiny, tiny bitty effort that you're making, because they know that the journey of a thousand miles begins with the first step. Those judgments are very aware. They have all of the intelligence of your mind because they were created by your mind. So they won't appreciate what little effort you're making, knowing what's yet to come. And so you'll have to be very strong to make a 60-second-a-day effort to free yourself from judgment.

Now that's your homework for the coming week. We'll see what it's like a week from today. Thank you.

MAY 22, 1980

CONSCIOUSNESS CLASS 212

Good evening, class.

It is stated the peace that passeth all understanding because peace is greater than understanding. Peace is greater than wisdom or any soul faculty for peace is the source and the power itself.

In your experiences and activities during your days, whenever you find a thought in your mind to be discordant, disturbing, or unpleasant, if you will pause in that moment and truly become receptive to the power of peace, you will bring about a balance in your mental world and therefore, by that balance, be freed from the control of the discordant thought. Now, I know that some of you have tried to establish some degree of peace during the times when you feel disturbed and not at ease. It is difficult, sometimes, to become receptive to that power, but it is never, ever impossible.

The balancing of the faculties and the functions is brought about by restoring your mental world to a state of peace. And that can only be accomplished, of course, by your own personal, daily effort.

The struggles of life are only struggles to our mental world. If we, through errors in our experiences, if we become over-identified with the mental world, then our struggles, indeed, seem to us to be insurmountable. But there is, of course, in anything, there is a way to restore balance, as I'm speaking to you this evening about the great power of peace. For peace is God and God *is* the power.

It is very difficult for our minds to relate to God, the word *God*. We have, from our earth experience, many judgments, many discouragements, and many false hopes relating to the word *God*. For somehow along the way we've had the expectations and the anticipations that this God would just wipe the slate clean, whatever seems to be bothering us at the moment. Because those judgments and experiences are indelibly recorded within our consciousness, we have great difficulty in expecting and in accepting and in believing the possibility that there is a power called God that can free us. But we are a bit more receptive to the word *peace*, because we have had, and do have, moments of what we understand to be peace.

When you truly, truly make the effort, not just to think the word peace, but to experience its true meaning, you will restore balance to your mental world.

We do not easily change our identifications in life. Now, the reason that we do not easily change our identifications in life is because we're constantly directing energy to the things that we identify with.

When we become concerned over anything in life, we direct a great amount of energy in the process of concern. If we are concerned about what is going to happen to us tomorrow, we direct this neutral, intelligent energy through limited thought patterns of our mind. Now, it wouldn't be so bad if we knew all about those thought patterns. But we don't know all about those thought patterns of ours because they have become so habitual that we have not, for long times, given conscious thought to them. Consequently, it certainly has proven, I'm sure, to all of us, that whatever we place concern, directed energy, to, we soon find we have problems with. Because that energy is limited in its expression to experiences of the past, then the past repeats itself for us year after year and century after century.

For many years the Spirit has recommended a daily process of flooding the consciousness with positive affirmation. I know we will all agree that each and every one of us are creating our realities in life. To some of us life is truly beautiful. To others, it is truly miserable. And to others, it's good and it's bad and we never know when. We are indeed captains of our ship and masters of our destiny when we consciously choose how and when it's going to be. That conscious choice, that being captain of our ship and master of our destiny, is our divine right. It is our birthright.

When you flood your consciousness with peace, you enter a state of universal consciousness. When that happens, you are no longer concerned about what you thought you were concerned about because you are no longer limited in your identity. The struggles are the effects of limited expression of the divine, intelligent energy. But we are the ones who limit the expression by limiting our interest. And in limiting our interest, we experience over-identification and concern.

In this philosophy it is clearly taught that each must face personal responsibility in life and each must do their part. Now, if our part and our personal responsibility were known in its totality by our limited minds, then certainly we're far from knowing our part.

It is only when we experience, through our efforts, that peace and we enter that state of consciousness known as universal consciousness and in that state we become fully aware that we are, in truth, a part of everything, inseparable, a united whole. That's when we free ourselves from these great wars within, from this great battle that our minds keep us moving, back and forth, century after century after century.

If you will permit yourselves to entertain the possibility that you have lost everything and you will permit your minds to accept that as a fact in that moment for you, then in that moment you will gain everything, for you will no longer be limited in your identification. You will no longer be concerned. You will no longer have the battle of your mind to hold, to garner, and to gather and to live in what the mind has to offer: a simple word, known as fear.

Now, fear, we understand, is what is called negative faith. It is faith in what the mind can do. For there is no mind in any universe that accepts that it can't do anything. Now, that may seem to be quite a shock to you. For we have said many times, "Well, I can't do this and I can't do that and I can't do something else." But that is only one of your levels justifying its way out of making some effort. The mind, which is designed to gather and to garner and to create, can and does do whatever it chooses to do. And we, today, are the living effect of its dictates in our life.

When you make that effort to truly experience peace, from that great fountain of intelligent energy, through that neutralizing process, the counter-balancing soul faculty to the sense function struggle that you are having will be called forth. You don't have to worry whether it's the faculty of duty or charity or gratitude or what the faculty is—or humility—because that is not something that you need be concerned about.

Your soul does not have the function of concern. Your mind has the function of concern. For if your mind did not have the function of concern, it would not have the glory of control.

So if you find the step to accepting peace in those moments and you still have the need to work with your mind and the mental realms, then all you have to do when you find yourself in great concern is to honestly ask your mind what it is that it demands to control. And it will answer. And it will tell you very clearly what its need is. Now, I'm only speaking to those of you who do not yet feel ready to move to the spiritual path of peace and still want to work with your minds and all of its justifications and its multitudes of deceptive methods that it uses to accomplish its ways. It will tell you what it needs to control. Then you talk to it as you talk to a child and ask your mind why it thinks it needs that control in that way.

The only thing that has any value is your true being. Our little temples of clay, they're already in a process of going back to where they came from, only to rise again. But you will not return into those old houses, those vehicles, that you have used. You'll not return into those. So what is so important—because, you see, my friends, birth and death are inevitable to all form, no matter what form it is. So if you hold with great tenacity to form, then you must pay the price of the suffering of decay. It is a struggle to be born. It is a struggle to die. To be freed from the struggle of birth and death—whether it's the birth of a thought or the death of a physical object, it doesn't matter. That is what creation or form has to offer. Now, the mind is creation. The mind is form. Thought is a part of that creative process. And so it's born and it dies.

If you truly aspire to be free from that struggle, if you really want to be free, then only by entering the spiritual realms of universal consciousness, through the power of peace—and don't worry about all the soul faculties. They'll be brought into balance according to an infinite law. They're not and cannot be controlled by minds, for they are not composed of mental substance. If you're ready for that spiritual step, then you will make the effort each day and in every way.

Look at what life has offered already. Many forms have come into your life and many forms have gone. And each and every moment there's a constant process of a new form of thought in your mind. It's going to go. You never know when. If you let it go now, then it may not leave you now. If there is something that you value and your value is very great, let it go in your mind and you won't have to worry about when it's really going to go. Now, that's how we get to live in the world and not become a part of the world. That's how we get to live with people and never become a part of people. That means we're free from the fruits of action; we're free from the bondage of attachment.

Many times we have discussed the great form of judgment. Well, of course, judgment is created by thought and it has the added power of concern and, in truth, is control.

We all agree, I'm sure, that we are indeed controlled by the judgments that we have made. And as we continue to be identified with the mental world, we get to reap the harvest of each and every judgment that we make. Because those judgments are filled with the force of creative energy, they are denials of the rights of others and they are inevitably our destiny.

Destiny is at our command when we are freed from the mental world.

To go to a mountain top and experience the peace that passeth all understanding is to weaken our very substance and character. It's like taking a little plant and putting it in a hothouse: it can only live in a hothouse. But to experience the beauty and the peace and the joy of living in the jungle and in the midst of the Philistines not only strengthens our character, but expands our soul faculties of courage, of duty, of gratitude, of patience, of wisdom.

It is so easy to move from one place to another ever in keeping with the dictates of our mind. Not to see certain people because we are so weak in our efforts that when we see those people, we go totally into the emotional forces, not because of the people we meet, but because of our weakness of our lack of effort at controlling our own emotions. It is better to be in the world and not a part of the world than to escape from the world, only to return to it a cripple and weakling to start all over again.

Now, we have in our evolution earned and merited getting this far, but this is not the place to stop. You don't stop when you find the way. That's when you move on.

And so, my friends, the heaven that we all are seeking—because we all know where we came from—that cannot be denied us; we know our home—is here now. It's not tomorrow. It is *not* tomorrow. It isn't after such and such and such and such and such and such has worked out in our life. That's not where heaven is. It's not at the end of that path, because, you see, that path, it never ends. Did you ever meet anyone that's really free from desire? I never did. I never even met a cockroach that was free from desire! So I'm sure none of the two-legged animals have yet evolved that far.

But I am always encouraged. When the struggle is the greatest, the victory is at hand. But not the victory of which your mind dictates. That's not the victory that's at hand. Because if the victory that was at hand is what your mind dictates—huh!—then all you're doing is going back into the old pattern to repeat it again and again and again. That is not the victory of which the Spirit speaks. When the struggle is the greatest, when you are totally over-identified with your mind to limited thought patterns and the experiences are becoming just too much to bear, then victory is at hand that you are willing your little soul to rise up and tell that mind it's had enough and from now on your little soul is going to take charge and not have all those experiences anymore.

Now, there have been times in your life when your little soul has risen up and it's let your mind know, kindly but firmly, who's taking charge, finally! But unfortunately, it doesn't seem to last too long. That simply means that you've got to go back on the treadmill again and again and again. And the ancient Hindus called that the law of karma. Well, I think we've had enough karma in our life and I think it's time that we get freed from what the Friends call the yo-yo: first you're up and then you're down. And then you're up and then you're down. It certainly is exhausting. I know it's exhausting for me just to watch it. I can just imagine what it is to be that yo-yo.

Now, so many beautiful, simple truths have been given. If you only applied three of them—well, let's reduce it to one, because one wouldn't take as much effort as three. If you just tried one of them in the Law of Continuity—now that means each and every day, in each and every way. You have eighty-one levels of consciousness. You have forty soul faculties to balance out forty sense functions, and you've got one eternal power, called Peace.

What happens to you when you're disturbed and someone says, kindly, "Now, just be at peace?" Why, the level's about ready to kill you. Of course, there's many ways of saying "Be at peace." So, depending on what level of consciousness it's coming from, you have many varied experiences.

But, you see, when you feel so blue and so discouraged, when everything seems to be a disaster, try peace, because peace works. Of course, if you're really stuck in the spin cycle of the level—it is a spin cycle, you know, because it keeps moving. I never saw a thought stand still yet. It moves. And unfortunately, if we really identify with it, we'll spin ourselves on a merry-go-round that just doesn't seem to ever stop. But you try peace. See if you get mad with yourself. You get to see how much force that thought really has.

The mental world can be beautiful when it's balanced with your spiritual world. But if it's not balanced, then you've got nothing but a struggle, not only now, but on and on and on and on and on. You see, there is something greater than thought. There's the power that sustains thought. You always choose your thought. I know ofttimes you may not be aware of the thoughts you've chosen, but your experiences in life are the mirror and they remind us of the thoughts that we have entertained.

But you can change all of that if it's not serving a good purpose. You can change it. But now is the time to change it, because tomorrow will never come. If it doesn't mean enough today, it won't mean enough tomorrow.

To stick with one thing, even a simple process of flooding the consciousness with the power of peace, even that seems to be a great chore, depending, of course, on what's got us in control at the moment.

You know, I, like all of you, can entertain many thoughts. I can think of the disasters or the possibility of disasters. I can think that everything is going to pot or it's already there and I'm just waking up to the fact. Of course, I can entertain that kind of thinking, but, you see, I've already entertained that kind of thinking and I had a lot of experience as the effect. And from that somehow I've merited to get a philosophy that really worked. Because—see, I know it works because it works for me. And if it works for one, it means it works for everyone. You know the philosophy. To have the experience of it working for you, you have to make the effort. You can't just make the effort for a little while and then go back to the other patterns that brought you the negative experiences in life.

We are, every moment—and I emphasize every moment—we are sending messages out into the universe. We are doing it day and night. Our mind never stops sending messages into the universe. And we never stop having experiences. Think of that. We never stop having experiences because we never stop broadcasting. Want new experiences? Want better experiences? Start broadcasting something by conscious choice. You can't expect it to work overnight because it didn't take overnight, you see, to bring you what you have. It took a lot of broadcasting.

I'm only trying to emphasize to you that it works. It really does work. And any of you that have been around any length of time at all know very well it works for your church; it works for the job that it has to do and it works very nicely. It works the same for you when you let it.

So why not put what you're spending so much time and effort to learn, why not put it to work? It's time to really put it to work. I've always been a firm believer in being practical—not cheap, I hope, but practical. There is a vast difference. Practical. Why spend money to study something and not apply it? What good's it going to do? It does, really, no good except in the sense of your eternity: it's recorded in your memory par excellence. But why not have it do something today? It's intended to do something if you will only apply it.

Now, I know very well many of you want to make some changes. And I know very well that this old world, that if we over-identify with it, then we have all of its problems and struggles on our shoulder. I have no intention of over-identifying with it. Be with it and not a part of it means not to identify with it. That's how you get to be in the world and not a part of it is through your identity process, you see. It's like two people. They live together. They get grounded in each other's universes. Well, what does that mean? It simply means they've over-identified with each other. With a microscope, they're picking each other apart and the honeymoon is long over. It's long over because they're over-identified.

Now, it's like this old money world. You over-identify with it and you start to experience all those different problems and struggles. You see, when you're really on the bottom of the barrel, your old mind's just tried everything and all that it's tried hasn't worked out, you're truly blessed. You've got nothing left in the mental world. There's no, no choice left. You've made it. You have to turn to the spiritual. You see, there's nothing left. That's when your opportunity is truly golden. That's when it's really knocking at your door, if you have a door left. You know, sometimes you don't even have a door left. But that's *really* when you have the opportunity.

Now, we'll all survive, but we have the conscious right to survive nicely. I don't believe in these barefoot gods. I never did. We're here in this world to enjoy the goodness in the world. And the goodness is there. But it's up to us to start taking control of what we want to identify with.

Now, if you saw a person that you felt was pretty miserable, would you consciously, immediately identify with that person? Well, you know very well you wouldn't. Nobody wants to be around misery. I mean, we'll all agree with that. Nobody wants to be around anyone that's in the depths of self-pity and, and all of that. Nobody wants to be around it. Why doesn't anyone want to be around it? Because they've got the level in themselves and they know what it's like and they're not about to go back down into it! That's why they don't want to be around it.

But you can look at it another way, you see. You can say, "Oh, thank you, God, for reminding me. Here comes another two-by-four over my head." And you work on yourself. As an opportunity, you see. A seeming bad experience ofttimes produces excellent results. It depends on what you do with the experience. Don't you see? No matter what experience you're having, or have had, whatever it is, you can always turn it around. There is a power flowing through you that can take the essence from it and make it very good for you.

I've said a few times—I say it again—I have truly—I truly feel blessed. I have a wonderful opportunity. I don't have to sit down and have a cup of coffee and think how miserable I am, somebody comes to remind me what my life would be like if I don't work on myself. I don't have to think about the disastrous economy today, because someone always comes to remind me. So, you see, in that sense I am very fortunate. I really am fortunate. I don't have to think whether or not I, I should be smiling more. I can't help but smile because I have so many frowns knocking at my door.

So, you see, you can do the same thing. You can turn it all around. I don't have to tell myself what a miserable, crummy world this is and how I've been left out of the good stream of life, because I have people to come to tell me what it's like. And isn't that beautiful. It really is. But I make very sure that in those moments I am working every single second, because I learned the hard way, from experience, that after they left, all of a sudden I felt miserable and I didn't understand why. And sometimes I'd be miserable for weeks. So I learned.

When misery knocks at your door, go to work right away, even though you think it's not your misery. Because if you don't, you see, misery knows its kind and it'll find it inside of you and it'll rise up to take control of you unless you make the conscious effort.

Now, I can't remember, really, how many years it's been since I felt sorry for myself in self-pity, because God has blessed me with a few members in the church that seem to have that need to express that depth of discouragement and hopelessness rather frequently. And so I must talk to myself and encourage myself of how great life is that I don't have to go out into the universe to dig up those levels of consciousness. They're right at my doorstep just waiting to express themselves and they usually do a very good job at it. You see?

I tell you it's a beautiful world. I never felt better in my whole life. I don't feel better because so many people are feeling so miserable. I feel better because they're reminding me I'd better work harder or look where I'm going to be. Now, that's the way you look at life and then you'll see how great life really is.

I no longer, like I used to when I was a kid, remind myself of the Chin—of the starving people in China, you know. There's not enough rice in China, because that's what I heard when I was a little kid. I don't have to think about that anymore. I have it knocking at my door: "There's not enough steaks to eat." No.

Let's do something with what we've got because we've got everything necessary—and I mean everything—to bring us all the good that we could possibly desire. It's not out there, friends. It's no farther than your finger tips. Tell your mind the truth: "It's not out there." You are the magnet. It will come to you. You have to know that. You have to get your mind straightened out. Whatever you desire is right where you are. And all you've got to do is tell that mind who's in charge, and you will see that like attracts like and becomes the Law of Attachment.

And if we think we need more, just remember, if we get too much, we'll just collapse under the weight of it all, called responsibility, you know.

So we think about our vacations in life. And we think about the things we have not. And we think about the struggles and the disasters and the crises that we're going through, and yet, all those things will pass. By the law that brought them, they will go. And we don't have to be a part of them. We don't have to be.

If we have a book and we lose it, and it's a book that we're fond of and attached to, we have an emotional reaction only because we didn't choose (our minds) to let it go. It's just like two people. Perhaps one of them decides to go on their own way. The one who decides to go, they don't feel so bad. It's the other one left behind who hadn't made the decision before the other one made the decision. So they've got a little ego problem, don't you see?

So really, it's all these thoughts of ours. That's all that it really is. And we can feel as joyous as we feel miserable. And isn't that wonderful? It's entirely up to us. And I'll tell you, you don't have to be a Scorpio in life to be tenacious.

Thank you, friends.

MAY 29, 1980

CONSCIOUSNESS CLASS 213

Greetings, friends. This evening I wish to speak with you on that state of consciousness known as divine flow.

Whenever we permit our thoughts to review the past, we guarantee, by the Law of Creation, to concern ourselves with the future. That process is directly contrary to the eternal flow of divine consciousness. In order to enter that harmonious flow of health, wealth, and happiness, it is absolutely necessary to gain control of the mental world in order that you no longer be controlled by it. As long as the mind is permitted to review the past and concern itself with the future, then the harmonious flow and the power of the Divine, which is experienced in the eternal moment of the now, cannot, *cannot* be realized.

Because our minds are so used to think of everything that enters into our realms of desire and because of the very nature of the human mind, being a part of the dual Law of Creation, man enters the divine flow by putting all his thought into the eternal present, where the great changes that he seeks, for him, are possible.

Whenever you permit your mind to tell you that things will be better tomorrow, it immediately rises up and tells you how it was yesterday. And so the battle in the mental world continues on and on and on. To bring about the transformation that you may enter the spiritual realms of peace and harmony, of unity and eternal goodness, then the eternal moment must ever be in your conscious mind. For your mind, being the vehicle for your spirit, is subject to your spirit. And your spirit, being eternal, your spirit is ever present. And present is the moment of the power of God.

Whatever it is you think of doing, do it in your consciousness in the moment you have the thought. Learn to accept the possibility of all goodness and then give it no more thought, for you build the obstruction to the eternal path to the presence which is your true spirit. One may discuss the experiences they have wandered through, but in so doing, one must have control over the mind that it may be done so in the level of consciousness known as objectivity, for only in that level of consciousness is one freed from the dual law, is one freed from the magnetic field of emotional attachment.

As we know that peace is the power, peace, the power, and presence are inseparable, for they are, in truth, one and the same. The peace, the power, and the presence can only be experienced in the divine flow, and you may enter the divine flow only when you have gained control and brought the past and the future into the present moment, where all goodness is yours for the receiving.

Wherever you go and whatever you do, the goodness is with you when your thought is in that eternal moment. Stop and think, my good students, how often do you enter the power and the peace and the presence? How often do you bring the perfect balance to the mental realm that you may experience that divine neutrality where you know you have always been, for that is, in truth, your true home.

This is the moment. All else is an illusion. All past is an illusion. All future is an illusion. Only the presence of the present moment, only that is truth and only that is eternal. All else is the effect of the principle of creative substance; all else is form. All past, all future is form. Only in the moment are you formless, are you free. Only in the moment can you experience the Life, the Love, and the Light. All else be an illusion of the substance from whence dreams are made, for that, in truth, is what all else really is.

It is good to enter the dream as the observer. It is bondage to enter the dream and become the dream. For each dream, being created from the principle of the Law of Duality, offers to you an experience in the world of experience: it offers you that dual law.

If you have joy, or think you have joy from the principle of creation, then by that false belief will you guarantee its opposite, known as sadness. For sadness and joy, created of the same substance, brings to you the same experience. The one beeth the soul faculty and the other beeth the mental function. They are sustained by that eternal presence, by that eternal power. And so man views life ever in keeping with his own beliefs, ever in keeping with the dreams that he alone is creating.

Some time ago we spoke to you on "Dreamer, dream a life of beauty before your dream starts dreaming you." [*The Living Light Dialogue, Volume 1* or *The Living Light*] Don't you see, my friends? Your dream starts dreaming you: that creative substance becomes the force in your universe when you forget the eternal moment. When you forget the eternal moment, you lose the power in that moment of the Divine. When you find your world filled with struggles and disasters, filled with trials and tribulations, pause. In the moment of pause, you enter the presence and that is the lion's strength.

What is to be done shall be done in the keeping with the law that you individually and alone establish. You don't need to become the victim of the dream. You, your eternal being, is the true captain. You may keep on dreaming, for that is the nature of the mental world, for that is the nature of creation. But only when you separate yourself from the past and you separate yourself from the future, only then do you go home to your true home, only then do you have the freedom and the power and the peace. Only to go out again, but in going out again if you remember the eternal moment, you will never again be the victim of the dream that you have dreamed. And because all of life is a dream and is the effect of your dreaming, you have that wonderful, divine birthright to choose the dream you wish to dream. Your reality is a dream. And because you are the dreamer, you can change the dream.

So many feel it's so difficult to change their dream, to change their reality. It is only difficult because you have permitted your mind to dictate how the changing of the dream, for you, is possible. You see, my friends, in the eternal moment of the presence, the peace, and the power, there is no dictate, for there is no form. There is no thought; there is no mental world. And that is when, and that is how, you have the peace that passeth all understanding.

There are no form or forms in the eternal moment of now. Therefore there are no obstructions to your formless free spirit. But there is the great beauty that is the true you.

Beauty, a soul faculty, is experienced in keeping with how you permit your mind to relate to it. It is our mind that creates the form; the beauty is ever present. Beauty, like joy, is not dependent on limit or form for its expression. We have made it dependent upon form for us. We have made the goodness of life dependent upon form for us to realize and experience it. It doesn't have to be that way. Things don't have to be better tomorrow, for they are better in the moment that you take control.

When you permit your mind to dictate how you will enter the divine flow of goodness of life, then only by your dreaming that dream and becoming the victim of that dream can you realize the goodness that has always been, that will always be, for it is. And because it is, you, too, are.

Heaven is an experience that is dependent upon your realization of it. It will take the illusion of time that you have created in the mental world for you, but it is in the eternal moment of now.

When you enter that eternity, the presence and the present, when you enter that eternity, all things *are*, if that is your choice. For you enter the formless and you enter the free. You return home and once again are the essence itself. You are then the true and pure cause of your reality. Therefore, in the presence, in that great power of eternity, you form, from the formless and the free, that of your choice. But that takes daily, daily effort. It is the true, pure spiritual realm that is yours, that is you. It is not in some distant future unless you dream your dream that way.

Let your moment be ever present that you may know beyond a shadow of any doubt that all things come and all things go. And because all things do come and because all things do go, in that awareness you are free. There is nothing, there never was, there never will be, that you can call your own.

We experience the passing of many events. To some, we try to hold and we suffer. To others, we let them flow; we enter the eternal moment and they pass on through our life and we are free.

My good friends, it is only the things you attempt to hold that bring you the suffering, the struggle, and the disasters in life. If you will only give them to the source that is the true source, you will enter the eternal moment and be free from the strife. For whenever we attempt to hold to that which is passing on the stream of consciousness, we interfere with the great river of life. We try to build a dam with all the force our mind can muster, but no force can withstand the power of the stream of consciousness. And as our little dam we have created of mental substance with our force weakens and breaks down under that great power of divine flow, we feel, we register and experience the pain.

Life was not designed to hold. Life, the eternal consciousness, is designed to flow. Hold not to thought. For whoever holds to thought guarantees the holding to form, for thought is form. It is the forms within your mental universe to let go. Let them go that they may flow on the stream of consciousness, and in so doing, new thought, new ideas, new forms, you will experience.

If you feel it's difficult for you to let go, that is only the level of consciousness of fear. Whoever fears has great struggle in letting go. Whoever depends and relies upon form shall pay the price of form: it's known as pain and suffering. But whoever relies upon the formless, free Spirit, whoever relies upon the eternal presence of the eternal moment of now will flow harmoniously in the Divine Consciousness. Though multitudes of experiences come and go, they shall not move from the principle of peace. That is life in its fullness.

Our reality, of course, is the effect of the forms of thought that we depend upon. And as we depend and rely upon these forms of thought, our reality, having its limits—the limits of our mind and the limits of our own judgment—becomes the boundary in which we may express. And sooner or later, we desire to leave that boundary, to cross over into something new. For we, slowly but surely, begin to realize that we have, in truth, created a little prison in which there seems to be no escape.

Move and breathe in the now. Become consciously aware of how many times your thoughts are yesterday or tomorrow. Free yourself from the thoughts of yesterday and you'll be free, I say again, from the concerns of tomorrow.

And remember, that doing one's part in life not only means personal responsibility, it means the willingness, the effort, and the ability to respond to your true being. And when we respond to our true being, we rely and depend upon the power that we can experience in the eternal moment of the now.

Next year will not be better because it is compared with what has been and nothing is ever the same in creation. Something will always be wrong in the worlds of the mind.

And now, my friends, we'll take a few moments for the questions you have prepared.

Thank you. Please go into deeper depth on the subject of odic energy.

In reference to this question on odic energy, it will be, of course, of no benefit unless the questioner is willing to make the effort to enter the eternal moment and experience the great power and healing of odic energy, which can only be experienced when the mind is still. And the mind is only still when it is in perfect balance. And how does man bring his mind into perfect balance? The thoughts of yesterday and the concerns of tomorrow neutralize each other and man frees himself in the moment and will experience fully the power of the odic energy which is the very sustenance of life.

Thank you. What is meant by the Summer Lands?

The Summer Lands. The Summer Lands brought about—a term in the Spiritualist movement for those souls who have entered the realms of repose to adjust to their new surroundings in the early realms—early in the sense of the first realms of light, the twilight, where they—healers of those realms, bring them to visit, to experience loved ones who have gone before them that they may feel more at ease and more at home as they are being prepared for their work and their duty in the spiritual realms of service. The Summer Land is not a land where one tarries for years or centuries. But it is designed to help the souls to adjust to these other experiences and to help send them to the halls of learning where they may serve the light of God.

Thank you. How does temptation lead us to God when all else fails?

Yes, indeed. You can be assured, as long as you have a mind that assures you that you are you, you can then be assured of temptation. The Lord's Prayer states "Lord, lead us not into temptation." It is a beseeching of the law, for by "Lord" we understand the word to mean law. It is a beseeching of the law to lead us not into temptation. But *we* are that law, for man is a law unto himself. And so it is a beseeching of oneself to have courage and strength that the law created by man may not lead him into the realms of temptation. And so I said, long ago to you, that temptation leads us to God when all else fails. And indeed, indeed it does. For as we experience temptation and we continue to experience the lack of its fulfillment, the moment in the illusion of time does come when there is nothing left, nothing left but the essence and the power itself known as God.

So when all form, all form does not fulfill our tempting mind, we are indeed led to the only thing that's left. And that, for the mind, is God, as we exhaust the mental activity and experience the peace of the eternal moment.

Thank you. Please explain the saying, "God's sadness is nature's joy."

Yes. God's sadness is nature's joy. For sadness, a mental function, and joy, a soul faculty—God's sadness is nature's joy. Whenever balance is brought about between nature, creation, and the power that sustains it, when the mind, in its duality, is brought into perfect balance, it is then possible for the balanced mind to meet the balanced spirit. For the spirit, being formless and free, *is* the perfect balance. So when the mind in balance meets the formless, free spirit, there is an amalgamation. And that amalgamation brings about a transformation. And that transformation is known as the individualized soul.

You see, my friends, without a vehicle of identity, the spirit, formless and free, cannot have conscious awareness. When the spiritual substance meets the mental essence, a soul is individualized from what is known as the Allsoul.

The mental world is not a world that you should look at as nothing but struggle and disaster. The mental world is struggle and disaster for he who has identified with imbalance. When there is balance in the mental world, the spirit and the mental meet and the soul expresses or speaks through the heart. So, bringing about a balance in your mental world is the true, true job and true effort of your soul's journey on Earth, the planet of faith.

I know you all have had moments in which you felt the peace that passeth all understanding. But those moments can indeed be more frequent if you will only bring balance into your mental world that your spirit, formless, may meet, that the amalgamation, the effect thereof, be the individualized soul, may express.

It is our holding, which is our identity, where all of the strife and struggle truly exists. We cannot—it is not possible to experience anything that we don't identify with. As long as you insist upon identifying, identify with the good that is within you. When you identify with the good within you, you attract the good in all of your experiences in life, for you identify or hold to the good within you. Anyone who has repeated disasters and experiences the lack of good in their life is holding to the opposite of good within themselves.

We have the power of divine will flowing through us. We can choose whatever we wish to choose to identify with. If you feel that you're having bad experiences in life, be rest assured, my good students, you are identifying with that which is—you have considered to be bad within you. You cannot experience without anything you are not first identifying with within.

No matter where you go and no matter what you do, if your experiences are not harmonious, pleasant, and beneficial, it is because of what you are identifying with in your own mental universe. If someone comes to you with a disturbing vibration, then you have identified with a disturbing vibration within you. You do not have to continue to identify with that disturbing vibration within you. You can recognize it as it comes to you and make the effort to gain control of what you are identifying within you and change your experience by changing your reality.

We must learn, my friends, in time, the great freedom of the level of consciousness known as objectivity. We must learn someday to speak, to discuss, and be free from identifying with it within. We must learn to be in a world of seeming turmoil and be the perfect peace that passeth all understanding.

If you find that you identify quickly and easily with certain negative things in life, then that is the area in which you need great work to learn to become objective, to truly accept God's manifestation of variety. But each time you permit your mind to blame a person, place, or thing for the way you feel, for your lot in life, each and every time you permit your mind to blame outside for the experiences that you have, each time you do that, my children, you weaken the very fiber of your spiritual character. Think about it, my friends. For each and every time you permit your mind to blame outside for your feelings, each time you do that, you not only weaken your spiritual fiber and character, but you become the slave and the victim of those forces of creation. And the bondage becomes very great in time.

Whenever you experience the thought that you don't feel good because of what someone else is doing or has done, take control of yourself in that moment and declare the eternal truth: It's your thought. It's your mind. If you have lost control of it, do not blame someone else for taking what you have not taken care of.

You see, my friends, if you don't take control of your mind, then you who will soon find there are multitudes who will take control of it for you. From our own lack of effort have we become the victims of others who control our minds. They control our minds because we did not bother to face our responsibility of taking care of the vehicle of our eternal being. And so someone else does it for us.

We go out into the world and we experience emotion and anger and temper and upset, not by our conscious thought—we don't go out and say, "I now choose to be furious at such and such a person." We don't do that, but we do something much worse. We go out in the world and we meet a person and we immediately give them power, give them control over our emotional body, give them power over our mental universe. And then they manipulate us. They soon learn what makes us angry. They soon learn what pleases us. And so we become the puppets of what their minds choose to do with us. To be the victims of their control because we make no effort to control ourselves.

Good night.

JUNE 5, 1980

CONSCIOUSNESS CLASS 214

In this evening's class, we will discuss the application of the Divine Healing Prayer that we just spoke forth. [*Please see the appendix for the text of that prayer.*] It clearly states, in the first line, "I accept that the Divine Healing Power is removing all obstructions from my mind and body."

Now, perhaps the difficulty, with some of us, in believing that truth is that we are wanting in a clear identification with what is meant by Divine Healing Power. Divine—that which is divine is neutral. That which is divine is infinite and intelligent. That which is divine does not need to be told what to do.

Now, in the many obstructions that we encounter in the path of our efforts in life, when we speak forth that Healing Prayer, we must also, with the spoken word, identify with the meaning and the essence of the prayer itself or it does not, of course, work for us. You see, nothing works for us that we do not identify with. Many people firmly believe and are convinced that God works for them. Of course, the infinite, neutral, intelligent Energy works when we identify with it.

What takes place when we speak forth that Healing Prayer and we properly identify with it and identify with a greater identification than we are identifying with the obstruction that we are experiencing in our mind is very simple: that neutral energy, intelligently flowing through us, brings about a balance between the soul faculties and the corresponding sense functions. And during that time there is an experience of peace, of harmony, an experience of goodness or godness. To speak it forth by rote does not bring its true benefit. You must learn to feel, by identification with that power in the moment that you speak it.

We all have the ability to identify and we have that ability firmly established in our mind. Because we experience many so-called negative experiences only because we identify with them.

Now, we all have free will. We all have choice in any moment of our eternity. And we all have the power within us to wisely choose what we wish to identify with. One can, in being the observer, view the passing of many events and not be affected by them. It is only when you identify with your magnetic body, with your emotion, that you experience the impact.

So, of course, the first step that has been discussed so many, many times in these classes in this philosophy is to gain, through daily effort, control of the multitude of desires that express in the human mind. For without the daily effort to gain some degree of control of these many desires in your mind, you soon will find that there is an imbalance in your life, that you don't remember things, that you have confusion in your mind, that you become so very forgetful. You see, my friends, no one, in truth, is forgetful. We have a memory par excellence that records everything. And when we say we forget things and when we say we don't remember things, it only reveals that we are in a level of consciousness that is blinding us by desires that we are not making the effort to control.

Now, it is very easy to tell whenever we are controlled by these multitudes of desires in our mind. Whenever we have a responsibility or something to care for and we say that we forgot or we use a multitude of justifications to excuse ourselves from the responsibilities that we alone have incurred, it simply reveals that we are not making the daily effort to gain control over these fluctuating desires in our mind. And so we find ourselves, sooner or later, with ears to hear and we hear not, with eyes to see and we see not.

You see, my friends, when you make the effort to gain some degree of control over your desires, over your mind, then you can give these desires that come into your mind, you can give them to God. You don't have to work in the mental realms of deception to fulfill your desires, because, you see, there is something greater that will bring the fulfillment. Every time we use the mind to fulfill our desires, we guarantee the loss of the goodness of the desire itself. Now, we all understand that desire is the divine expression. But when we go to use the various devices of our mind to fulfill desire, we, of course, open the door to judgments and, in so doing, we lose the goodness or the divinity of the desire itself.

Many times people will experience that everything they seem to touch turns to disaster, does not seem to work out, that one thing after another seems to fall apart. And it's very difficult when anyone is having those type of experiences. It's very difficult to accept personal responsibility. Now, we've spoken so many times on personal responsibility, but it's time to apply that Law of Freedom. For without personal responsibility, there's no freedom, there's no goodness, and there's no success in truth. So if we truly want this goodness of life that is our birthright, then we are going to have to come to terms with our own mind and make a daily effort, because it will not come to any of us any other way. A daily effort is the only way that it will come into our lives.

Because we spend our days—and thousands of times in the course of a day our mind directs energy outside to blame people, places, circumstances, and things for how we feel. As we continue on that path of error and ignorance, slowly but surely our universe and what goodness is in it begins to shrink. Because we are doing it by habit, we feel a certain way, we think a certain thing, and we blame outside. We give that wonderful power to other people and to things. We constantly do it with our health, with our wealth, and with our happiness. Now, when we stop—and we cannot stop unless we make the daily effort, because it is a very firm and rigid habit pattern. It has become a habit from untold years of usage. Therefore, it takes that constant being on guard.

Now I know, to entertain the thought of constantly being on guard at the portal of your mind seems as though it would rob you from the joy of life, but it's just the opposite. It is the very thing necessary to guarantee the continuity of the abundance and the good and the joy of life.

Our minds constantly, day and night, our minds are broadcasting messages out into the universe. Day and night they are returning to us constantly, showing us—if we will only be honest and read them correctly—showing us what we are doing to ourselves with our thoughts. For it is only our thoughts and our thoughts alone that are bringing us these negative experiences in life.

If you will take charge of your mind, if you will truly become the captain of your ship and send out messages into the universe that will return to you with the goodness in which you send them out—for the law is infallible: all experience in our life, all experience is an effect. It is an effect of our thought. It is nothing more and it is nothing less. Each of us, each and every moment, are creating our reality. Now, if we permit our mind to tell us that our experiences are the effect of someone else's action or act or thought, then what we are doing is creating a reality of total bondage, for that which is ours, by our divine birthright, we are constantly giving away freely to others. We are constantly giving them the power over our happiness, the power over our emotions, the power over our very soul.

There is no other way, except through daily, constant effort, there is no other way to gain what you are truly seeking: the fullness and the goodness of life itself. If you are willing to give up the error of thought in blaming outside for how you feel, in blaming outside for what you do or don't do, if you are ready and you are willing, then you are able. And if you do that, what is waiting for you to gain far exceeds in value anything you have yet experienced.

There is no magic wand. There is no one in any universe anywhere that can do it for you. Not even God, the divine, neutral, intelligent Power, can do it for you. No one can do it for you. Many people can show you the way, but the step is entirely dependent upon you.

If your experiences have been extremely negative, then remember this, when it is enough, the change will come. When your mind really declares that it's had enough, then the door of opportunity opens for you to step through. If you have not had enough, then there's still a ways to go. If you still find a need within yourself to use excuses to justify why you do not face the responsibilities in life that you alone have incurred, if you still find that need within you, it only reveals you're not yet ready. If you still find a need to use the mind and all of its devices to bring you the goodness of life, which is the God of life, then not yet are you ready.

But if you have had enough, if you have had enough experiences, if you have had enough sorrow, if you have had enough sadness, if you have had enough disaster, if you have had enough, then you are ready to take that step out of the mental world into the realms of spirit and yet be still in this earthly world, yet be with people, places, and things and never be a part of them. Then you are ready to do the work of your soul in the here and now, for the work of your soul is here. It's not waiting a thousand years from now in some other realm. Your soul is here now. And now is the time to accept the simple truth that you are as spiritual as you allow yourself to be.

It isn't, my friends, that we don't have enough in our mind. It's that we have too much in our mind. It's what we need to take out of our mind: all of the errors in the past; all of the various devices to get the things that we want. We look at little children. We watch them grow up and we see how quickly their little minds, how clever they are to get the things that they desire. And so in this earthly experience we learn very quickly and we make judgments very early what we should do to get what we want. And then time passes on and we grow up, at least physically. And sooner or later, we see those devices and those games, they don't work all the time, like they used to when we were little, bitty kids. And then our lives become filled with frustration.

And fortunately, our lives do become filled with frustration that we may return to the source of purity of thought, of honesty of act, that we may speak freely and open our mouths. And if we have desires to fulfill that we be honest with ourselves and we don't play these childish games, because, you see, we always lose. Whenever we go to work with our minds to gain this, to gain that, to get this, to get that, we always lose in the end. It never fails.

So if you find your life filled with justifications because you are not making the effort to face your responsibilities in life, then you know you're not yet ready to make the next step. It doesn't mean that someday you won't be ready, because you will be, someday. But, you see, my friends, that someday can very easily be this moment.

You know, when we find ourselves so concerned over what others do and we find it difficult to tolerate what they do, it gives us the golden opportunity to decide whether or not we want to stay in the bondage and control of others. I realize that it is difficult, but not impossible, for people who are emotionally attached to be free. Now, they can be just as free as anyone else, if they choose to be. It is more difficult for people who are emotionally attached only because the emotional attachment to the other person is greater than their love of God.

You can have feelings for people, but your feelings can never become a greater priority than your love for God. Because if your feelings become a greater priority and a greater value to you than your love of God, then you must pay the price. And the price tag is very high. It's known as the price tag of bondage. For whoever loves God first, last, and always will never be bound, nor controlled, by another mind. But if your love of God is not constant in your consciousness each and every moment, then you're on the slippery ladder of becoming the victim of another person's mind. And that always brings great disasters. It's never failed to do so and it never will fail to do so.

We've spoken also before on the need of the mind to control. But, you see, what it needs to control, of course, is *our* mind. Not your wife's mind. Not your husband's mind. Not your brother or your sister's mind. But our own mind. That's where the need really is.

You know, it's so easy to look out and to see what someone else should do. But it becomes difficult for us when we face responsibility and see what *we* should do. When we are with people who don't seem to be doing what they should be doing, it gives us great opportunity, great opportunity to see where we are. To speak firmly without emotion is to speak without fear. To speak firmly without emotion is to use the soul faculty of kindness. But, you see, my friends, your mind cannot be in control in so doing, because if your mind is in control in so doing, then your emotions and your functions, not your faculties, not your spirit, nor the divine healing power, is flowing.

We look out in the world and we see that some people can ask other people to do things and they do them. And someone else comes along to ask them to do something and they have an emotional reaction almost instantaneously. But we must become aware of where we are when we speak. Because, you see, if we become aware of where we are when we speak, we won't be so surprised when *they* speak. Because knowing where we are before we speak, we know what the reaction is going to be. And to be forewarned is to be forearmed.

It is not true, as a student of the past stated some years ago, that this philosophy is a philosophy that teaches to be without emotion. This religion and philosophy—because without the science and philosophy, you would not have the religion—does not teach to be without emotion; it teaches to use it wisely. But we cannot use wisely what we do not have control of. We can use wisely what we gain control of inside ourselves.

Now, life is truly a beautiful experience. And it is our right, our divine right, to express that goodness and beauty that is ours. It is not beyond the realms of possibility, nor probability, to gain control of ourselves. That's the way life has been designed to be.

All of us must pay the price of our errors of the past. But we don't have to continue on depriving ourselves of the goodness that is in the moment in which we choose to be.

This church and the classes that it offers, as you all know, is a very small church in numbers. It's designed to be that way because this is a very personal, very personal philosophy. It is a philosophy to be used each and every moment of each and every day. It is not a philosophy to be read and set aside. And so the Spirit of this church works with each of its members and students in a very personal way. More personal than your minds could possibly imagine.

And so it is not an easy path. It's not intended to be, because we don't—our minds—intend to make it easy. We don't let go of patterns in a moment. It's a gradual process. It is going to happen, and is happening, to all of us. It happens here in Serenity. It happens in other religions. Here it is very intensive. By having a very small church and organization, it can be more intensive. If we had a large membership, then the personal work, working with each soul intensively, could not be done.

Whatever your experiences in life, they are passing. They are in the process of passing. They can pass quickly or they can pass slowly. But remember, here we are today and everything needed to bring us here has taken place. And everything needed to keep us here, if that is what we choose, will also take place, for we alone establish those laws.

Let us identify with the joy and happiness of life. Ofttimes it seems difficult to identify with the happiness and joy of life because, my friends, we judge what it is. To he who does not judge what the joy and happiness of life is, the joy and happiness of life is ever available to him. Now, I would like you to think of that for a few moments. The joy and happiness of life is ever and readily available to he who does not judge what it is. It is only when we judge what happiness is that we have such great difficulty in experiencing it. Think of that.

How does your Healing Prayer work? [*Please see the appendix for the complete text of the prayer.*] It's so simple: it's totally free from judgment. Think what the words really mean: "I"— you immediately identify with you, the true you. Not the thought of I, but the true I. "I accept that the Divine Healing Power is removing all obstructions from my mind and body and is restoring me to perfect health, wealth, and happiness." Think of those words. When you feel them, then you will be them.

It takes more than thought: it takes your feeling. That is what places us in the spiritual realms of consciousness. When your spoken word is united with your feelings, then you experience that which is the goodness of your own heart. Be not dependent upon anything that is the Law of Duality. All things are the effect of the Law of Duality. If you permit yourself to be dependent upon the Law of Duality, then you must have sadness and its opposite. You must have want and its opposite. You must have need and its opposite. You must have sorrow and its opposite. But if you depend on that which is beyond the dual laws of creation and form, then you will always be free. You will always be free.

That does not mean that you will not fulfill the work that you have come to earth to fulfill. You will. But you will no longer be a part of that struggle, not the true you. When you awaken within you that true eternal being that is the real you, certainly, your dual being will have the experience of dual creation, but *you* will be separate from it. That's what they speak of when they say to separate truth from creation. You are the eternal truth. But unless you identify with it, you cannot experience it. You cannot.

And so life is, "Dreamer," you are the dreamer, "dream a life of beauty before your dream starts dreaming you." Take stock of your dependence in life. Become consciously aware upon who or what you have permitted yourself to become dependent upon. And if you find that you have allowed yourself, by the error of thought, to become dependent upon anything governed by the Law of Duality or Creation, then make the change and be free.

Because, you see, my friends, what we have today is in keeping with the laws we've established. What we have tomorrow will depend on what we do with what we have today. If you are not happy with your job and you change your job because you have made a judgment that your experiences and your unhappiness is because of the job that you have, then you may be rest assured, my good students, that you guarantee, by the law that you alone have established, to get another job somewhere down the road to prove to your mind that you were right all the time. Because—don't you see?—you have given your divinity, you have given the goodness that is your right, that is your true being, you have given it to the false god of creation by not accepting personal responsibility for your thought, for your feelings. That's the only way we'll ever be free.

We will grow or we will go. Whatever is in your sphere of action, whatever is your reality this moment, be rest assured, if you become the captain of your ship, if you take charge of your life, of your thoughts, of your feelings, of what you are dependent upon, if you take charge of that—that's called personal responsibility—in this moment, in this moment *you* take charge of that, you can be rest assured everything within your reality will grow or it will go. You need not be concerned because the law is clear: that like attracts like and becomes the Law of Attachment.

Now, if you take control of your reality, if you become the master of your destiny now, you need not be concerned of people, places, and things, for people, places, and things must harmonize with your reality. Or they change or they go. Only by accepting that you alone make your life, that you alone are sustained by the Goodness of life, known as God, and only by depending upon that Goodness, that Principle, that Divinity, only then can you be free.

Whether you are married or single is irrelevant, because you attract unto you in keeping with your thoughts and your feelings. Be not saddened by what you have attracted, because you have the freedom and the power to change your attractions. This is the moment in which you can do something. To permit your mind to think of that which has passed is only to continue the bondage that you experience. This is the moment that you have the power. Let not yesterday, nor the moment past, be your master ever again.

Thank you.

JUNE 12, 1980

CONSCIOUSNESS CLASS 215

Good evening, class. For this evening's discussion, we'll speak on the Law of Use or Abuse.

I'm sure we will all agree with the understanding of the philosophy that the lack of use is abuse. And whenever we study anything in life, whether it's a philosophy or a sport, and we do not apply what we study, then we are not using it. And that that we do not use, we abuse. And so it is at this time in our semester that we are discussing the Law of Use and Abuse.

Now, over the many years you have been given an untold number of affirmations to help you to face personal responsibility and be free from the many trials and tribulations that we encounter in creation. If you do not use, on a daily basis, what you are studying, then, for you, it cannot work. For by the lack of application you are abusing your own efforts in life.

And I speak especially this evening in reference to the Law of Freedom, which we know is the full acceptance of personal responsibility.

Some time ago you were given an affirmation that stated very clearly, whenever you are not happy with the experiences in life that you are having, if you will in that moment declare the truth and tell yourself, "I am not happy with this experience in my life. I accept fully the personal responsibility that it is an effect of a thought in my mind. And because it is an effect of a thought in my mind, I have the power and the right to change the experience that I find distasteful. I have that right and that power within me by changing my thought." [you will use the law.]

Now, we have spoken hundreds and hundreds of times on the Law of Personal Responsibility. And yet, we go out in our daily lives and we encounter many distasteful, discordant experiences because we are not making the daily application of what we are working so hard to study; the philosophy has no benefit, except that it is recorded in your memory par excellence waiting for you to use it and not abuse it.

I do not honestly know whether or not, after this semester is completed, whether or not there will be any future philosophy classes given, because that is not, of course, dependent upon me and my wishes. That is dependent on whether or not a majority of the student body in attendance makes the daily effort to apply the philosophy that they are studying.

I realize that for most of us, we make it very difficult, very difficult to make changes. And yet, change for all of us is inevitable.

When it is such a simple thing—truth and freedom is such a simple thing. It is so simple. It's such a small thing to ask of oneself, when they have these experiences that they permit a loss of control of their faculty of reason, of emotional trauma and upset, created by fear, and it's such a simple thing to stop in that moment, each and every day—because I've yet to meet anyone that says every one of the experiences in the course of their day, at work and at home and in the many activities therein, is always harmonious and pleasant and enjoyable and beneficial. It would certainly be an angel from heaven itself to have to have those experiences all day long. But we can and we must for our own sake. Because, you know, the church, your church, is not dependent upon giving classes to serve the purpose for which it was founded. Therefore, classes, they come and classes, they do go.

And if 51 percent, which is a majority of the student body, think enough of the philosophy to use it and stop abusing it, then, I am sure, in keeping with that demonstrable law, that there will, at some time in the future, be a continuation of the classes.

If the daily effort is not made, then we continue on what the Friends have, some time ago, called the yo-yo vibration: one minute we're up and the next minute, we're down. And, of course, we always find someone or something to blame when we're down. But when we're up, it's difficult to find anyone to give the credit to.

And it's most interesting that we only give the credit to other people, we only give the power to others when we're down in life. And when we're up, we seem to be on an island all by ourselves that all of the good that is happening in our life when we're up is an effect of the great effort, the great effort that we alone have been making. And yet, we don't stop to think when things are so terrible in our life of the great, great effort that we alone have made to put us down there. Because, you see, my friends, it takes just as much effort to lift you up as it does to put you down. So isn't it kind of ridiculous and a total waste to use all of this energy, this divine energy, to dig your hole deeper in life?

Now, we all know that our physical bodies, they're going to dig a hole for someday, and we don't know just the hour. But let's not go down with the body, because that's not where we need to be.

But we will, *we will* have to make daily effort. Great effort, now and then, when things are so bad you can't even see the light of day, that's not where it is. It's the Law of Continuity of effort, that's where it really is. That's what will put you on an even keel, where you can enjoy life and you can serve the purpose for your being here in the first place. But this up and down, this in and out, this now and then making some effort, you see, that is not the way to be free. That will not free you, because when you have this now-and-then effort when things are real tough for you, that's when those levels that you've made king and master of your life, that's when they are totally fed and they've had their feast, so they don't mind you making a little effort now and then. But it does nothing to change those patterns of life that have kept so much struggle on your path.

Now, does anyone know why, do you really know why you don't want to bother to make daily effort? Is it such a struggle? Is it really easier in life to blame someone else for your problems? Is that such an easy thing to do and to go around the universe with a whole baggage full of people's names, to pick out of your little suitcase or trunk whenever something doesn't go your way? Isn't this the very thing that parents make, hopefully, great effort to nip in the bud with their little children when they don't have their way and they find someone else to blame? Because if parents don't do that, they're going to live to see the day they wished that they had.

Because, you know, my friends, when you permit your ears to listen to anyone who denies the truth and you do not stand on principle and declare the truth, then you are supporting not only that level in that person, but you are supporting that level inside of yourself. And in so doing, you see, you become the victim, the victim of it. Stop and think how many times in the course of a day that you blame someone or something for your not feeling just right, for your not having your desires in life fulfilled. Think how many times you blame your employer, you blame your job, you blame the financial circumstances that you alone, of course, you alone have set into motion. Sure, it's a hard pill to swallow, but once we swallow it, then we can be free from it.

You know, if you have to take some medicine, it only makes it worse if you stand and look at it for the next hundred years, knowing that someday you're going to have to take it. So why live each day knowing that someday you will have to accept the Law of Personal Responsibility and look at it each day and turn away, only to look at it the next day and the next? Think of the years you've already had, the years of experience, just on this earth realm. Think of all of the things you've done, all of the things you wanted to do and didn't do, all of the frustrations you've created simply by giving away your divinity. Each time you blame outside, you give away your divinity. And each time you listen to someone else who blames outside for their problems, you not only give away your divinity, but you help them give away theirs.

Now just stop and think about that.

When you are really in a level of peace and harmony, then you have to work when you hear people blame outside for what they're doing inside, you have to work on yourself to have compassion, understanding, and tolerance. And then help them to be free from the level they've trapped themselves in.

I can assure you, my friends, there is no path of peace without accepting your life as you alone have created it. The moment you accept your life the way you alone have created it, then you are qualified to change it. But you cannot, no matter what your mind says, you cannot change your life until you accept that the life you have is an effect of what you already have done. So don't think about changing things for the better until you accept the way things are: that you alone have created them, you and you alone.

Now, if you will remind yourselves every day in every way that everything you experience is an effect that you alone and your thought create, and if you will do that each and every day, I assure you, you will, in a very short time, begin to see the life that you really want.

This is the number one thing in this entire philosophy. You can learn all about the faculties and functions, but you cannot bring them into balance until you accept your right, until you accept your divinity.

And in speaking on that, my friends, I'd like to once again mention that we get out of a thing whatever we put into the thing and not one iota more. Our spiritual efforts in life are spiritual when our functions don't dictate what spiritual is. So often, you know, our minds want to dictate what is spiritual in our life. And you can be rest assured when your mind dictates what is and what isn't spiritual, you're far indeed from the spiritual path. Because your mind, a limited vehicle, can only dictate the limit.

So let us make more effort to encourage ourselves to accept that which will bring the good in our lives. To stop blaming our jobs. To stop blaming our companions and our wives and our husbands and our relatives. To stop blaming the politicians. To stop blaming everything, *everything* outside, outside, outside until it just isn't even worth living anymore.

You'll have all the success that your heart desires, you'll have all the abundant good that you could possibly want, if you will only accept on a daily basis your divinity. Think of it, my friends, each time you think—you permit your mind to think and your mouth to speak that it's outside, each time you do that, you lose your divinity. You lose the goodness that is truly yours each and every time you permit your mind to deny the truth of personal responsibility; you shut the door to all the goodness that is your eternal right.

Now, the awakening of the faculties and the expansion of them—and beginning, of course, with duty, gratitude, and tolerance—doesn't take place by thinking about them. It's not quite how they work. Understanding, the very foundation of our soul, expands in our universe in keeping with accepting personal responsibility for all our experiences in life. And so personal responsibility is the number one interest if you want to be free from these different problems that no one, of course, but ourselves creates.

And the greatest service that we could do to ourselves—because, remember, physician, heal thyself. So if we don't do a good service to ourselves, we certainly are not qualified to grant it to anyone else. Because we only grant to others what we first grant to ourselves, no matter what our minds may tell us. And so the greatest service that we could possibly, spiritually, grant unto ourselves is whenever, whenever we hear a denial of the truth, we speak up, kindly, firmly, the truth. Because each time we do that, we not only help the person that is in the error of ignorance of the moment, but, of course, we help ourselves.

And we all know that God helps those who help themselves by helping others. Now, that's how simple it really is. See, God helps those who help themselves by helping others. And this is why it is taught, "To those who have, yea, even more shall I give. And to those who have not, yea, even that shall I take away." Think of that, my friends. "To those who have not, yea, even that shall I take away." How does it work? It's so simple. Man is a law unto himself. He declares the Law of Ingratitude. He declares the Law of Lack and experiences its effect. Even a hymn in our hymnal states, "Count your blessings." That which you place your attention upon you have a tendency to become. If you place your attention upon what you have not, then, yea, even that shall disappear in keeping with the law that you alone establish. If you will place your attention upon what you have, yea, that shall multiply and increase many, many fold.

Because in placing your attention upon the goodness that you already have, that neutral energy goes out into the universe, through the faculty of gratitude, and a never-ending abundant supply is always waiting for you. So each time you count the figures in your bank accounts and each time you permit your mind to say what you have not, you soon find, though you keep right on banking, that that, too, disappears. And what happens to it? It just seems to disappear. But that is in keeping with the impartial and beautiful, demonstrable laws of life.

Whatever you tell yourself and believe, you become. That's how simple it works. It's always worked that way. So if you remind yourself of what you have (the goodness of life) and you share that into the universe, it shall multiply and it shall increase. But you must pay the price of sharing. Whenever you share goodness, you must pay the price of that sharing. And that price is a very simple price: it's the error of ignorance known as the function of jealousy, envy, and greed. It can have no power over you unless you give power to it.

Now, remember, whatever it is, look inside, because that's where it is. Do not allow your mind to look out and see what someone else has in comparison to what you have not, because in so doing, you take what you have—even though you're ignorant of doing it—and you give it to that over there. And so you look a week later and you see they've even got more. You see, it's like a business man: he puts his attention on his competitor and how well his competitor is doing, his competitor even does better. Because his competitor is receiving all of this energy going out in the universe with his name tag on it and his competitor knows what to do with that energy, because his competitor's already demonstrated that intelligence. You don't have to be a business man to see what you're doing to yourself, friends. All you've got to do is stop and think on a daily basis.

That'd be like me sitting here on Sunday morning saying, "Well, let's see, I wonder how many people are in the Catholic church down the street. I wonder how many are over at the Lutheran church this morning." Well, I'd soon find out I'd probably be the only one here because I'd give it all to them, don't you see? Now that's what people are doing. And they're not honestly, consciously aware of what they're doing with that which is rightfully theirs.

If you look at your neighbor's yard and it looks better than your yard in keeping with your judgment, you can be rest assured your neighbor's yard is going to look even more beautiful as yours gets worse, because the energy necessary to keep yours beautiful is now going across the fence to your neighbor's. Think about that. That's really what happens. That's what happens in realms that your physical eyes cannot see. I've watched it for many years. I watch people give away their divinity and give away that which is rightfully theirs. They talk to a person and the person says, "Oh, yes, I, I just got a raise." "Oh, well you're making more money than I am!" Well, what they have done is given away a raise, possibly on the horizon for them. They've just given it to the person they just talked to. And because they are not making the effort to understand those laws, those things are happening all the time, you see.

Now, I wasn't born with a silver spoon in my mouth—not even a gold one. But I accept the possibility, even as old as I am, that it's there for me, if that's what I choose to have.

But think about it, my friends. Please make the effort to start thinking. And thinking each and every day with a little bit more awareness of what's really happening inside of yourself.

If you start to think that maybe you're losing your hair and you talk to someone else and theirs is growing beautiful, well, you start losing more and more and more. It goes on all the time. It really and truly does.

Now, when business is good, obviously, a person in business feels good or pretty good. Until the level wants to find something wrong with something else and then maybe they blame the wife, the family, or whatever. But business—the business of good living is the number one business that should interest all of us. The business of good living. And what is good living? It's when God is in our consciousness and everything is flowing harmoniously, not only around and about us, but through us. You see, as we make the effort to receive graciously, then we give graciously and there's a continuous flow of goodness in our life.

If we have a job and we decide that that job doesn't pay very much and we decide maybe we're worth more than what this job is paying, well, we've got a problem. We've got a real problem. Because, you see, why we have a problem is that there's a level within us that merited that particular job, you see. Now, it's that level within us that we have to awaken to our conscious mind, get it reeducated, and maybe we won't have to move anyplace, that a seeming miracle will take place and we'll get a few raises one right after the other. You see, all things to God are possible. All things to God are possible. They're only, of course, possible if we permit them for us.

We look around and see a lot of great things and good things happening to other people and stop and wonder when they're going to happen to us. Well, we can keep on wondering, because they're not going to happen until we stop looking at what somebody else is getting. We've got to—you see, my friends, you cannot see and you cannot experience what is yours as long as you keep looking at what is someone else's. Now, it's just not possible. There's no way possible for it to take place. It is not only the so-called sin of lust, but it's one of the greatest obstructions that we can possibly build for ourselves.

Now, our minds want many things. And our minds, they look out and they see many, many things. They're only ours when we stop denying somebody else their right to theirs, you see. Because when you look out and you have those feelings called jealousy, envy, or greed, that feeling is the effect of a denial made by your mind. You see, you look out and you see something that you desire and somebody else has it. And you have that feeling commonly known as jealousy, envy, or greed. Well, that is the effect of a denial that you are making in that moment. You are denying them their birthright—their right to have that goodness. And because you are denying them that birthright, you, in truth, are denying yourself, because you cannot grant to another what you have not first granted unto yourself, you see.

So remember that when you look around the world. Just stop and think, each time you have those feelings. They are but the effects of a denial and you're denying that goodness for you. And I don't think that that makes anyone very happy myself. I can assure you it wouldn't make me very happy.

But there's other ways, you see. When you have that feeling of desire, you look out—you see, you set yourself up. Say, you desire a new car. The next thing you know every time you look around, everybody you know has got a new car. You're the only one that doesn't have a new car. Everybody else has got a new car. Or you want a new coat. Or you want a new shirt. Or you want a new pair of shoes or something and every time you look around, you see, you keep setting yourself up. You attract it. That law goes out and you set yourself up. And you say, "They got a new coat. God, I've been wanting a new coat for five years. Opps! That one just got a new coat." You see, you keep denying yourself your new coat. Now, your new coat won't come until you stop that. And when you take control of your mind and you stop denying others their right, then all your rights will be very well served.

But please, friends, for your own sake, let's make some daily effort, daily effort to improve our lives. It's so easy to—you know, my shoulders get broader every day because I've merited, and I accept I've merited, you know—it's very easy to blame Richard. It's very, very easy. It's a little more difficult, they tell me, to blame the Spirit, because they can't talk to them direct—most of them. And so I get to be the fall guy, which is fine, because I'm just as good dishing it out as I am at receiving it. And I receive plenty. So I let plenty right back out again, you know. I don't believe in being the obstruction. I want to be as open a channel, as free a flow as I possibly can be. And if I didn't love you still, I wouldn't sit here after being blamed for everything you can possibly imagine that's bad. Be nice to blame me for something that's good for a change. That would be an interesting twist. But anyway, let's stop and think on a daily basis. That's really not asking that much of yourself. To stop and think, "Whoops, here I go again, giving away my freedom and the goodness in my life, blaming outside for the experience that I have."

Now, because that blaming outside has increased recently, once again—it's like the tides of the ocean that flux and flow. It's nice and calm and peaceful, then, all of a sudden, the storms come: blaming outside for what's going on inside. I can assure you, anyone that speaks to me with any problems immediately is granted the understanding of truth: that the problem is only because you're looking outside. The solution comes right away. The moment you turn around, inside, you see the solution. There is no problem, my friends, none whatsoever: if you will accept personal responsibility, the seeming problems will all disappear. They'll just melt into the nothingness if you will only daily accept personal responsibility for your life and everything that you encounter.

You have enough tape, I believe. [*This remark was spoken to the technician recording the class.*]

Hopefully.

Yes. Well, if it goes on a C-90, we'll just spend more money.

Anyway—where was I? Yes. Turning around inside. So if you come to me with any problems, I'll be more than happy to talk with you. But I can assure you, before you leave, you will have to look inside. Because that's the only place the solution ever is. The reason that the solution—and the only place the solution ever is—is inside is because the only place the problem ever was, is inside. It wasn't somebody over there. It wasn't some employer. It wasn't some bank or some financial thing outside. It was all created in here. And so, you see, that's the only place to go for the solution.

I mean, you can chase all over the world if that's what you want to do. But you're not going to find the solution. It's not there, my friends. Try to get that through your head. The sooner you do, the better you will feel. The solution is not outside because the problem is not outside. That's the delusion. The problem's inside. It's not your employer, nor your husband, nor your wife, or anyone else. It never was. It never was. And it never, ever will be. It's created by your mind and it's solved by your mind, hopefully, with God's help.

Thank you very much.

JUNE 19, 1980

CONSCIOUSNESS CLASS 216

Good evening, class.

This, I believe, is our ninth class of this semester, with only two classes remaining. And so we will have a little change of format this evening. You may turn your chairs, if you wish.

This evening we're going to have the opportunity to participate in asking the questions, whatever they may be, that are concerning you in reference to your application of the philosophy that you have been studying. Now, I'm going to begin with the group on my right. And if you will just raise your hands and, rather than mention any names, I will just call upon you as you raise your hands for any questions that you have in your efforts to apply the philosophy that you have studied, that it may work for you. Because we all know, of course, that nothing will work unless we apply it. And so this is your opportunity, this evening, as we come close to the ending of this semester, to participate. And so I will begin with the group on my right. Yes, please.

I've had difficulty determining when I'm using initiative—what I think is initiative—and when it is self-will.

Thank you very much. The lady is asking the question of a difficulty in understanding whether or not she is using initiative or self-will. Well, initiative can be an initiative that is considerate of all responsibilities or it can be an initiative motivated by a personal self-desire, whose consideration is totally concentrated upon the desire of the moment. So one has to, before moving with the spirit of initiative, to become aware of what they are being motivated by. Does it have consideration for everyone that would be involved or does it only have consideration for a particular desire of the moment? And if that is weighed out in consciousness, prior to going ahead with the initiative, you'll have no problem in discerning which is self-will of one particular desire out of eighty-one and which is a spiritual initiative. Thank you. Yes.

It seems easy to attach oneself to persons, places, and things, but hard to detach. Could you help with that?

Yes, in reference to attachment and detachment, as long as we permit our mind to rely upon persons, places, or things to bring us anything in life that we desire, then we will always have a struggle and difficulty with the principal of detachment. And so, of course, the thing to do is to become first aware of the reliance that our minds have upon persons, places, and things, then we will not become so easily attached and, therefore, will not have struggle with detachment. Thank you. Yes.

When we are detached, can we still feel warmth for the person?

We can feel warmth, but not control. Now, there's a vast difference between attachment and detachment. Attachment, in our mind, offers us the sense of control over that that we feel attached to. And detachment does not offer us that sense or feeling of control. There's the difference between attachment and detachment. Thank you. Yes.

I would like to know how to free myself from judgment. And also I have difficulty in communicating my feelings quite a lot of the time. And I would like help with that, too.

Thank you. Anyone who has difficulty, a struggle in freeing themselves from judgment, has great difficulty in communicating their true feelings. The reason they have difficulty in communicating their true feelings is because whatever they feel is constantly being censored by this judgment that rises up in the mind. Then, the true feelings do not get communicated because they're censored by judgment and controlled by pride.

So as long as you hold to pride, you will experience judgment. And as long as you hold to pride, experience judgment, you will have difficulty in communicating your true feelings and you will have difficulty with your relationships with people.

To free oneself from the error—errors of judgment—takes a daily effort. It takes a constant effort. It takes a constant effort because the mind is constantly in a process of making judgments. Not decisions, unfortunately, but judgments based upon the experiences that it has already had. So if you wish sincerely to be free from the bondage of judgment, then the daily effort must be made and not just once or twice a day. Thank you. Group two. Yes.

Concerning commitment, I know—I understand that the first step of a thing is most important. What I would like to know is when you should make a definite commitment and when you should wait on a commitment, specifically financial commitments.

Yes. The thing is, in reference to the spiritual Law of Commitment, commitment is something that one should weigh out very, very carefully, because to commit means to place your full responsibility into whatever you commit yourself to. So it is, of course—and many people do not like commitment, because they do not like, in truth, responsibility. Now, if you don't like responsibility, personal responsibility, then you're not going to like commitment, because they're hand in hand; they're one and the same.

In reference to commitment in the material world and specifically the financial world, that is something that each individual must weigh out very carefully. Ofttimes we declare that the truth—that God is the source of our supply—and we establish the very laws necessary to demonstrate the truth that we speak. If we will look at the struggles in life, whether they're in the material world or any mental world or in any other world, if we will look at them as an opportunity to direct our faith to a source where all things are possible, we will strengthen our faith in that source and things will flow more freely for us.

Now, evidently, there has been, from your question, some struggle in reference to making commitments in the financial world and then having to pay the price of responsibility. Would you understand that?

Ah . . .

Yes, you may speak.

Basically, when you're not absolutely certain, at the time, whether you could live up to the commitment, it seems that follows the commitment right down the line, is that true?

It does. Thank you very much. I understand the problem now.

You see, the mind can never, ever be absolutely certain. The reason that the mind can never, ever be absolutely certain is because for the mind to be certain is contrary to the very nature of the duality of the mind. The mind offers to us, for every question, it offers its answer, for every light, it offers its darkness. And so when we go into a commitment—and we go into it only with our mental world, only with our mind—then we can expect, as sure as the night follows the day, we can expect the struggle along the path.

Now, how does one get free from that Law of Duality in reference to commitment? Very simply by gaining control of the mind so their soul, their inner spirit may speak and either commit oneself or not commit oneself. But to make commitments with the human mind is a guarantee of the struggles of life. Does that help with your question? Thank you.

Yes, would you rise, please?

I would like a little clarification on how far can we go to prepare ourselves for our work and yet not put a damper on the spirit of spontaneity?

Well, that depends, of course, entirely, in reference to your question of how far we can go with our work and not put a damper on the spirit of spontaneity, that depends with each individual of how much control they have over their judgments. Now, if you have little control over your judgments, then you can be rest assured you're putting a great big, gigantic damper on your spirit of spontaneity. So that, of course, is ever dependent on the effort that is made for the individual to control their judgments. The more control of their judgments in their mind that they have, the more the spirit of spontaneity will flow. Does that help with your question?

Yes. Thank you.

Thank you. Are there anymore questions in group two? No, I'll go by group, thank you. I'll just stay with this group here a moment and give them a chance to gain control.

I'd like to know how to unclutter one's mind once they've lost the control and have become cluttered in their thinking.

Thank you. In reference to a way to unclutter one's mind, which is something that all of us have a great need to do on a daily basis, because on a daily basis we're filling so much rubbish into the human mind. And so it is something that should be done on a daily basis. Now, there are, of course, many affirmations of a positive nature and they are beneficial in gaining control over the human mind. Now, we all know that repetition is the law through which change is made possible. And so if you choose wisely an affirmation and you repeat it frequently, you will bring about a change in consciousness, which simply means that your soul, which is experiencing a level within you where there is clutter and confusion, your soul will rise to a different level of consciousness and you will no longer experience the clutter.

Now, the clutter does not leave. It exists in consciousness on one or more of the many levels through which our soul is expressing. But by making the effort—the repetition of positive affirmation—you lift your soul where you no longer experience that level of consciousness and you can do that at any time that you are willing to make the effort.

Thank you.

You're welcome. Yes.

Quite often, when I'm faced with decisions, I find that I often want to do a decision that's not in my best interest. And it seems that after I've asked for guidance and stuff, I always have a feeling in my stomach of a heavy, kind of like a wanting to back off. Now, should I be guided in making decisions instead of having to ask and try to be guided by what I feel, instead of going through the mental gymnastics of going back and forth of just looking at the physical aspect of my choice?

Thank you. Most feelings that people are expressing are an effect of mental gymnastics, unfortunately. Fortunately, not *all* feelings, but most feelings are an effect of mental gymnastics. Now, you have a decision to make in life. Unless you make the effort to pause, to give your soul the opportunity to go through the many levels of consciousness, if you do not make that effort, then what happens is what you have been experiencing. One level tells you to do such and such or maybe three levels or maybe even ten. Then, after you have done it, your soul moves into other levels of consciousness, because there is not the conscious control of these different levels. And these are the levels—they were never asked in reference to the decision. And they're furious.

And so until the effort is made on a daily basis to gain control of the human mind—in order that you may consciously choose to move to certain levels of consciousness to see what they have to offer, to become consciously aware with these varying levels of the human mind—then you'll always experience these making decisions and then, after the decision is made, slipping into another level of consciousness and being very unhappy because, on those levels, you never even considered them. And they're not happy about it and they probably would have voted against you in the first place.

So now, when you ask, in reference to should one go by their feelings, one should go by their feelings if one knows that their feelings are not the effect of mental gymnastics. So it goes right back to the very ancient teaching, "O man, know thyself and you shall know the truth and the truth shall set you free." But for a person to say, "Well, shall I go by my feelings for my guidance?" I could not possibly recommend such a thing when there is no control over the mind to be assured of which level of consciousness you are going to be on when you experience the effect of the level which is known as a feeling. Does that help with your question?

Yes—

Yes, certainly.

How does one consciously go through their levels to see if they're in harmonious agreement with the choice?

By, number one, making the daily effort to be aware of their levels. That's number one. Because, you see, you cannot consider something—one cannot consider something that one is not aware of. So first, one must make the daily effort to become aware of themselves. Then they will, by making that effort, become aware of the eighty-one levels of consciousness through which their soul is expressing. Having become aware of these many levels from daily effort, then one can gain control over themselves and bring balance into their life. Does that help with your question?

Yes.

Fine. Thank you. [*After a short pause, the Teacher continues.*] Well, if there are no more questions from group two, I will move to group three, please. Yes, would you stand, please?

We're told to look within for the answers. But we're also told that self-reliance is a mark of pride. And I would like to see what the distinction is between the two.

Did you say soul reliance or self-reliance?
Self-reliance.
Yes.
Could you help me with the distinction?

I will certainly make that attempt. Now, the lady is speaking in reference to go within for the answer, for that's where the question came from and there's where the answer lies. And she also understands self-reliance is a mark of pride and, of course, indeed it is. But evidently there is some misunderstanding between going within and self-reliance.

Now, self-reliance, you ask anyone and they will tell you, "Yes, that is the reliance upon what my mind has to say." Now, that is not what we're talking about when we're talking about going in for the guidance in one's life. The going in, is going in to their own soul and in to the spirit and not to the covering, you see. So there is a vast difference in that respect. When you go in to your spirit and to your soul, there is total consideration not limited by the earthly experiences of the human mind.

You see, the human mind, as I have said many times, serves a very good purpose, but it is limited in its service. It is limited to a mental world. It is limited to what it has already experienced. So when you go into self-reliance, you're going into the human mind. And the human mind can only offer you what it has already experienced and the censorship of what is trying to enter your mind. Because anything that tries to enter your mind—and anyone's mind—is censored by the accepted judgments that the human mind has already made.

So, you go out into the world and you say, "Well, I have new experiences." But if you will take a look at these so-called new experiences, you will see that there is a basis in your experiences that you have already had that is related to the new experience. Otherwise, your mind would flatly refuse it. So we see from that simple demonstration that all of us can make at any time we choose, we see that the human mind is not only very limited in what it can accomplish and what it has to offer, but that it censors every new experience that it encounters depending upon what it has already accepted. Surely, that is not the place to go for guidance in eternity. But beyond that, beyond the human mind is the eternal spirit that is deep within. That is the eternal moment. It's all of the past and all of the future and it offers you the power of the present, not limited, nor censored by mental activity. Does that help with your question?

Yes. Thank you.

You're welcome. Yes. Would you please rise, please?

We have been taught that we come down to this earth to learn certain lessons. And does it mean then that when you see somebody making a mistake that maybe you could help them with or, without controlling them, could we help somebody? Or how far can we go without interfering with their lessons?

Yes, thank you very, very much. That goes to the basic principle revealed in our philosophy many years ago: Solicitation is the law—presence—pardon me. Presence is the Law of Solicitation. Now, if someone is within your presence, the law clearly states that solicitation is established. Therefore if you are living with someone or someone is in your universe frequently, they're in your presence and opportunity is constantly before you. Now, there is a fine line in this presence—the Law of Solicitation—and discernment, spiritual discernment of when to offer one's hand. That, each individual must become aware in their efforts to help another, because, you see, one must first help oneself.

The law is very clear. The natural law of life is very clear in that respect. One must first help oneself, then they may help another. So at the moment of solicitation, at that moment, one must help oneself in that moment before speaking or acting. If they do not do so, if they do not do so, then the danger of their establishing the Law of Transgression, for themselves, is very great.

And I am sure those of you who have made effort to counsel and talk with people and to help others, I'm sure you're very, very aware that time and again you've tried to talk to help someone who is in your presence, through the Law of Solicitation, and when they left, they felt great and you just felt horrible. What happened? The Law of Transgression was established by not first making the effort, in that moment, before you ever speak, before you ever act, you see. Then, you won't have to experience that transgression, known as picking up their package. But if that is not first done—and it can be done in a split second. It doesn't take five or ten minutes or an hour. You see, it doesn't take that long to go through one's own levels and to gain control within. But one must work on themselves first and one must constantly work on themselves in order to be qualified to be the instrument of the divine Spirit to help another.

So as one is counseling oneself, one must, in the process, counsel themselves in order to remain a clear, free channel for the Spirit and not pick up the package, so to speak, when the counseling is finished. Does that help with your question?

Yes. Thank you.

You're welcome. Yes, if you will rise, please.

Could you help me on organizing my mind to do my spiritual commitments and also my own personal commitments and continuity?

Yes, thank you very much. In reference to organization, one must understand, first, that system and order is the divine law of the universes. System and order. Now, always in life the demonstration is the revelation. No matter who we are, no matter where we are, the demonstration is always and forever the revelation. If one truly desires to bring system and order into their lives, the first step, the most important step and the very first step is the total acceptance of personal responsibility. Without that first step of totally accepting the divine Law of Personal

Responsibility, there cannot be system and order, the effect of which is organization and success.

If you are willing to make the daily effort to accept personal responsibility—and how does one make that effort? We've given many different ways to make that effort. Whatever thought you become aware of in your mind, to tell yourself the truth, "Thank you, God, this is my thought. This is my mind. I alone have created it. I alone am responsible for it. If I don't like it, I alone can change it." To flood one's consciousness with that great truth on a daily basis, sooner or later one is bound to fully accept the Law of Freedom, known as personal responsibility.

Now, man is freed only when he is fully in system and order. We have said it many, many different ways. The effect of self-control is freedom. But one cannot have self-control until one accepts personal responsibility, you see. So it all begins with personal responsibility. Then, what happens as one is working, accepting that demonstrable truth of personal responsibility, one takes a look and sees clearly, "I'm not organized. Things are all cluttered around me." And as the effort continues to be made within on personal responsibility, a great urge rises up from the soul to put everything in its place and everything—a place for everything. Because those are beginning steps of system and order. And from personal responsibility to system and order comes organization. And from organization comes the joy, the blessing, and the heavenly state of freedom itself. Does that help with your question?

Very much.

You're welcome. Yes, would you rise, please?

I would like to ask, How can I better help myself through fear?

Would you repeat that, please?

How can I better help myself when I'm in fear?

Thank you very much. By becoming consciously aware, consciously aware that you're in the mental world. Because only in the mental world, only in self-thought, the thought of I, can fear exist. Without the thought of I, you cannot experience what you call fear. For it is the thought of I that establishes the mental identification. And you cannot experience what you are not identified with. Now, many times the Spirit has recommended to redirect your energy, to change your identification, you see. Because you must first mentally identify in order to experience fear. And in order to mentally identify, you must first establish the thought of I, which is the separation.

The thought of I is the separation from the whole. And when we separate ourselves from the whole, then we begin to experience fear because we've identified through that thought of I. So when you are experiencing what you call fear, make the effort to tell your mind, "Yes, I have this fear because I have entered the thought of I and in entering the thought of I, I have identified with the Law of Separatism. I have separated my soul from its universal Source and in so doing, I experience fear."

Now, it's like so-called death. Many people have great fear of so-called death, but if they make the effort to free themselves from the thought of I, they'll no longer have any fear at all. It'll be nonexistent, because it cannot exist. Fear cannot exist, and does not exist, in the realms of the true spirit. Do you understand?

Yes. Thank you.

So when you have this fear—the fear of this and the fear of that—immediately go to work on re-identifying, removing the thought of I, and you will, once again, become a part of the universal whole and have no experience of fear whatsoever, for you have left those realms. Thank you.

Yes. Would you rise, please?

Quite often people fall into realms of lack of enthusiasm and lack of impetus to take on their responsibilities and commitments and just a general lack of interest in life around them. How can they free themselves of that and find their way back, find their way back to interest and enthusiasm?

By accepting the simple truth that they entered those realms of consciousness because they tried to escape from the Law of Personal Responsibility. So often we try so many things to escape from responsibilities in life—only *our* responsibilities. No one gave them to us. No one made them for us. We all made them, of course, for ourselves. And there are many, many devices that the human mind will use to escape from its own responsibilities. Some people they'll take different types of narcotics and different things to escape from their responsibilities. Others will resign themselves and say, "I have no enthusiasm at all. There's nothing I really want to do. I just want to lay around and bask in the sun, like a toad." It's only because they're trying to escape from the laws that they, and they alone, have set into motion.

Now, is your question that you are trying to help someone around you that is in that?

Yes.

Well, I can only tell you the effort that I would make. They would hear day and night, around the clock the Law of Personal Responsibility. And if life was so miserable, why didn't they flush out you know where along with their misery? Because you didn't need it. You see, you can't be soft-pedaled, you know. You can't be a dumb daisy with that level of consciousness. You see, when you have that type of a vibration, which is the epitome of self-pity, which is the great, great con game to be freed from the laws that they, as individuals, alone have set into motion.

Remember, there is never, ever, ever any struggle greater than our ability to grow through it, you see. And if you want to help a person, you must learn to communicate that within yourself. Nothing is impossible to God. When man is out of the thought of I, man is in God, whole and complete and perfect, not separated from the source. You see, our problems begin when we separate ourselves from the source. That's the only time our problems begin and they begin because we, at times, unfortunately through our merit system in entering this earth realm, through our early education in life and our early experiences, we spend so much effort trying to escape from the responsibilities in life that we, *we* alone have set into motion, you see.

So if you really want to help a person, help yourself, knowing deep inside yourself, nothing ever in life is such a burden, is such an obstruction that God cannot move through it. No matter what it appears to be. And to be in God, one must be out of the thought of I, in the beautiful realms of personal responsibility.

Now, I've had some experience with these levels of so-called self-pity and, of course, I have also worked on myself. Because if you don't work on yourself, then you certainly can't be an instrument or qualified to work with someone else. But one must make it very, very clear, you see. Self-pity cannot exist unless it has an ear to bend. And if you give it company, then you must, in order to give it company, be in rapport with it within. Do you understand? So if you don't want it around you, all you have to do is make sure that you're not in rapport with it within. And that that is around and about you will grow or go. It's quite simple. The law is so clear in that respect. Thank you.

Now I will go to group four, which is over there, please. If you have any questions—yes, would you rise, please?

I was wondering about helping other people. And when you find that you're helping them and not getting much return and you start feeling like you're getting taken advantage of—now, is there such a thing as being taken advantage of or should you just accept helping them without a return?

Thank you very much. Oh certainly, we take advantage of ourselves in so many ways, in so many ways. We take advantage of ourselves thousands of times a day. Now, first of all, we have to ask ourselves the question, "Do I accept, O God, the Law of Personal Responsibility?" That's number one. If the answer is yes, if it's affirmative, then we must ask ourselves the question, "Do I accept the demonstrable law that like attracts like and becomes the Law of Attachment?" If the answer is affirmative, then we must move on and say, "What level inside of me, O God, is attracting these freeloaders into my life?" Do you understand?

Now, we may not, it is true, be freeloading in that particular way. Do you understand? But we must be setting that law into motion in order to attract it out of the universe into our life. So, of course, in keeping with the demonstrable Law of Freedom, known as personal responsibility, we start working on ourselves, do you understand? And we ask ourselves, "Now, I have been working helping these people and I seem to be getting no return. O God, what was my true motive in helping these people in the first place? Obviously, it must have been selfish for I am experiencing the effects of selfishness." Do you understand? Now, it's a hard pill for all of us to swallow. Don't feel rejected or sensitive, because we all have that level of consciousness within us. And as we become aware of it, then we can work with it.

So, you see, our motive in life is revealed to us a million times a day in a million different ways, because life itself is the mirror reflecting back to us what we are putting out into it. So therefore, if we will be honest with ourselves—for only honesty will lead us through the jungles of life—if we will be honest with ourselves, then we will see, "Oh yes, in some things, yes, I have established that law. I never would have dreamed, though, it would have come back the way it's coming." Do you understand?

Yes.

And if you—in making your efforts in personal responsibility, you will find a great freedom. And as you make those changes within, on these various levels, you will find no more problems with people who you understand are freeloading off your efforts, you see? Because you will do what is right to be done because it is right to do it and you will not be one bit concerned where they go or how they grow.

Because, you see, all effort is rewarded. It is the very law of the Divine. But, you see, when we dictate through what channel the reward to us shall come from our efforts, then we have very serious problems in life. That's why we do what we know is right to do because it's right to do it. We're not concerned about the reward because we know the law. Therefore we're not sitting around holding our breath waiting for it to enter into our universe, because we know it's on its way. We have no concern. We have no worry and we're free. And we don't tell God how it's to get to us. Then, it's sure to come. Thank you.

Any other questions in group four, please? Yes.

We are taught that we set laws into motion and for them to manifest, we should concentrate on that which we feel is the right thought. Often times though, I find that I may establish a law, or several laws, that—some are beneficial and others are not. In time, I find that out. But I then wonder maybe it's better not to think and to ask for guidance and not set laws consciously, because of being at another place in time. Do you—

Yes, I certainly do. Now, the thing is, friends, we're setting laws into motion all the time. The only difference is by becoming consciously aware, we then know the experiences that are yet to return into our lives. Do you understand that? All we are doing is making the effort to become consciously aware. The laws are being established by our mind all the time. And because, you see, as it says, "Man is a law unto to himself," [*The Living Light Dialogue, Volume 1*]. And what are we doing with the law that we are?

We must also remember that there is something greater than the mental laws that man establishes and experiences. And that something greater we understand to be the spiritual realms, which we are in this moment if we are out of the mental realms, you see. We have these mental realms here that all of us are most familiar with. And then we have this peace and harmony of the spiritual realms. By not being so concerned, then one is not so disturbed in reference to these laws until they gain more control over their mind, which sets these laws into motion in the first place. So it is not necessarily beneficial for a student on the path in the early steps of unfoldment to become overly concerned with the laws that they are setting into motion, because by so doing, they lose whatever joy of life that they could possibly be having. It's slow steps are sure steps. So one should not become overactive mentally in understanding and applying a spiritual philosophy. Does that help with your question?

Yes. Thank you.

You're welcome. Any other questions in group four? Yes.

I'm trying to have an understanding. When you say God is our only source and bringing that kind of expansiveness down to a very detailed practical living in the mundane.

Yes, you see, as one makes the constant effort to declare the truth that God is the true and only source of their supply, what happens is very simple, very simple: the mind is dictating constantly that "If I do this, I will get that" and it is constantly reinforcing the Law of Limitation by the judgments that the mind is constantly making based upon past experiences. Now, here we are, our souls, expressing through these mental realms that are constantly, right around the clock, reinforcing the laws of limitation. As we make this great effort—great to many people, small to others, it depends upon the individual—but as we make this effort to flood our consciousness with God as the source of our supply, our reliance gradually, slowly but surely begins to shift from the limitation that the human mind has to offer to the wholeness of the Divine Spirit.

And as our mind begins to make this turnover, this shift, our faith starts to be directed in the spiritual—do you understand?—that is without limit because it is without judgment. Now, in order to have limit in life, you must have judgment. You cannot have limit without judgment. So our minds offer us limitation. Our minds offer us judgment, restrictions, adversities, and go on down the list. But our spirit offers us the freedom from all limit, the possibility of all good. And that's what you're really doing when you make that daily effort. Does that help with your question?

Yes. Thank you.

You're welcome. Now we will have group five, please, our final group here. If you have any questions, please raise your hands. I'm sorry—Did I miss this group here? Please raise your hand. That is group five right there. Yes, thank you.

Would you rise, please? Sorry.

I find myself caught up in the flow of conversation with people and I find myself saying things that moments after I have said them I wish I hadn't said them. But I have a very difficult time in breaking that pattern before it happens.

Thank you very much. I understand the situation. When compassion leaves the guiding hand of reason, it inevitably opens the door of credulity, which means credulity: easily imposed upon. Do you understand? You have a universal motherhood consciousness. And that universal motherhood consciousness does not have the guiding hand of reason. And compassion, you see, opens the doors to move into the flow of people and their particular problems. You hear?

Now, that is not an exclusive struggle in life or cross for you. There are many people who do have that particular struggle. If you accept, truly accept, "Well, now, Lord, I accept for myself the law of total full personal responsibility. I have compassion for this soul that is going through this particular struggle, but it is only an effect of the law that they alone have established. Therefore, I have no emotion. I am not controlled by my functions as I talk with this individual." Then you will not have, in life, that problem, because your little spirit will be alert, awake, and aware. And it will say to you, deep inside, "That's enough!" And at that moment, you move on to the other duties that you have. Does that help with your question?

Thank you.

Thank you. Yes, now we have group six, please. Are there any questions in group six? Yes, would you rise, please?

Yes, I was wondering what is meant exactly by accepting one's divinity.

Accepting—

Could you elaborate on that?

Accepting what?

Your divinity.

Accepting one's divinity. Yes. It's most interesting because, you see, total acceptance, total acceptance *is* the Divinity. And so accepting one's divinity is a total acceptance under the light and guidance of personal responsibility.

Now, unfortunately, sometimes we create for ourselves confusion where the path is very simple and the path is very clear. We do that from a feeling of insecurity. Now, everyone, *everyone* everywhere who relies upon the mind for the goodness in life experiences insecurity. Some of us seem to have more experiences with insecurity than others, at times in our lives. But when one is experiencing insecurity—and usually in this old mundane world it's financial insecurity—turn it around and see the golden opportunity to strengthen your faith in the only Source that will never fail you. Because, you see, you have merited in life, you've merited this wonderful opportunity to feel financially insecure or emotionally insecure or whatever insecurity you want to call it. You have in your evolutionary incarnation merited that experience. In other words, you've set yourself up and, of course, we set ourselves up for many things in life. But let's take the best out of what it has to offer.

And we can take the best out of these feelings of insecurity by saying, "Look at this. Look how insecure I feel. I don't know what's going to happen to me. I don't know where I'm going to go. I don't know where I'm going to live. I don't know if I'm going to have anything to eat." And all that the mind has to offer in the feelings of insecurity. And I don't know of anyone with any common sense that wouldn't sooner or later turn away from that level of consciousness, from that mental activity, and just maybe take a chance that there is such a thing as God and that to this such a thing called God all things are possible, including the feeling of security. So, you see, that's taking the good from the experience.

In life, we encounter many, many, many experiences. Each and every one of them contain an essence. Now, stop and think. The Divine Power called God, the Infinite Eternal Energy sustains any and every thought that we think. Now, all experiences, all form is the effect of thought. It is sustained by the Infinite Divine Intelligence, called God. Now, when we have experiences, which are forms created by thoughts, sustained by God, and we don't like the experience, don't push it away. Because, in so doing, you deny it and in denying, you make it your destiny. Accept its right of existence. And in so doing, you place yourself in a position to take the essence or God that is sustaining the experience and use it to your greater good.

Our time has passed. Thank you very much. Thank you.

JUNE 26, 1980

CONSCIOUSNESS CLASS 217

Good evening, class.

I believe that this is the tenth class of this semester, which means we have one more class to go for this semester.

Now, last week, we didn't quite finish with the opportunity for you to ask your questions and so we will conclude with that this evening. We haven't discussed much on meditation simply because it is in everyone's best interest to first make the effort to gain some degree of control of their thoughts before attempting a regular, daily meditation. Because so often it has been proven that people who are not making any effort to gain some degree of control over their thought process are not really benefited by some effort of meditation. You can, of course, however, take some time, when you awaken in the morning, to have a few moments of peace and to gain some degree of self-control.

Now, I do want to conclude here with the questions. And I believe we were in this group or the last group. Someone had a question from last week. Yes.

I understand that humor is the salvation of the soul. And my question is in regards to the way I approach humor at times. I find that I say things jokingly and people will laugh. And it has always made me feel good to see people laugh. But I wonder if it's really always in their best interests—do you understand what I mean?—the way in which I make my humor.

Thank you very much for your question. If there is concern of the mind in reference to how a person will react in our efforts to share humor, the salvation of our soul, then it is not the humor or salvation of our soul that is being expressed at the moment. Because it is controlled by a judgment and, therefore, that soul faculty, humor, does not flow freely. You see, there has to be a judgment of the mind in order for there to be a concern of how a person will react to what we have to share. Do you understand? Now, when there is a judgment which creates the concern, then the gift is without the giver and it is, in truth, a loan and not a gift at all.

Yes, if you have further question—yes.

It's not—it wasn't necessarily that I had concern about if they found humor in what I said or not, but I just wondered, sometimes things are said kiddingly and people will laugh. They understand that it's, I believe, for the humor aspect of it, and then they laugh. But is that a laugh that is in their interest?

Yes, the concern of whether or not it is in their interest, you understand, is created by a judgment which censors the free flow of the faculty of humor. So if one will first free themselves from the judgment that creates the concern, then the spiritual flow will be unobstructed. One should not be concerned when they have something to share that brings goodness to them, you see. Because in bringing goodness to them—and they share that—only goodness can come from it no matter who is receiving it. Now, if they receive it censored, then that is their right, you understand?

Yes.

Yes. Now, some time ago, we spoke on concern and on self-concern. It's a very important subject to discuss. The more concern that we have over any endeavor that we are trying to work on, the more restricted is the spiritual flow through our soul. Now, I have watched this not only with human beings, but with humans and their interests or concern with their animals, with their plants, with their trees, or any living thing.

You see, the statement to put God in it or forget it means the flow of the Divine Spirit through us without any restriction of judgment of mental activity. Now, you see, when you're working with anything, whether you're interested in a healing for an animal or a human or you're interested in a healing for a plant or a tree or a blade of grass, if you permit your mind to emanate the vibration of concern, then it is that mental vibration, that electromagnetic energy, that dual activity of creation that you are sending and directing to whatever you are interested in being healed.

It is difficult, I am sure, for many of us, at times, to be interested in the fulfillment of our desires whether we want an animal to be healthy, a human, or a tree or a plant, it is difficult to gain control of the mind and accept that what we are interested in is a living entity, sustained by the same divine, intelligent Energy that is sustaining us.

You see, a tree does not grow by the benefit of the human mind. Whether or not there is a human mind in the universe is of no import to a tree. It will grow and it will fulfill the purpose for which it is designed. Now, if we would like it to grow better, if we would like the animal to be more healthy, then we must first accept that the same energy, the same intelligence that is sustaining us at this very moment, is sustaining the tree. Now, when we accept that, you see, then we become the instrument through which that may flow unobstructed into the universe over everything that we see, everything that we hear, and everything that we touch or sense.

It is very important, for it is our concerns in life that create so much of our difficulties. Now, if we are concerned about things outside, then we have to understand that we are very concerned about everything inside. Now, the blood flows through our veins unobstructed until our minds become concerned over whether or not it is flowing at the proper speed. Then, when we start becoming concerned over exactly how it's flowing, science has proven repeatedly that that mental activity creates an obstruction to that natural, divine flow. Now, it works whether or not we're concerned about our blood or whether or not we're concerned if we are breathing just right.

Now, all you've got to do is be still for a moment and think, "Now, let me see, am I breathing at the proper rhythm?" and start getting some mental activity over just how you're breathing. You will very soon find out that you are not satisfying your mind the way that you're breathing, for your mind is going to find something wrong. And all it will take is just a moment. So we will take a moment of stillness so you can check to see exactly how you're breathing. Now I can assure you, of all those within the sound of my voice, someone or some of you are going to find something is not just satisfactory to your mental judgment about the way you're breathing. Now once that judgment is made, the next step is for the mind and its great curiosity to dictate what is wrong with you. So let's take a moment of silence. [*After a pause of only a few moments, the Teacher continues.*]

That's long enough because some of you already started to have a little palpitation there in your chest, which simply reveals how our minds interfere with the divine, natural flow in life. We interfere with our breathing. We interfere with our blood. We interfere with the flow in all of our activities. Think, just think, my friends, how much we interfere with that which flows naturally and beautifully without our judgments.

Now, if we will take that very simple demonstration and, seeing what concern does to our breathing, what concern does to the flow of blood, then we can understand what is causing these obstructions in our path in life. It's only, only our concern. We're concerned whether or not this job will work out, and in that concern, we immediately relate to the experiences of all the jobs we had before. We're concerned whether or not we're going to have enough bread in our mouth tomorrow, you see? And in that concern we are creating all of these mental obstructions on our path. And so we go on that wheel—they call it the karmic wheel—over and over and over and over, again and again.

Now, I know that we have been brainwashed, but we're the ones that did the brainwashing. And because we're the ones that did the brainwashing, then, of course, we're the ones that are going to have to undo it.

Now, here at one of our classes, there was a question on organization. It is an important question, because most people find that they are not organized the way they would like to be. But, you see, the truth of the matter is we're all organized. Some of us are organized in harmony and some of us are organized in confusion. And the only difference between the two is, as we've stated before, is personal responsibility. Now, you take a person who says, "Well, take a look at me, I'm not organized at all." But it is not true. You will find that their whole universe is filled of half do's. There is a multitude of things around them waiting to be finished, you see. And all those strings are still attached.

Now, that's called a state of confusion, you see. It's really quite simple. We're organized in harmony or organized in confusion. And we have the choice moment by moment.

If you want to be organized in harmony—"The Law of Harmony," remember, "is my thought." Many of you I don't think are aware of the "Total Consideration" affirmation. And I wonder if any of my students still remember it. Perhaps—yes, do you remember it? The "Total Consideration" affirmation? [*Turning to another student, the Teacher continues.*] I'm sure you do. Would you rise and speak it forth to those who have yet to hear it?

I am the manifestation of Divine Intelligence. Formless and free. Whole and complete. Peace, Poise and Power are my birthright. The Law of Harmony is my thought and guarantees Unity in all my acts and activities, expressing perfect Rhythm and limitless flow throughout my entire being. Without beginning or ending, eternity is my true awareness and sees the tides of creation as a captain sees his ship. As the Light of Truth is sustained by the faculty of Reason, I pause to think and claim my Divine right. Right Thought. Right Action. Total Consideration. Amen. Amen. Amen.

Thank you very much.

Now, that is a very important affirmation that was given to us many years ago: Total Consideration. "The Law of Harmony is my thought." Now, does anyone know what the Law of Harmony is? Yes. Would you rise, please?

Faith, poise, and humility.

Thank you. Anyone else have an answer to, What is the Law of Harmony? [*After a short pause, the Teacher continues.*] You have—we all have forty soul faculties and forty corresponding sense functions. When each faculty and each corresponding function is in balance, then you experience the Law of Harmony. For what that really is—when they are in balance, there is a perfect, unobstructed flow of the divine intelligent Energy.

Now, how does one go about to bring forty soul faculties and forty sense functions into a state of balance? Any thought, any thought that you entertain in your mind that disturbs your peace of mind is directly related to a sense function which is out of balance with the corresponding soul faculty.

Now, you have been given a few of the triune soul faculties and sense functions. You've only been given a few for a very, very good reason. And that reason is simply stated in, Man values only that which he makes an effort to attain, and the value of his attainment is measured by his effort.

Now, when you have a thought that disturbs your peace of mind and your state of being of goodness, of feeling good, you can very easily with honest, honest investigation, you can very easily trace that thought to the sense function that gave it birth. Once knowing the sense function, your own inner being will clearly show you the balance to that function. Now, if you make that effort, and you make that effort daily, then you're going to bring these faculties and functions into balance, and you're going to experience the Law of Harmony, which is your thought. It becomes your thought when you make that effort.

Then, when you speak your word forth into the universe knowing that it shall not come back to you void but accomplish that which you send it to do—that only works in the Law of Harmony. That's when it works. You can speak your word forth many times—and many people have and it has returned unto them void because it left them void. When it went out to the universe, it was void. It did not have that power with it because there was not the Law of Harmony. So whatever it is that you want and whatever it is that you want to do, before you do it, before you think of it, then put that power to work.

Do not dictate what the results of your efforts in life will be. And if you will refrain from dictating what the effects of your efforts in life will be, then you will not have to pay the price of creation, that dual law. If you will do what you know is right to do because it's right to do it, you'll be free from concern. If you permit your mind to continue to dictate what the possible effects of your efforts in life will be, then you will always be in concern, you'll always be in judgment—for concern is the child of judgment—and you'll always be controlled by the Law of Creation, by the duality of creation.

Here, we have come, hopefully, to learn and to apply the separation of truth from creation. For it is only truth that frees us and it is only creation that binds us. We're here to learn to be in creation and never a part of creation, to be with a person, place, or thing and never a part of a person, place, or thing. Surely, it is easy to be attached. And it is only easy to be attached because we've made it so very easy to judge. If we didn't make it easy for us to judge, then we would not easily experience the bondage of attachment.

All things in creation are sustained by the same intelligent, divine energy that is sustaining our thought this moment. It is here for us to use, not to be attached to—the effect, again, of judgment—but to use it, not abuse it, and to ever move onward and upward on the spiritual path of constant expansion. Because this is what we are here on this earth realm—this is what we are doing. This is what is happening to us each and every moment. Our consciousness is constantly expanding. Now, we call that expansion "experiences." We're constantly filling our universe with a multitude of experiences. And that process goes on and on and on and on, for our consciousness is God encased in form. Its very purpose is the expansion of form and that expansion process is constantly taking place.

Now, he who holds to form will experience pain, for form is limit and the limit is constantly being expanded by the consciousness or God within us. So if you have pain, if you have discord, if you have struggle, and if you have difficulty, it is your mental resistance to the expansion of consciousness that is inevitable that is taking place at all times.

So it is not, of course, wise to try to stop the inevitable. The expansion process *is* inevitable. The Divine Consciousness within *is* evolving the form. You see, when we think of form usually we just think of some physical body. We look at ourselves and that's all that we see. But what you don't see is that it's a house. It's a house not only for you, your soul, but for all of the nature spirits who live there. That's their house, too. Because you do not see them in no way denies the truth of their existence.

Now, when the Law of Harmony is your thought, then these elementals and these nature spirits representing the water, fire, earth, and air of which your body is composed, then they are in harmony, you see, and all things are brought into balance for the greater good of the whole. Now, this is taking place at all times in your house, your personal house, called your body. But it's also taking place all around and about us. It's taking place in nature. It's taking place with the flowers and the trees, because those, those spirits are everywhere that there is form, you see.

Then, of course, we have those and we have the nature spirits. We have the elementals. We have the astral forms and we have the thought forms. You see, my friends, we have such a busy house. We have no time to be concerned, really, with someone else's house because our house is so full and our house is so active. And there is so much going on and there is so much taking place. We have a great responsibility to take care of the house that we live in—a great responsibility. It's really a full-time job—twenty-four hours, right around the clock. The full-time job is for our minds not to interfere. That's where the full-time job is. So the work of the Divine can be conducted harmoniously in keeping with its true, original purpose.

Now, there was brought to my attention the other day some interest in reference to the process of aging. And for those of you who were not present at the house that day, I'd like to share with you something that all of you can see what causes the process of aging. Now, I know especially, usually, the women are interested in it. The men are extremely interested, but they find it unmanly to discuss it. So we'll just let them go by. But anyway, when you find yourself emotionally disturbed, when you find yourself unhappy, when you find yourself concerned, when you find yourself intolerant, when you find yourself sad, and any of those mental activities that are not harmonious or bringing you the feeling of goodness, when you feel that way, look in the mirror. And I can assure you, if you will do that, you will know beyond a shadow of any doubt what causes people to age.

The aging process is simply being out of the Law of Harmony. Now, you know what the Law of Harmony is. So if you want the fountain of youth, it's available to you. It's very simple. And when you see how much you age when you're in the forces, when you honestly look in the mirror, you can be rest assured, the horror that you see in your face will help to inspire you to make greater effort to have feelings of joy, of peace, of harmony and happiness, because it just is not worth it.

Now, why do these contortions and things happen and implant all these wrinkles in a person's face? How does this work? Well, your face is a part of your house, of your temple of your soul. And the responsibility of keeping that in good working order is primarily the responsibility of you, your soul. But it has a multitude of nature spirits working on the skin, the bone structure, and go on down the list, working on the element of water and the fire and heat within your being and the air, you see—and the earth and all of those things. Now, there are literally hundreds of these little nature spirits that are living in your universe, in your home. And they have a lot of work to do, a lot of work to keep your house clean and neat, you see?

Now, when you permit your mind to be upset, what you do is disturb all of those nature spirits who are very busy working. Say, for example, you get emotionally upset. Now, which of the four elements is affected by your emotional upset? Do any of you know? Is it earth, fire, water, or air? Do any of you know? Do you know?

I think fire.

A person says fire. Anyone else?

Would it be air and water?

A lady says air and water. Yes.

Water.

Water. What you do, when you get emotionally upset, you are the direct cause of a war, a battle that takes place between the nature spirits of the element fire and the nature spirits of the element water. Now, what happens when you mix fire and water? You get steam, don't you? Explosions. Now that's exactly what happens when you permit yourself to be in the forces. And then, slowly but surely—because it takes time—slowly but surely, you begin to see this so-called early aging process taking place in your face, in your eyes. Because when the fire spirits go to work and battle a war with the water spirits, they affect the air and the earth spirits. And they all take sides.

You see, the elementals and the nature spirits, they have an intelligence. You have to understand that. And they have a purpose to serve. They have an area, an element to protect. Do you understand? And when you cause them, any of them, to war against each other, you pay the price and that house starts its decaying process.

Now, some people, they explode. The fire and water spirits are at war and they explode and they express it. It has just as much effect, of course. Those nature spirits are still at war and it's expressed out there. And some other nature spirits that it landed on, perhaps they rise up and the same thing happens. Then you have the other kind of people who stand there like the Sphinx and explode inside. Well, which is the best? They both make you old. They both disturb nature.

You know, they say that some people have green thumbs and some have brown—or maybe it's black. But I want to share with you, if we all had a pink thumb, we wouldn't have to worry about anything growing, pink being divine love. Remember, when you want something to grow, whether it's a blade of grass or a dollar bill, if you want it to grow, if you really want it to grow, make God your highest priority. You see, my friends, when any desire that our mind entertains becomes greater than our desire for God, then the good does not return to us. It's like one of our young members of this church. He said he wanted a paper route real bad and maybe he would get it. And I said, "How bad do you want that paper route?" He said, "I desire it really, really bad!" I said, "Well, when you desire God as much as you desire the paper route, at least equal, hopefully more, then you'll have your paper route." Well, I guess he really did want it bad, because he got it.

So, you see, my friends, it's that way with everything, whatever your desire is. You know, sometimes, you see, of course, desire strikes a blow to our mind and our little old body reacts. But, you see, when you have the greatest of the greatest desires for something—God knows, we can't seem to pass a day without that insatiable desire for something—take that something and put it over here, and put God there, you see. Let God be your greatest desire. Then, all of these other great desires banging at your head, they'll come harmoniously and bring good with them.

So often we have such great desire and when it comes to us, it comes void. We no longer have the enjoyment from it that we thought we would get from it. It's like a person, they go to the store—they're impulse buyers. And they just go and they get an impulse. The desire takes total control of them. They go into the store, they buy it, and by the time they get it home, if they're lucky enough to get that far, they wonder why they bought it. You see? What are they doing with that? They didn't need it anyway. How come they got it in the car? Sometimes they'll turn right around and take it on back. It only gets—serves to show us, you know, how much control we really have.

But if you want true fulfillment from your desires, which are the divine expression—until this old thing gets a hold of it and makes it something else—if you really want fulfillment with your desire, put God in front of your desire. And remember, now when you put God in front of a desire, you know, that's not the end of doing your part. That's only the beginning. That's just the beginning.

So the first step is, you put God ahead of the great desire that you have. Then you look and take an example of how God works. Does anybody ever see God sleeping? Does anybody ever see God on vacation? Does anybody ever see God off duty? Does anybody ever see God tired and exhausted worn out and frayed? Well, if you did, you wouldn't have the energy to think, because that's where the energy comes from, you see? Now—but what do we see God doing? We see God, the divine Infinite Intelligence, demonstrating twenty-four hours a day, moment by moment, split second by split second, the Law of Continuity of Effort—the continuity of effort, ceaseless, never stopping.

Now, so we now know the desire, as great as it is, must take second place to our desire for God. After that has happened, we have to take an example of how God fulfills desire. God does it through us, not to us. We don't believe in a God that does things to us. We believe in a God that does things through us. And there is a vast difference. And so as God does things through us, it causes the Law of Continuity of Effort. So you want something to grow in your life, you want your desire to be fulfilled, to grow? Then you must demonstrate the Law of Continuity of Effort, no matter how you feel.

This is why, when you have desire, weigh it out. "Is this really what I want, because by wanting this, I am the father or mother of it. I am responsible for it. It must be cared for. It must be fed. And I can't let it go spasmodically. Maybe today I feel like feeding this child of mine and a couple of days later I don't feel like feeding it for two or three weeks. I've got other desires in my head." Well, you can be rest assured, then all your desires treated that way will fizzle like an Alka-Seltzer. You'll hear it for a time and then that's it, you see. It goes *plunk* in the bottom of the glass.

So a wise person, they weigh out all these desires and they say, "Let's see. Yeah, I really want that. Fine. I've got to put God first. The desire is second. Then I've got to demonstrate the Law of Continuity of Effort. Then, after I get it, I have really got to face personal responsibility. Because this is a child that I, by my own efforts, my own desires, have brought into my universe." Then—don't you see, my friends?—you'll soon find out as you face those three steps—putting God first, continuity of effort, and personal responsibility—you'll say, "Just a moment! No, I don't need any more kids in my universe. Look at all I have now!" You see? And you will, slowly but surely, see your desires lessen. It's miraculous how it works. You won't be concerned about all of these things, because you've got so many things, so many kids already to take care of. They're big responsibilities, you see. They must be fed. They must be cared for. Do you understand?

And then you'll understand what is meant when it's said, "When of naught desire is, in vain doth sorrow speak [*Discourse 2*]." The sorrow being, of course, our resistance to personal responsibility for what we desired in the first place.

Treat your children well and you will live to see the day when they will treat you kindly. Now, I'm not just talking about two-legged children running around the universe. Every desire that you call forth into your universe is your child. You and you alone are responsible for it. You and you alone have given it birth. And you and you alone shall give it death. Painless and free or slow, struggling death. Because we give desire birth, we also give it death. If we have given it a joyous birth, then let us not forget to give it a joyous death. Now, what does that mean? You have your desire. You get it fulfilled. You take care of it, for it's yours. You alone chose it. You alone brought it to you and you alone must care for it. Then, your children of desire, indeed, they will care for you.

Now, you also know, When the tools no longer serve the worker, the worker begins to serve the tools. So if you don't keep things in order, if you don't care for things, then you will soon be the victim of that effort.

My friends, it takes effort not to care for something. It takes less effort to care for something than it does not to care for something. And I'll tell you why. Very simple. Whatever you have in your universe, you alone have brought through your desires. And you look at it and you have other desires. And so you don't care any longer for what you had brought before. So your child lays there waning and crying. Your conscience knows. And it takes great effort on your part—and great energy—to constantly deny your conscience, for it's your child. It's in your possession. Now, just because you've done it, perhaps, for a lifetime and you're not consciously aware of this denial that you're doing, that denial is still taking energy. And that denial becomes your destiny.

So it takes more out of you not to care for the things you have brought into your life than it does to care for them. And that's really the truth of the matter. So if you find you have brought from your desires too many children into your home, then I just want to remind you we always have a garage sale. [*Many students laugh.*]

Thank you very much. Thank you.

JULY 3, 1980

CONSCIOUSNESS CLASS 218

Good evening, class.

Now, this is, as you know, the final class of this semester. There will, in the future, be other classes. I am not at liberty at this time to give the exact dates, but you will be informed in plenty of time when another semester is to begin.

I realize that over these years you have gained a great deal of knowledge in reference to what the philosophy has to offer. And I think one of the most important opportunities that has been granted to the class and to the people who attend this church is the spiritual benefits being derived from your efforts to apply daily what has been termed the Serenity Plan. [*Please see the appendix for the Serenity Plan.*] So many of us, unfortunately, when this plan was given to a group of students at the house, have thought of it as some kind of deprivation and some kind of discipline. Discipline, it is. And the benefits to be reaped from any constructive discipline are great and many.

You see, my friends, truth is taught through indirection, demonstration, and example. And we should all see that when our desires for anything are great enough, we always find a way. And so it is by working with the desires of each individual, the desire of their personal self-image, many people, many students are applying the Serenity Plan and reaping the benefits of a form more in keeping with their judgments.

Now, I haven't yet met a person who is totally free from judgment here in this earth realm. And so that's something, of course, that we're all working with. You know, as I said to one of my students today, if we would only take a lesson from the postage stamp, we certainly would be much better off. And what is the lesson from a simple postage stamp? Well, it's quite simple, really. It sticks to something 'til it gets what—where it's supposed to be. Now that's something that most of us seem to have great difficulty in doing: to stick to something until we get where we want to go. Because on any path that is beneficial, we are easily distracted.

I am well aware that there are a few, very few—because the plan was not their original thought—who have yet to see its benefits by application of it.

But what does it really do for us besides take a few pounds off that we would like to take off? To some, those few pounds are many. What does it really do? It gives us the daily opportunity to gain control of our mind. It gives us the incentive, for our desires are great, our pride is very great. And our desires related to our self-image and our pride will, in this case, serve a very good purpose if we will permit it to do so. Each day we have the opportunity of taking control of a thought in our mind that tells us we're hungry and we've got to stuff our stomach.

Now, long ago it was given to you, the different parts of the anatomy and their spiritual meanings. And the stomach, as you will recall, represents affection. And as we look across our land and see so many people, we quickly realize that most everyone is starved for affection, for most everyone is overweight. Why does a person permit themselves to be starved from—starved for affection? Because they have dictated how they will receive the affection that they need. And because we have made these many dictates and because these judgments rule our lives, we suffer. And we suffer with overweight. We suffer with many different things.

As you continue on with the plan, you're going to find many changes taking place in your consciousness, not just related, directly, to eating. You're going to find a clearer thinking. Because, you see, as most of you already realize, you feel lighter. Whether you have lost a half a pound or twenty pounds, you all have the same feeling: you feel lighter. That is an effect, my friends, of clearer, cleaner thinking.

Now, how do you get this clearer and cleaner thinking? Because you have to work consciously—and you're doing that—to control these habitual tapes that have been running your life for so long. And because you are making that effort, you are beginning to become aware—a little bit more aware—of your thoughts. And just think, out of the mud of earth grows the lotus of heaven: a seeming bad thing ofttimes produces good results. And when there was no other way, no other way to help you to become aware of your thoughts and to make that effort, think what your overweight has done for you: it has helped you to begin to think. That's when you take a seeming bad experience and you take the good out of that seeming bad experience. Now, that very same principle, that very same law applies to everything in your life. It's not limited to your weight. It applies to any and everything that you choose to apply it to.

Most of you are aware of the needs of some minds. The immediate need was to deviate, of course, from the plan. Now, whenever you're offered anything in life, unless you have control to some degree of your mind, the first thing that your mind will attempt to do is to change whatever you have received. Because by changing, it has made the judgment that it makes it its own. But if it doesn't get to change it, then it's never really theirs. Now, what this reveals to us is separatism in consciousness. It reveals that we have separated ourselves from the divine, universal, infinite whole. And because we have separated ourselves from the whole, we cannot have anything that is ours unless we introduce a change to it. If we become aware of that process, then we're on the first step of becoming a part of the divine, united whole.

Whenever we suffer, whenever we struggle, it's only because we have denied the truth. The truth being that we are inseparably a part of the whole, the Divine Consciousness.

When we find that we can't go anywhere without the constant thought of self, we soon find what is known in this philosophy as time-pressure. There's never enough time to get done what we want to do. There's never enough time for ourselves. Well, my friends, of course, there never will be enough time for ourselves because the time is being used up by the thought, the constant thought of the self.

You see, you take in a certain amount of energy and you use up a certain amount of energy. And anytime you use up more energy than you take in, you're going to start losing what is known as fat or weight. We all have a super abundance of energy stored up in our batteries. Some of our batteries are a little small, perhaps; some are very large. But it's all sitting there waiting to be used. Now, it's up to us to make the effort. When we feel bad enough, we make the changes in anything that we feel bad enough about.

But it does seem that two of the many problems that seem to beset us in life is the constant thought of self and the unwillingness to demonstrate the very Law of Success: the continuity of effort. Why do we have such difficulty in taking a lesson from the postage stamp? And we can't seem to get where we want to get. And we can't seem to be a success in what we want to be a success in. Because we've gone so many years of our life on this earth—and even the ones before—we've gone so many years without any effort to control our mind. We all know that freedom is the direct effect of self-control.

We come to the Spirit and we ask for many things. We want an improvement in our health, but our judgments stand in the way of that improvement. We know more than the Spirit that we have asked. And because we know more than the Spirit that we have asked, that obstruction has a higher priority in our consciousness. And God, or the devil, cannot get through. So we have to take an assessment of ourselves and our desires in life and not bother to ask when we are not willing to bother to receive. I think that makes good sense to all of us. You see, when our judgment knows more than the help that is waiting for us to receive, when are judgments are the higher priority, then it must be our judgments that we ask for the answers to our problems. But unfortunately, that's not what usually works. We ask because we want support for the judgments that we have made. And when we don't get the support for the judgments that we've already made, then we get very upset.

Now, if we decide that we have a certain health problem, for example, and we ask here and we ask there for help and the help we ask for is not in keeping with the judgments that we've already made, we have all kinds of problems—not problems with the people we've asked. That's not where the problem lies. We have a problem with the judgments that we have made and insist upon making. You see, it doesn't matter whether you ask one person or many persons, the judgment will ever censor what you receive. You can ask—stand face-to-face with God himself—but your judgment will either totally obstruct what is available to you or at least censor it and distort it until it's no longer recognizable for what it was originally attend—intended to accomplish.

How interesting our minds are as they look about the universe and constantly justify, known as excuses, for not doing this or not doing that. We can all spend our time telling ourselves how very busy we are, how much we have to do, how tired and exhausted we are, we can all spend our time doing that and reaping the harvest of that type of thinking. We all already have experienced what those levels of consciousness have to offer.

So as we conclude this semester, what is it, you must ask yourself, that you're taking with you? Because we all know we're going to take with us what we put in. For that's what we get out of a thing—is only what we put into the thing. So whatever you have put into this semester, that's what's going to go with you—not one iota more and not one iota less. If you have put a lot in, then you're going to take a lot out. And a lot is going to go with you. You can be rest assured of that. But if you have put in very little, if you have only put in your physical presence and a microscopic portion of your mental being and, hopefully, at least 1 percent of your spiritual being, then that's what you will take back out. That's what life is all about: we get out of a thing what we put into a thing and never one iota more.

So, my friends, to those of you who know deep in your hearts how much you're getting out of it, you can be rest assured, without egotism and in all humbleness, how much you're really putting into it. And it will show. Of course, it will show in your daily activities. It will show in your jobs. It will show in your health. It will show in your life and the abundant good that's available to all of us.

I have spoken many times that the greatest gift you can give to life is the gift of self. There is no greater gift you can give. Though you have all the treasures that earth has to offer, they are as of nothing compared to the gift of self. Think of that. Think of what it really means to give the greatest gift of all: the gift of self. When you give the gift of self, there's no longer any thought of that which you have given, because you either give the gift of self or you loan it. And if you loan it, then your mind is filled with self, self, self. When you are ready, you will give the greatest gift you have to God: the gift of self.

And your benefit from that gift—what you will receive back—is as clear as the day follows the night: you will receive freedom. For having given the gift of self, the thought of I and the thought of self no longer, for you, exist. And when the thought of I and the thought of self no longer exist for you, then you're free. And being free, you have everything. There's no thought and no desire for things, because you are free. And being free, you are a part and parcel of all. No longer will you suffer from the delusion of need. No longer will you suffer from the delusion of lack or the delusion of limitation. No longer will you suffer from the delusion of time-pressure, for you have given the greatest gift you have to God. You no longer have identification with self, for God now has the self and, in return, you have the freedom. No longer will you have the need to worry and fret over your health, your wealth, and your happiness, for all of that goes with the package that you've given to God. Now, that's the next step in our evolution.

And you know, each one of us knows when we've given the great gift of all gifts. And each one of us will know when we made it a loan for a time.

I assure you, my friends, the only obstruction, as I have stated many times, the only obstruction to all the goodness you desire is the constant thought of I. There is no other obstruction in the universe. For it is the thought of I, that delusion, that takes you out of the stream of consciousness of the divine eternal flow. Whether it's your health, your wealth, or your happiness, the only thing that stands between you and all of that goodness is your thought of I.

So what, then, are we giving to God? We are not giving something that a man of common sense could possibly treasure. Who would treasure the struggles of life? Who would treasure illness? Who would treasure poverty? Who would treasure lack and limitation? That's what self offers. And that's what we have the opportunity to give. It is not something that, when we stop and think, we want to hold on to, especially with such tenacity.

So where, then, is the problem in giving this gift? Let us pause for a moment that we may see honestly why we have waited so long to give this gift back to God. Why have we waited? Because having been so long in self, we're not quite sure that God exists. That's the sadness, my friends. Because we're not quite sure that God exists, we can't possibly give up what we are so attached to. Because, not being sure that God exists, we therefore have no guarantee. We think we know what we have, but I assure you we never know in life what we have until we give it up. And when we do give it up, we're truly amazed at what returns.

How are we going to make these changes that we all know we must make someday? How are we, once again, going to declare our birthright and our divinity? How are we, once again, going to direct this beautiful soul faculty of faith to the source that really sustains it? Only from effort. Daily, conscious effort.

When our priorities are so high in our consciousness, that, my friends, is when we are truly blessed, for that is when we have the greatest opportunity to really redirect back to God our faith. When you really want something with all your being and you give it with the thought of I, you give it up, that's when you'll start to really grow. But you must, you must want it as a number one priority in your life. Whatever your desire is, it has to be your highest priority. It has to really gnaw at your consciousness for its fulfillment. And when it starts to gnaw at you daily, that, my friends, is when to give it up. Now, we can do that now, today or we can procrastinate and serve the theft of all time. And we can wait, until we get on the other side, as one of my students said, to be sure.

My friends, if you don't find God now, you are not about to find God when you leave your physical body. Because your mind—no one's mind changes like that. There's not that kind of a change that takes place. You have fear before you go; you have fear after you get there. And people there have to work with you to cast the light of reason and common sense over that error of ignorance.

So if you want to wait 'til you leave earth, then be rest assured and be prepared: your waiting will not be years; it will be centuries, for it takes much longer over there than it does over here. Here, we have a physical body acting as a buffer. And things and experiences, though seemingly intense to us, are nowhere near as intense as when you lose your physical body. For there, when you desire, you are really a part of the desire. There, when you are attached to a thing, you are the thing itself. Here, you have this buffer. There, you do not.

Now, if we believe that God is the source of our supply, if we truly believe that God is all our health, wealth, and happiness, then it stands to reason it is only our lack of effort to experience

God to have the health, wealth, and happiness that is God. That we must all agree to. We can't cry for God when things are tough and forget God when we think things are going so good. Because that's not how it works, my friends. You see, what happens is, when things go good, we take the credit. And when things go bad, we don't take the credit and we cry for God. That's all that reveals. It means at one time with one experience we accept personal full responsibility, and at another time with another experience, we totally deny personal responsibility. Now, we know why we cry for God when it's tough and we forget God when things are so smooth. Interesting how our little minds work, isn't it? But we cannot help but face that simple truth.

So is it not better for us to have the struggles of life that we may cry for God and maybe find God? Is it not better to be hungry, is it not better to be without funds, is it not better to have poor health, if in all of those things we find God? In fact, some religionists have so believed in its benefits that they have taught and practiced self-sacrifice in order to find God. This philosophy does not teach you ways to sacrifice yourself. We're doing a good job on that without anybody teaching us. [*Many students laugh.*] But it shows us how we can be freed from that foolishness, if we choose to do so. But we alone must make that conscious choice.

Long ago, when this philosophy first came to this world, this teacher said, "O suffer senses not in vain for freedom of your soul is gain." So, as we suffer along with our little self, running into all types of detours and getting so discouraged and so disgusted because our little self can't get things worked out, think what happens: we turn to God, at least temporarily. But if we mess things up enough, then we'll cry for God a lot more often—you understand?—and finally, sooner or later, we're bound to find God and get free.

So when I see these struggles around and about me, it doesn't mean I don't have, hopefully, some compassion. But I feel very good inside, because I know that the student, or students, I know they will grow or go. And I see the wonderful opportunity that they have right in front of them. When everything else fails, the door opens. But not the door of self. The hinges already blew off that door. [*Many students laugh.*] It's the other door that I am talking about.

How fortunate we are when we suffer. I remember many times the students call me to tell me how much they're suffering. And I said, "Gee, that's wonderful. I hope you continue." Because I meant that very sincerely because I know, I know, sooner or later, when the suffering is sufficient, we do find God. I do know that. And I don't know it from reading a book. I know it from walking the path. I know what it has to offer. So I do feel good when they cry the loudest. They say the squeaky wheel gets all the grease. Well, the only grease they're getting from this source is the grease of God. And they better get that through their consciousness, because I hear a lot of crying in my work. A lot of crying. And the philosophy is very clear: nip it in the bud.

But you can be rest assured when a person is in the depths of the pity of self, if they don't have an ear to bend, they'll get very angry and, be rest assured, they'll begin to make some changes.

Now, I'm sure all you women that are married, or have been married, are very, very familiar with husbands coming home crying how hard they work. Well, sooner or later, you hear enough of it. And sooner or later, you let them have it. And when you let them have it, some changes come about for the better. Because, you know, there is what is known as a saturation point. And nothing reaches its saturation point any faster than self-pity. I don't know of anyone, even the people in self, who want to listen to somebody else's self-pity around the clock. I know of no one who enjoys it. So you see how beautifully things do balance out.

Now, many times I've made it very clear with my students. I've said, "You've got so much of *you* in the way, God can't even get in. Now, when you get a little bit of *you* out of the way, then

God or goodness will move in, because your cup runneth over. It's filled with self. There's no room for God to get in."

How beautiful life really is. And it's beautiful when we choose to see it that way. Now, we can see it that way every morning upon arising. We can see beauty everywhere, if that is what we want to see. We can see its opposite everywhere if that is what we want to see. And so life truly is ever as we take it and it is just the way we make it. And that's all there is to it.

Now, I went to the doctor—what is today? Thursday?—yesterday. And he had been away on lecture tours for a month or two. And I happen to prefer, like a barber, I like to go to the same doctor. And so he's away. So I decided, fine, I'll wait 'til he gets back. And so I did. So I went in and I had a very busy schedule, I thought, yesterday, with the things that had to be done. And he said, "Mr. Goodwin, I never saw you looking so fine." I said, "Good. I'm feeling great." So he runs his little check there, you know. And, of course, I am grateful because I was prepared: I did have someone upstairs say, "Well, you know, Richard, your spine's been out of whack for about a month and a half. You'll have to have an adjustment." And I said, "Well, that's—I don't need any adjustment." So he says, "Well, Mr. Goodwin, you've got to have an adjustment."

I said, "Well, could I go right home after?" I could lay down at home. No. Got to stay upstairs two hours. I said—well, I won't say what I said, but anyway I said it. And he said, "Well . . ." And I said, "Oh, no. No, I'm not going to go through all that foolishness again. I'll go up there."

Two hours. Well, it's very—I have made it very difficult for me. I haven't had many adjustments. I don't believe in many adjustments. So I haven't had many. But I have made it difficult for me to have to lie down on that table for two hours and stay wide awake. For some unknown reason I decided, when I first started, it wasn't the place to sleep; and so I've never slept there. And, of course, for some unknown reason, I'd forgotten my watch. So I didn't know what time it was. And I lay there and, of course, I thought about everything.

But then, I had to say, "Now this is a wonderful opportunity for me to say my affirmations." Well, after saying about ten thousand, I figured two hours *must* be up. [*Quite a few students laugh.*] So I walked downstairs and I said, "Two hours up?" She says, "Only an hour and a half." I said, "Well, I'm already up, so what's a half hour?"

So anyway, what I'm trying to point out very simply: no matter what it is you experience, you can make it beautiful. You really can. Even if you have to lay perfectly still on your back for, well, an hour and a half, it can be beautiful, you see.

And when you hear the wails and crying and the wailing of the self-pity and what great struggles people are having around and about you, you know, and how horrible things are and go on down the list, you can hear, you see, but not listen. Now, you know, we all have had the experience with people hearing us and not listening. Well, that's one time to use that habitual talent that we all seem to have. That's one time to consciously use it. In other words, a person that hears lets it in this ear and zoom on out that ear. It means that we're not affected emotionally—you understand?—because we're consciously in control here. Something's working inside of us, you see. Otherwise, what happens to us is, we find ourselves right down there where they were. Of course, they walk away feeling a lot better, you know, if the judgment has got any satisfaction at all. But I'll tell you one thing, when you're working with people, if the judgments don't get satisfaction, they don't leave very happily. Not at all.

Now, all of us can do a lot more than what we're doing for the part of us that's going to last. Call it your spirit or your soul, it doesn't make any difference. That's the part of you that's been around a long, long time. It was wide awake long before you came to earth and it'll be wide awake long after you're gone. So let's start to think about spending a little bit of time—a little more than what we've been spending—on that part of us that's enduring and lasting, that we're living with throughout eternity.

This is the earth journey. Believe me, it's a real short one. Maybe you don't think so. You're not yet to my age. But you will. Time passes very quickly. You know, before you know it, Christmas will be here. And then there's another year and another year and another decade. So all of this goes very, very quickly. The things that you race around and rush after, stop and pause a moment and see how well those things are really serving you.

And how much, really how much time out of twenty-four hours are you really spending on your spirit within? How much time are we really spending in sel*fless* service, service without return to the self? See? Now, many people don't understand self*less* service. But that's what it means. Service with no return to the self. And that is the only service that benefits the part of you that's eternal.

All this other self-service, that takes care of your functions for a time. But any of you, familiar with self-service, are very well aware the functions are forever greedy; they never get enough. You give it one; it demands two. It gets two; it demands twenty. It's never enough, my friends.

And those of you on the Serenity Plan are well aware, now, that this constant habit of grabbing the refrigerator door and stuffing the mouth constantly twenty-four hours, day and night—you're now becoming aware of, you see. Of course, our fat reveals how much stuffing's going on. But, my lord, how greedy can our tapes be? That we've got to shove something in our mouth every time we turn around.

You know, some of my students used to, the first thing, when they got up to the house, you know, to come for self*less* service—service without the return to self—the first thing, they came through the kitchen door, the minute they got through the kitchen door, their hand was out headed towards the refrigerator,

12 feet away or 10 feet away. You see, their hand couldn't even wait until the feet got to the refrigerator door. The hand was always moving ahead, like that. Now, stop and think of that, my friends. And we tell ourselves that we're going to Serenity for self*less* service? When our hands are ahead of our feet to get the food to shove into our mouth? We must take stock of these experiences. Indeed are they wonderful opportunities to see what we're doing to ourselves, you see.

Now, when we're doing self*less* service—service without interest or return to the self—then self has nothing to say, *nothing* to say about the self*less* service that we're doing. Because if self has something to say about the self*less* service that we're doing, then it's not self*less* at all, you see. Now, I think we ought to really think about that one.

Considering, all the students know that if they have an interest in supporting their church, they make a little something for the bazaar. They check it out with the Council, the Spirit of the church, because there's a lot to weigh out. If you're making something to support your church, then surely the eighty-one souls that founded it—and do pretty good at the business of operating it, I would think, maybe some wouldn't agree with me—certainly know something about whether or not we already have too much of those items. Or whether or not this is the quality that would sell and do well and support the church. But, you see, you've got to really get into selfless service to make those kind of steps. And you can't be dictating that you'll do so much and no more. And you can't be dictating that you've got so many other self desires that to fit in the selfless service one—no, that's pretty low on the self desire list. You see, it's on the wrong list! The service is on the wrong list. It's on the self list, not the self*less* list. Vast difference, my friends. Great, big vast difference.

So let's become more consciously aware when we tell ourselves that we're doing self*less* service that we do not, hopefully any longer, delude ourselves. Because no one really wants to be deluding themselves.

Now, I said selfless service means service without interest of return to the self. And when you are truly doing service without interest of return to the self, God is your return. And what greater good could you have than God? You don't have to worry about *things*, no matter what they are, when you're doing self*less* service. You don't have to be concerned of how much money you have or don't have, or how much you're going to get out of this or get out of that.

I've been in this business for forty years now and I've found many interesting things, to say the least. But I think the most interesting of all is how we delude ourselves in what is known as self*less* service. I have had many students come and go. And some here in these classes, they'll be around a long time. Some will go. Some will stay.

But I have had many come and go. And they were absolutely sure they were going to get their money's worth out of me—every drop of energy they could—while they were around. Well, they got a rude awakening. I'm a very practical person. I believe firmly, wholly, and completely in the Law of Balance. First of all, I believe, beyond a shadow of any doubt, that the workers win. Because I believe that and have for many, many, many, many years, I make great effort to spend my time, whatever time that I have, with the workers. Only makes good sense, doesn't it? If you believe that the workers win and you're willing to be a worker yourself, why would you spend any time with people who are not workers? What inside of you could possibly stimulate you to spend time with anyone who isn't a worker? Now, one doesn't have to make a judgment. All one has to do is be observant. Either we work or we don't work.

So long ago, having made that decision, I stick to it. I have for many, many years refused to ask another to do anything that

I was not first willing, ready, and able to do myself, whether it was typesetting your church programs, which I happen to have done some time ago, when another student decided to leave all of a sudden, or any other job. If you are willing first to do the job yourself and to make that effort to qualify yourself, then, don't you see, my friends, when you speak your word forth and you ask another to do it, there's no doubt in your mind, because if they don't, then you will. That's when you can speak with authority. When you first make the effort to become the living demonstration, when you first make the effort to be the example, then you'll have no problems speaking from a level of authority. There will be no doubt and no question, because you're willing to do it first yourself. But that demonstration we all have to make someday.

You have received much. To those who receive much, much shall be demanded by Life herself. Neither your church, nor I, demand anything from you. But in keeping with the law whatever you have received, you must, in your way, give forth. For if you do not, it shall be taken from you in ways that your mind knows not. Because by holding the good that you receive in life, by holding it, you obstruct the flow. Goodness flows from an eternal spring. Whoever receives it and holds it guarantees the law to lose it. So for each good that you have stored in your consciousness, let it flow in keeping with the law. But cast not your pearls before the swine. He who casts his pearls before the swine is controlled by the thought of I and the motive is not pure. And the motive, not being pure, the results are never good.

Give what you have to give. Care less what they do with it. And in so doing, you're freed from self. Your motive, then, is as pure as the Light itself. And only the good can return to you.

So whatever it is you have judged is disturbing you this moment and this day, give that judgment, with the package known as self, to God. Then you will have no concern, nor interest, whether or not God is working, because there's nothing here left to be concerned. You've given this up. Now, you won't become an idiot by giving this thing up. You'll finally become wise.

But whether or not we doubt the existence of God doesn't change God. And we're all going to awaken fully, surely, wholly, and completely to that demonstrable truth. For each morning at 4:00 a.m., I hear the cries of many of my students. [*Mr. Goodwin meditated every morning at 4:00 a.m.*] I hear the cry for this and I hear the cry for that. And I hear and see God's ministering angels waiting and watching for the judgment, the self, the only wall of obstruction, to bow. And when it bows, those angels of the Light, they move into that universe and the healing takes place. Not the way the self dictates. God forbid, no. Because the dictates of the self are changing around the clock.

But it does take a redirection of the Law of Acceptance. We've already accepted the obstruction. How about trying to redirect and accept the way? Take stock of how many obstructions you have on your path. If you find many, it just goes to show you've got to cry a lot louder and a lot more often, because they're still there, you see. But when we cry loud enough and long enough, finally the doors open. It's really a beautiful thing to witness. And our minds, they cannot dictate how long and how intense our suffering must be. It's not our soul that suffers, you can be reassured of that. It's only our senses that are having the experiences, because only our senses created them.

And remember, it's never our soul that dictates whether or not God's ministering angels are on duty doing their job. We don't have to worry about that. They're on duty twenty-four hours a day and night. They don't need sleep. They don't even have a time clock. They're not worried about how little time they have to serve God. That thought never enters their mind. They're not worried about how they're going to fit God's work in a couple of minutes a week or a couple of minutes a month. Well, they don't have any thoughts like that. They're too busy working. No, you don't have to worry whether or not God's angels are doing everything they can to help you.

The only interest or concern you have to have is lower those obstructions you built up from your judgments and your constant thought of I. Don't you understand? God's ministering angels cannot, and will not, if they could, but they cannot, go contrary to divine, natural law. For your very obstruction is sustained by the power of God. It's called doing our part. Let us lower the obstructions in our path. And we all know how to do it. Then, God's angels, waiting to do their part, will show you what a beautiful world it really is.

And there is nothing, nothing in all of the universes that is good, that your heart can possibly desire that is not waiting for you this very moment. All we have to do is to accept that simple truth. That's all we have to do. Because the moment we accept that truth, we won't have to worry about doing our part. We did it in the moment of acceptance.

Thank you. Thank you.

JULY 10, 1980

APPENDIX

The Divine Healing Prayer

I accept that the Divine Healing Power
Is removing all obstructions
From my mind and body
And is restoring me
To perfect health, wealth, and happiness.
My heart is filled with gratitude
For the Divine Law of Acceptance
That is healing both present and absent ones
Who are in need of help.
Peace, the power that healeth,
Is guiding my thoughts, acts, and deeds
As God and I go hand in hand
Living a life of joyful abundance.

The Total Consideration Affirmation

I am the manifestation of Divine Intelligence. Formless and free. Whole and complete. Peace, Poise, and Power are my birthright.

The Law of Harmony is my thought and guarantees Unity in all my acts and activities, expressing perfect Rhythm and limitless flow throughout my entire being.

Without beginning or ending, eternity is my true awareness and sees the tides of creation, as a captain sees his ship.

As the Light of Truth is sustained by the faculty of Reason, I pause to think and claim my Divine right.

   Right Thought. Right Action. Total Consideration.

      Amen. Amen. Amen.

Divine Abundance

Thank
(Gratitude)

You
(Principle)

God
(Divine Intelligence)

I'm
(Individualizing)

Moving
(Rhythm)

In
(Unity)

Your
(Realization)

Divine
(Total)

Flow
(Consideration)

Serenity Plan
The natural way of weight reduction
(This is NOT a diet.)

Phase I
During this phase you may eat a full breakfast of any foods you desire, preferably very nutritious ones, no later than 9 a.m. You may also eat a full dinner of anything you wish, except beer or alcoholic beverages, between the hours of 5:30 and 9 p.m. This is important to allow the proper time span between breakfast and dinner. The entire meal should be consumed at one sitting.

Though you may be used to eating lunch and snacking in between meals, it will not be difficult to give up both lunch and snacking, as you may drink all the V-8 cocktail juice (not the hot or clam variety), tea or coffee you wish. It is preferable to purchase the 6 oz. cans of V-8 which may be refrigerated, but you should add no ice, lemon or salt. You should drink each can all at once. You may add milk to your coffee or tea, but no sugar, except with meals. It is recommended that you drink no more than two glasses of plain water each day. It is strongly advised NOT to drink liquids while eating, as this interferes with nature's chemical process in digesting your foods. Foods not properly digested produce fatty tissue.

Each and every morning upon awakening, weigh yourself that you may experience the conscious awareness and joy of your weight reduction.

Phase II
During this phase, a 20-minute daily Waltham walk is advised. The great benefit of this walk is to redistribute the fatty tissue in your body, and aid in weight reduction in the proper areas. The Waltham walk is a rhythmic walk on level ground where the arms are swung in unison with the stride. As the left foot

steps forward, the right hand swings forward the same distance as the stride, so the forward hand and foot are the same distance out. The left hand is swung back the same distance as the right foot. Flat shoes are necessary. This simple movement exercises every muscle in your body, producing a beneficial and invigorating result. No other exercises are necessary, though you may continue other exercises if you are in the habit of doing them.

Phase III
When you are ready to move into Phase III, you may speed up your weight reduction by skipping dinner one night, but NOT more than two nights per week. The nights should not be consecutive.

Phase IV
Now that you have progressed to this point, you will notice that your food intake has automatically reduced by two-thirds of your original intake. One or two times per week, but no more than two, you may eat two slices of bacon and two eggs for breakfast. And for dinner, you may have a SMALL tasty salad consisting of lettuce and tomato only, with the dressing of your choice.

Phase V
By the time you enter this phase, you will be chewing your food VERY slowly and thoroughly, savoring each and every morsel. Each meal should take at least 30 minutes to consume. Remember, the slower you chew your food, the less you eat, the more weight you lose, and the happier you become.

© Serenity – June 11, 1980

www.ingramcontent.com/pod-product-compliance
Lightning Source LLC
Chambersburg PA
CBHW020634300426
44112CB00007B/110